People and places

A 2001 Census atlas of the UK

Daniel Dorling and Bethan Thomas

The POLICY PRESS

First published in Great Britain in May 2004 by

The Policy Press
University of Bristol
Fourth Floor, Beacon House
Queen's Road
Bristol BS8 1QU
UK
Tel no +44 (0)117 331 4054
Fax no +44 (0)117 331 4093
E-mail tpp-info@bristol.ac.uk
www.policypress.org.uk

ISBN 1 86134 555 0 paperback
A hardback version of this publication is also available

British Library Cataloguing in Publication Data
A catalogue record for this report is available from the British Library

Library of Congress Cataloging-in-Publication Data
A catalog record for this report has been requested

Daniel Dorling is Professor of Human Geography at the University of Sheffield, and **Bethan Thomas** is a Researcher in the Department of Geography, University of Sheffield.

Cover design by Qube Design Associates, Bristol
Photographs in atlas kindly supplied by Mary Shaw
Printed in Great Britain by Alden Press, Oxford

Acknowledgements

We would like to thank John Pritchard of the University of Sheffield for his assistance in working with the initial data and maps used here. Helen Durham of the University of Leeds worked on checking the population cartograms and we are grateful for her assistance. David Gordon of the University of Bristol provided details of the Breadline Britain index and indicators of high income and wealth from his earlier publications, which enabled us to revise them here to include with 2001 Census data. Richard Mitchell of the University of Edinburgh and David Martin from the University of Southampton worked with us on a project to correct the 1991 Census data, which allowed the comparisons over time to be made. We are also grateful for the assistance in this of Ludi Simpson from the University of Manchester, and to Mary Shaw of the University of Bristol who took the photographs and advised on the style and content of the atlas. Finally we owe thanks to Dawn Rushen, Dave Worth, Helen Bolton and Julia Mortimer at The Policy Press who initially thought this atlas should be published, agreed to print it in full colour, typeset the text, maps, footnotes and tables, and helped enormously in clarifying the message!

The Census data used in this report was obtained from the Office for National Statistics, the General Register Office for Scotland and the Northern Ireland Statistics and Research Agency. Information derived from the population censuses of the United Kingdom and digital boundaries are reproduced with the permission of the Controller of HMSO. We are grateful to these agencies for providing the data needed in a timely fashion, and for instigating a programme of correcting the output before publication to allow for expected under-enumeration in 2001. In particular we would like to acknowledge the work of Ian Diamond, now of the Economic and Social Research Council, which helped to ensure that the 2001 Census was the most accurate census released to date in the UK. Without that work, and of course the good will of the people who filled in their census forms, it would not have been possible to have made accurate comparisons over time within just a few months of the release of the data.

Finally we would like to thank our colleagues at the Universities of Newcastle, Bristol, Leeds and Sheffield, where we worked in collaboration on a variety of projects, many of the results of which were needed in order to produce this atlas.

Reference maps

The following pages provide key maps and cartograms for each country of the UK and each Government Office Region (GOR) of England. All local authority districts are listed below, alongside a letter that which indicates which region they fall in, as follows:

A	North East	F	West Midlands	K	South West
B	North West	G	East of England	N	Northern Ireland
D	Yorkshire and the Humber	H	London	S	Scotland
E	East Midlands	J	South East	W	Wales

These regions and countries are shown opposite in the map and cartogram to the left. On the right the major cities of the UK are highlighted.

Regions and countries
East Midlands
East of England
London
North East
North West
Northern Ireland
Scotland
South East
South West
Wales
West Midlands
Yorkshire and the Humber

Major cities
Aberdeen
Belfast
Birmingham
Bradford
Bristol
Cardiff
Edinburgh
Glasgow
Inner London
Leeds
Liverpool
Manchester
Newcastle upon Tyne
Outer London
Sheffield

North East (p x)	North West (p xi)	Yorkshire and the Humber (p xii)	East Midlands (p xiii)	West Midlands (p xiv)	East of England (p xv)
London (p xvi)	South East (p xvii)	South West (p xviii)	Northern Ireland (p xix)	Scotland (p xx)	Wales (p xxi)

Regions and countries

Major cities

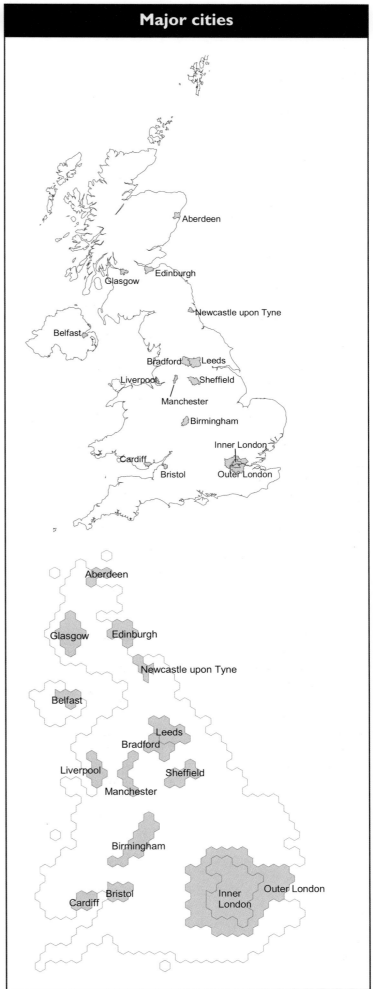

People and places

GOR	Local Authority	GOR	Local Authority	GOR	Local Authority	GOR	Local Authority
S	Aberdeen City	G	Cambridge	S	East Ayrshire	E	High Peak
S	Aberdeenshire	H	Camden	G	East Cambridgeshire	S	Highland
J	Adur	F	Cannock Chase	K	East Devon	H	Hillingdon
B	Allerdale	J	Canterbury	K	East Dorset	E	Hinckley & Bosworth
A	Alnwick	K	Caradon	S	East Dunbartonshire	J	Horsham
E	Amber Valley	W	Cardiff	J	East Hampshire	H	Hounslow
S	Angus	B	Carlisle	G	East Hertfordshire	G	Huntingdonshire
N	Antrim	W	Carmarthenshire	E	East Lindsey	B	Hyndburn
N	Ards	K	Carrick	S	East Lothian	S	Inverclyde
S	Argyll & Bute	N	Carrickfergus	E	East Northamptonshire	G	Ipswich
N	Armagh	A	Castle Morpeth	S	East Renfrewshire	W	Isle of Anglesey
J	Arun	G	Castle Point	D	East Riding of Yorkshire	J	Isle of Wight
E	Ashfield	N	Castlereagh	F	East Staffordshire	K	Isles of Scilly
J	Ashford	W	Ceredigion	J	Eastbourne	H	Islington
J	Aylesbury Vale	E	Charnwood	J	Eastleigh	K	Kennet
G	Babergh	G	Chelmsford	B	Eden	H	Kensington & Chelsea
N	Ballymena	K	Cheltenham	S	Edinburgh	K	Kerrier
N	Ballymoney	J	Cherwell	S	Eilean Siar	E	Kettering
N	Banbridge	B	Chester	B	Ellesmere Port & Neston	G	King's Lynn & West Norfolk
H	Barking & Dagenham	E	Chesterfield	J	Elmbridge	D	Kingston upon Hull
H	Barnet	A	Chester-le-Street	H	Enfield	H	Kingston upon Thames
D	Barnsley	J	Chichester	G	Epping Forest	D	Kirklees
B	Barrow-in-Furness	J	Chiltern	J	Epsom & Ewell	B	Knowsley
G	Basildon	B	Chorley	E	Erewash	H	Lambeth
J	Basingstoke & Deane	K	Christchurch	K	Exeter	B	Lancaster
E	Bassetlaw	H	City of London	S	Falkirk	N	Larne
K	Bath & North East Somerset	S	Clackmannanshire	J	Fareham	D	Leeds
G	Bedford	G	Colchester	G	Fenland	E	Leicester
N	Belfast	N	Coleraine	N	Fermanagh	J	Lewes
A	Berwick-upon-Tweed	B	Congleton	S	Fife	H	Lewisham
H	Bexley	W	Conwy	W	Flintshire	F	Lichfield
F	Birmingham	N	Cookstown	G	Forest Heath	N	Limavady
E	Blaby	B	Copeland	K	Forest of Dean	E	Lincoln
B	Blackburn with Darwen	E	Corby	B	Fylde	N	Lisburn
B	Blackpool	K	Cotswold	A	Gateshead	B	Liverpool
W	Blaenau Gwent	F	Coventry	E	Gedling	G	Luton
A	Blyth Valley	N	Craigavon	S	Glasgow City	B	Macclesfield
E	Bolsover	D	Craven	K	Gloucester	N	Magherafelt
B	Bolton	J	Crawley	J	Gosport	J	Maidstone
E	Boston	B	Crewe & Nantwich	J	Gravesham	G	Maldon
K	Bournemouth	H	Croydon	G	Great Yarmouth	F	Malvern Hills
J	Bracknell Forest	G	Dacorum	H	Greenwich	B	Manchester
D	Bradford	A	Darlington	J	Guildford	E	Mansfield
G	Braintree	J	Dartford	W	Gwynedd	J	Medway
G	Breckland	E	Daventry	H	Hackney	E	Melton
H	Brent	W	Denbighshire	B	Halton	K	Mendip
G	Brentwood	E	Derby	D	Hambleton	W	Merthyr Tydfil
W	Bridgend	E	Derbyshire Dales	H	Hammersmith & Fulham	H	Merton
F	Bridgnorth	N	Derry	E	Harborough	G	Mid Bedfordshire
J	Brighton & Hove	A	Derwentside	H	Haringey	K	Mid Devon
K	Bristol	D	Doncaster	G	Harlow	G	Mid Suffolk
G	Broadland	J	Dover	D	Harrogate	J	Mid Sussex
H	Bromley	N	Down	H	Harrow	A	Middlesbrough
F	Bromsgrove	F	Dudley	J	Hart	S	Midlothian
G	Broxbourne	S	Dumfries & Galloway	A	Hartlepool	J	Milton Keynes
E	Broxtowe	S	Dundee City	J	Hastings	J	Mole Valley
B	Burnley	N	Dungannon	J	Havant	W	Monmouthshire
B	Bury	A	Durham	H	Havering	S	Moray
W	Caerphilly	H	Ealing	F	Herefordshire	N	Moyle
D	Calderdale	A	Easington	G	Hertsmere	W	Neath Port Talbot

GOR	Local Authority	GOR	Local Authority	GOR	Local Authority	GOR	Local Authority
J	New Forest	J	Reigate & Barnstead	B	South Ribble	J	Tunbridge Wells
E	Newark & Sherwood	S	Renfrewshire	F	South Shropshire	A	Tynedale
F	Newcasle-under-Lyme	K	Restormel	K	South Somerset	G	Uttlesford
A	Newcastle upon Tyne	W	Rhondda Cynon Taf	F	South Staffordshire	W	Vale of Glamorgan
H	Newham	B	Ribble Valley	A	South Tyneside	J	Vale of White Horse
W	Newport	H	Richmond upon Thames	J	Southampton	B	Vale Royal
N	Newry & Mourne	D	Richmondshire	G	Southend-on-Sea	D	Wakefield
N	Newtownabbey	B	Rochdale	H	Southwark	F	Walsall
S	North Ayrshire	G	Rochford	J	Spelthorne	H	Waltham Forest
K	North Cornwall	B	Rossendale	G	St Albans	H	Wandsworth
K	North Devon	J	Rother	G	St Edmundsbury	A	Wansbeck
K	North Dorset	D	Rotherham	B	St Helens	B	Warrington
N	North Down	F	Rugby	F	Stafford	F	Warwick
E	North East Derbyshire	J	Runnymede	F	Staffordshire Moorlands	G	Watford
D	North East Lincolnshire	E	Rushcliffe	G	Stevenage	G	Waveney
D	North Lincolnshire	J	Rushmoor	S	Stirling	J	Waverley
G	North Norfolk	E	Rutland	B	Stockport	J	Wealden
F	North Shropshire	D	Ryedale	A	Stockton-on-Tees	A	Wear Valley
K	North Somerset	B	Salford	F	Stoke-on-Trent	E	Wellingborough
A	North Tyneside	K	Salisbury	N	Strabane	G	Welwyn Hatfield
F	North Warwickshire	F	Sandwell	F	Stratford-upon-Avon	J	West Berkshire
E	North West Leicestershire	D	Scarborough	K	Stroud	K	West Devon
K	North Wiltshire	S	Scottish Borders	G	Suffolk Coastal	K	West Dorset
E	Northampton	A	Sedgefield	A	Sunderland	S	West Dunbartonshire
G	Norwich	K	Sedgemoor	J	Surrey Heath	B	West Lancashire
E	Nottingham	B	Sefton	H	Sutton	E	West Lindsey
F	Nuneaton & Bedworth	D	Selby	J	Swale	S	West Lothian
E	Oadby & Wigston	J	Sevenoaks	W	Swansea	J	West Oxfordshire
B	Oldham	D	Sheffield	K	Swindon	K	West Somerset
N	Omagh	J	Shepway	B	Tameside	K	West Wiltshire
S	Orkney Islands	S	Shetland Islands	F	Tamworth	H	Westminster
F	Oswestry	F	Shrewsbury & Atcham	J	Tandridge	K	Weymouth & Portland
J	Oxford	J	Slough	K	Taunton Deane	B	Wigan
W	Pembrokeshire	F	Solihull	A	Teesdale	J	Winchester
B	Pendle	S	South Ayrshire	K	Teignbridge	J	Windsor & Maidenhead
K	Penwith	G	South Bedfordshire	F	Telford & Wrekin	B	Wirral
S	Perth & Kinross	J	South Bucks	G	Tendring	J	Woking
G	Peterborough	G	South Cambridgeshire	J	Test Valley	J	Wokingham
K	Plymouth	E	South Derbyshire	K	Tewkesbury	F	Wolverhampton
K	Poole	K	South Gloucestershire	J	Thanet	F	Worcester
J	Portsmouth	K	South Hams	G	Three Rivers	J	Worthing
W	Powys	E	South Holland	G	Thurrock	W	Wrexham
B	Preston	E	South Kesteven	J	Tonbridge & Malling	F	Wychavon
K	Purbeck	B	South Lakeland	K	Torbay	J	Wycombe
J	Reading	S	South Lanarkshire	W	Torfaen	B	Wyre
H	Redbridge	G	South Norfolk	K	Torridge	F	Wyre Forest
A	Redcar & Cleveland	E	South Northamptonshire	H	Tower Hamlets	D	York
F	Redditch	J	South Oxfordshire	B	Trafford		

NORTH EAST

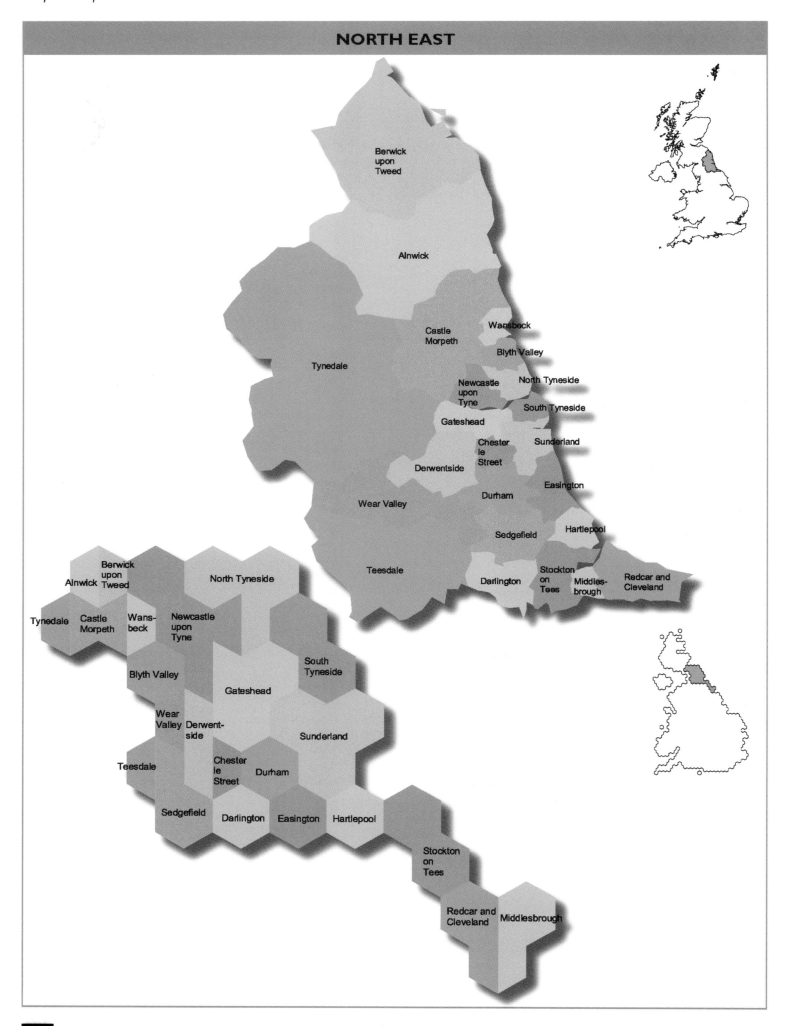

NORTH WEST

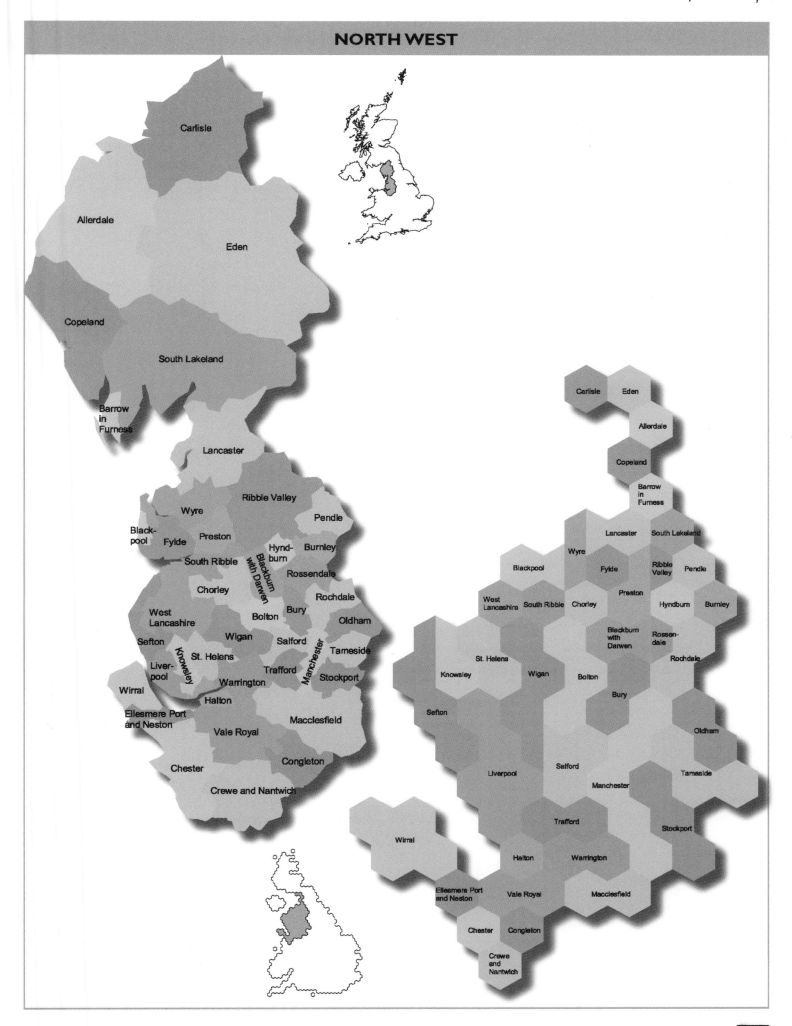

YORKSHIRE AND THE HUMBER

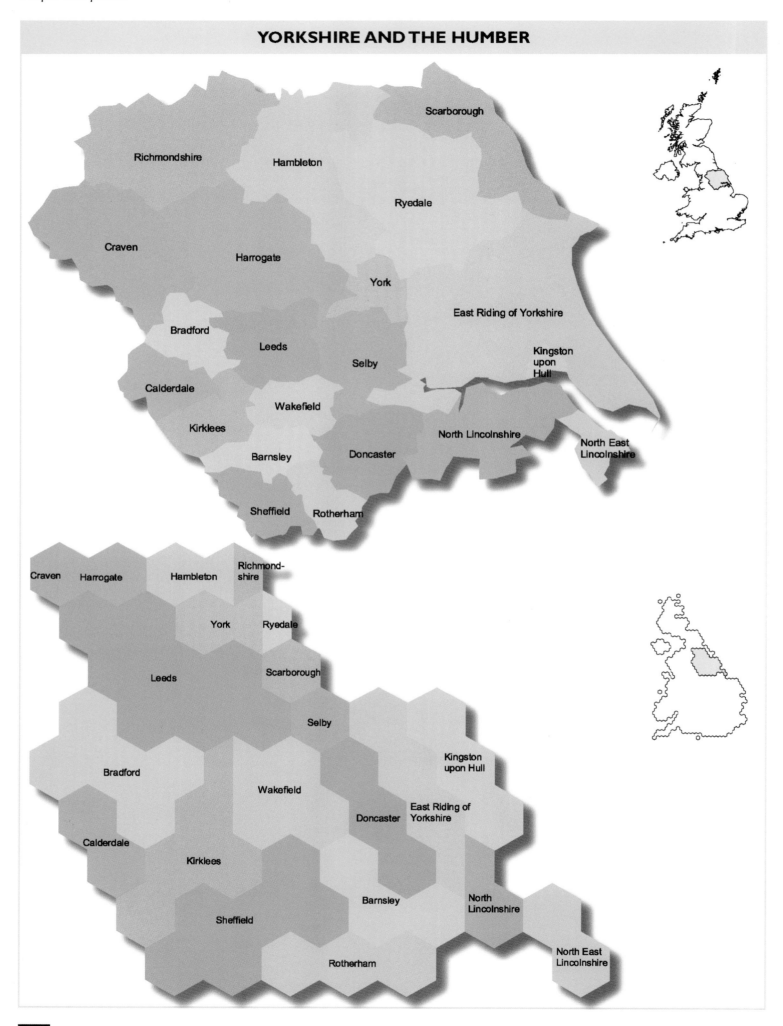

EAST MIDLANDS

WEST MIDLANDS

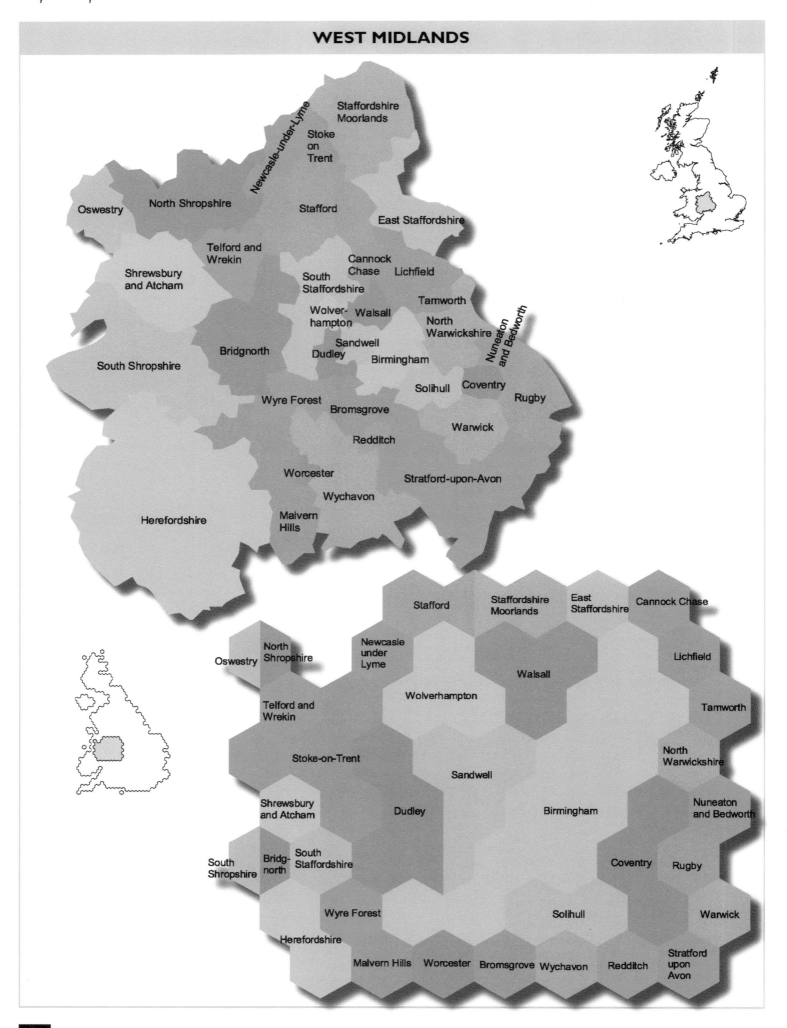

EAST of ENGLAND

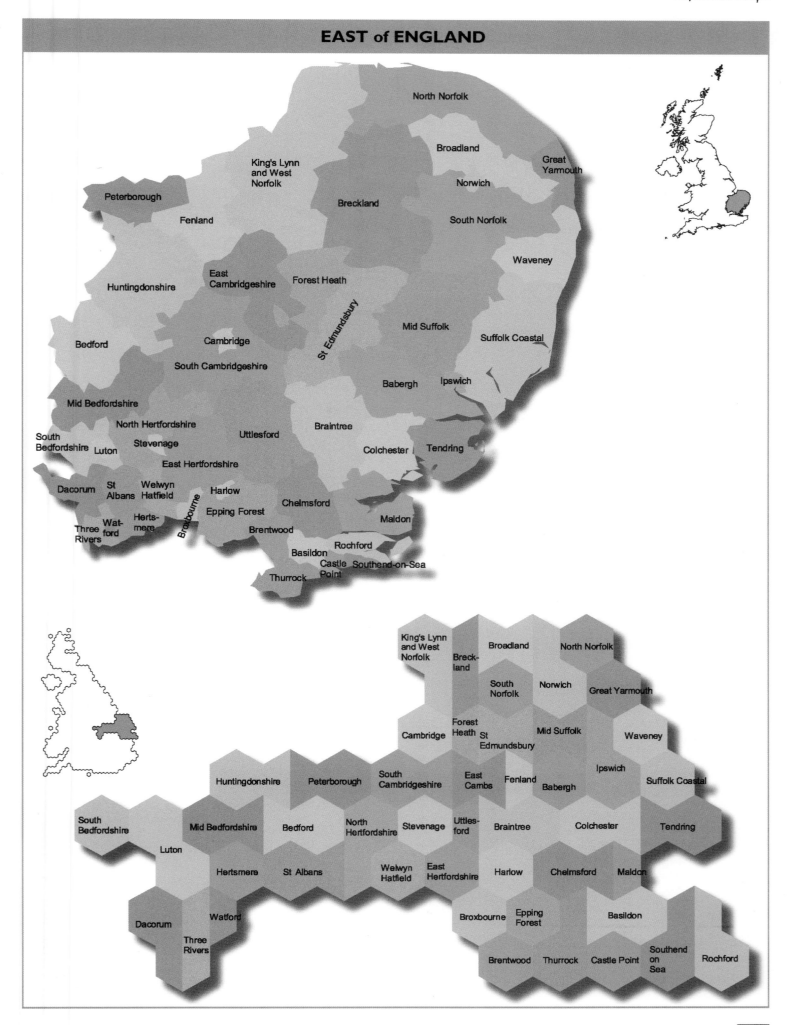

LONDON

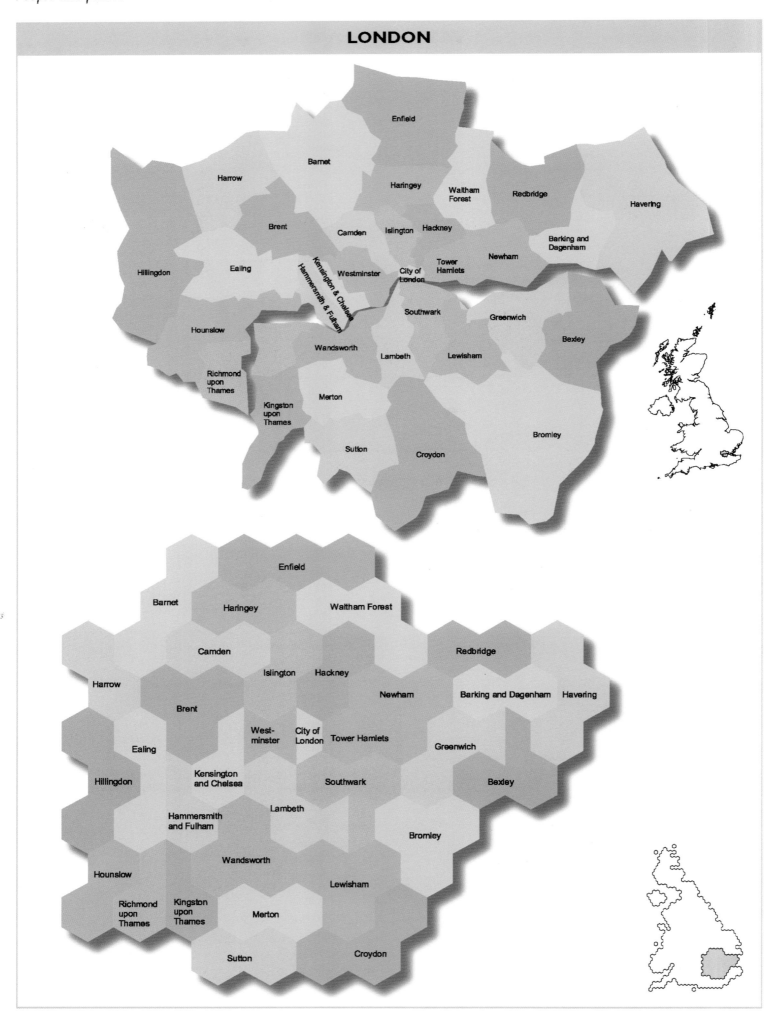

SOUTH EAST

SOUTH WEST

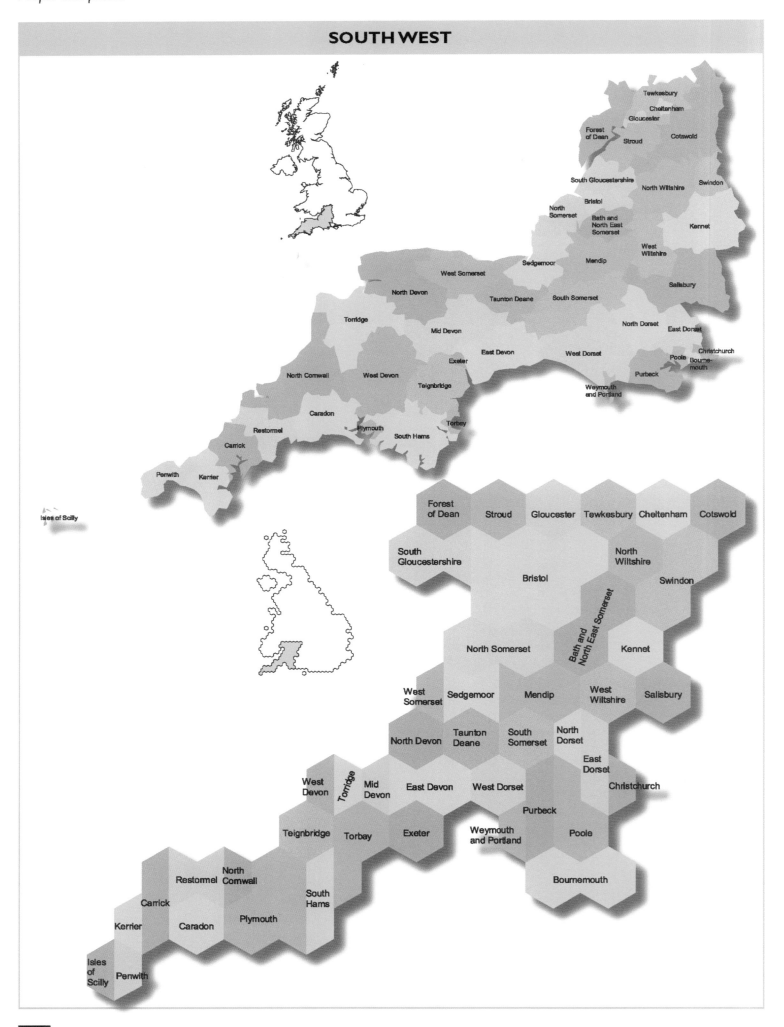

NORTHERN IRELAND

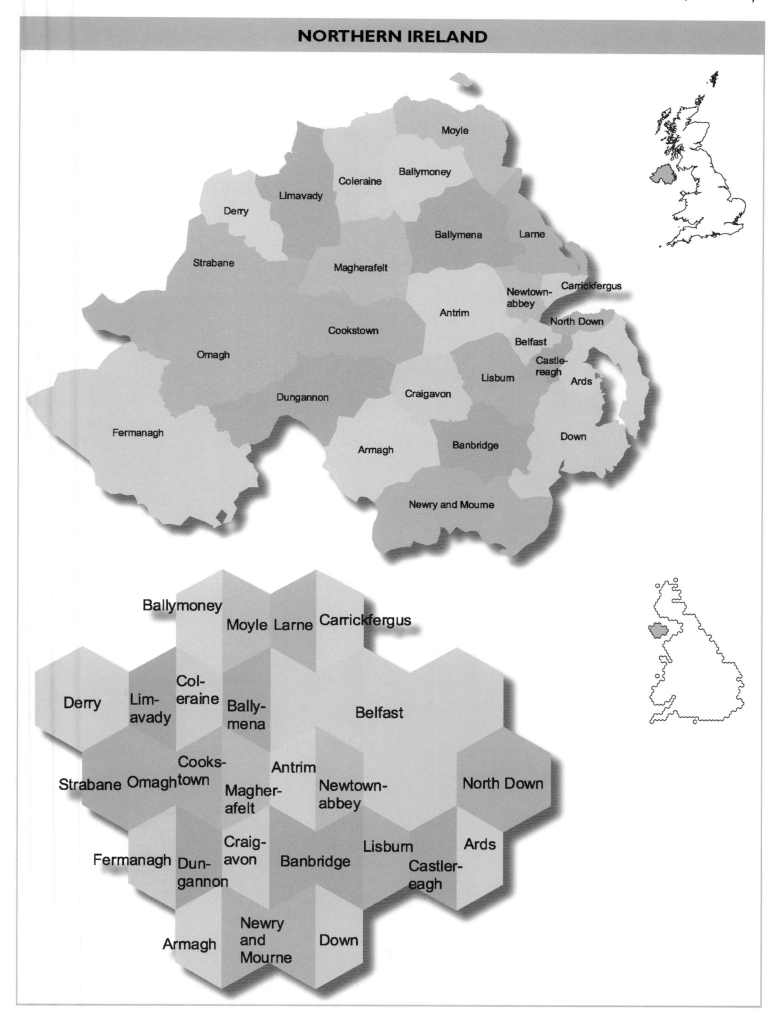

SCOTLAND

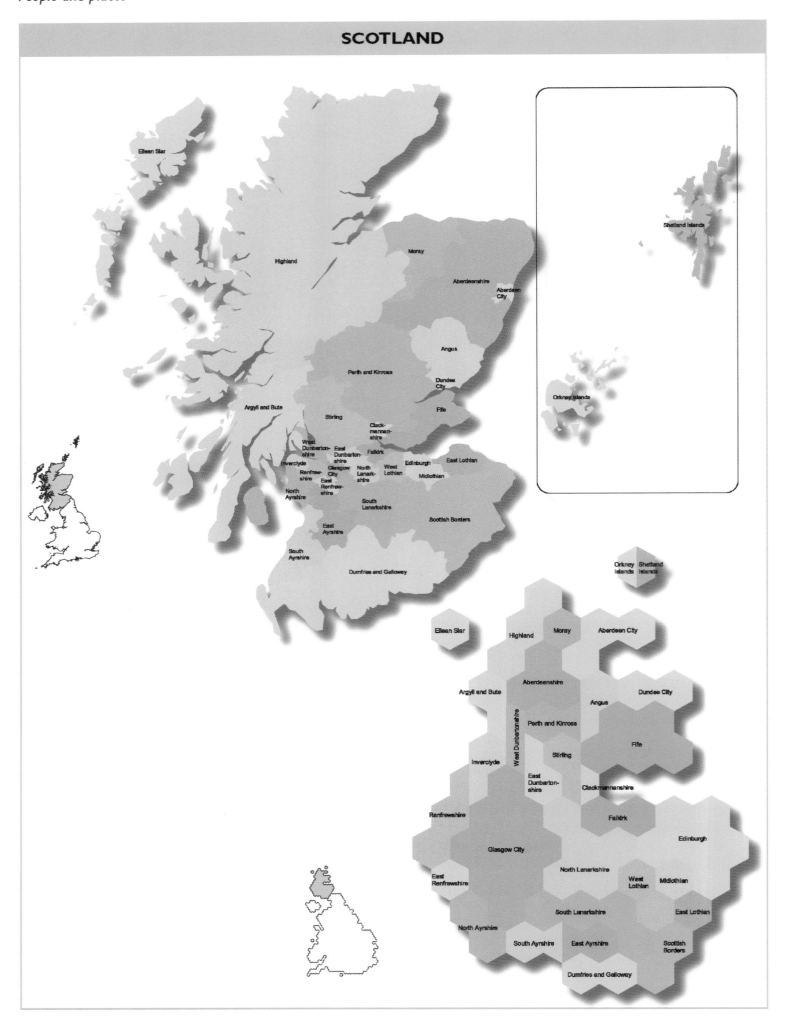

WALES

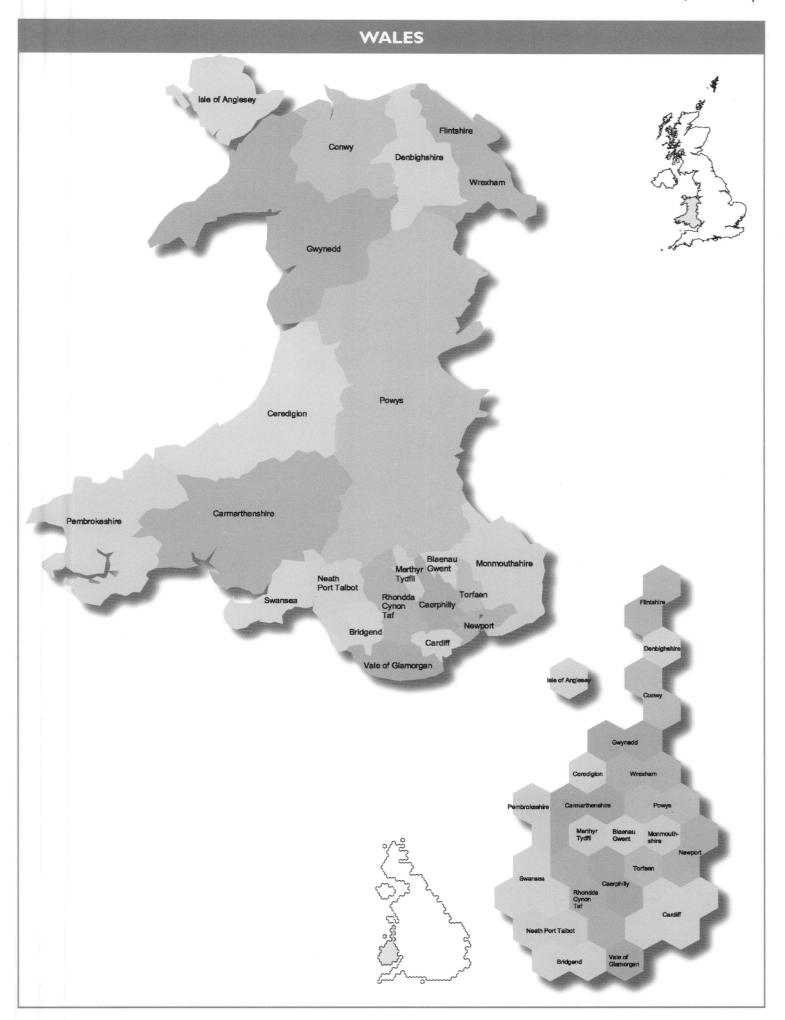

Introduction and overview

Maps in this section include:

People and places 2001 is the first published atlas that aims to depict the detailed human geography of the whole of the United Kingdom. It is also the first atlas of its kind:

- to include well over 500 separate maps and cartograms;
- to map so many aspects of life in the UK in a single volume;
- to show how almost all of those aspects to the geography of life are changing over time;
- to use a single population denominator throughout;
- to simultaneously depict every pattern graphically both from the point of view of people, and of the land.

The remit for writing *People and places 2001* was to provide a wealth of information on both the current state and changing human geography of the UK, with detailed commentary and analysis. The atlas is restricted to only including information released, or which can be derived or estimated from, the 2001 and 1991 Censuses of the population. The atlas is further restricted in that only the local authority scale is used throughout, in the limited space available for commentary, and in the need for analysis to be easily interpretable and to not obscure the overall picture. Thus most analysis appears in footnotes at the end of each chapter and provides just a taste of what can be studied from these sources. The last two censuses of the UK alone supply enough information for a dozen more atlases to be produced, in much finer geographical detail than is shown here, and with far more analysis. Data from earlier censuses and a huge range of other sources is also now available which could be used to illustrate better those aspects of life not well measured by a census. Nevertheless, we believe that we have presented here the most comprehensive account of the human geography of the UK available to date, and a more complete record than has been produced before in any single publication.

Taken as a whole, the atlas shows a nation of social divisions expressed through the changing patterns of where different groups of people in the UK live. The *increased dominance of London and the South East of England* is the single most striking image conveyed when all these maps and cartograms are considered as a whole. The *economic and social revival of Northern Ireland* is a similarly persistent theme.

Patterns of both polarisation in some aspects of life and of a nation coming together in other ways run through all the maps in this atlas. The atlas provides both a snapshot of a moment in time and a picture of how that snapshot came to be, and thus of where current trends are heading. The 2001 Census of the UK revealed a nation very different from that depicted by the 1991 Census. Although a majority of the population were included in both censuses, many of those people have changed the work they do, gained a job when they had none before, retired early, gone to university, bought cars or their home outright, in numbers never seen before. While many people have become richer and wealthier, more are poorer. Geographically, the population continues to move slowly and relentlessly southwards.

Other trends are changing more rapidly. The human geography of the UK is becoming transformed, driven by the economic needs of London, of finance, of the wealthy, the educated and the able, to the detriment of the periphery, of traditional industries, of the poor, and of those without qualifications. Only through charting the changing fortunes of hundreds of places, through a hundred thousand variables, summarising just a few aspects of millions of lives, can we begin to see this wider picture. The UK is a nation within which the human landscape varies widely, and many of those geographical variations are becoming more evident, more distinct, over time.

David Rhind and his colleagues drew the first detailed atlas of the UK census, using data from 1971 and the new but expensive technology of laser plotting (Census Research Unit et al, 1980). The atlas depicted the population for only three dozen variables, but in incredible spatial detail for the time, using pioneering technology to individually colour every kilometre square of the country according to the social characteristics of local residents. Many of the conventional maps shown here appear very similar 30 years

later. The use of local authority boundaries in this atlas has little impact on the patterns' appearances. However, the use of population cartograms do show a very different country to that depicted by conventional mapping; and we can now include Northern Ireland and change over time data almost universally throughout these pages, which was far more difficult to do in the 1970s.

New technology greatly simplifies the production of censuses atlases and thus results in more being produced following each successive census. Following the 1981 Census of population separate atlases were drawn of the different countries of the UK, but none of the UK as a whole, and many using what was then called a 'line plotter' to colour areas through 'hatching' (for England and Wales, see Champion, 1983; for Northern Ireland see Horner et al, 1987). A later publication also explored the use of mapping with unconventional areas, but again changing the areas being mapped had little impact on the patterns seen (Champion et al, 1987).

By 1991 technology had moved on again but line plotters were still employed to produce the first census atlas published almost immediately following release of the census data, the direct precursor of this volume: *People and places 1991* (Forrest and Gordon, 1993; Gordon and Forrest, 1995). A little later the Ordnance Survey, then under the direction of David Rhind, also produced an atlas based largely on the 1991 Census. Their atlas shaded areas with continuous colour and was the first of a census in the UK to be printed in full colour and to include Northern Ireland in places, although often as a single spatial unit (Ordnance Survey, 1995). Two more detailed atlases were drawn of the same census and of changes since 1981, both including some cartograms, but both excluded Northern Ireland and used only two colour separation in their printing (Dorling, 1995a; Champion et al, 1996). One used local authority wards rather than districts as its basic spatial unit. Yet again, that had little effect on the patterns shown. It is only now that costs of production have fallen

sufficiently that a full-colour atlas can be drawn of the whole of the UK without the financial sponsorship of a national mapping or census agency.

In the remainder of this introduction we explain why particular design decisions were taken to produce the maps shown here, and how they can best be understood.

The inherent structure to the human geography of the UK is so rigid, the differences between places so great, that the patterns seen are little altered whether that geography is mapped through kilometre grid squares, wards, functional regions, or the very wide variety of other boundaries now available. The last 30 years of census atlas production in the UK has demonstrated that the spatial units used have little impact on the patterns seen at the national scale. Because of this, and because we wished to start work on this atlas as soon as the first 2001 Census data was released, we use 2001 local authority boundaries throughout this atlas, 434 areas in all – 354 in England, 22 in Wales, 32 in Scotland, and 26 in Northern Ireland. The Province is only excluded in a very few cases where no comparable data was made available for that country. Scotland is only excluded in one set of maps as a question on particular professional qualifications was not asked there.

In most cases where the entire UK cannot be mapped this affects only a few maps of change as these required data from the 1991 Census, and that was less complete for the Province. We also fail to show change from 1991 entirely again in a few cases where no comparable information was available for all of the UK to that recorded for the first time in 2001. When there is data only collected in Northern Ireland, on adherence to particular religions, we have mapped that here just for the Province. The inclusion of Northern Ireland added disproportionately to the work involved in creating these maps, but showed some of the most dramatic local changes within all the UK to have occurred there in the 1990s. Nationally, the overriding story is of a growing dominance of the capital and its hinterland. The growing dominance of the South East is only made clear when censuses are compared[1]. We return to that observation, in detail, in our conclusion to the atlas.

What does make a huge difference to the patterns seen in any atlas of any census is the projection used for mapping

[1] In work with many colleagues we saw glimpses of these changes through analysing different contemporary sources of spatial data throughout the 1990s, but without the 2001 Census we often had to guess in the conclusions to our books and papers as to where these trends were heading. It was in studying the changing patterns to mortality in Britain that we first saw evidence that a pattern of increased spatial polarisation may be forming: Davey Smith and Dorling, 1996, 1997; Davey Smith et al, 1998, 2001; Gordon et al, 1999; Mitchell et al, 2000; Shaw et al, 2002a; Dorling and Gunnell, 2003.

the census data. Here we have used both a conventional map of the UK and an equal population cartogram.

An *equal population cartogram* is part map, part graph; it is a map projection which attempts to keep areas together which neighbour each other and the overall shape and compass orientation of the country roughly correct while simultaneously ensuring that every area is drawn approximately in proportion to its population. On the cartogram each individual is given roughly equal weight, the variations within cities are revealed, while the variations in the countryside are reduced in size so as not to dominate the image and divert the eye away from what is happening to the majority of the population. For this atlas we created a cartogram by hand using pencil and graph paper. The process of creating the cartogram took over a year to complete.

We began with a computer-created cartogram of parliamentary constituencies. Each constituency contains roughly the same number of people and each was drawn as a hexagon because, on average, areas tend to have just less than six geographical neighbours each. By using hexagons we were able to minimise the number of places that neighboured areas that did not touch on the ground and the number that failed to touch areas that they should have. Nevertheless a great many geographical inconsistencies were created. These could have been removed by using more complex shapes, but that would have created a far more visually complex cartogram than we wished for.

Having created the constituency cartogram as a mesh of hexagons we next assigned parts of each constituency to each local authority. Some local authorities are made up of many constituencies, such as Glasgow and Leeds; in other places two local authorities fit within a single constituency. Most often there is a more complex relationship between the two geographies. We simplified this by deciding that constituencies could only be split in two at most, and if so, only vertically. Local authorities had to be contiguous units and to neighbour as many other authorities that they were contiguous to on the ground, on the cartogram, as was possible. This required numerous revisions to the cartogram to be made, all again by hand. Next, with colleagues, we added the geographies of health authorities (of various incarnations), of former standard and current GORs, of travel-to-work areas, old counties and other ways in which the UK can be divided up, such that the cartogram presented just for one set of areas in these pages could be used to depict as wide a range of different types of areas as possible in the future. Although many attempts have been made to create an automated solution to this kind of mapping, there is still no computer algorithm that can do this; a painstaking manual process

is required to create the jigsaw that forms the underlying base map of people in the UK[2].

In the 'Reference map' section that precedes this Introduction and overview, summary maps of the entire cartogram of the UK are included, together with a list of all local authorities and a series of key maps for each GOR, which also allow areas on the conventional map to be identified. To do this, locate the area on the conventional map, and it will be shaded the same colour on the cartogram; and on both the cartogram and the map each area is also named. To understand the equal population geography of the UK requires taking a little time to study these key maps.

Large local authorities form distinct shapes on the cartogram. Glasgow appears as a diamond, Nottingham and Leicester as a pair of triangles that neighbour on the cartogram, if not in reality. When you look at the cartogram you are seeing a map that shows in most detail the places where most people live, and how those places are related to each other in terms of how many other people live, between them. When you look at conventional maps you mostly see places where almost no one lives, and places that appear to be near to each other, for instance boroughs either side of London, are in population reality often very far apart. Of course, unless you have extremely good eyesight you cannot see how London boroughs are coloured at all on the conventional map. The conventional map tends to hide most the places where the population is poorest, where people are not almost all White, where people travel to work on the bus, where they live in terraced housing or flats, and where they are often least powerful. The conventional map shows a country dominated by agriculture, not an urban nation dominated by a world city within which there are large pockets of poverty as well as affluence.

A further advantage of the cartogram over the conventional map is that it is easy to interpret the colours shown on the cartogram. If half the cartogram is coloured a particular shade, then the social characteristic associated with that colour apply to the areas within which half the population of the UK live. For each area the characteristic is simply an average – it will not apply to many of the people living there, but it does typify those people as a group. Where there are blocks of colour on the map or cartogram, then the geographical group being typified is larger. The real boundaries on these maps and cartograms are not those of the local authorities used to demarcate the data dissemination units, but the boundaries formed

---

[2] For some work conducted during the 1990s working towards and further explaining this form of mapping, see Dorling, 1992a, 1993, 1995b, 1996a, 1998; Champion and Dorling, 1994; Dorling and Fairbairn, 1997.

by the blocks of colour shown in these graphics; some are complex and others are very simple.

Furthermore, in every chapter of this atlas (save this one) a single denominator is used for calculating rates for every single map: the entire population of the local area. This is a break from past mapping traditions that has important implications for reading the atlas. Every rate can be compared with every other on all maps (except for those in this chapter) because all the rates use the same denominator in their calculation. This denominator is different in 1991 as compared to 2001, so that at both points in time every rate is 'per head' and every living person at that point in time is used in its calculation. Thus we do not show rates of unemployment only for people of working age, or people in the labour market, or rates of youth unemployment as a percentage of everyone out of work in an area. Instead we show the rates of unemployment as a proportion of the entire population, and the rate of youth unemployment as a proportion of the entire population in a local area. These decisions result in the rates being shown often appearing very small. We have tried at all times not to differentiate between differences of less than 0.1% of local populations or of less than 100,000 people nationally. We are showing how common each social category is in the population as a whole, not as a proportion of some sub-group of that population. There are drawbacks to having made this decision, but we believe it is more important to ensure that almost every map in an atlas can be compared with every other, rather than to try to identify a particular most appropriate population denominator for each variable.

There are also benefits to having made this decision that we did not foresee. To be able to map social characteristics such as tenure and car ownership we had to measure the number of people, not households, living in housing of a particular tenure or having access through a member of their household to a car. The resulting maps are very different to what would have been seen had households rather than people been mapped, particularly the maps of the changes to these characteristics over time. All these decisions help us to focus on *people in places*. As the millennium turned, numerous studies were presented of how life in Britain had changed over the preceding century[3]. Here we have tried to add the detail to that last decade of change in a way that allows all the changes to be compared, and their potential impact in the future (were these trends to continue) to be gauged in their respective levels of importance through the numbers of people each change affects.

As well as trying to draw as simple a cartogram as possible, we have also tried to use the simplest colouring schemes available to shade these diagrams. This chapter is the only one to use more complex shading that illustrates how complex such shading can be by using all colours of the rainbow. In the seven chapters that follow, only five shades, each a single primary colour of the rainbow, are used to shade the maps and cartograms of 2001. Identical shading is used on each, and so only one key is needed for both map and cartogram. A map and cartogram are placed alongside these two graphics, showing how the variable being mapped changed during the 1990s. Here, where there have been decreases in that variable, a second contrasting shade of colour is used to indicate that, and again, only five shades are used in all. The use of the contrasting shades helps to identify where polarisation may have occurred, where a particular group of the population is becoming more spatially concentrated.

Social polarisation has continued to rise in the UK in the 1990s in many aspects of life. For polarisation to be occurring geographically, falls or slow rises must occur where a characteristic is relatively rare, while either the slowest falls or the fastest increases must have occurred where it was most common to begin with. Thus both the static and change maps need to be compared simultaneously. There were great swings in value of housing, in employment rates and in migration taking place throughout the 1990s, but, in general, these have led to the UK becoming a more divided nation than ever seen before (Dorling et al, 1994; Pattie et al, 1995, 1997; Dorling and Woodward, 1996; Shaw et al, 1998, 1999; Davey Smith et al, 2000, 2002; Dorling and Simpson, 2001; Dorling and Rees, 2003a, 2003b, 2004).

Throughout the atlas we have measured change over time as 'percent point change'. That is, we have subtracted the proportion of all people having a characteristic in 1991 from the same proportion as measured in 2001. This method of calculating change produces far less dramatic statistics than do measures of relative change, but again this choice makes all the change statistics in the atlas comparable. The larger a change shown in this atlas, the more people it involved. Because in many places the rate of underlying population change is much slower than of social change, the maps of change are very similar to much simpler maps of changing absolute numbers of people (only the first map in this chapter shows those), but taking into account the widely different populations of local authorities across space. Some of the fastest changes may well have taken place within parts of the largest local authorities and here our use of this geography will disguise that. In other cases, local changes in rural areas may only be apparent because of small local authorities adding to the variety of rates shown in those areas, but we have shrunk those areas on the cartogram to reduce their visual impact.

---

[3] With colleagues we contributed to the millennium speculation; had we known what the maps in this atlas reveal, we might have been a little less optimistic: Dorling et al, 2000; Gregory et al, 2001; Shaw et al, 2002b; Dorling, 2003; Tunstall et al, 2004.

Had we used a more evenly populated set of places for these maps, such as parliamentary constituencies, each cartogram would appear as a honeycomb of hexagons and identifying individual constituencies would have been very difficult without a great deal of extraneous information being added. Had we measured change using a relative scale we would have highlighted those changes that affected the areas with the fewest people. Furthermore it would not have been clear what our denominator should have been. If measuring change in the number of people working in banking for instance, after subtracting the numbers in 1991 from those in 2001, do you divide the result by the numbers initially working in 1991 only, by the entire population of the area in 1991, or by some average of either, combining both 1991 or 2001? The percent point measure of change is simplest, most robust to errors in the data and actually tells you for every one hundred people how many more or less are now of the characteristic being shown.

Despite using a robust measure of change, we still required good quality information. Where changes involve only relatively few people they are much more sensitive to measurement error than are larger changes or just depictions of the situation at one point in time. The 2001 Census was corrected before it was released by the census authorities to ensure it was representative of each area of the country. There have been debates over its accuracy, but these have been very minor as compared to those which followed the release of the 1991 Census statistics. With colleagues we have corrected the results of the 1991 Census to include all the people thought at that time to have been missed by the census authorities (Dorling and Simpson, 1994; Simpson and Dorling, 1994; Pattie et al, 1996; Martin et al, 2002; Mitchell et al, 2002). At the time of writing the census authorities are still debating exactly how many people there were in the UK in 2001, but are quibbling over only a few tens of thousands in a few places; they are also debating whether as many were missed as we thought in 1991. We believe that the results of these deliberations would have no discernable impact on these maps. The 1991 Census results, corrected to the 1991 mid-year estimate, are used here in all cases except for some variables for the City of London, where the uncorrected results appeared more reliable. In hindsight, had we been attempting this exercise again we might have merged the City and a similarly tiny authority, the Scilly Isles, with their most appropriate neighbouring districts. Some of the most extreme changes seen in many maps are for these two areas of the country. Part of the reason for that will have been measurement error at either census.

However, another part of the reason is that the City has been in the centre of a maelstrom of rapid social change in London. We believe its social characteristics have changed rapidly. Furthermore, the Isles of Scilly are in some ways also changing rapidly. But both areas, due

partly to having hotels and other unusual forms of housing, are disproportionately affected by changes in the ways successive censuses count people as being resident or as living in an area. Overall, the change in the definition of residence has little influence on our maps as we are using the 1991 Census corrected to both incorporate the people who were missed by that census and to move people around the country to where they would have been counted using 2001 Census definitions.

All this pedantry may appear a little unnecessary. Unfortunately, creating a clear picture is only achieved through worrying through all the details, repeatedly correcting and checking the data, and looking one further time when anything appears a little 'odd'. Undoubtedly, however, some errors will have slipped through.

The census data is not produced in a form that is simple to use. For 1991 it was disseminated according to the district boundaries in place in that year. We took the data at output area level and re-aggregated it to 2001 areas (which, incidentally, used December 2002 boundaries). Data from the 2001 Census was released in different formats, by each of the three main census authorities. The stitching together of these various sources took a great deal of time, patience and care. A suspicious person may think that the 'powers that be' did not want an atlas of change of the whole UK drawn at all!

Having collected the data, cleaned it, re-amalgamated it to make it comparable by area, checked which variables could be compared over time, drawn our new base maps, and decided on what shading schemes we would use, what types of measures of change, and which denominators, we were finally able to choose what to map and how to structure the atlas.

We have tried to include almost every variable that can be most simply mapped as a count of people from both of the last two censuses and some of the new measures of the characteristics of the population introduced into the 2001 Census. We rejected variables where the patterns of change or of the situation in 2001 were not of interest or appeared to have been too influenced by measurement error. This mainly influenced the residents of communal establishments and thus we include no maps of the populations of prisons, nursing homes, nor student halls of residence, hostels, nor of the homeless who were poorly counted at both censuses.

We have divided the atlas into seven chapters following this introduction and overview. These are easily identified through the blocks of colour of their maps, and each begins with a brief summary of the topic covered. The chapters are: Age and sex (red), Religion and ethnicity (orange), Birthplace and migration (yellow), Qualifications and employment (green), Occupation and industry (blue),

Families and households (indigo) and Homes and cars (violet). Each chapter thus addresses a common pair of themes, usually with other related information inserted. The maps to each chapter are also all accompanied by commentary, and in many cases, some analysis of the figures in footnotes. In many cases we have simply listed where the most interesting changes have occurred due to lack of space and time to investigate each trend further. However, some particular themes are taken further in the footnoted analysis which is amalgamated at the end of each chapter, including the implications of the changing sizes of birth cohorts, changing levels of residential segregation, and of industrial agglomeration. The comments we make on what is seen are partly guided by these brief analyses, but are mainly made through extending the implications of more detailed work we have published with others elsewhere (Dorling, 1991, 1992b, 1994, 1996b, 1997, 1999; Champion and Dorling, 1993; Dorling and Atkins, 1995; Shaw and Dorling, 1998; Dorling and Simpson, 2000; Johnston et al, 2001, 2003; Dixie and Dorling, 2002).

In the remainder of this introduction and overview we draw seven far more detailed maps than those included in the rest of this atlas. These are the only seven maps which are not using total population as their denominator, and most are not simply derived from census data but require some more calculation. However, the patterns shown in these maps help to explain some of the most important underlying changes that have occurred to the geography of UK society in recent years.

The first three pages of maps show, respectively:

- how many people lived in each place in 2001 and how the number of people in each place have changed over time;
- the population density of each area and how that has altered;
- how the population potential of each area has altered to be as it is now, and how it is now.

Population potential is a measure of how many people live near each place, and its calculation is explained in the text that accompanies that map. The three maps show how the population has grown most in the South, has become more densely populated in London than before, and how those changes have resulted in the centre of population moving southwards, with there now being fewer people living near the cities of the North West and North East of England, despite the overall growth in population.

In all the maps that follow these underlying population changes are removed by standardising rates for each area by the population living there at each point in time. Such standardisation allows the changing characteristics of the population to be studied, but it is important to remember that the number of people involved is changing in each area too.

The next three maps depict estimates of the current rates of poverty, income and wealth in the UK, and how those patterns have changed in recent years. These are the only maps and cartograms in the atlas that map households rather than people, as poverty, income and wealth are best estimated at the level of households. We have included the maps here as earlier versions were included in the 1991 volumes of *People and places* (Forrest and Gordon, 1993), but we have updated their measurement as more data is now available (see the Appendix).

The rate of poverty is an estimate of the proportion of households in each area living in what the majority of people in Britain at each point in time would consider to be poverty: not having access to the money or resources to have a decent standard of life. Over time, the expectations of the population of Britain rise, and as income inequalities in the UK have increased, the proportions living in poverty measured in this consensual way have risen too.

Two successive surveys of poverty in Britain were used to ascertain how best to estimate the number of households in each area living in poverty at each point in time. Those surveys were used to produce a model of how best to combine census variables to make that estimate[4]. The original *People and places* volumes also include a 'fat cat' index. We have replaced that here with two simple models. The first, termed 'rich'[5], which estimates the proportion of households living on high incomes, and the

---

[4] For the estimate of the number of households living in poverty in 1991 the following households were combined, each weighted by a proportion: 21.7% of households with no car + 20.3% of households renting + 16.0% of lone-parent households + 15.9% of households headed by a person in social class IV or V + 10.8% of households containing a person with a limiting long-term illness + 9.4% of households containing a person who is unemployed.

For the estimate in 2001 the combination of variables used was: 13.6% of households with no car + 19.7% of households renting + 21.8% of lone-parent households + 5.9% of households headed by a person in a low social class + 9.9% of households containing a person with a limiting long-term illness + 13.8% of households containing a person who is unemployed + 36.6% of overcrowded households + 8.5% of households with adults with no qualifications.

[5] We producd a simple regression model to predict the number of households in each area with recourse to an annual income of over £60,000 a year using data released by Barclays bank shortly after the 2001 Census. The same model was applied in both census years: 22.6% of people in high earning occupations (Corporate Managers, Science and Technology Professionals, and Business and Public Service Professionals) + 0.8% of households with access to three or more cars, less 1%.

second, termed 'wealth'[6], that estimates the proportion of households with recourse to substantial wealth. These three pages of maps are thus the only three pages of modelled estimates in this atlas. They will inevitably be subject to a higher degree of error than the remainder of the maps that tabulate actual census variables, but we feel they provide a useful summary of how poverty and affluence appear to be rising across much of the UK, but especially in London. It is London too where the richest people live and where their incomes have risen most, but it is around London where most wealth is concentrated and where that concentration is becoming ever more evident. This introduction ends by showing the map and cartogram of how the national census agencies have typified each place in the country by giving it a label dependent on its census characteristics in 2001. The UK is made up of hundreds of distinct towns and cities, each surrounded by unique hinterlands of villages, hamlets and farmlands. However, there is a structure to this variety that can be used to both typify each place, and which is repeatedly revealed when a myriad of individual characteristics of the population are plotted and compared. In each place there is much greater variety than can be shown in these pages, but people within each place are generally becoming more like each other and less like those who live in very different parts of the country. Beneath the divisions that the simple census maps and typologies reveal are deep-seated and growing spatial inequalities in poverty, wealth and income. Only in London do large numbers of both rich and poor people live, and within that great world city they too are spatially segregated, but at a much finer scale than can be revealed here.

We conclude the atlas, in a final chapter following all the maps, by summing up the major changes to the UK population that highlight most what has changed during the 1990s, and hence where we can expect the population to change the most in the near future and in which ways.

Our conclusion is that the country is being split in half. To the South is the *metropolis of Greater London*, which now extends across all of southern England in its immediate spatial impact. To the North and West is the *archipelago of the provinces*, a series of poorly connected city cluster islands that appear to be slowly sinking demographically, socially and economically.

There is great variation in this simple picture, but this is our overall impression of where current trends are taking the UK geographically. For the detail to this summary,

each chapter that follows is preceded by an overview in which all the changing patterns shown are considered. Within each chapter there is commentary to each pair of maps and cartograms that usually states the total number of people in the UK being counted at both points in time, and the proportion of the UK population they constituted in both censuses. We often list individual districts that contain the highest concentrations of a particular group, concentrations over a particular threshold, or which have seen the most extreme changes over time. In many cases these lists appear in footnotes to the maps, at the end of each chapter.

We have tried to use the official names of all local authorities, and to present them in the same order throughout, starting with the London boroughs, then moving through England in old county order, ending with Wales, Scotland and Northern Ireland. Where a district has two names we have adopted the convention of replacing 'and' with '&' so that it is clear that a single place is being labelled.

We hope you find our analysis, the maps and cartograms of interest, relatively simple to understand and revealing a picture of the UK that highlights what is most unusual while still depicting the more subtle and often smaller changes that are slowly occurring everywhere. All the data that this atlas is based on was available at the time of writing through various official and research websites. The cartogram base has also been made available for general use on the web. It may take a little time to find the relevant information, but if there is a map you wish to see which is not shown in the pages that follow, it is very likely that you could now find the information to draw your own. Thirty years ago only the national census agencies had the resources to do this, 20 years ago just a few dozen academics were able to do so and had access to the data required, a decade ago there were still severe restrictions on who could access census data, use mapping software and even draw these boundaries. Today all those obstacles are gone, and in 10 years' time there may be little need for an atlas such as this. You will be able to draw your own. Nonetheless, if current socio-spatial trends continue, then in 10 years' time a much bleaker image of the UK will be revealed.

People depend more than ever on the places they are living in for the quality of their lives, and those places are collecting together ever more distinct groups of people. The Kingdom is now as far from a collection of united countries and regions as it has ever been. On the maps shown here, the UK is looking more and more like a city-state and its provincial archipelago of allegiance. It is a Kingdom united only by history, increasingly divided by its geography.

---

6 We produced a simple regression model to predict the numbers of households in council tax bands G and H in each area and applied it to each census: 16.1% of households with access to three or more cars + 15.7% of households living in homes with seven or more rooms.

References

Census Research Unit, OPCS (Office of Population Censuses and Surveys) and General Registrar Office (Scotland) (1980) *People in Britain: A census atlas*, London: HMSO.

Champion, A. (1983) *England and Wales '81*, Sheffield: The Geographical Association.

Champion, A. and Dorling, D. (1993) '1991 Census figures by tenure and ethnic group', *Housing Review*, vol 42, no 4, p 66.

Champion, A. and Dorling, D. (1994) 'Population change for Britain's functional regions 1951-91', *Population Trends*, vol 77, pp 14-23.

Champion, A., Green, A., Owen, D., Ellin, D. and Coombes, M. (1987) *Changing places: Britain's demographic, economic and social complexion*, London: Edward Arnold.

Champion, T., Wong, C., Rooke, A., Dorling, D., Coombes, M. and Brunsdon, B. (1996) *The population of Britain in the 1990s: A social and economic atlas*, Oxford: Oxford University Press.

Davey Smith, G. and Dorling, D. (1996) '"I'm all right John": voting patterns and mortality in England and Wales, 1981-92', *British Medical Journal*, vol 313, pp 1573-77.

Davey Smith, G. and Dorling, D. (1997) 'Association between voting patterns and mortality remains', *British Medical Journal*, vol 315, pp 430-1.

Davey Smith, G., Dorling, D. and Shaw, M. (eds) (2001) *Poverty, inequality and health: 1800-2000: A reader*, Bristol: The Policy Press.

Davey Smith, G., Shaw, M. and Dorling, D. (1998) 'Shrinking areas and mortality', *The Lancet*, vol 352, pp 1139-40.

Davey Smith, G., Shaw, M., Mitchell, R., Dorling, D. and Gordon, D. (2000) 'Inequalities in health continue to grow despite government's pledges', *British Medical Journal*, vol 320, p 582.

Davey-Smith, G., Dorling, D., Mitchell, R. et al (2002) 'Health inequalities in Britain: continuing increases up to the end of the 20th century', *Journal of Epidemiology and Community Health*, vol 56, pp 434-5.

Dixie, J. and Dorling, D. (2002) 'New questions for the 2001 Census', in P.H. Rees, D. Martin and P. Williamson (eds) *The Census data system, Part VI, Planning for 2001 Census outputs*, Chichester: John Wiley & Sons, ch 20, pp 283-93.

Dorling, D. (1991) *The demand for housing in Britain 1971-2001*, North East Regional Research Laboratory Research Report, Newcastle upon Tyne: Centre for Urban and Regional Development Studies, University of Newcastle upon Tyne.

Dorling, D. (1992a) 'Visualizing people in space and time', *Environment and Planning B*, vol 19, pp 613-37.

Dorling, D. (1992b) 'Stretching space and splicing time: from cartographic animation to interactive visualization', *Cartography and Geographical Information Systems*, vol 19, no 4, pp 215-27, 267-70.

Dorling, D. (1993) 'Map design for census mapping', *The Cartographic Journal*, vol 30, no 2, pp 167-83.

Dorling, D. (1994) 'Visualizing the geography of the population with the 1991 Census', *Population Trends*, vol 76, pp 29-39.

Dorling, D. (1995a) *A new social atlas of Britain*, London: John Wiley and Sons.

Dorling, D. (1995b) 'Visualizing changing social structure from a census', *Environment and Planning A*, vol 27, no 2, pp 353-78.

Dorling, D. (1996a) *Area cartograms: their use and creation*, Concepts and Techniques in Modern Geography Series No 59, Colchester: Environmental Publications, University of East Anglia.

Dorling, D. (1996b) 'Be cheerful, strive to be happy, identifying disadvantaged areas: health wealth and happiness', *Radical Statistics*, vol 62, pp 8-21.

Dorling, D. (1997) 'Regional and local differences in the housing characteristics of ethnic minorities', in V. Karn (ed) *Ethnic minorities: Education, employment and housing*, OPCS, London: The Stationery Office, ch 8, pp 147-69.

Dorling, D. (1998) 'Human geography – when it is good to map', *Environment and Planning A*, vol 30, pp 277-88.

Dorling, D. (1999) 'Who's afraid of income inequality?', *Environment and Planning A*, Commentary, vol 31, no 4, pp 571-4.

Dorling, D. (2003) 'A century of progress? Inequalities in British society, 1901-2000', in D. Gilbert, D. Matless and B. Short, *Geographies of British modernity: Space and society in the twentieth century*, Oxford: Blackwells, Part 1, Ch 2, pp 31-53.

Dorling, D. and Atkins D.J. (1995) *Population density, change and concentration in Great Britain 1971, 1981 and 1991*, Studies on Medical and Population Subjects No 58, London: HMSO.

Dorling, D. and Fairbairn, D. (1997) *Mapping ways of representing the world*, London: Longman.

Dorling, D. and Gunnell, D. (2003) 'Suicide: the spatial and social components of despair in Britain 1980-2000', *Transactions of the Institute of British Geographers*, vol 28, pp 442-60.

Dorling, D. and Rees, P.H. (2003a) 'A nation still dividing: the British census and social polarisation 1971-2001', *Environment and Planning A*, vol 35, pp 1287-313.

Dorling, D. and Rees, P.H. (2003b) 'A nation ever more divided', *Town and Country Planning*, vol 72, no 9, p 270.

Dorling, D. and Rees, P.H. (2004) 'A nation dividing? Some interpretations of the question', *Environment and Planning A*, vol 36, pp 369-73.

Dorling, D. and Simpson, S. (1994) 'Gone and forgotten? The census's missing one-and-a-half million', *Environment and Planning A*, Commentary, vol 26, no 8, pp 1172-3.

Dorling, D. and Simpson, S. (2000) *Statistics in society: The arithmetic of politics*, London: Arnold.

Dorling, D. and Simpson, L. (2001) 'The geography of poverty: a political map of poverty under New Labour', *New Economy*, vol 8, Issue 2, Oxford: Blackwell Publishers, pp 87-91.

Dorling, D. and Woodward, R. (1996) 'Social polarisation 1971-1991: a micro-geographical analysis of Britain', monograph in the *Progress in Planning Series*, vol 45, no 2, pp 67-122.

Dorling, D., Gentle, C. and Cornford, J. (1994) 'Negative equity in 1990s Britain', *Urban Studies*, vol 31, no 2, pp 181-99.

Dorling, D., Mitchell, R., Shaw, M., Orford, S. and Davey Smith. G. (2000) 'The ghost of Christmas past: health effects of poverty in London in 1896 and 1991', *British Medical Journal*, vol 7276, pp 1547-51.

Forrest, R. and Gordon, D. (1993) *People and places: A 1991 census atlas of England*, Bristol: SAUS Publications, University of Bristol.

Gordon, D. and Forrest, R. (1995) *People and places 2: Social and economic distinctions in England*, Bristol: SAUS Publications, University of Bristol.

Gordon, D., Davey Smith, G., Dorling, D. and Shaw, M. (1999) *Inequalities in health: The evidence*, Bristol: The Policy Press.

Gregory, I., Dorling, D. and Southall, H. (2001) 'A century of inequality in England and Wales using standardised geographical units', *Area 33*, vol 3, pp 297-311.

Horner, A., Walsh, J. and Harrington, V. (1987) *Population in Ireland: A census atlas*, Dublin: Department of Geography, University College Dublin.

Johnston, R., Pattie, C., Dorling, D. and Rossiter, D. (2003) 'The Conservative century? Geography and Conservative electoral success during the twentieth century', in D. Gilbert, D. Matless and B. Short (eds) *Geographies of British modernity: Space and society in the twentieth century*, Oxford: Blackwells.

Johnston, R., Pattie, C., Rossiter, D. and Dorling, D. (2001) *From votes to seats: The operation of the UK electoral system since 1945*, Manchester: Manchester University Press.

Martin, D., Dorling, D. and Mitchell, R. (2002) 'Linking censuses through time: problems and solutions', *Area*, vol 34, no 1, pp 82-91.

Mitchell, R., Dorling, D. and Shaw, M. (2000) *Inequalities in life and death: What if Britain were more equal?*, Bristol/York: The Policy Press/Joseph Rowntree Foundation.

Mitchell, R., Martin, D., Dorling, D. and Simpson, S. (2002) 'Bringing the missing million home: correcting the 1991 SAS for undercount', *Environment and Planning A*, vol 34, pp 1021-35.

Ordnance Survey (1995) *Statlas UK: A statistical atlas of the United Kingdom*, Southampton: Ordnance Survey.

Pattie, C., Dorling, D. and Johnston, R. (1995) 'A debt-owning democracy: the political impact of housing market recession at the British general election of 1992', *Urban Studies*, vol 32, no 8, pp 1293-315.

Pattie, C., Dorling, D. and Johnston, R. (1997) 'The electoral geography of recession: local economic conditions, public perceptions and the economic vote in the 1992 British general election', *Transactions of the Institute of British Geographers*, vol 22, no 2, pp 147-61.

Pattie, C., Dorling, D., Johnston, R. and Rossiter, D. (1996) 'Electoral registration, population mobility and the democratic franchise: the geography of postal voters, overseas voters and missing voters in Great Britain', *International Journal of Population Geography*, vol 2, pp 239-59.

Shaw, M. and Dorling, D. (1998) 'Social exclusion', in M. Bartley et al (eds) *Social determinants of health: The solid facts*, Copenhagen: World Health Organisation Regional Office for Europe.

Shaw, M., Dorling, D. and Brimblecombe, N. (1998) 'Changing the map: health in Britain 1951-1991', in M. Bartley, D. Blane and G. Davey Smith (eds) *The sociology of health inequalities*, Oxford: Blackwell.

Shaw, M., Dorling, D. and Davey Smith, G. (2002b) 'Editorial: Mortality and political climate: how suicide rates have risen during periods of Conservative government, 1901-2000', *Journal of Epidemiology and Community Health*, vol 56, no 10, pp 722-7.

Shaw, M., Dorling, D. and Mitchell, R. (2002a) *Health, place and society*, Harlow: Pearson Education.

Shaw, M., Dorling, D., Gordon, D. and Davey Smith, G. (1999) *The widening gap: Health inequalities and policy in Britain*, Bristol: The Policy Press.

Simpson, S. and Dorling, D. (1994) 'Those missing millions: implications for social statistics of non-response to the 1991 census', *Journal of Social Policy*, vol 23, no 4, pp 543-67.

Tunstall, H.V.Z., Shaw, M. and Dorling, D. (2004) 'Places and health', *Journal of Epidemiology and Community Health*, vol 58, pp 6-10.

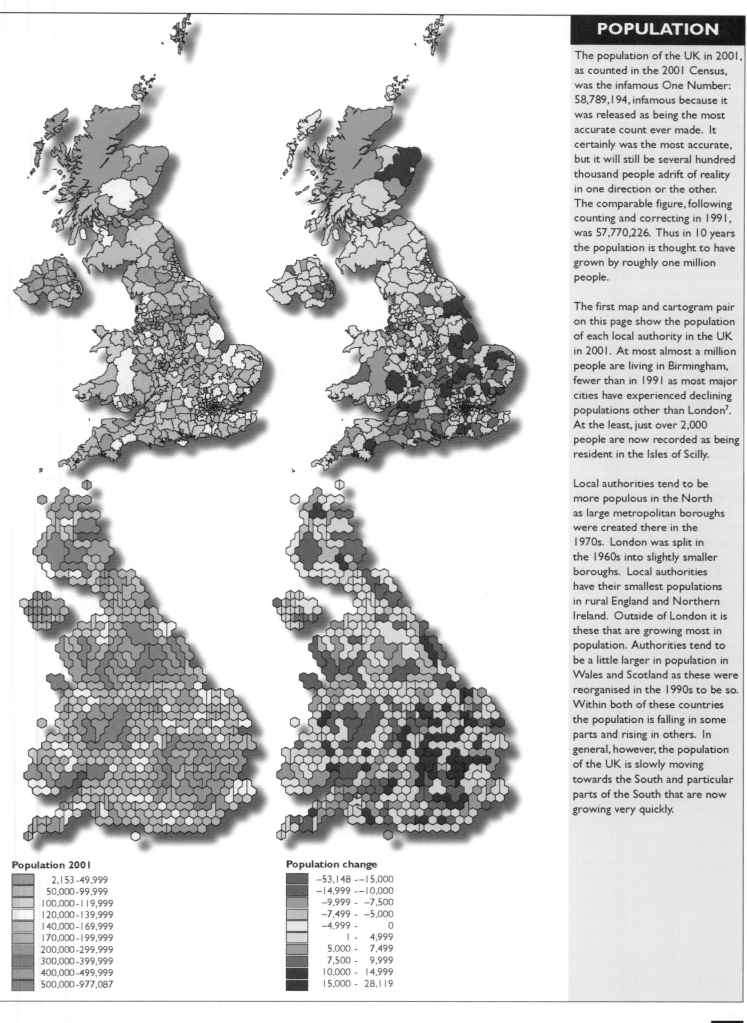

POPULATION

The population of the UK in 2001, as counted in the 2001 Census, was the infamous One Number: 58,789,194, infamous because it was released as being the most accurate count ever made. It certainly was the most accurate, but it will still be several hundred thousand people adrift of reality in one direction or the other. The comparable figure, following counting and correcting in 1991, was 57,770,226. Thus in 10 years the population is thought to have grown by roughly one million people.

The first map and cartogram pair on this page show the population of each local authority in the UK in 2001. At most almost a million people are living in Birmingham, fewer than in 1991 as most major cities have experienced declining populations other than London[7]. At the least, just over 2,000 people are now recorded as being resident in the Isles of Scilly.

Local authorities tend to be more populous in the North as large metropolitan boroughs were created there in the 1970s. London was split in the 1960s into slightly smaller boroughs. Local authorities have their smallest populations in rural England and Northern Ireland. Outside of London it is these that are growing most in population. Authorities tend to be a little larger in population in Wales and Scotland as these were reorganised in the 1990s to be so. Within both of these countries the population is falling in some parts and rising in others. In general, however, the population of the UK is slowly moving towards the South and particular parts of the South that are now growing very quickly.

Population 2001

	2,153-49,999
	50,000-99,999
	100,000-119,999
	120,000-139,999
	140,000-169,999
	170,000-199,999
	200,000-299,999
	300,000-399,999
	400,000-499,999
	500,000-977,087

Population change

	−53,148 −−15,000
	−14,999 −−10,000
	−9,999 − −7,500
	−7,499 − −5,000
	−4,999 − 0
	1 − 4,999
	5,000 − 7,499
	7,500 − 9,999
	10,000 − 14,999
	15,000 − 28,119

DENSITY

Local authorities vary greatly in their physical area as well as in their populations. Those that are small in physical area tend to contain the most people. Population density is shown here as simply the number of people living in a district for every hectare of land in the district. There are one hundred hectares in a square kilometre and 243,073 square kilometres of land in the UK. Nationally, population density rose slightly, from 2.38 persons per hectare to 2.42 between 1991 and 2001. Population density is highest in London, peaking at 131 people per hectare living in Kensington & Chelsea, which also was the most densely populated borough a decade ago, but then with only 120 people living, on average, in every 100m x 100m grid square. Population density is lowest, at 0.08 people per hectare in the Highland Council Area of Scotland, a rate unchanged on that of a decade ago, 1,600 times fewer people for every square kilometre of land than live in the royal borough.

Change in population density is entirely caused by change in population because we are using identical boundaries to compare these areas over time. As the population have moved southwards, densities have increased most in London and the South East, with the largest rise being in Tower Hamlets[8] Population density has fallen the most in Manchester, large inner areas of which were redeveloped in the 1990s to replace high density housing with lower density homes. Almost all the falls in density have been outside of the South East except for two London boroughs[9].

Density 2001

	0.1- 1
	2 - 4
	5 - 7
	8 - 10
	11 - 15
	16 - 19
	20 - 39
	40 - 49
	50 - 89
	90 - 131

Density change

	-3.9 - -2.1
	-2.0 - -1.1
	-1.0 - -0.1
	0.0
	0.1 - 0.6
	0.7 - 1.5
	1.6 - 2.7
	2.8 - 5.6
	5.7 - 8.9
	9.0 - 14.2

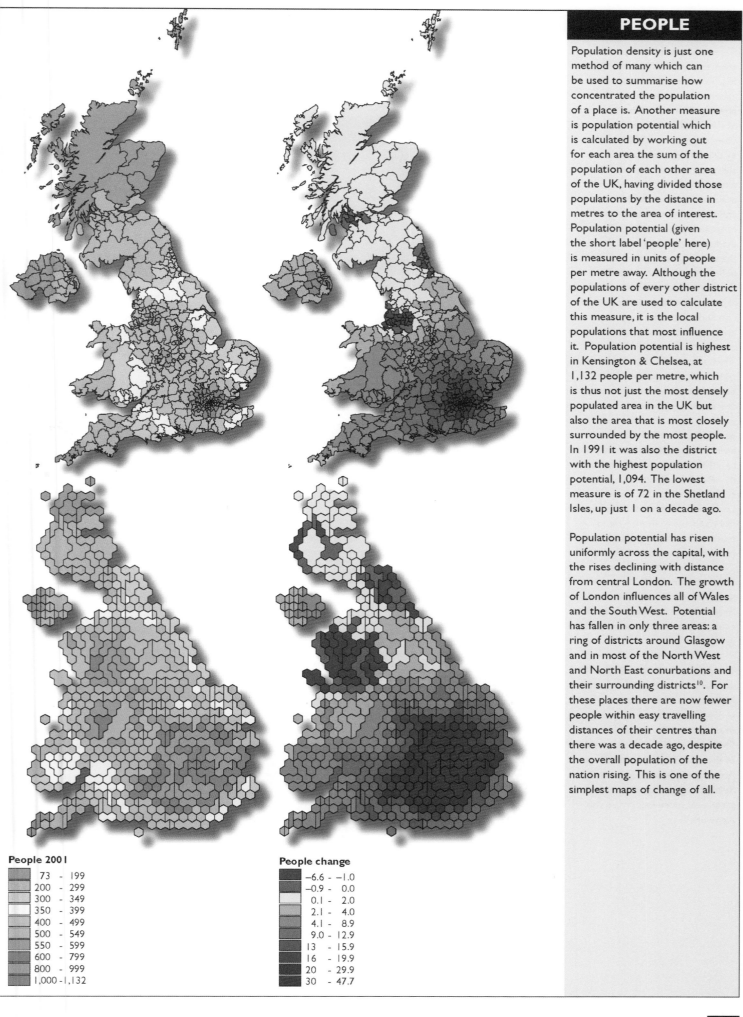

Population density is just one method of many which can be used to summarise how concentrated the population of a place is. Another measure is population potential which is calculated by working out for each area the sum of the population of each other area of the UK, having divided those populations by the distance in metres to the area of interest. Population potential (given the short label 'people' here) is measured in units of people per metre away. Although the populations of every other district of the UK are used to calculate this measure, it is the local populations that most influence it. Population potential is highest in Kensington & Chelsea, at 1,132 people per metre, which is thus not just the most densely populated area in the UK but also the area that is most closely surrounded by the most people. In 1991 it was also the district with the highest population potential, 1,094. The lowest measure is of 72 in the Shetland Isles, up just 1 on a decade ago.

Population potential has risen uniformly across the capital, with the rises declining with distance from central London. The growth of London influences all of Wales and the South West. Potential has fallen in only three areas: a ring of districts around Glasgow and in most of the North West and North East conurbations and their surrounding districts[10]. For these places there are now fewer people within easy travelling distances of their centres than there was a decade ago, despite the overall population of the nation rising. This is one of the simplest maps of change of all.

People 2001

	73 - 199
	200 - 299
	300 - 349
	350 - 399
	400 - 499
	500 - 549
	550 - 599
	600 - 799
	800 - 999
	1,000 - 1,132

People change

	−6.6 - −1.0
	−0.9 - 0.0
	0.1 - 2.0
	2.1 - 4.0
	4.1 - 8.9
	9.0 - 12.9
	13 - 15.9
	16 - 19.9
	20 - 29.9
	30 - 47.7

POOR

Censuses can aid the estimation of rates of poverty in the UK, but do not contain sufficient information alone to measure poverty. Here we show estimates of the proportions of households living in poverty in 2001 made by combining census data with surveys explicitly designed to measure poverty. Note that the measure of poverty here and hence the rates are for households, not people. The poverty measure used is the Breadline Britain measure that defines a household as poor if the majority of people in Britain, at the time of calculation, would conclude that the resources available to that household constituted living in poverty. Thus, as overall living standards rise, poverty can also rise if society becomes more unequal and more people lack what the majority come to consider to be necessities. In 1991 21% of all households in the UK were poor; by 2001 that proportion had risen to 24%. Poverty is now most concentrated in East Central London and Glasgow[11]. Poverty has risen everywhere save in much of Northern Ireland. It rose the least in Britain in North Tyneside (by only 0.3%) and in Cotswold (by 0.9%). It rose the most in London and in other large urban areas as well as some coastal resorts, and fastest by 13% in Newham.

The method used to calculate this measure of poverty is explained further in the Introduction above (see footnote 4), and was implemented for this atlas by David Gordon at the University of Bristol. This is a preliminary mapping of poverty in 2001. A definitive mapping will require a great deal more work (see the Appendix).

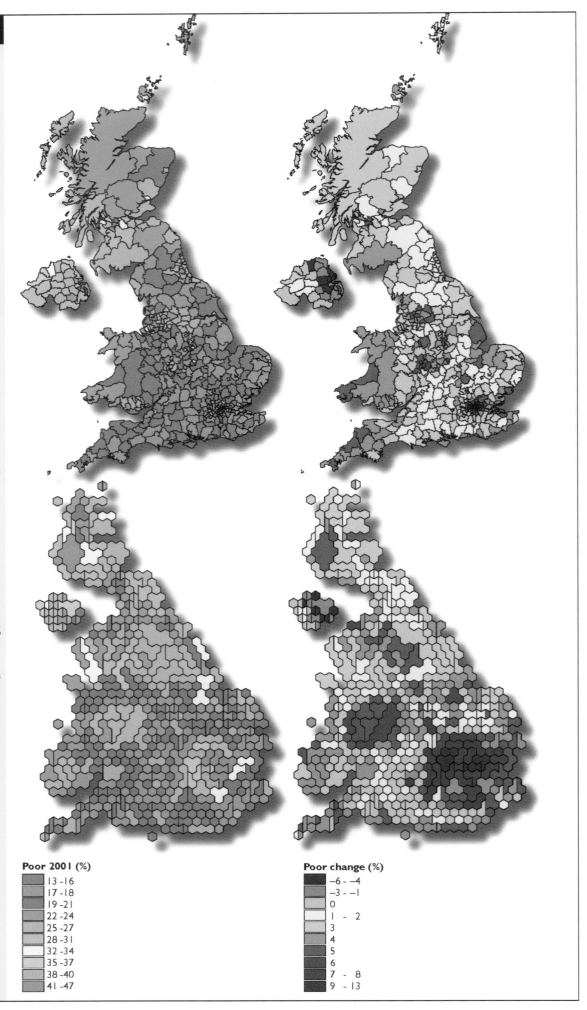

Poor 2001 (%)

	13 –16
	17 –18
	19 –21
	22 –24
	25 –27
	28 –31
	32 –34
	35 –37
	38 –40
	41 –47

Poor change (%)

	−6 – −4
	−3 – −1
	0
	1 – 2
	3
	4
	5
	6
	7 – 8
	9 – 13

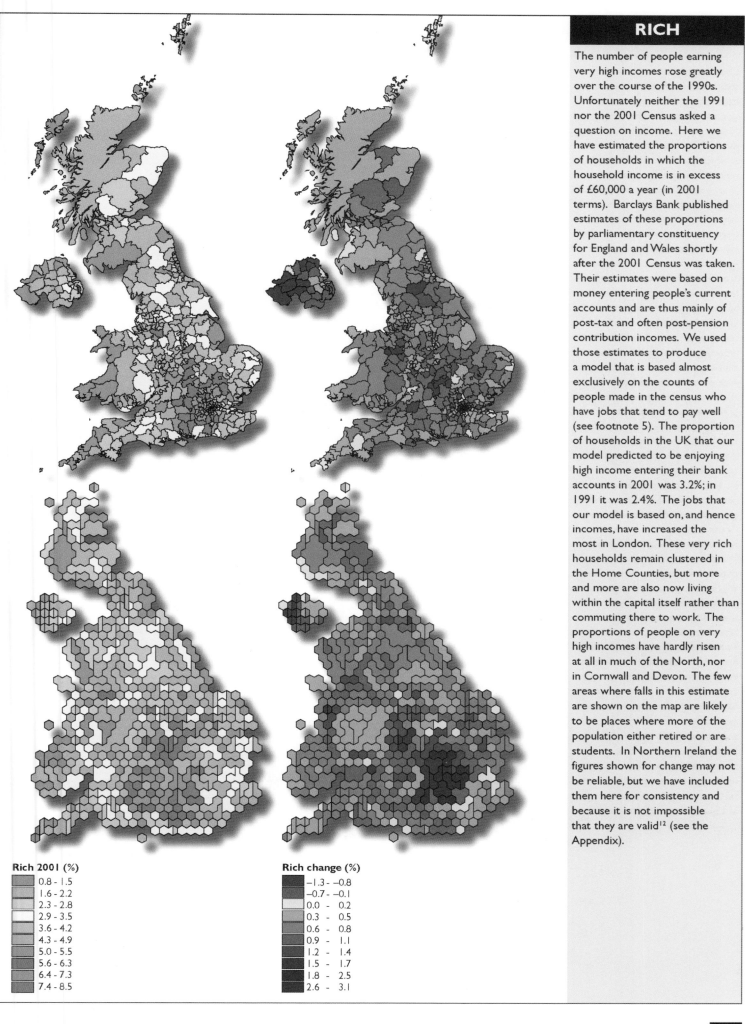

RICH

The number of people earning very high incomes rose greatly over the course of the 1990s. Unfortunately neither the 1991 nor the 2001 Census asked a question on income. Here we have estimated the proportions of households in which the household income is in excess of £60,000 a year (in 2001 terms). Barclays Bank published estimates of these proportions by parliamentary constituency for England and Wales shortly after the 2001 Census was taken. Their estimates were based on money entering people's current accounts and are thus mainly of post-tax and often post-pension contribution incomes. We used those estimates to produce a model that is based almost exclusively on the counts of people made in the census who have jobs that tend to pay well (see footnote 5). The proportion of households in the UK that our model predicted to be enjoying high income entering their bank accounts in 2001 was 3.2%; in 1991 it was 2.4%. The jobs that our model is based on, and hence incomes, have increased the most in London. These very rich households remain clustered in the Home Counties, but more and more are also now living within the capital itself rather than commuting there to work. The proportions of people on very high incomes have hardly risen at all in much of the North, nor in Cornwall and Devon. The few areas where falls in this estimate are shown on the map are likely to be places where more of the population either retired or are students. In Northern Ireland the figures shown for change may not be reliable, but we have included them here for consistency and because it is not impossible that they are valid[12] (see the Appendix).

Rich 2001 (%)

	0.8 - 1.5
	1.6 - 2.2
	2.3 - 2.8
	2.9 - 3.5
	3.6 - 4.2
	4.3 - 4.9
	5.0 - 5.5
	5.6 - 6.3
	6.4 - 7.3
	7.4 - 8.5

Rich change (%)

	−1.3 - −0.8
	−0.7 - −0.1
	0.0 - 0.2
	0.3 - 0.5
	0.6 - 0.8
	0.9 - 1.1
	1.2 - 1.4
	1.5 - 1.7
	1.8 - 2.5
	2.6 - 3.1

WEALTHY

While a high income might make a household rich, it does not necessarily imply that they are also wealthy. Wealth is accrued income, amassed in the form of savings, and can be held in a variety of forms. The main form in which most wealth in the UK is held is in housing equity. The older a rich person is, the more likely they are to own their house outright, and the richer they were when they were young, the more that house may now be worth. We have estimated the proportions of households who are very wealthy from census data by modelling the proportions of households living in council tax band 'G' and 'H' homes (the most expensive), given census data on the proportion of homes with seven or more rooms in each area and the proportion of households with access to three or more cars. Nationally in 1991, 4.4% of all households fell into the wealthy category as defined here (see footnote 6). By 2001 that proportion had risen to 5.7%. The rise in wealth was concentrated in the Home Counties where the wealthy were most likely to live in the first place. As with our estimate of people on high incomes, there are limitations to how a model based on census data can predict these distributions, and those limitations become most clear when looking at the changes over time. Although Northern Ireland experienced an economic boom in the 1990s, it is unlikely that it now contains as many households as wealthy as the cartogram and map of 2001 would suggest. Similarly it is unlikely that the rises in wealth have been as great there. It is more possible that rates of wealth have fallen in parts of London[13] (see the Appendix).

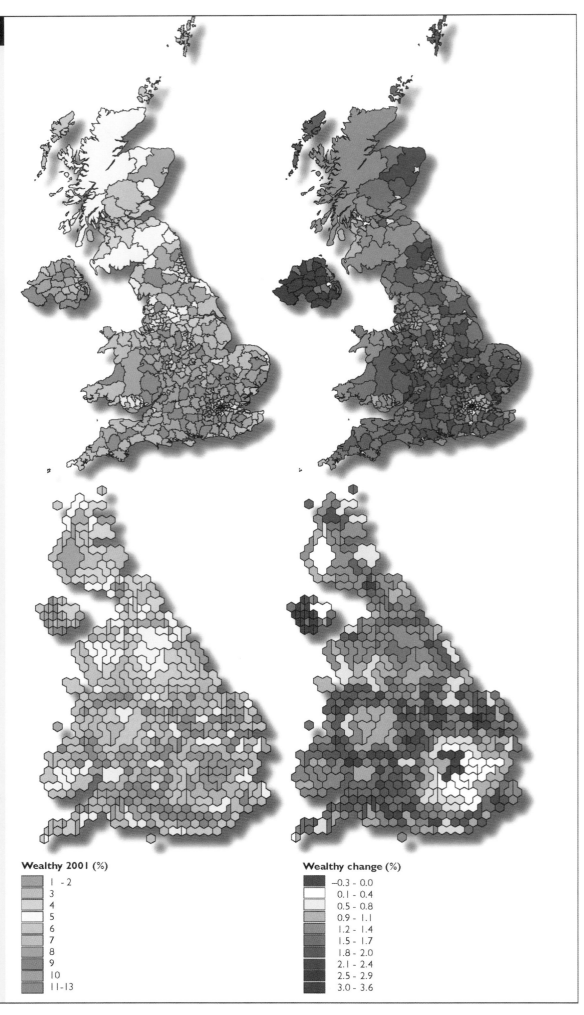

Wealthy 2001 (%)

- 1 - 2
- 3
- 4
- 5
- 6
- 7
- 8
- 9
- 10
- 11-13

Wealthy change (%)

- −0.3 - 0.0
- 0.1 - 0.4
- 0.5 - 0.8
- 0.9 - 1.1
- 1.2 - 1.4
- 1.5 - 1.7
- 1.8 - 2.0
- 2.1 - 2.4
- 2.5 - 2.9
- 3.0 - 3.6

PLACES

Following each of the last four censuses, the national census agencies or civil servants working in collaboration with them have produced classifications of areas which use census data to group similar areas together that are then labelled. These classifications are made independently following each census, using differing methodologies at each time, and hence are not easily comparable over time. They also result in places being given labels that differ, so here we show only the 2001 classification of place in the UK. Although the conventional map of places is widely available, the cartogram of the same data shown below is not, and shows a very different picture of the UK.

At the core of the UK is 'London centre', surrounded by 'London cosmopolitan' and 'London suburbs' districts (including Slough and Luton). Encircling the capital is the 'Thriving London periphery', 'Prospering Southern England' and 'New and growing towns'. The official labels seen in conjunction with the cartogram describe how life in the UK is now organised on the ground. Large urban areas outside of London are 'Regional centres', or, where there is still some manufacturing, 'Centres with industry'. Much of the remainder of southern England is filled up with 'Prospering smaller towns' surrounded in turn by the 'Coastal and countryside' districts (with a special classification for those areas in the Province). The remainder of Wales, the North of England and Scotland is either made up of 'Manufacturing towns' or 'Industrial hinterlands', areas slowly dropping away from the rest[14].

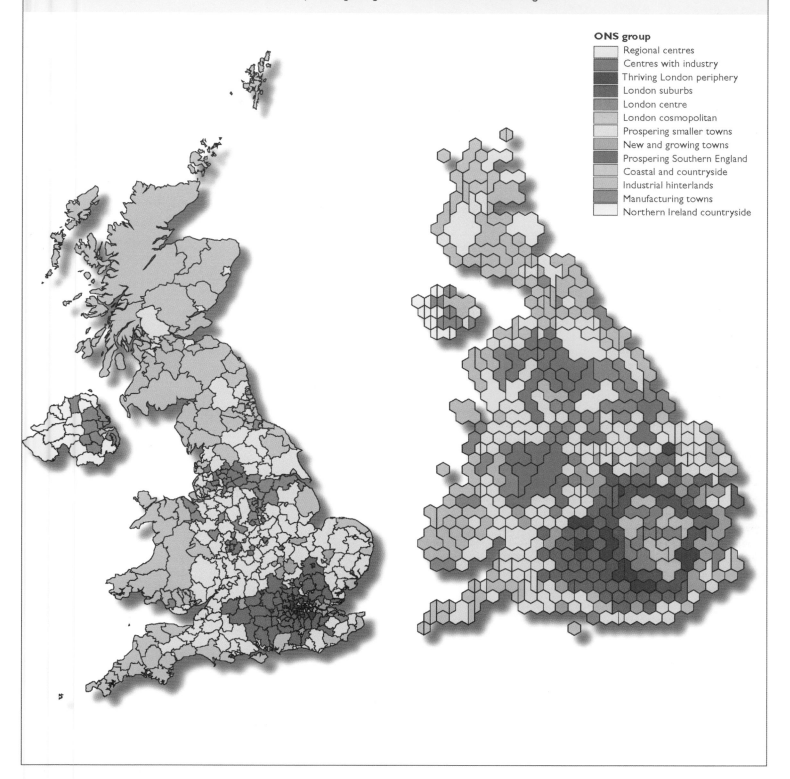

ONS group
- Regional centres
- Centres with industry
- Thriving London periphery
- London suburbs
- London centre
- London cosmopolitan
- Prospering smaller towns
- New and growing towns
- Prospering Southern England
- Coastal and countryside
- Industrial hinterlands
- Manufacturing towns
- Northern Ireland countryside

NOTES

[7] For the 10 local authorities with the largest populations recorded in 2001 (and how those have changed) see Table 1.1.

Table 1.1: Population

	2001	1991	Change	% change
Birmingham	977,087	1,005,764	−28,677	−3
Leeds	715,402	716,760	−1,358	0
Glasgow City	577,869	631,012	−53,143	−8
Sheffield	513,234	528,708	−15,474	−3
Bradford	467,665	475,192	−7,527	−2
Edinburgh	448,624	438,916	9,708	2
Liverpool	439,473	480,196	−40,723	−8
Manchester	392,819	437,717	−44,898	−10
Kirklees	388,567	381,416	7,151	2
Bristol	380,615	396,559	−15,944	−4

[8] Population density has risen by two or more people per hectare in: the City of London, Barking & Dagenham, Brent, Camden, Ealing, Hackney, Hammersmith & Fulham, Kensington & Chelsea, Kingston upon Thames, Lambeth, Lewisham, Merton, Newham, Southwark, Tower Hamlets, Luton, Slough, Southampton and Worcester.

[9] Population density fell by one person per hectare or more in Wandsworth, Westminster, Manchester, Salford, Liverpool, The Wirral, Newcastle upon Tyne, Sunderland, Birmingham, Sandwell, Wolverhampton, Bristol, Plymouth, Kingston upon Hull, Blackpool, Norwich, Middlesbrough, Nottingham, Stoke-on-Trent, Dundee City and in Glasgow City.

[10] Population potential has fallen in: Bolton, Bury, Manchester, Oldham, Rochdale, Salford, Stockport, Tameside, Trafford, Wigan, Knowsley, Liverpool, St Helens, Sefton, Wirral, Gateshead, Newcastle upon Tyne, North Tyneside, South Tyneside, Sunderland, Ellesmere Port & Neston, Halton, Macclesfield, Warrington, Chester-le-Street, Derwentside, Durham, Easington, Hartlepool, Stockton-on-Tees, Chorley, Fylde, Rossendale, West Lancashire, Blyth Valley, Castle Morpeth, Wansbeck, East Dunbartonshire, East Renfrewshire, Inverclyde, North Ayrshire, North Lanarkshire, Renfrewshire and West Dunbartonshire.

[11] Over a third of all households in the following districts lived in poverty in 2001: City of London, Brent, Camden, Hackney, Hammersmith & Fulham, Haringey, Islington, Kensington & Chelsea, Lambeth, Lewisham, Newham, Southwark, Tower Hamlets, Westminster, Manchester, Liverpool, Dundee City, Glasgow City, Inverclyde, North Lanarkshire, West Dunbartonshire, Belfast, Derry and Strabane. In 1991 only eight areas were in that list: Hackney, Islington, Southwark, Tower Hamlets, Glasgow City, Belfast, Derry and Strabane.

[12] In Northern Ireland the number of people working in the highest paid occupations in 1991 had to be estimated from the total number of professional and managers working in 1991 in the province, as the data was not separately tabulated in that census. The most probable reason for the apparent fall of high incomes shown on the map is that a disproportionate number of managers and professionals working in Northern Ireland in 1991 were employed by the state on incomes below £60,000 (in 2001 terms), and thus the apparent fall is simply the overestimation of earnings in the past. We have included Northern Ireland in these maps for completeness and because it is just possible that as the population in much of the Province has risen, due to fewer people leaving than before, there are, on average, fewer very rich people living there. Independent data on the changing income distribution in Northern Ireland would need to be consulted to verify this speculation.

[13] As the population of London becomes younger, an increasing number of people are renting their homes or have just begun to buy their homes and have little equity in them. The wealth of London housing is largely owned by older people living outside of the capital, either directly as landlords or through their pension funds, which are partly invested in the banks and building societies that lend money to younger people for their mortgages and other loans. In Northern Ireland, there was a boom in house extensions during the 1990s. The number of households living in houses with seven or more rooms rose from 107,000 in 1991 to 160,000 in 2001. There is certainly much more wealth being invested in the Province than before, but perhaps not as much as this model would predict. Nevertheless, for many decades the social geography of the Province has not been compared to the mainland, and so we have again included Northern Ireland, despite having doubts over the extrapolation of our model there.

[14] See Table 1.2.

Table 1.2: Places

Population change by places	% change	2001	1991
Northern Ireland countryside	7	649,287	605,479
London cosmopolitan	6	1,686,643	1,593,234
London centre	5	1,342,935	1,281,285
Prospering smaller towns	5	12,695,199	12,125,006
Prospering Southern England	4	4,966,654	4,756,252
London suburbs	4	2,801,538	2,689,339
New and growing towns	3	3,029,024	2,927,557
Coastal and countryside	3	5,852,626	5,658,656
Thriving London periphery	3	1,503,847	1,454,127
Manufacturing towns	1	5,320,803	5,256,569
Centres with industry	−2	5,635,993	5,756,256
Regional centres	−2	6,154,780	6,301,190
Industrial hinterlands	−3	7,149,865	7,366,136
UK	2	58,789,194	57,771,086

Age and sex

Maps in this section include:

By the turn of the millennium, the UK has become a country where local geography has structured society more than at any point in its recent past. In the 1950s and 1960s, almost all areas of the country had more similar populations. This is most easily seen in the age and sex structure of the population, which has now become highly differentiated across the land.

Fifty years ago older people lived alongside young people. Men and women were more equitably distributed in each local area. In each area were found similar proportions of people who were rich and poor, who had received a good education or almost no education at all, who were living in comfortable housing or who were dealing with very poor housing conditions.

There were variations, but most of the variations were to be found within local areas rather than between them. Particular industries did dominate particular areas, but there was near full employment of men everywhere, and everywhere required the services of professionals to very similar degrees, who tended to live locally.

That country is now no more. It was no utopia, but it was a place where local geography mattered less. Ironically it is the increased ease of movement between places that has led to places now mattering more. Rapid road building and growth in car ownership has allowed people who can to live much further from their workplace than before. Long distance migration has become more common, breaking up families and creating places which cater more specifically for people of different ages than was the case in the past.

The growth in work for women, the widespread use of contraception and the legalisation of abortion has meant that the sexes are no longer as paired up and evenly spread across the country as before. Women's continued emancipation has helped greatly to break that past near certainty as cities become more feminised, while their

relatively faster growth in life expectancy and lower emigration rates have further increased the differences in sex ratios seen across the country. Women are also the major beneficiaries of the rise in student numbers that have significantly changed the age profiles of many areas. And they are choosing to have children, on average, much later than ever before, and this is altering the geography of childhood immensely.

The declines in primary and manufacturing industries have continued almost unabated from the 1970s and 1980s, while the service sector booms. Some people move home at increasing rates across the country to take advantage of these changes, while a socially and demographically different group are increasingly likely to be left behind in areas of depopulation. People can change many of their social characteristics where they reside, for example, they can get a job, change their area of employment, or buy their home from the state, for instance. But it is mainly increased selective migration that has fuelled the continued polarisation of the UK space; it is only when we consider the changing geographical pattern of the age and sex of the population that we are looking at changes that are almost solely the result of differential rates of migration.

Young women are moving in unprecedented numbers to take up work in most of the major cities of the UK. They leave behind a rural and poorer northern urban agglomeration of areas where men make up almost half of the population. The South, however, contains the only large groups of areas where men come near to being a majority of the population, and then, generally only in the most affluent parts of the South. Babies are now born in their greatest numbers in the South of England, most in places where women have moved the most, and particularly where those who delayed childbirth are now having their children (and more babies are boys than girls). The numbers of children are also rising most in the South and falling fastest in Northern Ireland, which has experienced an abrupt demographic shift over the course of the last decade. Nationally, unprecedented numbers of students are filling up university towns, emptying most of the rest of the country of people aged around 20. The students go on to move southwards or to leave the country, maybe just for a year, maybe for longer, while many others at these ages come in from abroad to take their places.

The census revealed that a huge number of men had left the country in net terms over the course of the last decade. When the Census results were released it became apparent that there were roughly one million fewer men living in the UK than had previously been assumed by the Office for National Statistics. For those who stay it is only around the Home Counties that men are just in the majority, and it is to London that people now aged between 30 and 44 have flocked as never before, women more than men. This mass migration has resulted in London and other large cities emptying out of people in their late middle age, with many retiring or entering semi-retirement early.

As new areas become chosen as being favourites for retirement, the population there becomes more female. The retired population have moved away from the cities and almost the entire hinterland of London too, to make space for the young. By the last decade of life the very old have been pushed and have pulled themselves to the coast, particularly the southern coasts, as never before.

Retirement areas are the only places where a majority of the population are still married. In many city centres the rate of marriage has almost fallen to be only a quarter of all people. Had you said, in 1950, that this would be the future, few people would have believed you. If this population shift were to continue to 2050 then many areas will become known by the age groups they most exclusively accommodate. Student, retirement and middle age districts will emerge, where currently we talk only of neighbourhoods with these particular demographic characteristics.

The processes which have driven these rapid changes to the demographic geography of the UK are not driven by a huge desire of people of different ages to live apart, but by acceleration in the speed of transactions in various markets.

The market for higher education has grown and now processes millions of students a year, moving them geographically as well as socially. The market of school exam results that emerged as they were first nationally published in the 1990s encourages those who can to further segregate their children geographically.

The job market has boomed and sucks in labour of the particular ages it most requires, with much less preference for men than ever before. The housing market encourages people in late middle age to leave the large parts of the

UK where demand for young and skilled labour is highest, and to retire to where they can best afford now to live. The marriage market has nothing like the power it once wielded to encourage couples to conform to a norm that resulted in everywhere being so much more similar in the past. People's choices over where to live are constrained and made increasingly by changing markets. Individually, we may feel that we made the choices we thought we had. Collectively, we are acting in ways that the censuses reveal to be the product of wider underlying influences, and which are leading to a country more divided by its geography than ever before.

This polarisation by age should be of concern both for its revealing other processes of division that it is a reaction to, and for the implications of the polarisation itself. Although the pattern of polarisation is not universal, most districts have become more distinct in their age and sex profiles over time. The footnotes to the text that follows (at the end of each chapter) chart the more complex story of changing birth cohorts that also contribute to the patterns seen. The results of these changes are that distinct large areas are beginning to cater for distinct groups of the UK population, leading to spatial concentrations of particular industries and services that support these populations. Those who can move to where they are increasingly supposed to be, given their age: to university, the South, and the coast. Those who cannot are increasingly out of place.

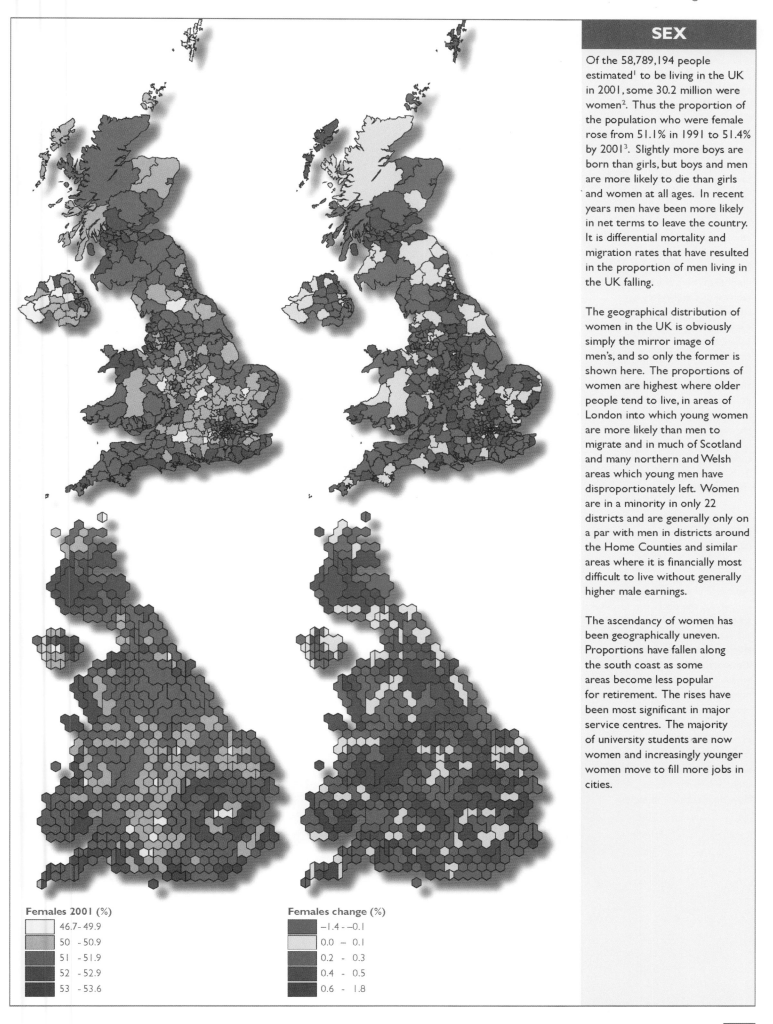

SEX

Of the 58,789,194 people estimated[1] to be living in the UK in 2001, some 30.2 million were women[2]. Thus the proportion of the population who were female rose from 51.1% in 1991 to 51.4% by 2001[3]. Slightly more boys are born than girls, but boys and men are more likely to die than girls and women at all ages. In recent years men have been more likely in net terms to leave the country. It is differential mortality and migration rates that have resulted in the proportion of men living in the UK falling.

The geographical distribution of women in the UK is obviously simply the mirror image of men's, and so only the former is shown here. The proportions of women are highest where older people tend to live, in areas of London into which young women are more likely than men to migrate and in much of Scotland and many northern and Welsh areas which young men have disproportionately left. Women are in a minority in only 22 districts and are generally only on a par with men in districts around the Home Counties and similar areas where it is financially most difficult to live without generally higher male earnings.

The ascendancy of women has been geographically uneven. Proportions have fallen along the south coast as some areas become less popular for retirement. The rises have been most significant in major service centres. The majority of university students are now women and increasingly younger women move to fill more jobs in cities.

Females 2001 (%)
- 46.7 - 49.9
- 50 - 50.9
- 51 - 51.9
- 52 - 52.9
- 53 - 53.6

Females change (%)
- −1.4 - −0.1
- 0.0 - 0.1
- 0.2 - 0.3
- 0.4 - 0.5
- 0.6 - 1.8

BABIES AND TODDLERS

There were 2.0 million children aged under three resident in the UK in 2001[4]. Ten years earlier there were 2.3 million. People are choosing to have fewer children and many are delaying childbirth to much later in life. Despite this, there are still twice as many babies and toddlers per person in Hackney as compared to West Somerset, or in Newham as compared to East Devon.

Babies are born in greatest numbers where there are most women of childbearing ages, although as that age range expands, the geography of where babies are most likely to be born becomes more diffuse. London, Birmingham, the Pennine towns and Northern Ireland continue to dominate the map of where early years are most likely to be lived. However, as the proportion of the UK population who are babies or toddlers has fallen from 4.1% to 3.5%, that map has altered quite remarkably.

There have been actual increases in the proportions of people aged 0-2 in six London boroughs, and two districts near London[5] where older women are now having their first children at rates which cancel out the decline in fertility among younger women. Due to similar factors, rates have hardly fallen around suburban London. Instead, they have fallen most where there were the lowest numbers of childless middle-aged women in 1991. It is unlikely that what we see here, in eight areas in and around London, is the start of a national trend, but it is not impossible that more births to older women in the future might slow down the fall in fertility.

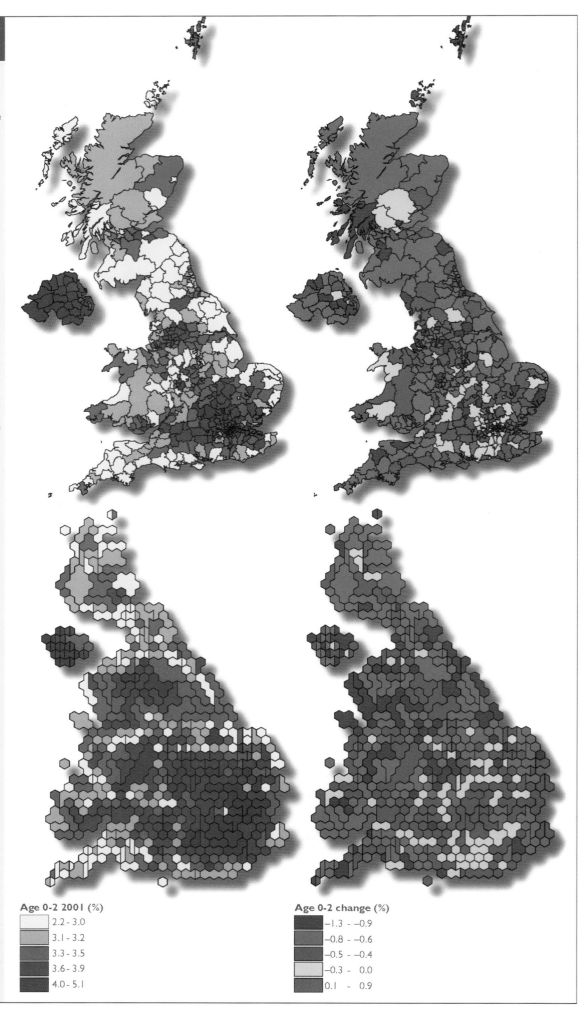

Age 0-2 2001 (%)

- 2.2 - 3.0
- 3.1 - 3.2
- 3.3 - 3.5
- 3.6 - 3.9
- 4.0 - 5.1

Age 0-2 change (%)

- −1.3 - −0.9
- −0.8 - −0.6
- −0.5 - −0.4
- −0.3 - 0.0
- 0.1 - 0.9

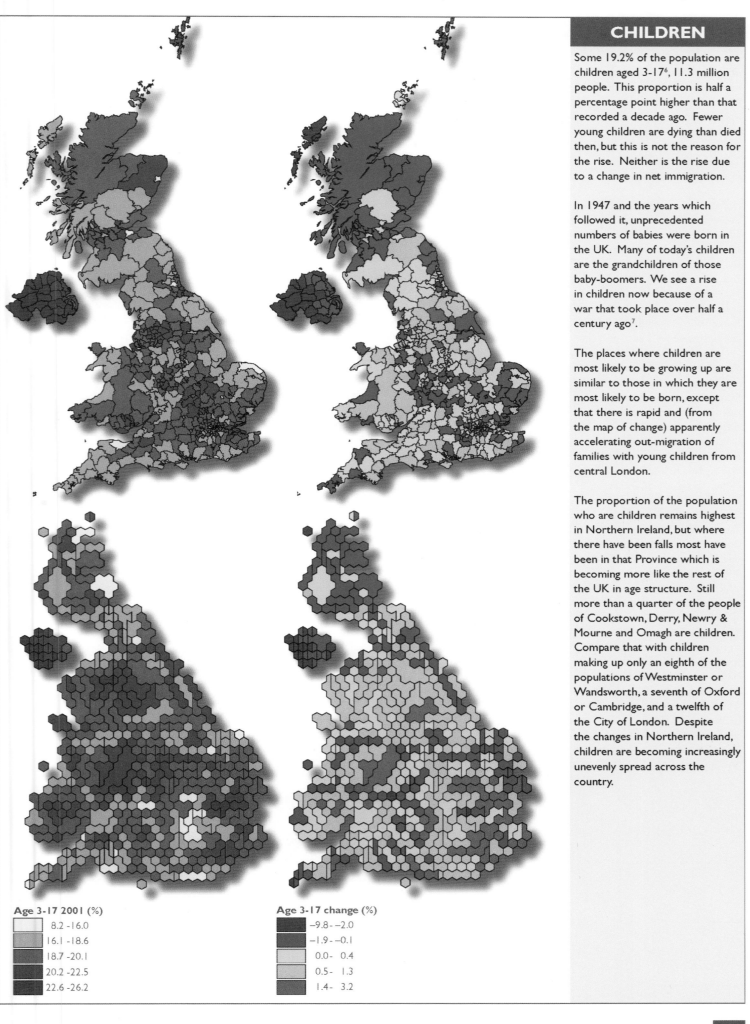

CHILDREN

Some 19.2% of the population are children aged 3-17[6], 11.3 million people. This proportion is half a percentage point higher than that recorded a decade ago. Fewer young children are dying than died then, but this is not the reason for the rise. Neither is the rise due to a change in net immigration.

In 1947 and the years which followed it, unprecedented numbers of babies were born in the UK. Many of today's children are the grandchildren of those baby-boomers. We see a rise in children now because of a war that took place over half a century ago[7].

The places where children are most likely to be growing up are similar to those in which they are most likely to be born, except that there is rapid and (from the map of change) apparently accelerating out-migration of families with young children from central London.

The proportion of the population who are children remains highest in Northern Ireland, but where there have been falls most have been in that Province which is becoming more like the rest of the UK in age structure. Still more than a quarter of the people of Cookstown, Derry, Newry & Mourne and Omagh are children. Compare that with children making up only an eighth of the populations of Westminster or Wandsworth, a seventh of Oxford or Cambridge, and a twelfth of the City of London. Despite the changes in Northern Ireland, children are becoming increasingly unevenly spread across the country.

Age 3-17 2001 (%)

	8.2 - 16.0
	16.1 - 18.6
	18.7 - 20.1
	20.2 - 22.5
	22.6 - 26.2

Age 3-17 change (%)

	−9.8 - −2.0
	−1.9 - −0.1
	0.0 - 0.4
	0.5 - 1.3
	1.4 - 3.2

COMING OF AGE

Ages 18, 19 and 20 are now years of demographic dislocation, as up to a third of teenagers go to university at 18, most leaving home to do so. In 2001 there were 2.2 million people in these three years of their lives, some 3.7% of the population, down from 4.2% a decade earlier[8].

It is at these ages that we first see the widest differences emerging across the country in who lives where by age. At one extreme this group makes up 9% of Oxford and Cambridge, 8% of Durham, 7% of Nottingham, Ceredigion (where Aberystwyth University is located), Southampton, Exeter and Lancaster, and 6.5% of Manchester.

When the other extreme is considered, it is fairly clear from where these university towns find their entrants most disproportionately. This group constitutes less than 2.5% of the population of South Bucks, Macclesfield, Christchurch, West Dorset, South Shropshire, Elmbridge, Mole Valley and Eilean Siar (formerly known as the Western Isles of Scotland). With the exception of the latter, these districts are among the most affluent areas of the country from which teenagers are most likely to leave to go to university.

The map of change in the size of this age group shows, in general, the suburban and semi-rural rings from which universities increasingly draw students and, in red, the districts into which particular universities have attracted the greatest increases[9], causing the distribution of 18- to 20-year-olds to polarise further[10].

Age 18-20 2001 (%)

	2.4 - 2.9
	3.0 - 3.1
	3.2 - 3.5
	3.6 - 4.3
	4.4 - 9.2

Age 18-20 change (%)

	−1.7 - −1.1
	−1.0 - −0.8
	−0.7 - −0.6
	−0.5 - 0.0
	0.1 - 3.6

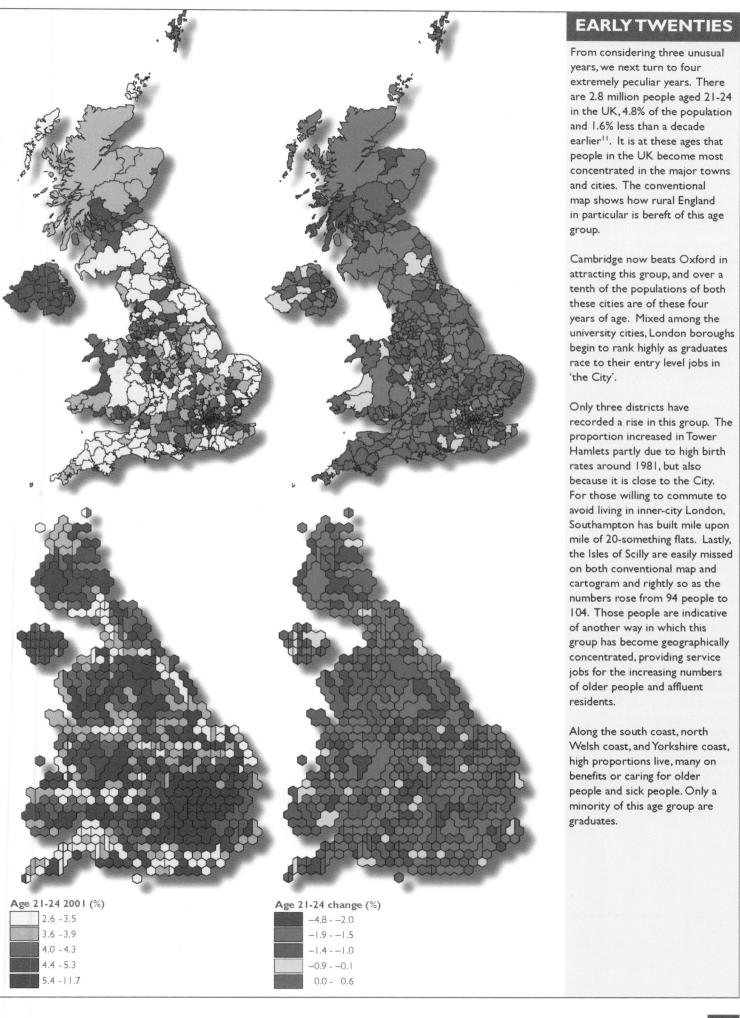

EARLY TWENTIES

From considering three unusual years, we next turn to four extremely peculiar years. There are 2.8 million people aged 21-24 in the UK, 4.8% of the population and 1.6% less than a decade earlier[11]. It is at these ages that people in the UK become most concentrated in the major towns and cities. The conventional map shows how rural England in particular is bereft of this age group.

Cambridge now beats Oxford in attracting this group, and over a tenth of the populations of both these cities are of these four years of age. Mixed among the university cities, London boroughs begin to rank highly as graduates race to their entry level jobs in 'the City'.

Only three districts have recorded a rise in this group. The proportion increased in Tower Hamlets partly due to high birth rates around 1981, but also because it is close to the City. For those willing to commute to avoid living in inner-city London, Southampton has built mile upon mile of 20-something flats. Lastly, the Isles of Scilly are easily missed on both conventional map and cartogram and rightly so as the numbers rose from 94 people to 104. Those people are indicative of another way in which this group has become geographically concentrated, providing service jobs for the increasing numbers of older people and affluent residents.

Along the south coast, north Welsh coast, and Yorkshire coast, high proportions live, many on benefits or caring for older people and sick people. Only a minority of this age group are graduates.

Age 21-24 2001 (%)

  2.6 - 3.5
  3.6 - 3.9
  4.0 - 4.3
  4.4 - 5.3
  5.4 - 11.7

Age 21-24 change (%)

  −4.8 - −2.0
  −1.9 - −1.5
  −1.4 - −1.0
  −0.9 - −0.1
  0.0 - 0.6

LATE TWENTIES

We next move from considering four years to five years of life: the late twenties. Some 3.9 million people are aged 25-29, 6.6%, 1.7% down on 1991[12]. Here the main story is London. The top 12 districts, each with over a tenth of their populations at these ages, are all boroughs in the capital[13]. Of the next 12 a majority are in London and the rest within easy commuting distance of London[14]. Even three of the next 12 districts most popular with 25- to 29-year-olds are in London[15].

London has far more than its fair share of late 20-somethings. Given that, it is even more remarkable that outside Northern Ireland and the Isles of Scilly these proportions are actually rising in the City of London, Camden, and Tower Hamlets, all to 13%, and in Wandsworth to 16% of the population. One in six people in Wandsworth is now aged between 25-29.

Outside of these ghettos of the nearly middle-aged, rates have fallen least where numbers were highest to begin with, in the rest of London, in commuter towns and in cities near London, and around Bristol and Edinburgh to a much lesser extent. Numbers are falling most rapidly in other major cities and in South East London, which is becoming much less the place to be at these ages.

The other remarkable story of this age group is that events in Northern Ireland have finally abated the normal exodus by these ages, at least between 1991-2001. That population is now nearly stable.

Age 25-29 2001 (%)

- 3.5 - 5.1
- 5.2 - 5.7
- 5.8 - 6.2
- 6.3 - 7.1
- 7.2 - 16.1

Age 25-29 change (%)

- −3.3 - −2.1
- −2.0 - −1.7
- −1.6 - −1.4
- −1.3 - −0.1
- 0.0 - 4.8

EARLY MIDDLE AGE

Traditionally people can expect to live 'three score year and ten', although that is now a little low given current life expectancies in the UK. Halve the figure and you get the category we label 'middle age', ages 30-44. Traditionally too these are often seen as boring years and in one way they are in that the patterns of location vary little between them, so here we have amalgamated 15 years of life. Some 13.3 million people are early middle aged, 22.6% of the population, up 1.4% on a decade ago[16].

The most middle-aged place in the UK is Lewisham. Almost a third of people in Lewisham are middle aged. This capital of the middle years is in close competition with another 11 London boroughs that top the table, all having over 27% of their populations in this category[17]. These are the places to which many of the late 20-somethings move out. Others move slightly further afield, but overall continued city living is either becoming more popular or increasingly a necessity for this age group.

Further out from London again and a ring of green districts can be seen on the cartogram of change, where this group is falling in its share of the local population. In the South West, North Wales and remoter areas elsewhere, falls can be seen despite the rising numbers of this second baby boom generation (the children of the children born just after the war). This age group is also slowly and steadily becoming more geographically polarised.

Age 30-44 2001 (%)

- 16.9 - 21.0
- 21.1 - 21.9
- 22.0 - 22.7
- 22.8 - 23.7
- 23.8 - 29.2

Age 30-44 change (%)

- −2.5 - 0.0
- 0.1 - 0.7
- 0.8 - 1.3
- 1.4 - 2.2
- 2.3 - 8.4

LATE MIDDLE AGE

Just when life appeared to be getting dull, everything changes. Late middle age is defined here as the 15 years from 45-59. By 2001 this group comprised some 11.1 million people, 18.9% of the population, up 2.5% on a decade earlier; but note that changing mortality rates begin to influence these maps[18].

London does not hold its charms forever, and with ever growing numbers of young people fighting to enter the Capital, between early and late middle age is the time to leave. Similar trends are seen in other cities such as Manchester, Leicester and Nottingham. This flow, between early and late middle age, from the cities has been long recognised. However, something changed during the 1990s and what was a trickle became a flood.

A dividing line is emerging between the places to leave and the places to head for. As people enter late middle age they leave London, the greater Birmingham, Manchester and Leeds conurbations, Glasgow, Edinburgh, Belfast and the districts east of Cardiff. For those that could afford it, early retirement began in earnest during the decade of change shown here. Those, who could, moved to the South West, Mid Wales, the more rural Midlands and East Anglia, Cumbria and northern Scotland.

Just as the young were leaving the countryside, the old entered, or forced the young out, by buying the homes the young people might have bought. Additionally, or alternatively, older people may have left the cities in greater numbers because so many more young people were entering. We cannot be sure of the precise drivers but whatever went on occurred in a way that is now clear to see in its effect.

Age 45-59 2001 (%)
- 11.3 - 15.7
- 15.8 - 18.1
- 18.2 - 19.8
- 19.9 - 21.1
- 21.2 - 23.2

Age 45-59 change (%)
- −1.5 - 1.9
- 2.0 - 2.6
- 2.7 - 3.0
- 3.1 - 3.6
- 3.7 - 6.4

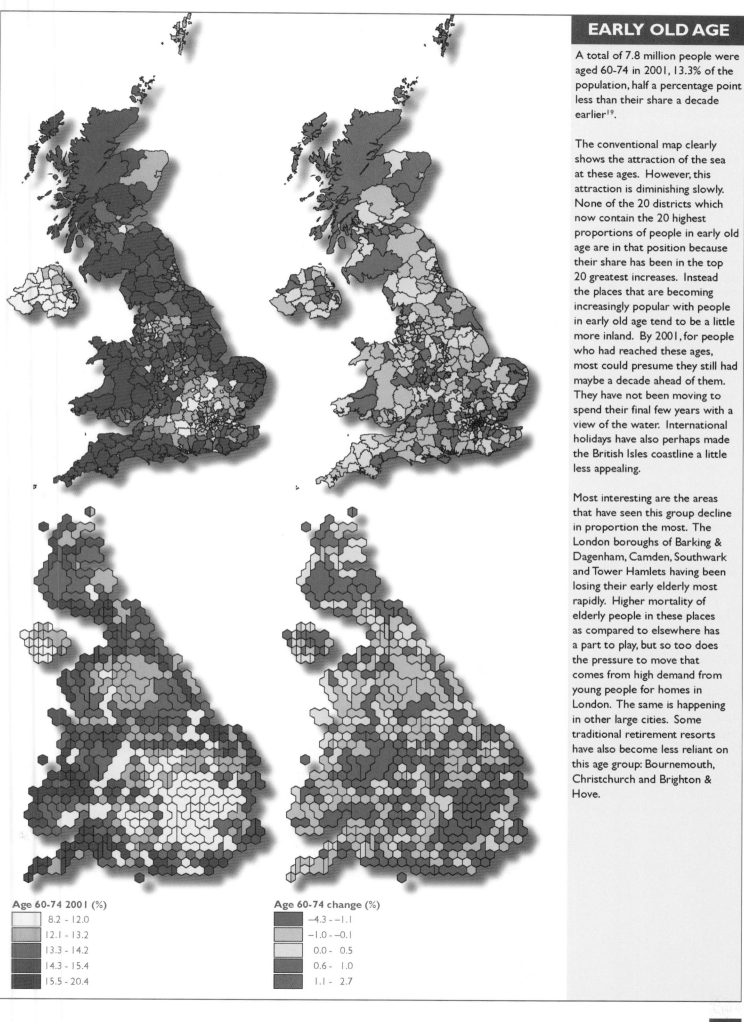

Age 60-74 2001 (%)

	8.2 – 12.0
	12.1 – 13.2
	13.3 – 14.2
	14.3 – 15.4
	15.5 – 20.4

Age 60-74 change (%)

	−4.3 – −1.1
	−1.0 – −0.1
	0.0 – 0.5
	0.6 – 1.0
	1.1 – 2.7

EARLY OLD AGE

A total of 7.8 million people were aged 60-74 in 2001, 13.3% of the population, half a percentage point less than their share a decade earlier[19].

The conventional map clearly shows the attraction of the sea at these ages. However, this attraction is diminishing slowly. None of the 20 districts which now contain the 20 highest proportions of people in early old age are in that position because their share has been in the top 20 greatest increases. Instead the places that are becoming increasingly popular with people in early old age tend to be a little more inland. By 2001, for people who had reached these ages, most could presume they still had maybe a decade ahead of them. They have not been moving to spend their final few years with a view of the water. International holidays have also perhaps made the British Isles coastline a little less appealing.

Most interesting are the areas that have seen this group decline in proportion the most. The London boroughs of Barking & Dagenham, Camden, Southwark and Tower Hamlets having been losing their early elderly most rapidly. Higher mortality of elderly people in these places as compared to elsewhere has a part to play, but so too does the pressure to move that comes from high demand from young people for homes in London. The same is happening in other large cities. Some traditional retirement resorts have also become less reliant on this age group: Bournemouth, Christchurch and Brighton & Hove.

LATE OLD AGE

Much has been written about the rise of older people, but a great deal of that rise has still to occur. 4.0 million people were aged 75-89 in 2001, 6.6% of the population, increasing their share by a third of a percentage point from 1991 when 3.8 million had attained this age[20].

Attachment to the coast for this older group is even stronger, and to southern coasts in particular. Most people in much of the North of the UK, especially men, still cannot expect to reach the age of 75. However, even for this group, population growth has been most rapid just inland from the coast. As the numbers of elderly slowly grow, the coastline becomes saturated and new bungalows need to be built further inland.

The most interesting story concerning the geography of late old age is not where people are now choosing to live, but from where they are leaving most rapidly. Deaths count for a great many exits at these ages but upon death many elderly people's homes are re-occupied by similar if slightly younger people. Such a process is not occurring as it has traditionally done across a swath of country from the North of London down to the Hampshire and Sussex coastlines. Across the rest of the country there are similar if smaller blocks of contiguous districts in which the very elderly are not being replaced when they leave. If current trends continue, the patterns revealed in 2001 are set to become much more entrenched. Local authority districts are becoming increasingly distinctive in their age profiles. Mixed communities by age are disappearing.

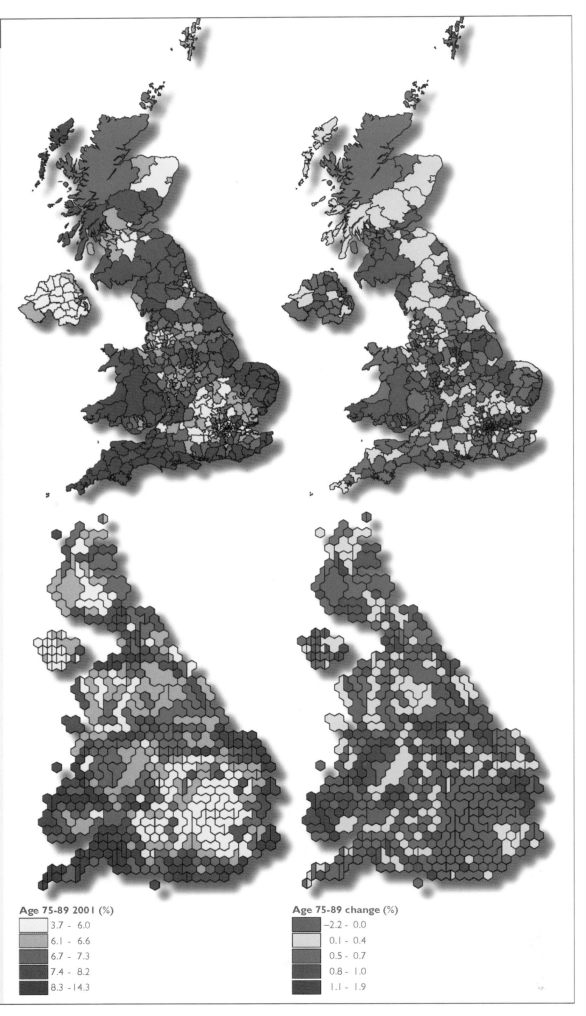

Age 75-89 2001 (%)

	3.7 - 6.0
	6.1 - 6.6
	6.7 - 7.3
	7.4 - 8.2
	8.3 - 14.3

Age 75-89 change (%)

	-2.2 - 0.0
	0.1 - 0.4
	0.5 - 0.7
	0.8 - 1.0
	1.1 - 1.9

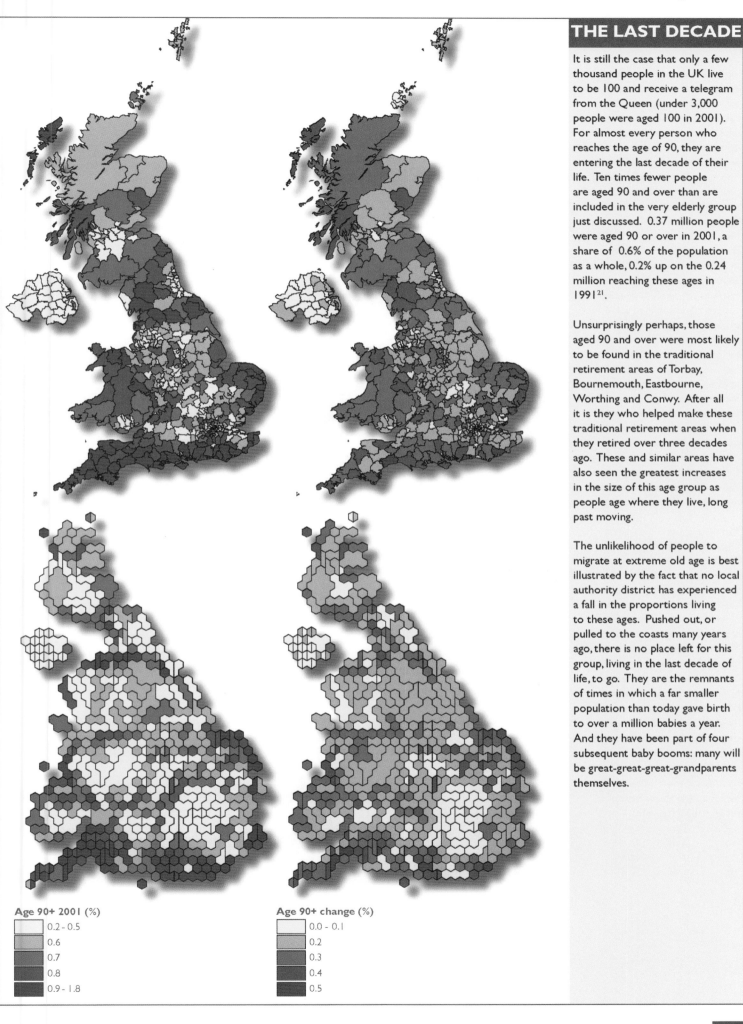

Age 90+ 2001 (%)

- 0.2 - 0.5
- 0.6
- 0.7
- 0.8
- 0.9 - 1.8

Age 90+ change (%)

- 0.0 - 0.1
- 0.2
- 0.3
- 0.4
- 0.5

THE LAST DECADE

It is still the case that only a few thousand people in the UK live to be 100 and receive a telegram from the Queen (under 3,000 people were aged 100 in 2001). For almost every person who reaches the age of 90, they are entering the last decade of their life. Ten times fewer people are aged 90 and over than are included in the very elderly group just discussed. 0.37 million people were aged 90 or over in 2001, a share of 0.6% of the population as a whole, 0.2% up on the 0.24 million reaching these ages in 1991[21].

Unsurprisingly perhaps, those aged 90 and over were most likely to be found in the traditional retirement areas of Torbay, Bournemouth, Eastbourne, Worthing and Conwy. After all it is they who helped make these traditional retirement areas when they retired over three decades ago. These and similar areas have also seen the greatest increases in the size of this age group as people age where they live, long past moving.

The unlikelihood of people to migrate at extreme old age is best illustrated by the fact that no local authority district has experienced a fall in the proportions living to these ages. Pushed out, or pulled to the coasts many years ago, there is no place left for this group, living in the last decade of life, to go. They are the remnants of times in which a far smaller population than today gave birth to over a million babies a year. And they have been part of four subsequent baby booms: many will be great-great-great-grandparents themselves.

MARRIAGE

Lastly in this chapter on basic
identity we turn to marriage.
Age and sex are recorded first
through birth certification and
subsequently at censuses and
finally upon death. Marriages are
certified when they occur, and
are again recorded at censuses.
The same laws of registration
cover marriage as deal with births
and deaths (and thus sex and
age), and so we include marriage
here[22]. Legal marriage below
the age of 16 in the UK has not
been possible for many years and
although polygamous marriages
are now recognised for purposes
such as claming benefits, they
cannot be conducted in the UK.
Same-sex marriages are not yet
formally recognised here.

In 2001, 25.0 million people were
married, 43% of the population,
down 4% on a decade earlier.
Given that roughly a fifth of the
population are too young to
marry, this proportion means that
a majority of those that can marry
still do and remain married or
re-marry.

People are more likely to be
married the older they are.
Compare the current distribution
shown opposite with the
cartograms of the population
now in late middle age and
older. London is the home of
the young and the antithesis of
marriage. Outside of Northern
Ireland, Eilean Siar and the Isles
of Scilly, marriage rates continue
to fall everywhere[23]. Marriage
is currently least common in
Islington and Lambeth, where
only 26% of the population are
now married, down from 32%
and 30% respectively in 1991. To
understand more of this pattern
we next turn to consider the
geography of religion.

Married 2001 (%)
- 26-31
- 32-37
- 38-42
- 43-48
- 49-54

Married change (%)
- −8 - −6
- −5 - −4
- −3 - −2
- −1 - 0
- 1 - 2

NOTES

[1] The 2001 Census used a process called 'capture-recapture' to attempt to count more accurately the population of the UK than had been achieved before. The figures it produces are estimates rather than counts, but for ease of description we use 'counts' from here on. At the time of writing there is some controversy as to the accuracy of the census. It may have missed several hundred thousand people, most of them men. Such errors would have almost no effect on the maps shown here. However, because of this uncertainty, we generally give numbers from here on as millions to one decimal point. It is the accuracy of the digit or digits following the decimal point that cannot be assured.

[2] The census gave people no option such as 'confused', and the question referred to 'sex' not 'gender'.

[3] We use the 1991 Census results corrected for under-enumeration in 1991. The release of 2001 Census data cast doubt on those corrections, but the uncertainty is still less than that concerning 2001 data.

[4] We have chosen to consider all children aged under three as a single group as it is at these ages that most children are looked after at home, and because single year of age change figures are less reliable due partly to very high levels of migration around the time of birth. Also people often miss new-born infants off census forms. However, both the 1991 and 2001 sources of data that we use have been corrected for this known source of error. What is unknown is the extent to which there might have been a slight rise in this group due to some international migrants preferring to give birth in the UK slightly more than they used to (raising birth registrations slightly), which may influence the change cartogram.

[5] City of London, Camden, Kensington & Chelsea, Richmond upon Thames, Wandsworth, Westminster, St Albans, and Epsom & Ewell; coloured red on the cartogram of change.

[6] We considered mapping different age ranges of children but found that the maps were too similar to be of value to reproduce. Ages 3-17 are the ages at which most children are in nursery care or some form of education. Almost no people aged under 18 have children themselves in the UK anymore. There are hardly any teenage mothers in the UK, for instance, and almost all of them are aged 18 or 19. It is at 18 that we see the greatest change to maps by age distribution.

[7] Put simply, the baby boom lasted from mid-1946 until births returned to 1945 levels in 1951. Those births resulted in a second baby boom between 1963 and 1968 (when births returned to 1962 levels). Later and less predictable childbearing lead the third baby boom to be far more spread out, but over three quarters of a million children were born each year between 1985 and 1994 in the UK. Such numbers had not been born a year since 1973. Fewer children are now born a year than at the lowest point in the depression (1933), or even during the lowest previous post-war baby slump (1977).

[8] 2.17 million children were born in the years 1981-83 in the UK as compared to 2.52 million born between 1971-73. The fall is thus lower than the reduction in birth cohort size would predict. Given populations of 2.17 and 2.42 million in the 2001 and 1991 (corrected) Censuses, it would appear that for every child that has died in the UK before the age of 18, born between 1981-83, one (net) has entered this country; whereas 100,000 children of these ages in 1991 were 'missing from the UK' as compared to the birth figures for that cohort. What appears to be a fall is a rise!

[9] These being in order of most increase first: Cambridge, Durham, Oxford, Ceredigion, Southampton, Lancaster, Nottingham, Exeter, Manchester, Runnymede, Cardiff, Norwich and Newcastle upon Tyne.

[10] Because we are using the 1991 Census results corrected to agree to the 1991 mid-year estimates, students are being counted at their term-time address at both points in time.

[11] For those still following the birth cohort story here is the episode for this age group. Between 1967 and 1970, 3.73 million babies were born in the UK; by 1991, 3.65 million people aged 21-24 were here, a fall of 0.08 million. Coming forward a decade, between 1977 and 1980, 2.83 million babies were born, but by 2001, there were 2.80 million people aged 21-24, a fall of only 0.03 million. By the time you get to such tiny numbers of people, adjusting for the impact of calendar and census years becomes important although uncertainty over census counts is too high to really warrant this for this age group in particular. Nevertheless, allowing for the numbers of people born 21 to 24 years ago in the UK, this group has not declined in number as fast as its predecessor group a decade ago. Increasing numbers of overseas students may make up a little part of the reason for this.

[12] For 2001 and 1991 respectively, the birth cohort sizes were 3.73 million (1972-76) and 4.96 million (1962-66), the groups at ages 25-29 numbered 3.87 million and 4.79 million. Thus more people are now living in the UK than were born in the UK in this cohort despite deaths and in contrast to a decade earlier.

[13] City of London, Camden, Hackney, Hammersmith & Fulham, Haringey, Islington, Kensington & Chelsea, Lambeth, Southwark, Tower Hamlets, Wandsworth and Westminster.

[14] In London: Brent, Ealing, Hounslow, Lewisham, Merton, Newham and Waltham Forest. Commuting distance from London: Reading, Slough, Cambridge, Watford and Oxford.

[15] In London: Barnet, Greenwich and Kingston upon Thames. Outside London and still popular with those aged 25-29: Manchester, Bristol, Brighton & Hove, Rushmoor (in Hampshire), Southampton, Norwich, Aberdeen, Edinburgh and Limavady (Northern Ireland).

[16] 14.06 million people were born between 1957-71 as compared to 12.87 million between 1947-61. These groups do now, of course, overlap, and some of the former will be the children of the latter, but it is still possible to compare the size of age groups in 2001 and 1991 with the numbers born in the UK who would now be of those ages. The 2001 population is 13.27 million, just under 800,000 fewer than were born. The 1991 population was 12.22 million, only 650,000 fewer than were born. Here, what looks like a rise in the size of a group is actually a fall when birth cohorts are considered. One reason for the fall in group size, when adjusted for birth cohort size, is the change in immigration controls and emigration desires for children born in the 1960s as compared to the 1950s.

[17] City of London, Hackney, Hammersmith & Fulham, Haringey, Islington, Kensington & Chelsea, Lambeth, Richmond upon Thames, Southwark, Wandsworth and Westminster.

[18] 12.62 million babies born between 1942-56 largely resulted in 11.12 million people being of ages 45-59 in 2001. A decade earlier 11.36 million babies born between 1932-46 largely resulted in 9.50 million people of ages 45-59 in 1991. Thus, assuming no net effect of migration, some 1.50 million of the later babies died before they could be enumerated in late middle age in 2001 (12%), and 1.86 million of the earlier born babies died before they could be enumerated in late middle age in 1991 (16%). This simple estimate suggests that a person's chances of dying and missing being enumerated at these ages in a census fell by a quarter over 10 years. Of course, it could be due to factors operating many years ago. The later group, born earliest in 1942, will all have benefited from rationing and then for most of their childhood from the introduction of the NHS in 1948. Children's rations in war time were much more nutritious than the food the average child born in the 1930s received.

[19] Between 1927 and 1941, 11.0 million babies were born in the UK of which, ignoring migration, 7.8 million or 71% survived to 2001. Between 1917 and 1931, 12.7 million babies were born (including those in the Irish Republic prior to 1922), 8.0 million or 63% survived in the UK to 1991. Again rates of mortality for this cohort, as compared to its counterparts born a decade earlier, have declined by a quarter in a decade. The numbers reaching this age may be slightly lower but the proportions surviving from birth to this age are much higher. The reason for the decline is because today's 60- to 74-year-olds are too young to have been born during the baby boom that resulted from the end of the First World War, with births peaking, in what was then the UK, at 1.1 million in 1920 alone.

[20] 13.9 million babies were born between 1912-26, only 4.0 million survived to 2001. Again we are assuming no net effect of migration and ignoring those surviving who were born in Ireland before 1922. This survival rate of 29% can be compared to the fortunes of the 15.8 million babies born between 1902-16, of whom only 3.8 million survived to 1991, some 24%. The improvements in mortality at very elderly ages have not been as dramatic as those seen by other elderly groups. That is not surprising given that children born in the later period were likely to spend much of their childhood living through the deprivations of the 1930s economic depression. Also, somewhat different diseases tend to cause more deaths among the very elderly, diseases for which there have been fewer improvements in treatment over time.

[21] Of people aged 90 and over in 2001, figures from the Government Actuary's Department suggest that more than half are aged 90, 91 or 92. Taking the births from those three years of life, just over 3 million babies were born between both periods: 1909-11 and 1899-1901 (the year Queen Victoria died). Doubling that gives a population at risk of about 6 million. Thus the 0.37 million survivors in 2001 constitute roughly one in 16 of all births among that groups, and the 0.24 million survivors in 1991 constitute just one in 25 of their birth cohort. By 2001 a person's chances from birth around the start of the last century of reaching the age of 90 were 8%; of reaching the age of 93: 4%; 95: 2%; 97: 1%; 99: 0.4%; 101: 0.16%; 103: 0.05%; 105: 0.02%; 106: 0.01%. Put another way, only one in 10,000 people born in 1895 were alive in 2001, roughly 100 people (of whom only four were men).

[22] We do not include maps of divorce because they largely reflect the age structure. Where there are more elderly people, more people are likely to have been divorced. Maps of changes to divorce are confused by the changing proportions of people who remarry, tabulated in 2001 but not in 1991.

[23] The proportion of all people who are married has fallen fastest in Southampton, by 8% to be 35%. A further eight out of every hundred fewer people are now married there than were in 1991. In the following lists the proportion married in 2001 is shown in brackets. The simple marriage rate has fallen by 7% in Brighton & Hove (to 32%), Nottingham (31%), Lincoln (37%), Norwich (34%) and Barking & Dagenham (37%). It has fallen by 6% in Islington (26%), Greenwich (34%), Exeter (37%), Manchester (28%), Blackpool (39%), Lancaster (40%), Bristol (35%), Belfast (35%) and Ceredigion (41%). It is not falling because a greater proportion of people are having children in these places and children cannot marry. It is falling most in these cities and university towns because the share of young adults in these places is rising and young adults are increasingly unlikely to marry young. The smallest fall outside of the Islands and Northern Ireland has been in Rutland, of 1%, but even there a minority of all people are now married as compared to a majority in 1991.

Religion and ethnicity

Maps in this section include:

The previous chapter ended by showing how marriage continues to decline in popularity across the UK, falling in popularity everywhere, but slightly faster where the population is rapidly becoming younger. Only in the west of Northern Ireland and on two small islands is the crude rate of marriage increasing, and only because there are relatively fewer children (too young to marry) there. The decline in marriage in the UK is largely a reflection of the continued and very long-term decline in the power of the established church. Although the majority of marriages that take place in the UK are now civil ceremonies, the continuation of marriage largely reflects a continuation in practises established by the church. It was the continued decline in the influence of the established church, coupled with lobbying from the other religions of the UK, which lead to the 2001 Census being used to take the first official survey of the religious beliefs of the population held since 1851. Ironically, while the 1851 religious census was concerned with the differing numbers of people practising different forms of Christian belief, in England and Wales in 2001 all the various Christian denominations were amalgamated.

The census showed that Christianity was strong when measured in this way only in a few parts of the North West of England. Large numbers of people in Scotland and Wales clearly now object to being asked their religion through a census. The non-Christian religions were most dominant in the major city regions, London, the Midlands, the Northern conurbation, Glasgow and in Cardiff. Here, too, people were most likely not to state their religion when asked (an option given on the form). In Scotland very high numbers stated they had no religion, similar to the districts with the very highest proportions with no religion in Northern Ireland, and perhaps stating so for similar reasons.

Other than Christianity, no religion holds sway over large groups of the UK population, but people are more likely to tick allegiance to another religion because of adherence, rather than simply because they have once or twice been in a church.

Muslims are in a small minority in every district in the UK. In the three districts with the highest proportions they only number just over a third of the population, just under a quarter and just under a fifth. Outside of these few places with significant numbers the proportion of the population who are Muslim reach a tenth only in a few cities, northern towns and boroughs of North London.

People declaring an allegiance to the next largest religion in the UK, Hinduism, are fewer still. They make up less than a fifth of the population in the area in which they are most concentrated. Hindus make up only a tiny proportion of the population as a whole, living mostly in the suburbs of London and some Midland towns and cities.

The Sikh and Jewish populations are even smaller, more dispersed and less concentrated too, again in specific urban and suburban areas.

Allegiance to any other religion (other than in Scotland) and Buddhism is clearly a southern phenomenon. Adjusting for the relative sizes of each religious group, Muslims are most concentrated geographically, followed by Hindus, religious Jews, Christians, Sikhs, people with no religion and then Buddhists, a religion not strongly associated with any ethnic group in the UK and hence less with any place. Degree of concentration tends to reflect the concentrations of people of ethnicities most associated with each religion, and hence is reflecting a pattern that is probably of religious dispersal over time as, although religious belief was not asked in 1991, ethnicity was, and so it is possible to measure the changing geographies of ethnicity.

While many aspects of society in the UK became more polarised geographically over the course of the 1990s, this was not generally the case for people's ethnicity. In most cases minority ethnic groups became slightly less geographically concentrated over time although that is difficult to see from the maps (you have to read the footnotes). This is largely due to the particular points at which these ethnicities have been counted and the types of ethnicity that were included in the last two national census forms. We have had to compare these categories as best we can and explain the detail in the footnotes to the following text.

In short, all the smaller ethnic groups were associated with waves of immigration to Britain that had peaked long before the 1991 Census was taken. By measuring the changing geographies of ethnicity in the 1990s we are mainly measuring the dispersal of people and their children and grandchildren out from areas where many people first settled in the UK. In the footnotes to the text describing the maps and cartograms of ethnicity that follow, we have also presented calculations of the changes to various indices of segregation and isolation which show how numerically there has been an overall dispersal of smaller ethnic groups across the districts of the UK during the 1990s. The maps and cartograms also show this, but they highlight where groups are still most concentrated and where any concentrations of people by ethnicity have risen within the country.

The UK remains a White desert with a few oases of colour, but these oases are spreading out. The Indian, Chinese and Other Asian populations are moving out of the cities to more distant suburbs and small towns. The Black Caribbean population behave similarly, despite declining in number (due partly to emigration). People of Pakistani and Bangladeshi origin remain very concentrated in particular areas of initial settlement, but they too become more dispersed out of these areas during the 1990s. Most districts in the country also saw small rises in the proportions of their population who were Black Africans or ticked the Black Other census box. The only group who may not be spread out more are the group of miscellaneous ethnicities labelled as 'Other other' by the census authorities, as these include many people associated with very recent small waves of immigration mainly living in the South of England. Increased segregation by ethnicity is not a feature of mainland Britain. To find any evidence of that you have to cross the Irish Sea.

Various White ethnicities allied with religious identities have mattered most in recent decades in the UK in Northern Ireland. The patterns to these identities are changing slowly over time, but there is no sign of any reduction in the concentration of people by identity in particular areas of the Province (treating all Protestants as a single group and allowing for the changing sizes of population groups). While the proportion of the population who are Catholic has risen, so too and more quickly has the proportion who are unwilling to state any religious adherence. Thus despite there being little evidence of any major changes to levels of residential segregation in the Province, there are changes occurring coincident with the rapid demographic reorientation of that area described in Chapter 2 and the economic turnaround described in more detail in several chapters of this atlas to follow (Chapters 5 and 6). Again it is markets that may be leading these changes. More young people unwilling to declare a religious affiliation are staying to live in Northern Ireland than before. In Britain, too, as minority ethnic groups improve their economic situations from those often associated with first generation immigration, the housing and job markets spin increasing numbers of people out of the city centres, into which other groups are now being pulled.

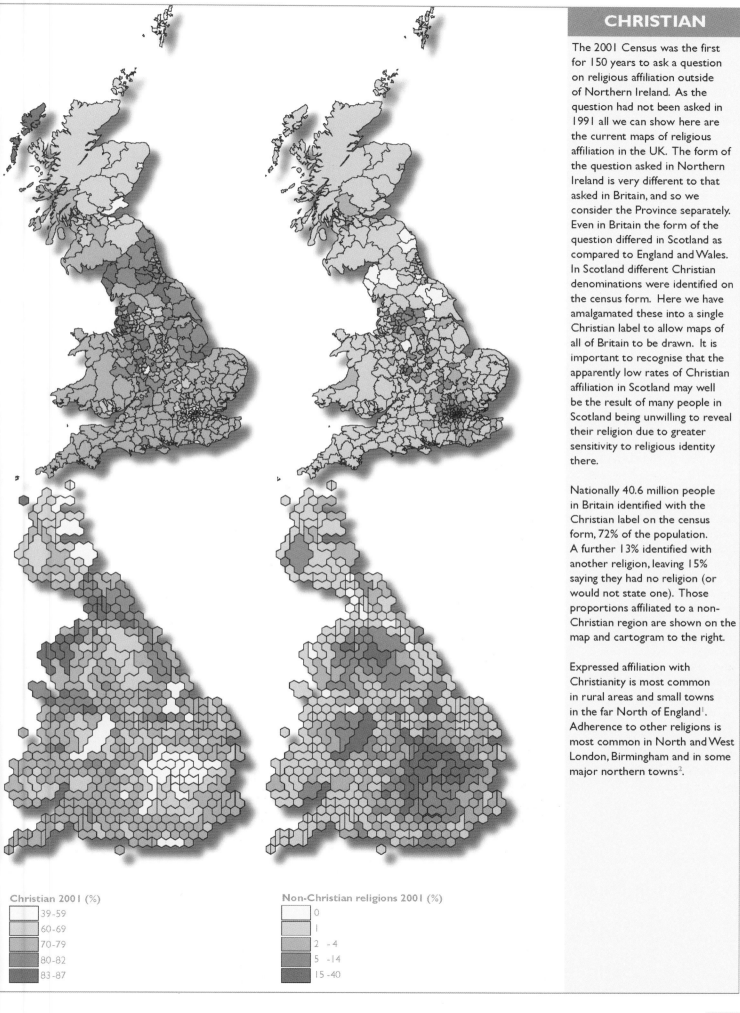

CHRISTIAN

The 2001 Census was the first for 150 years to ask a question on religious affiliation outside of Northern Ireland. As the question had not been asked in 1991 all we can show here are the current maps of religious affiliation in the UK. The form of the question asked in Northern Ireland is very different to that asked in Britain, and so we consider the Province separately. Even in Britain the form of the question differed in Scotland as compared to England and Wales. In Scotland different Christian denominations were identified on the census form. Here we have amalgamated these into a single Christian label to allow maps of all of Britain to be drawn. It is important to recognise that the apparently low rates of Christian affiliation in Scotland may well be the result of many people in Scotland being unwilling to reveal their religion due to greater sensitivity to religious identity there.

Nationally 40.6 million people in Britain identified with the Christian label on the census form, 72% of the population. A further 13% identified with another religion, leaving 15% saying they had no religion (or would not state one). Those proportions affiliated to a non-Christian region are shown on the map and cartogram to the right.

Expressed affiliation with Christianity is most common in rural areas and small towns in the far North of England[1]. Adherence to other religions is most common in North and West London, Birmingham and in some major northern towns[2].

Christian 2001 (%)

- 39-59
- 60-69
- 70-79
- 80-82
- 83-87

Non-Christian religions 2001 (%)

- 0
- 1
- 2 - 4
- 5 - 14
- 15 - 40

NO RELIGION

A total of 8.6 million people are recorded as having no religion by the census in Britain, and a further 4.2 million as having chosen not to state their religious affiliation. These groups between them constitute 22.6% of the population. However, they include a large number of people who wrote in their religion as Jedi. Jedi was Britain's fourth largest religion in 2001. This upset the census authorities and so in a fit of pique they did not publish the geographical details of this group. Similarly significant numbers of people in Scotland objected to being asked their religion, thus Scotland stands out as distinctive on these maps and the maps bear little relation to actual beliefs and adherence in Scotland[3].

Outside of Scotland the highest proportions of the population declaring no religion, all of over a quarter, are found in Cambridge, Brighton & Hove, Norwich, Blaenau Gwent and Rhondda, Cynon, Taf. The first three areas contain many university students and similar young people who were particularly likely to affiliate with the Jedi. The two areas of Wales with high rates are likely to be in this list for similar reasons to most of Scotland. Scotland similarly records very low rates of religion not being stated. People were least likely to be prepared to state their religion in particular boroughs of London and some other towns and cities[4]. These maps tell us more about dissent from census taking and official intrusion than they do of religion. Nevertheless the patterns seen are informative and distinct. They are geographies of those who do not want their religious geographies revealed.

No religion 2001 (%)

6 - 9
10 - 14
15 - 19
20 - 24
25 - 42

Religion not stated 2001 (%)

4 - 5
6 - 7
8
9
10 - 12

The two largest non-Christian religions in Britain are Islam and Hinduism, with 1.6 and 0.6 million people affiliated to each respectively, 2.8% and 1.0% of the population. It is for these religions that the census question is most likely to have produced results that can be clearly interpreted. The largest part of the Christian religion is affiliated with the state churches, and thus many people may tick the Christian box without actually holding many Christian beliefs or taking part in many Christian practises. The same is unlikely to be true to the same extent for other religions.

People affiliated to the Muslim religions are most likely to be found in North London, Birmingham, Leicester and in some Pennine towns. Just over a third of the population of Tower Hamlets are Muslim, the next largest proportion is just under a quarter of the population of Newham, then just under a fifth of Blackburn with Darwen (in Lancashire)[5]. After Islam, Britain's third largest religion, Hinduism, has most of its followers living in suburban London, Leicester and Oadby & Wigston (in Leicestershire)[6]. The geographical locations of these two religious groups are closely linked to geographies of Bangladeshi, Pakistani and Indian ethnic groups, as can be seen from the following maps in this chapter. However, there is no simple mapping from ethnicity to religion, and thus the differences between the maps of ethnic and religious identity highlight where religious affiliations are less easily attributed to ethnic identity.

Muslim 2001 (%)
- 0.0- 0.1
- 0.2
- 0.3- 0.9
- 1.0- 9.9
- 10 -36.4

Hindu 2001 (%)
- 0.0
- 0.1
- 0.2- 0.9
- 1.0- 2.9
- 3.0-19.6

SIKH AND JEWISH

After the Jedi these are Britain's fifth and sixth largest religions. Respectively, they each have 0.34 and 0.26 million people affiliated to them in Britain, 0.6% and 0.5% of the population. Being so small each of these religions is hardly found at all in some of the more remote areas of Britain where only a handful of people, less than 0.1% of the population of a district, identified themselves as Sikh or Jewish. Where an area is labelled as 0 on the map there can be up to 100 people following a particular religion, but usually there are a dozen or less.

The highest proportion of the population labelling themselves as Sikh are to be found in Slough (9.1% of the district's population), Hounslow (8.6%), Ealing (8.5%), Wolverhampton (7.6%) and Gravesham (in Kent, 6.7%)[7]. If the cartogram of Sikh affiliation is compared to the map of Indian ethnicity the similarities are striking[8].

The highest proportions of the local population with Jewish religious affiliations are in Barnet (14.8%), Hertsmere (in Hertfordshire, 11.3%), Harrow (6.3%), Redbridge (6.2%), Camden (5.6%) and Hackney (5.3%)[9]. Outside of London and the northern Home Counties, the proportion of people adhering to this religion only just exceeds 3% in East Renfrewshire and Bury. Jewish secular ethnic identity was not asked for in the 2001 Census and so it is not possible to compare these distributions of religion with any ethnic distribution.

Sikh 2001 (%)

- 0.0
- 0.1
- 0.2 - 0.9
- 1.0 - 1.9
- 2.0 - 9.1

Jewish 2001 (%)

- 0.0
- 0.1
- 0.2 - 0.9
- 1.0 - 2.9
- 3.0 - 14.8

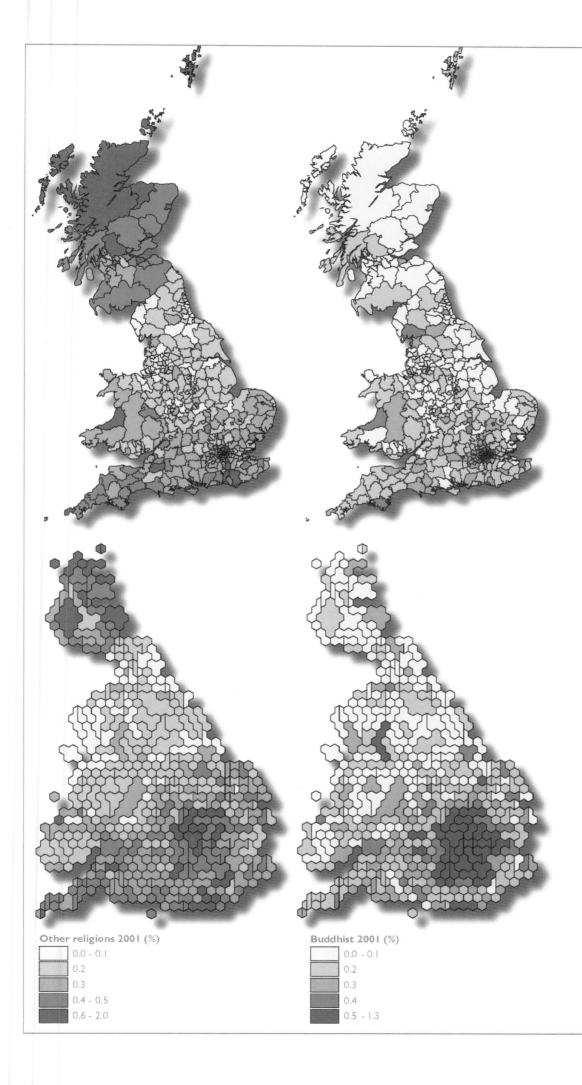

OTHER RELIGION AND BUDDHIST

The seventh and eighth largest religions in Britain are all other religions that the census authorities accept as religions, combined, and then Buddhists, which is the smallest separately identified religious affiliation. A total of 0.17 million people affiliate with the unnamed religions as compared to 0.15 million Buddhists in Britain. As proportions of the population, these both represent just 0.3% of all people. Both groups have very distinct geographies. The combined religions are concentrated in and around London and in Scotland. It is very likely that most of the other religions in Scotland are various versions of Christianity whose adherents wished to specify their particular affiliation and did not wish to be labelled alongside other Christian groups. The Buddhist adherents are almost all to be found inside the capital, with the only notable concentrations outside being in Cambridge (1.0%), Oxford (0.8%), Brighton & Hove (0.7%) and Manchester, Epsom & Ewell, Reading and Elmbridge (all at 0.5%). But Buddhists can be found almost everywhere, thus Clackmannanshire is the only district in the country with nearer to none than 0.1% Buddhists. In contrast to the other non-Christian religions (see footnotes 5, 6, 7, 8, 9), almost 50 districts have to be combined to contain over half of all Buddhists. The level of dispersal of each religion can be measured in various ways. In England and Wales the most segregated group are Jewish, the most isolated are Christian and the least integrated group are Muslim; while Buddhists, other minor religions, atheists and agnostics are most dispersed[10].

Other religions 2001 (%)

- 0.0 - 0.1
- 0.2
- 0.3
- 0.4 - 0.5
- 0.6 - 2.0

Buddhist 2001 (%)

- 0.0 - 0.1
- 0.2
- 0.3
- 0.4
- 0.5 - 1.3

CATHOLIC AND PRESBYTERIAN

In Northern Ireland a religious question has been asked for many decades in the census. The 2001 Census reported 0.68 million Catholics, 0.35 million Presbyterians, 0.26 million Church of Ireland, 0.06 million Methodists, 0.11 million of other denominations and 0.23 million stating no religion. Thus 40% of the population are directly affiliated to the Catholic Church, 40% to the Protestant Churches and 20% to other denominators or to no religion. Because the balance of religions is so fine and religion is of such importance in the Province, questions on religious background are also asked, but we will not consider them here, nor attempt to assign the non-Trinitarian Churches and other groups to one side or the other.

In 1991 Catholics made up 38% of the population. They have risen in proportion in all districts but three: Ards, Ballymoney and Carrickfergus. Here and in Ballymena, Banbridge, Castlereagh, Coleraine, Larne, Lisburn, Newtownabbey and North Down, they constitute less than a third of the population. In Cookstown, Derry, Down, Dungannon, Fermanagh, Limavady, Magherafelt, Newry & Mourne, Omagh and Stabane, they constitute the majority. Conversely Presbyterians have shrunk by over half a percent of the population to 21% in 10 years and in all but five districts. In all those five districts this growth has been at the expense of other Protestant religions, and the proportions of Catholics has also grown. To understand whether these changes are leading to more or less spatial divisions at the district level some social statistics have to be calculated[11].

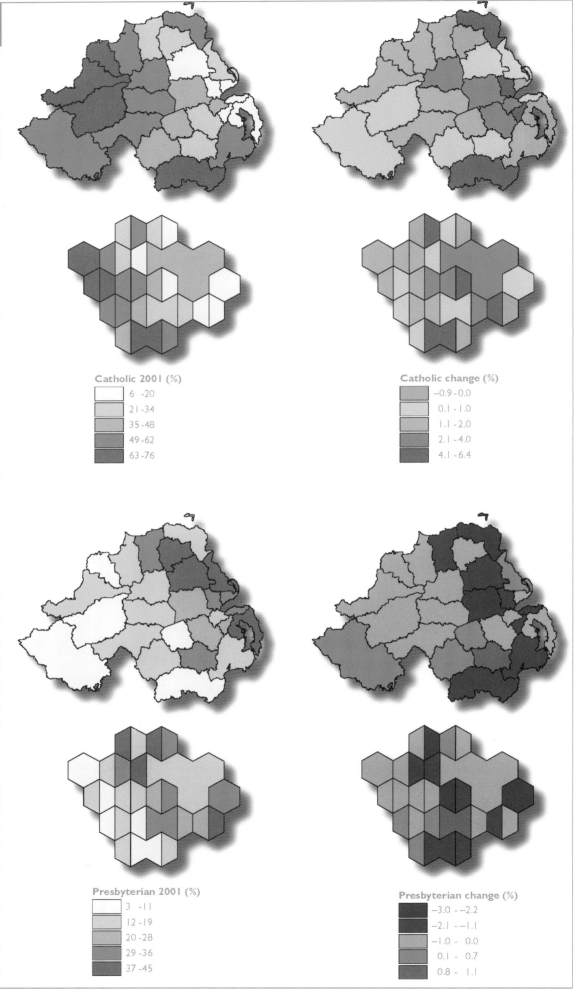

Catholic 2001 (%)
- 6 - 20
- 21 - 34
- 35 - 48
- 49 - 62
- 63 - 76

Catholic change (%)
- −0.9 - 0.0
- 0.1 - 1.0
- 1.1 - 2.0
- 2.1 - 4.0
- 4.1 - 6.4

Presbyterian 2001 (%)
- 3 - 11
- 12 - 19
- 20 - 28
- 29 - 36
- 37 - 45

Presbyterian change (%)
- −3.0 - −2.2
- −2.1 - −1.1
- −1.0 - 0.0
- 0.1 - 0.7
- 0.8 - 1.1

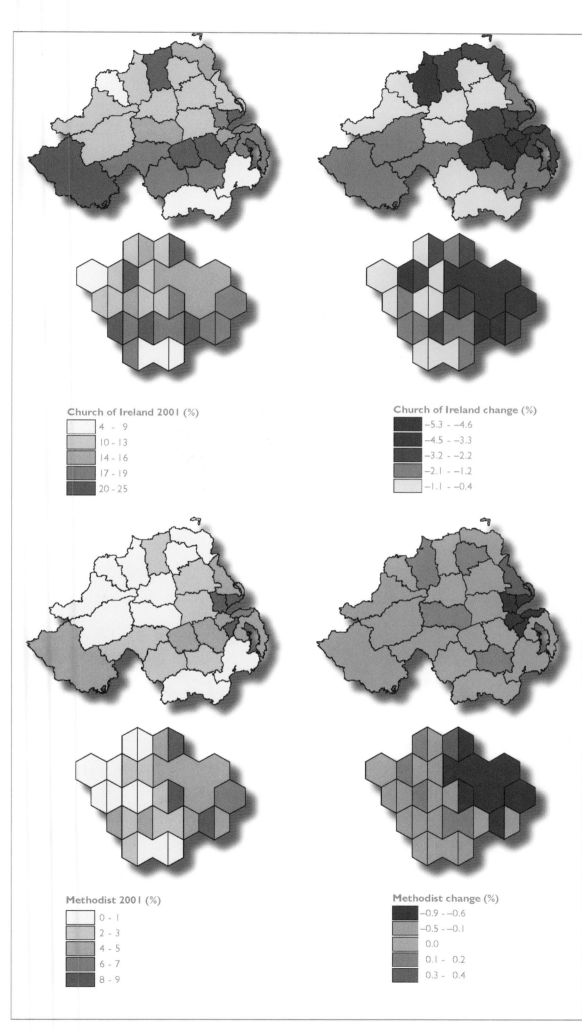

MINOR PROTESTANT RELIGIONS

Church of Ireland 2001 (%)
- 4 - 9
- 10 - 13
- 14 - 16
- 17 - 19
- 20 - 25

Church of Ireland change (%)
- −5.3 - −4.6
- −4.5 - −3.3
- −3.2 - −2.2
- −2.1 - −1.2
- −1.1 - −0.4

Methodist 2001 (%)
- 0 - 1
- 2 - 3
- 4 - 5
- 6 - 7
- 8 - 9

Methodist change (%)
- −0.9 - −0.6
- −0.5 - −0.1
- 0.0
- 0.1 - 0.2
- 0.3 - 0.4

The Church of Ireland had the allegiance of 15% of the population of Northern Ireland in 2001, 2% less than in 1991. The Methodist Chapels had the allegiance of 4%, a third of a percent less than in 1991. Both have very distinct geographies to their popularity and relative decline.

The Church of Ireland is the largest of the Protestant Churches in Armagh, Cookstown, Craigavon, Dunganon, Fermanagh (where it is strongest and where there are the lowest numbers of Presbyterians), Lisburn and Omagh. However, its greatest decline has been in Lisburn, where 5% of the population left the church in 10 years in terms of population share, resulting in a 4% rise in the share stating they had no religion to declare. Its share of the population fell significantly in all its other most popular districts in line with increases in non-affiliation. How these changes alter the pattern of religious mix in the Province again require some reference to separately calculated statistics[12]. The church's share fell least to the West and where it was low to begin with.

For the Methodist groups Carrickfergus, Castlereagh and Newtownabbey are the most populous districts, but they never constitute even a tenth of the population. Their share of the population is falling in these three districts and in another 12, mainly to the east of the Province. In the areas with the very highest proportions of Catholics there are only a handful of Methodists. The decline is strongest where the group was largest and in the few districts where Presbyterianism is becoming slightly more popular.

OTHER RELIGION AND NONE

A total of 6% of the population of Northern Ireland, 1% less than a decade ago, subscribe to other minor religions. These include all the religions counted in England and Wales and a plethora of small, usually quasi-Protestant, groups. Other denominations are most common in the districts with the least Catholics. Just over a tenth of the populations of Carrickfergus and Castlereagh are affiliated to these religions. However, these two districts have seen some of the largest falls in their support. Other religions are only growing in popularity in Limavady as this is an area with a rapid rise in young adults (see Chapter 2, footnote 15).

The proportion of the population of Northern Ireland who refuse to state or do not have a religion rose from 11% to 14% in the 1990s. It is now highest in the West and North and constitutes a quarter of the population of North Down and Carrickfergus. As stated before, these are districts with low proportions of Catholics where religions other than Presbyterianism are more likely to prosper. In both these areas an additional 7.5% of the population decided to state no religion in 2001 as compared to 1991. The proportion of the population not stating a religion only fell in Newry (with the highest Catholic share of 76%) and did not rise in Magherafelt (62% Catholic). The religious composition of Northern Ireland is changing quickly, but most rapidly where it was most mixed to begin with. It is worth comparing the province to the mainland, however, as some divides are not as great as they appear[13].

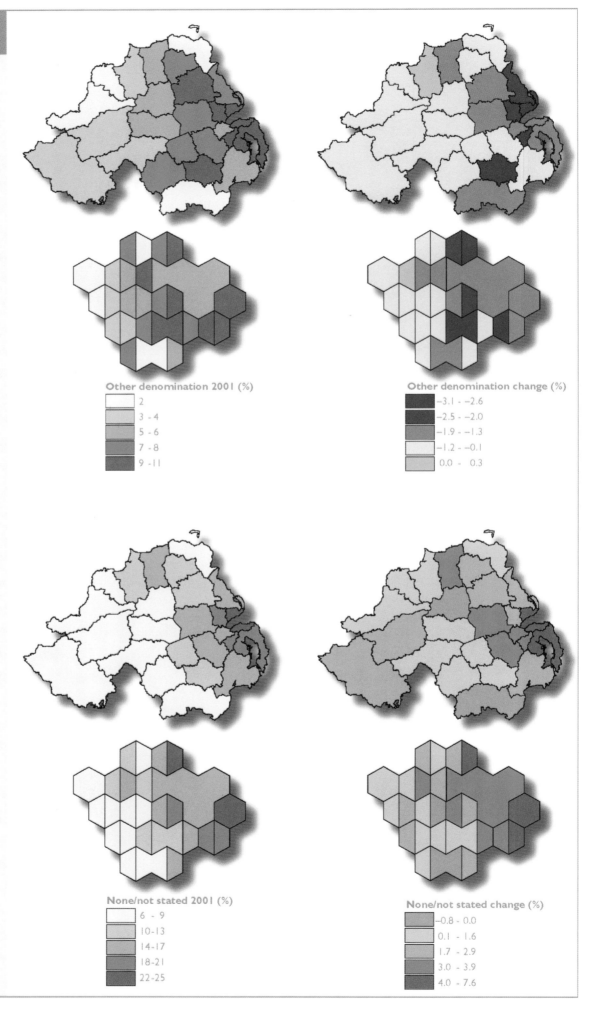

Other denomination 2001 (%)
- 2
- 3 - 4
- 5 - 6
- 7 - 8
- 9 - 11

Other denomination change (%)
- −3.1 - −2.6
- −2.5 - −2.0
- −1.9 - −1.3
- −1.2 - −0.1
- 0.0 - 0.3

None/not stated 2001 (%)
- 6 - 9
- 10 - 13
- 14 - 17
- 18 - 21
- 22 - 25

None/not stated change (%)
- −0.8 - 0.0
- 0.1 - 1.6
- 1.7 - 2.9
- 3.0 - 3.9
- 4.0 - 7.6

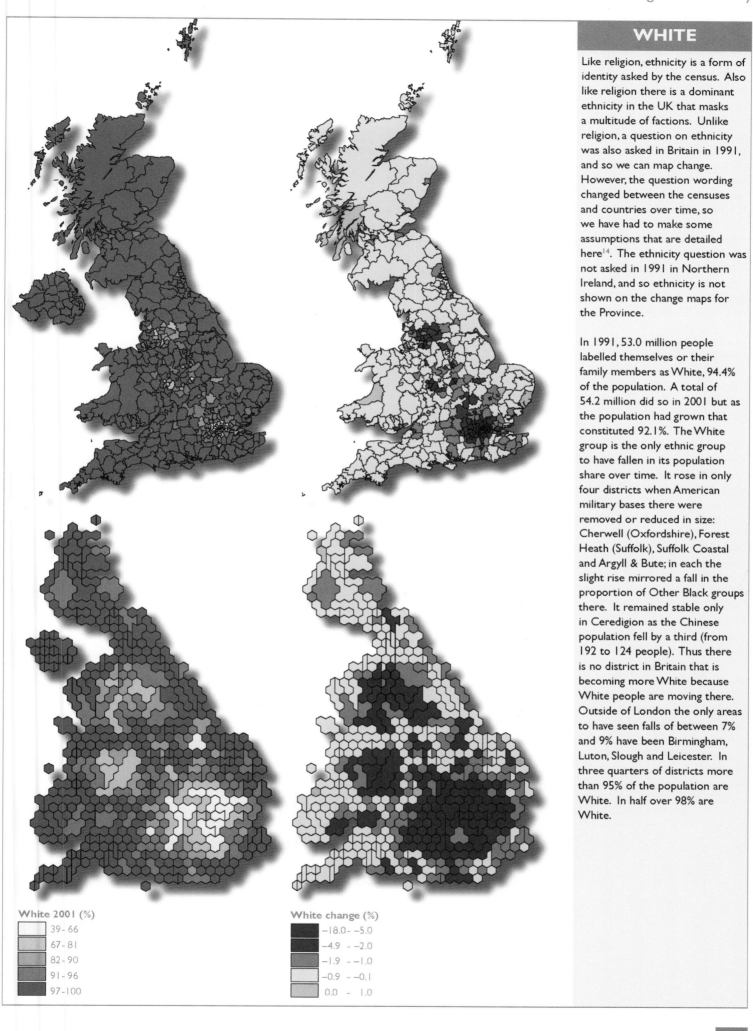

WHITE

Like religion, ethnicity is a form of identity asked by the census. Also like religion there is a dominant ethnicity in the UK that masks a multitude of factions. Unlike religion, a question on ethnicity was also asked in Britain in 1991, and so we can map change. However, the question wording changed between the censuses and countries over time, so we have had to make some assumptions that are detailed here[14]. The ethnicity question was not asked in 1991 in Northern Ireland, and so ethnicity is not shown on the change maps for the Province.

In 1991, 53.0 million people labelled themselves or their family members as White, 94.4% of the population. A total of 54.2 million did so in 2001 but as the population had grown that constituted 92.1%. The White group is the only ethnic group to have fallen in its population share over time. It rose in only four districts when American military bases there were removed or reduced in size: Cherwell (Oxfordshire), Forest Heath (Suffolk), Suffolk Coastal and Argyll & Bute; in each the slight rise mirrored a fall in the proportion of Other Black groups there. It remained stable only in Ceredigion as the Chinese population fell by a third (from 192 to 124 people). Thus there is no district in Britain that is becoming more White because White people are moving there. Outside of London the only areas to have seen falls of between 7% and 9% have been Birmingham, Luton, Slough and Leicester. In three quarters of districts more than 95% of the population are White. In half over 98% are White.

White 2001 (%)
- 39 - 66
- 67 - 81
- 82 - 90
- 91 - 96
- 97 - 100

White change (%)
- −18.0 - −5.0
- −4.9 - −2.0
- −1.9 - −1.0
- −0.9 - −0.1
- 0.0 - 1.0

INDIAN

After White, the second largest ethnic group in Britain is Indian. A total of 1.1 million people now claim this ethnic identity, 1.8% of the population, 0.2% more than in 1991. Despite this overall increase, the most striking image from the maps and cartograms opposite is an apparent fall in the already very small proportions of Indian people living in rural areas. Part of this fall may be statistical artefact as many of these areas have seen slight rises in the Other Asian group (see below), and we have assigned Asian/White people in 2001 to that group (see footnote 24). However, what we are not seeing is any great dispersal of people of Indian origin into rural Britain. Just over half a million (47.5%) of all Indian people in the UK live in just 13 districts[15]. One of those districts, Newham in London, has seen its proportion of Indians fall by 1% of its population. In 1991 these 13 districts contained 49.8% of all Indians; there is thus very slight dispersal occurring, but it is to particular places. The Indian population is rising most outside of London in Harrow (+6%) and in Oadby & Wigston (+5%, see footnote 6 and accompanying text on Hindu religious adherence on page 39).

What is most stark about the geography of Britain's second largest ethnic group is how in the large majority of the country there is almost no one to be found who is Indian. In some 23 districts there are 23 or fewer people of Indian origin[16]. Almost a million people live there, 0.04% are Indian, 50 times fewer than the national average proportion[17]. In 10 years the total number rose by nine people.

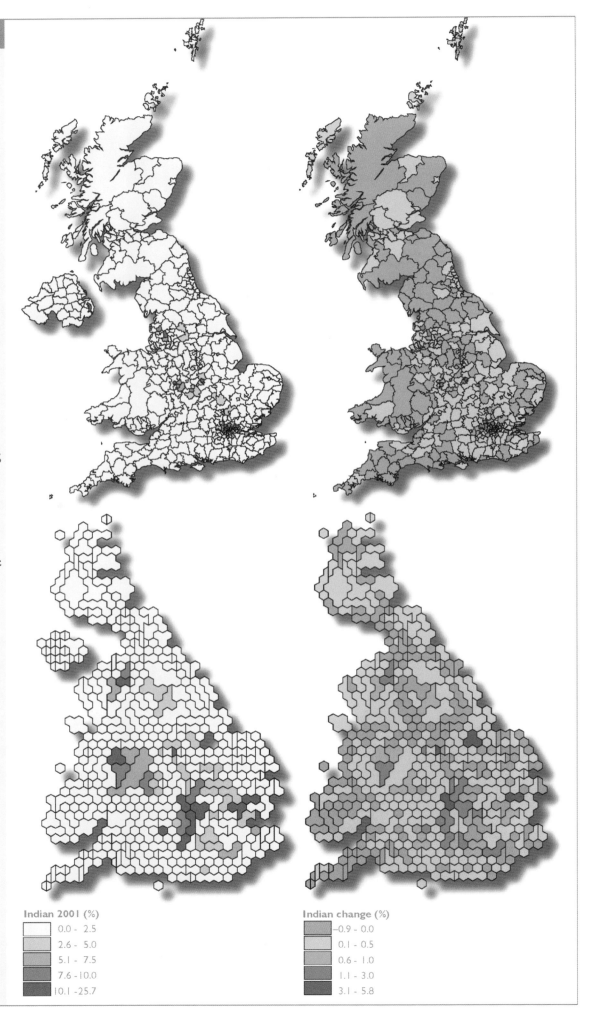

Indian 2001 (%)

	0.0 - 2.5
	2.6 - 5.0
	5.1 - 7.5
	7.6 - 10.0
	10.1 - 25.7

Indian change (%)

	-0.9 - 0.0
	0.1 - 0.5
	0.6 - 1.0
	1.1 - 3.0
	3.1 - 5.8

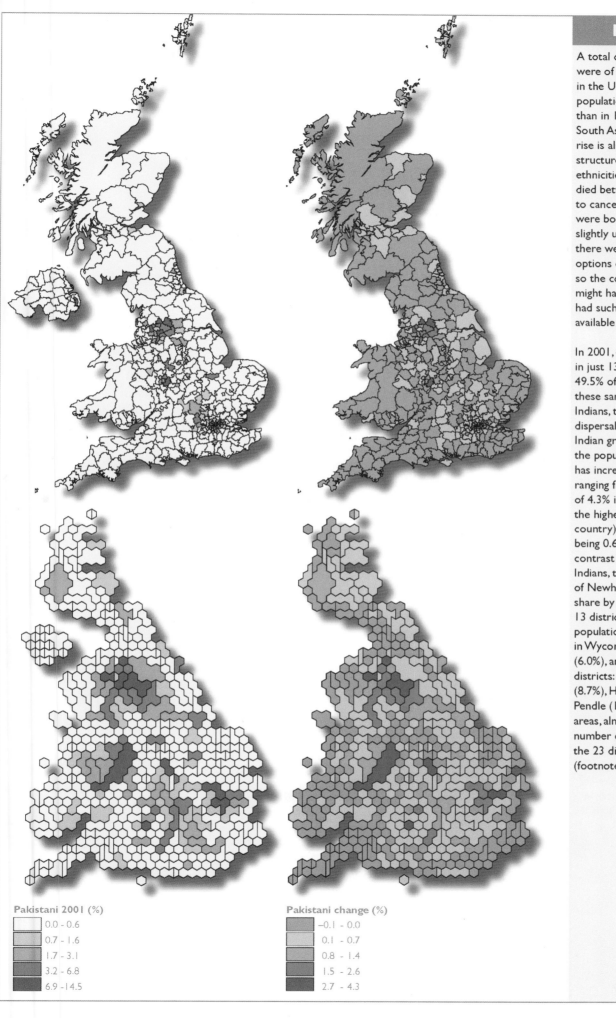

A total of 0.75 million people were of Pakistani ethnic origin in the UK in 2001, 1.27% of the population and 0.38% more than in 1991. Like the other South Asian ethnic groups, this rise is almost all due to the age structure of people of these ethnicities, meaning that very few died between the census years to cancel out the children who were born. The increase may be slightly underestimated as in 1991 there were no mixed ethnicity options on the census form and so the count of Pakistanis then might have been somewhat lower had such labelling options been available in the past.

In 2001, 49.0% of Pakistanis lived in just 13 districts[18]. In 1991, 49.5% of Pakistani people lived in these same areas and so again, like Indians, there has been very slight dispersal[19]. However, unlike the Indian group, the proportion of the population who are Pakistani has increased in all these 13 areas, ranging from an increase in share of 4.3% in Bradford (to 14.5%, the highest proportion in the country), to the lowest increase being 0.6% in Leeds (to 2.1%). In contrast to the declining share of Indians, the Pakistani population of Newham has increased its share by 2.6%. Outside of these 13 districts more than 5% of the population are now Pakistani in Wycombe, Buckinghamshire (6.0%), and in three Lancastrian districts: Blackburn with Darwen (8.7%), Hynburn (6.7%) and Pendle (13.4%). As for the remote areas, almost an identically small number of people are Pakistani in the 23 districts identified above (footnote 16).

Pakistani 2001 (%)
- 0.0 - 0.6
- 0.7 - 1.6
- 1.7 - 3.1
- 3.2 - 6.8
- 6.9 - 14.5

Pakistani change (%)
- −0.1 - 0.0
- 0.1 - 0.7
- 0.8 - 1.4
- 1.5 - 2.6
- 2.7 - 4.3

BLACK AFRICAN

In 2001, 0.57 million people were of Black African or White/Black African ethnicity. We have combined these two categories to allow comparison to be made with the number of Black Africans in the UK in 1991 (0.23 million). It is very important to note that a large part of this rise will be due to the inclusion of the mixed group here in 2001. Many people who would have chosen this option, had it been offered in 1991, may instead have chosen the White or Black Other labels at that time. Thus the rise in proportion of 0.56% from 0.40% to 0.96% of the population is partly due to changing labels on the census forms.

The highest proportions of Black African people are all found in a few London boroughs where more than a tenth of the population now tick these boxes: Hackney (12.8%), Lambeth (12.4%), Newham (13.8%) and Southwark (16.9%). Some 51.1% of all Black Africans lived in their most populous 13 districts in 2001[20]. In 1991 these 13 areas contained 54.0% of all Black Africans in Britain, and so again we see geographical dispersal of a small population through large relative rises for very small populations in many areas[21]. Outside of London the Black African population has increased by just over a percent of the population in only six places: Manchester (to 2.3%), Luton (to 2%), Reading (to 1.8%), Slough (to 2.1%), Watford (to 1.2%) and Leicester (to 1.4%). Part of these increases will be due to the inclusion of the mixed category in our comparisons. Less than a tenth of one percent of the population were Black African in 150 districts in the UK in 2001.

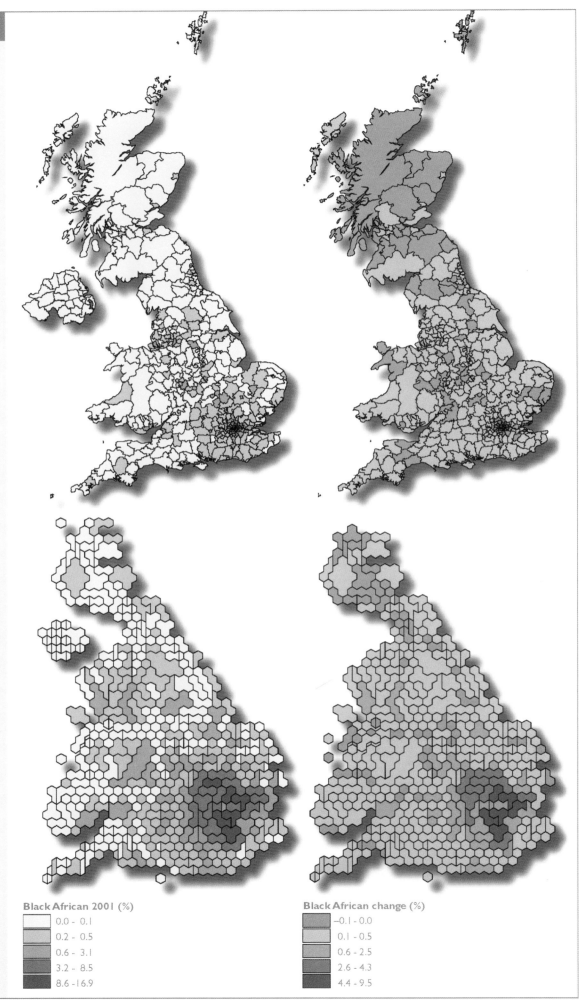

Black African 2001 (%)

	0.0 - 0.1
	0.2 - 0.5
	0.6 - 3.1
	3.2 - 8.5
	8.6 - 16.9

Black African change (%)

	-0.1 - 0.0
	0.1 - 0.5
	0.6 - 2.5
	2.6 - 4.3
	4.4 - 9.5

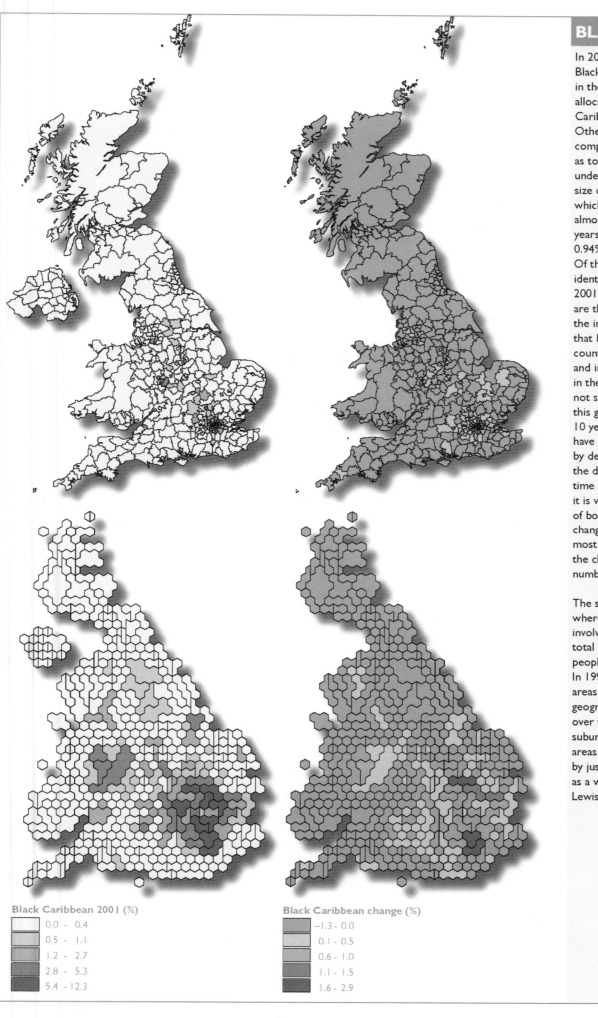

BLACK CARIBBEAN

In 2001 there were 0.53 million Black Caribbean people living in the UK. We have chosen to allocate the mixed White/Black Caribbean category to Black Other for the purposes of comparison (see footnote 22 as to why), and so we may be underestimating the rise in the size of this group over time which, as measured here, has been almost static over the last 10 years, rising ever so slightly from 0.94% to 0.96% of the population. Of the smaller ethnic groups identified by both the 1991 and 2001 Censuses, Black Caribbeans are the oldest in terms of both the international migration flows that brought many people to this country in the 1950s and 1960s, and in terms of people established in the UK before then. It is thus not surprising to see the size of this group remain static over the 10 years. Births and in-migration have been almost cancelled out by deaths and out-migration, if the definitions at both points in time are comparable[22]. However, it is very likely that the majority of both the map and cartogram of change indicate decreases across most of Britain due to changes in the choice of labels of a very small number of people living there.

The statistics are most robust where the numbers of people involved are not minuscule. A total of 53.4% of Black Caribbean people live in 13 districts[23]. In 1991, 52.7% lived in these areas so there has been a slight geographical concentration over time, albeit with a slight suburbanisation as the only two areas to have seen their share rise by just over 2% of the population as a whole are Croydon and Lewisham in South London.

Black Caribbean 2001 (%)
0.0 - 0.4
0.5 - 1.1
1.2 - 2.7
2.8 - 5.3
5.4 - 12.3

Black Caribbean change (%)
−1.3 - 0.0
0.1 - 0.5
0.6 - 1.0
1.1 - 1.5
1.6 - 2.9

OTHER ASIAN

In 2001, 0.44 million people ticked the Other Asian and White/Asian boxes on the census form. We have combined these two categories here as we believe that they are the most comparable, when combined, to the 1991 Other Asian group[24].

With the exception of White, this group is more geographically spread out than the five larger ethnic groups considered already. Only 30.8% live in the most populous 13 districts for this group as compared to around half for the previous four groups. Ten years ago for these same areas this ratio was 33.5%, and so, just as for the named Asian groups, there has been geographical dispersal. Given that this group is such an amalgam of ethnicities it is not surprising to find it appearing to be more spread out. The highest proportions of people with an Other Asian ethnic identity are where they constitute more than 4% of the population in Brent (5.8%), Ealing (5.1%), Harrow (6.2%) and Merton (4.5%). In the first three of these London boroughs more than a sixth of the population are Indian, and these are also among the four with the largest rises (see below). In Merton 2.1% of people were born in Sri Lanka and 2.1% in other Far East countries.

The largest rises in the share of the population who are South Asian are in Brent (2.2%), where 18.5% of the population are Indian, Ealing (2.5%), where 16.5% of the population are Indian, Harrow (3.9%), where 21.9% of the population are Indian and Redbridge (2.5%), where 14.0% of the population are Indian and 6.2% are Pakistani.

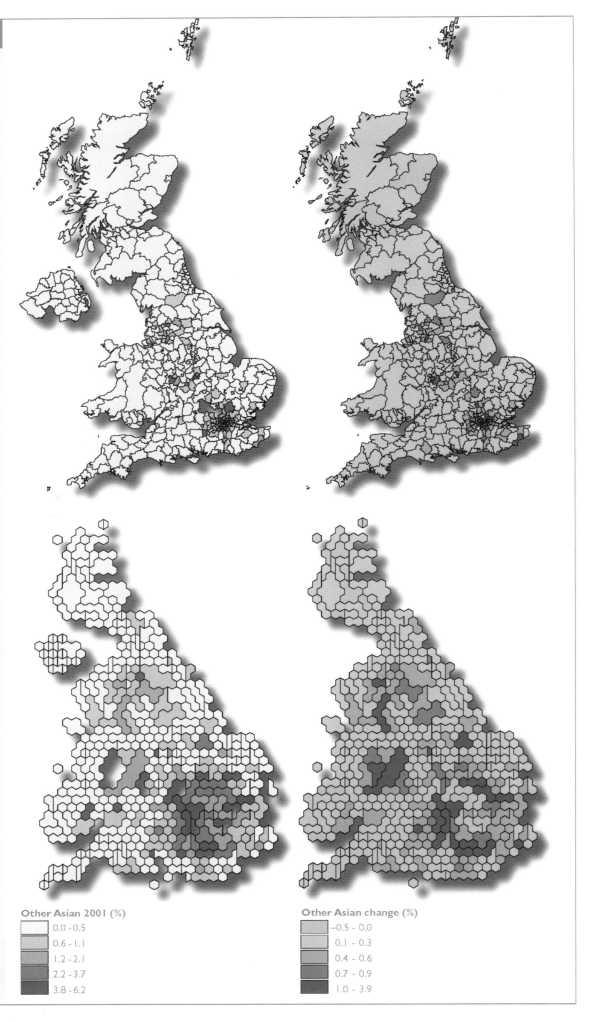

Other Asian 2001 (%)

- 0.0 - 0.5
- 0.6 - 1.1
- 1.2 - 2.1
- 2.2 - 3.7
- 3.8 - 6.2

Other Asian change (%)

- −0.5 - 0.0
- 0.1 - 0.3
- 0.4 - 0.6
- 0.7 - 0.9
- 1.0 - 3.9

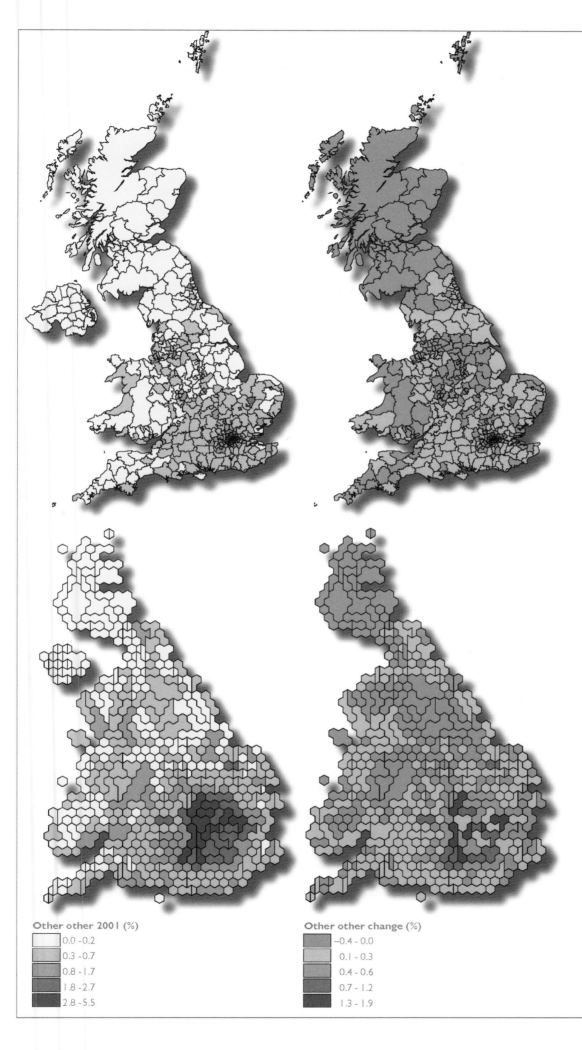

OTHER ETHNICITY

The seventh largest ethnic group in the UK is a catch-all category for people who described ethnicities for themselves which did not fit neatly into the boxes on the census forms. It is important to remember that more boxes were available in 2001, and so we might have expected this group to reduce in size due to that[25]. However, in 1991 there were 0.31 million people labelled 'Other, other' by the census and in 2001 the 'Other ethnic group' category counted 0.38 million. Thus the group has grown, despite the changing options, by 0.1% to make up 0.64% of the population of the UK in 2001.

Clearly London and large city orientated, this group of people appears far more cohesive geographically than the amalgam of labels that would constitute it would suggest. The pattern to its growth is also geographically clear, with faster growth in the capital, but also in specific districts. Outside of London, rates of growth have been greatest in Surrey in Epsom & Ewell (+1.2%, mainly of ethnicities associated with the Far and Middle East), Elmbridge (+0.8%, Africa and Far East), and Forest Heath (+0.7%), with similar rates of growth being seen in Oxford (+0.7%).

The areas with highest proportions of the population being of these other ethnic groups are all found in London, the very highest being in Westminster (5.5%), Kensington & Chelsea (5.3%) and Ealing (4.1%). These groups are both growing fastest and are highest in some of the most affluent areas of the UK.

Other other 2001 (%)

- 0.0 - 0.2
- 0.3 - 0.7
- 0.8 - 1.7
- 1.8 - 2.7
- 2.8 - 5.5

Other other change (%)

- −0.4 - 0.0
- 0.1 - 0.3
- 0.4 - 0.6
- 0.7 - 1.2
- 1.3 - 1.9

BLACK OTHER

In England and Wales, three groups have been combined to attempt to replicate who would have been most likely to have chosen the Black other category, had the 1991 Census form been used in 2001. These were the Other Black, Other mixed and White/Black Caribbean mixed groups which, combined, constituted 0.33 million people in 2001, much more than the 0.19 million in 1991, partly due to the groups which are being compared. Many of the Mixed White/Black group may have chosen White or Caribbean and many of the Other mixed group might have no association with Black. Nevertheless, given the limited options available this is the best combination of groups we can combine to make a comparison at this point (an even more complex grouping was used in Scotland, see Table 3.5 in the notes at the end of the chapter). In 1991 many young Black people wrote 'Black British' on the census form that was converted to this label.

Despite the growth in this group, both map and cartogram show areas of no change or slight decline. The declines are only of over half a percent of the local population where American armed forces have left Cherwell in Oxfordshire, and Forest Heath and Suffolk Coastal in Suffolk. Rises in population share of just over 3% have only been recorded in Hackney, Lambeth, Lewisham and Southwark. To see whether what appears to be a spatial polarisation on the map is in fact such a change requires some statistics and a large note of caution regarding the different labels being compared at these two points in time[26].

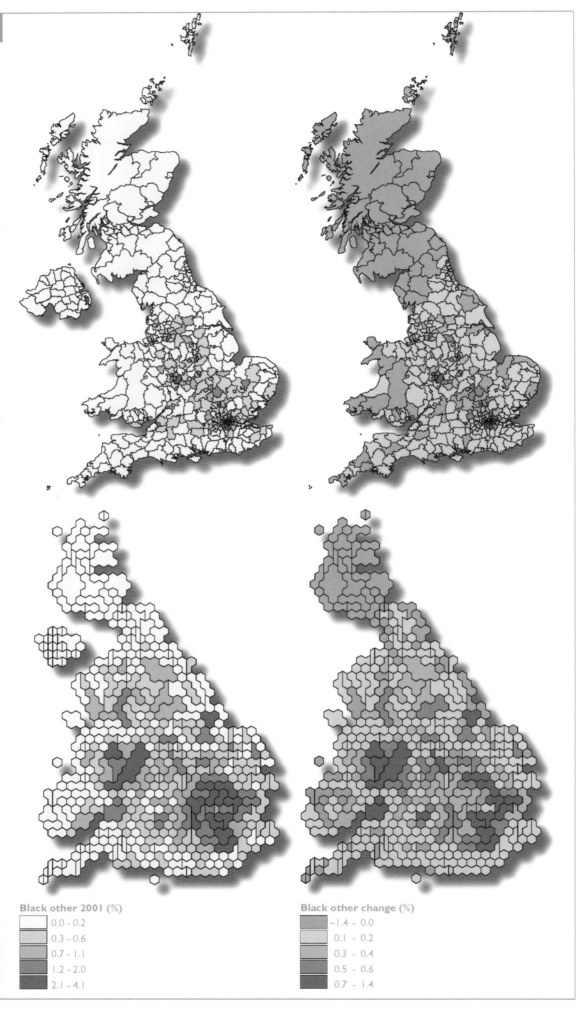

Black other 2001 (%)
- 0.0 - 0.2
- 0.3 - 0.6
- 0.7 - 1.1
- 1.2 - 2.0
- 2.1 - 4.1

Black other change (%)
- −1.4 - 0.0
- 0.1 - 0.2
- 0.3 - 0.4
- 0.5 - 0.6
- 0.7 - 1.4

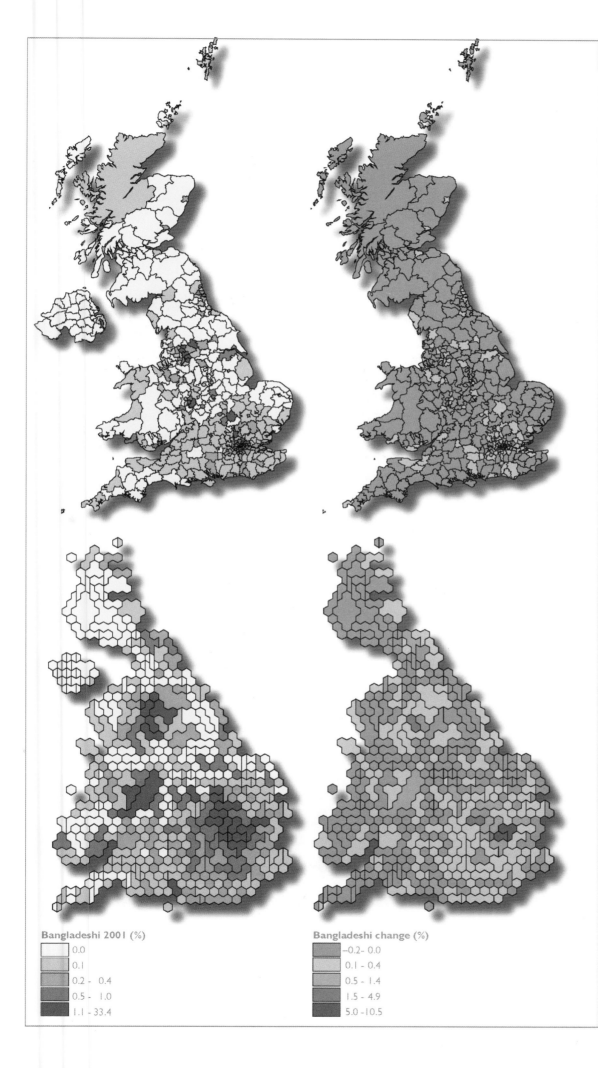

BANGLADESHI

The ninth largest ethnic group in the UK in 2001 were the 0.28 million Bangladeshis, up from 0.17 million in 1991. These figures may again be a slight underestimate due to the increased options on the 2001 form.

In 1991, 22.5% of Bangladeshis in the UK lived in Tower Hamlets. By 2001 that had risen to only 23.2%, despite the number of Bangladeshis in Tower Hamlets increasing by 70% over these 10 years due largely to young adults having children and very few older adults dying. Thus, the proportion of Bangladeshis living outside of Tower Hamlets rose faster in many places, and so we see slight dispersal yet again, but still growth in the core area of initial settlement. Again, to gauge whether this is a general trend and in which ways these geographical changes are occurring, some statistics are needed[27].

A total of 58% of Bangladeshis live in the 10 districts with the highest proportions, which, in descending order are: Tower Hamlets (33.4%), Newham (8.8%), Camden (6.3%), Oldham (4.5%), Luton (4.1%), City of London (3.8%), Hackney (2.9%), Westminster (2.8%), Islington (2.4%) and Birmingham (2.1%). Outside of these areas the largest rises in the local population share of this group have been in Redbridge (0.9%), Portsmouth (0.7%) and Rossendale in Lancashire (0.5%). The only significant drop in the proportion of the population who are Bangladeshi has been in Haringey, of 0.2% of the local population share.

Bangladeshi 2001 (%)

- 0.0
- 0.1
- 0.2 - 0.4
- 0.5 - 1.0
- 1.1 - 33.4

Bangladeshi change (%)

- −0.2 - 0.0
- 0.1 - 0.4
- 0.5 - 1.4
- 1.5 - 4.9
- 5.0 - 10.5

CHINESE

In 2001, 0.25 million people stated that their ethnicity was Chinese, making this the smallest separately identified ethnic group in the UK, but still larger than the 0.16 million the group constituted in 1991, a rise from 0.29% to 0.42% of the population. Again this might be a slight underestimate as people had more options to tick in 2001. The proportion of the population who are Chinese grew the most, by between half a percent and almost one percent in the following 12 areas: the City of London, Barnet, Kensington & Chelsea, Kingston upon Thames, Merton, Southwark, Tower Hamlets, Westminster, Manchester, Milton Keynes, Cambridge and Oxford. The growth was highest in the two university cities. It is noticeable also that there has been a rise in Cardiff, Belfast and Edinburgh. Changes in the distribution of ethnic groups in Scotland should not be ignored[28]. Outside of the 12 areas that have experienced the largest increases, the only other two areas where more than one-and-a-half percent of the population are of Chinese ethnicity are Camden and Islington.

It is interesting to compare the distribution of people claiming Chinese ethnicity with the much smaller group of people living in Britain who were born in China, as shown towards the end of the next chapter. Many people of Chinese ethnicity were not born in Britain, but hardly any of those who were not, were born in China. Nevertheless, there are similarities in the maps (see Chapter 4, footnote 18).

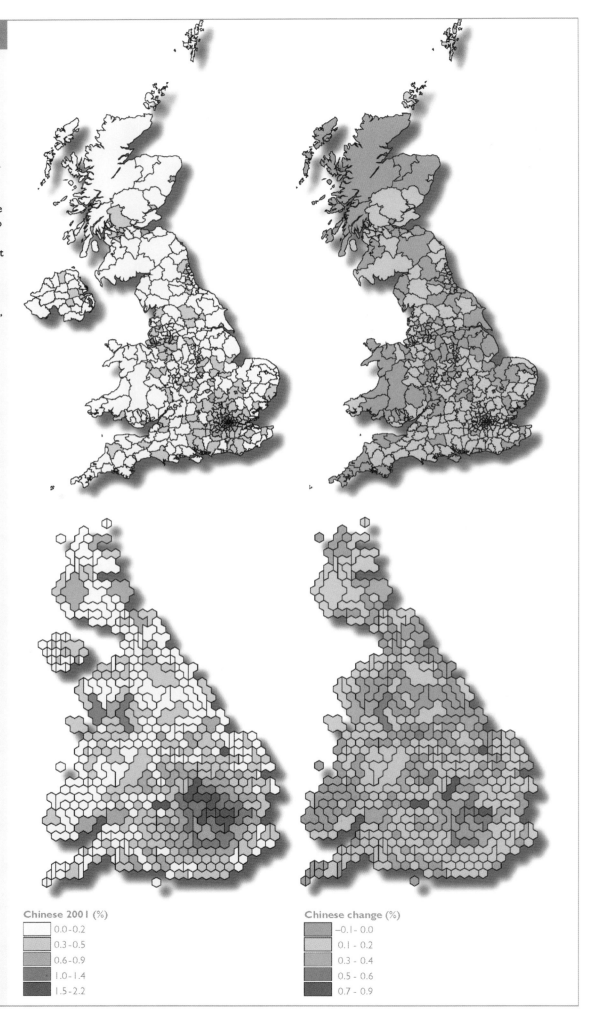

Chinese 2001 (%)

0.0 - 0.2
0.3 - 0.5
0.6 - 0.9
1.0 - 1.4
1.5 - 2.2

Chinese change (%)

−0.1 - 0.0
0.1 - 0.2
0.3 - 0.4
0.5 - 0.6
0.7 - 0.9

NOTES

[1] The 10 areas with the highest proportions of the population identifying with Christian affiliation, all over 85%, are Wigan, Knowsley, St Helens and Sefton boroughs of the North West; Allerdale and Copeland in the Lake District; Easington and Wear Valley in the North East; and Ribble Valley and South Ribble in Lancashire. Eight of the 10 areas with the lowest levels are in London, all at less than 50%. The other two areas are Leicester (45%) and Aberdeen (50%).

[2] Eight of the 10 areas where non-Christian religions are most popular, all at over 27%, are in London. The other two areas are Leicester (31%) and Slough (28%). In all of the top 10 areas where other religions are least popular, over 80% of the population affiliates themselves to Christian religions. Thus the two maps above mirror each other to an extent. Where they are not mirror images, large proportions of people are unwilling to state a religion or say they have none (such as in Aberdeen).

[3] Of the 65% of Scotland's population who did state that their religion was Christian, 42% identified with the Church of Scotland, 16% with the Roman Catholic Church and 7% with Other Christian denominations. The Church of Scotland was most popular in Angus, Dumfries & Galloway, East Ayrshire, Orkney Islands, Scottish Borders and South Ayrshire, where just over half the population identified with this label. Over a quarter of the population identified with Roman Catholicism in Glasgow City and over a third in Inverclyde, North Lanarkshire and West Dunbartonshire. Some 28% of the population of Eilean Siar identified with other Christian denominations, followed by just over a tenth of the population of Argyll & Bute, Highland, Moray and the Shetland Islands.

[4] These were the London boroughs of Camden, Hackney, Haringey, Islington, Lambeth, Lewisham and Southwark; and also most common in Nottingham, Forest Heath (Suffolk) and Blaenau Gwent.

[5] A total of 801,000, the majority of Britain's Muslims, live in just 20 districts. Within London these are Brent, Camden, Ealing, Enfield, Hackney, Haringey, Newham, Redbridge, Tower Hamlets and Waltham Forest. Outside London they are Manchester, Oldham, Sheffield, Birmingham, Bradford, Kirklees, Leeds, Luton, Blackburn with Darwen and Leicester. These are not all the areas with the highest proportions of the population being affiliated to Islam, but with the highest absolute numbers.

[6] A total of 289,000, the majority of Britain's Hindus, live in just 13 districts. In London these are Barnet, Brent, Croydon, Ealing, Enfield, Harrow, Hillingdon, Hounslow, Newham and Redbridge. Outside of London they include Birmingham, Wolverhampton and Leicester.

[7] A total of 171,000 people, the majority of the Sikh population, are found in just 10 districts: Ealing, Hillingdon, Hounslow, Redbridge, Birmingham, Coventry, Sandwell, Wolverhampton, Slough and Leicester.

[8] The proportion of the population who are of Indian ethnicity is, of course, much higher than that who are of Sikh religion, and many more people of Indian ethnicity are of Hindu, Christian and Muslim religions in particular districts. Note also that these maps can be compared with the map of birthplace for those born in India (which uses the boundaries of India in place before independence).

[9] A total of 132,000 people, a majority of the religious Jewish population, live in just nine districts: Barnet, Camden, Hackney, Harrow, Redbridge, Westminster, Bury, Leeds and Hertsmere (in Hertfordshire).

[10] Table 3.1 shows three indices of dispersal by district for each group in England and Wales. The first (1) is the index of segregation, the proportion who would have to move district to be evenly spread; the second is the index of isolation (2), the chance of a person of a particular religion meeting another person of their religion, at random by district; the third (3) is an index of separation, the index of isolation adjusted for the national size of the religious group, which can vary from 0% to 100%.

[11] The three statistics of dispersal calculated for the English and Welsh religious groups can also be calculated for the six Northern Irish groups and are shown in Table 3.2, but for both censuses: Index 1 is 'segregation'; index 2 is 'isolation'; and index 3 is 'separation' (see footnote 10). The Protestant column at the end provides the results for the three main Protestant religions combined.

[12] Table 3.3 shows the 2001 dispersal table of footnote 11 less the equivalent 1991 table. It provides a summary of which groups are becoming more or less dispersed in which ways.

The most segregated group in 2001 were Methodists, but that level of segregation, where 27.87% would have to move district to be evenly spread, is 0.20% less than a decade ago. The most isolated group in 2001 were Catholics and that level of isolation has risen by 1.92%. The group that is most separated from the rest of the population, given its size, is also Catholics, and again that level has risen. However, at the district level, Catholics are becoming slightly less segregated and Protestants slightly less isolated. The only group becoming less dispersed on all three measures are those with no religion.

[13] Outside of Northern Ireland the only area of the UK where Christian denomination was asked for was in Scotland. The table for Scotland, Table 3.4, can thus be compared to that for the Province, Table 3.2.

In 2001, by district, Catholics were more segregated in Scotland than in Northern Ireland, the Church of Scotland more isolated than the Church of Ireland, and other Christian religions more separated from the rest of the population than were Methodists in the Province. Hindus, religious Jews, Muslims and Sikhs are all more segregated in Scotland than are the Christian religions in Northern Ireland. They are even more segregated in England and Wales than in Scotland (see Table 3.1). Only those with no religion are more segregated in Northern Ireland than elsewhere, and even they are less isolated.

[14] In 2001 several mixed White/and Other groups were added as options to the form. We have assumed that no one who chose one of those options would have chosen a White-only option had the mixed options not been available. In doing this we will overestimate the decline of the White group slightly. We have also assumed that everyone who chose the White British, White Scottish, Irish or Other White options in 2001 would have ticked a White box if that were all that was available in 2001. They would not all have done so and so this assumption will to an extent have cancelled out our previous assumption. The meaning of ethnic labels changes over time and people can change their ethnicities just as they change their religions. Given this, any comparisons made over time are problematic.

[15] Barnet, Brent, Ealing, Harrow, Hillingdon, Hounslow, Newham, Redbridge, Birmingham, Coventry, Sandwell, Wolverhampton and Leicester.

[16] Many of these districts contain just a handful of people who label themselves as Indian. Just over half of these places are in Northern Ireland, the rest are in rural and remote England and Scotland, none are in Wales: Caradon, Eden, West Devon, Purbeck, Teesdale, Alnwick, Berwick-upon-Tweed, Eilean Siar, Orkney Islands, Shetland Islands, Ards, Armagh, Ballymoney, Banbridge, Carrickfergus, Cookstown, Down, Dungannon, Fermanagh, Larne, Limavady, Moyle and Newry & Mourne.

[17] The district whose local proportion matches the national average is Cambridge, where 1.79% of the population are Indian; in 1991 that proportion was only just over 1%, only two thirds of the British mean average then of 1.55%.

[18] Only three of these were in London: Newham, Redbridge and Waltham Forest; eight were northern or midland metropolitan boroughs: Manchester, Oldham, Rochdale, Sheffield, Birmingham, Bradford, Kirklees and Leeds; and two were towns with commuting distance of London: Luton and Slough.

[19] The slight dispersal is mainly due to a very rapid increase, albeit still of small numbers, of people who are Pakistani from zero in the following districts: Isles of Scilly, Eden, Berwick-upon-Tweed, Oswestry and West Somerset; the numbers have risen by more than ten-fold in Forest Heath, Restormel, Caradon, North Dorset and Penwith; by more than five-fold in West Oxfordshire, Cotswold, South Northamptonshire, Newark & Sherwood, Rutland, North Devon, Kerrier, Adur, Mendip, North West Leicestershire, West Lancashire, Bassetlaw, Isle of Wight, Derbyshire Dales, West Wiltshire, Tendring and East Lindsey. In all of these places the numbers are still tiny.

[20] All of these were in London: Barnet, Brent, Camden, Croydon, Enfield, Greenwich, Hackney, Haringey, Lambeth, Lewisham, Newham, Southwark and Waltham Forest.

[21] A long list of places has seen the number of Black Africans rise more than five-fold: Isles of Scilly, Wansbeck, Alnwick, Powys, Carrick, City of London, Tynedale, Castle Morpeth, South Oxfordshire, Barking & Dagenham, North Shropshire, Purbeck, Richmondshire, East Hertfordshire, Monmouthshire, Oadby & Wigston, Broxbourne, Poole, Southend-on-Sea, Allerdale, Vale Royal, South Holland, Crawley, Thurrock, East Lindsey, Fenland, Kennet, Telford and Wrekin, Milton Keynes, Daventry, North Tyneside, South Hams, West Dorset, Horsham, North Kesteven, Slough, Wellingborough, Luton, Hillingdon, Barrow-in-Furness, Hertsmere, Restormel, West Lancashire, Caradon, Carmarthenshire, Harlow, South Bucks, Chiltern, Leicester and South Cambridgeshire.

[22] In 1991 many of the children of people who had migrated to the UK from the Caribbean chose the label Black Other, or wrote in Black British that was converted to Black Other as a label. This is part of the rationale for not including Mixed White/Black Caribbean people here as many will be young and so we could assume would have behaved in the same way had they been presented with the 1991 Census form in 2001.

[23] All but one of these are in London: Brent, Croydon, Ealing, Enfield, Hackney, Haringey, Lambeth, Lewisham, Newham, Southwark, Waltham Forest, Wandsworth and Birmingham.

[24] In the absence of a Mixed White/Asian option on the 1991 Census form many people who would have ticked this box then, had it appeared, might have ticked the Indian, Pakistani, Bangladeshi or Chinese options, and thus, by making this assumption, we may be reducing the apparent sizes of all those groups in 1991 for the purposes of comparison. Other issues that we have ignored here are that people can change their label over time; and that children are almost always labelled by their parents on census forms and may choose a different label when they come to fill out the form. Also of importance are the ways in which the 1991 Census has been corrected here to sum to the mid-year estimates for that year. This was done using ward age/sex profiles. Corrections that include information on under-enumeration by ethnicity add roughly another 7,000 people to this group. If we are fortunate many of these errors and assumptions cancel each other out.

[25] For the 10 ethnic groups used to create these maps showing 2001 categories which are combined, see Table 3.5.

[26] Table 3.6 shows three indices of dispersal by district for each group in England and Wales as defined in footnote 10: the index of segregation (1), the index of isolation (2), and an index of separation (3). Just over 60% of Caribbeans, Africans, Pakistanis and Bangladeshis would have to move district to be evenly spread. The other groups are less segregated. The White group is by far the most isolated and is also more separated from the rest than is any other group, followed by Bangladeshis then Indians. Black others, along with the Chinese, Asian others and Other others are the least separated of all the ethnic groups in England and Wales, having allowed for their sizes.

[27] Table 3.7 shows the changes in the three indices of dispersal for England and Wales by ethnic group between 1991 and 2001. The only groups that have become more segregated, ever so slightly, are White and Other other. However, the White group is the only group to have become less isolated (isolation tends to increase as groups grow in size mainly where they were before). The third index, of separation, does suggest that there has been some increase in the level of separation over time for some of the groups. That is taking into account their changing population sizes, the chances of people in the groups of meeting people from other groups, by area, is reducing slightly over time; most for White, next for Bangladeshi and African, next for Pakistani and least for Indian.

[28] Table 3.8 shows the 2001 levels of the three indices of dispersal for Scotland by ethnic group. The only change that has occurred since 1991, when decimal points are not shown, is that there has been a single percentage point drop in the degree of separation experienced by Pakistani people in Scotland. We treat Scotland here separately from England and Wales because slightly different questions on ethnicity were asked in Scotland. Again the most isolated group is White, but their levels of isolation are now near the maximum of 100%. The most segregated group is Pakistani, followed by the Other Asian groups, but lowest among these is the level for Chinese, lower again only for Caribbean and Other ethnic groups. In England and Wales, the Chinese are the least segregated after White (see footnote 26). The smallest groups are not necessarily the most segregated.

Table 3.1: Indices of dispersal of religion for England and Wales, 2001

Index	Christian (%)	Buddhist (%)	Hindu (%)	Jewish (%)	Muslim (%)	Sikh (%)	Other (%)	None (%)	Not stated (%)
1	4.8	29.8	56.2	62.1	54.2	62.5	19.5	10.2	4.7
2	72.9	0.5	6.4	5.1	10.3	3.9	0.4	15.8	7.8
3	3.9	0.2	5.4	4.6	7.6	3.3	0.1	1.2	0.1

Table 3.2: Indices of dispersal of religion for Northern Ireland, 1999 and 2001

	Catholic (%)	Presbyterian (%)	Church of Ireland (%)	Methodist (%)	Other (%)	None (%)	All Protestant (%)
1 (2001)	20.75	20.85	14.01	30.13	16.90	15.96	10.49
2 (2001)	50.20	25.69	17.03	5.18	7.40	15.77	30.09
3 (2001)	16.65	6.29	2.04	1.73	1.11	2.20	2.48
1 (1991)	21.37	20.77	13.43	30.50	15.60	13.64	9.93
2 (1991)	48.61	26.45	19.71	5.63	8.90	12.12	31.70
3 (1991)	16.59	6.48	2.44	1.93	1.23	1.22	2.45

Table 3.3: Change in indices of dispersal of religion for Northern Ireland, 1991-2001

	Catholic (%)	Presbyterian (%)	Church of Ireland (%)	Methodist (%)	Other (%)	None (%)	All Protestant (%)
1 (1991-2001)	−0.73	0.09	0.27	−0.20	1.76	2.53	0.56
2 (1991-2001)	1.92	−0.12	1.52	−0.20	−0.88	2.67	−1.61
3 (1991-2001)	0.31	−0.01	−0.13	−0.08	−0.01	0.51	0.03

Table 3.4: Indices of dispersal of religion for Scotland, 2001

	Church of Scotland (%)	Catholic (%)	Other Christian (%)	Buddhist (%)	Hindu (%)	Jewish (%)	Muslim (%)	Sikh (%)	Other (%)	None (%)	Not stated (%)
1 (2001)	6.56	25.99	17.01	21.24	40.34	55.56	43.78	44.82	18.38	8.43	8.78
2 (2001)	49.68	24.43	9.21	0.12	0.16	1.37	1.40	0.25	20.84	20.84	4.28
3 (2001)	2.25	7.65	1.54	0.02	0.08	1.27	0.80	0.16	0.09	1.01	0.17

Table 3.5: The ten ethnic groups used to create maps showing which categories are combined

	Britain 1991[a]	England and Wales 2001	Scotland 2001
1	Chinese	1 Chinese	1 Chinese
2	Black other	2 Other Black; 3 Other mixed; 4 Caribbean/White	2 Black Scottish; 3 Other Black and *
3	Asian other	5 Other Asian; 6 Asian/White	4 Other South Asian and *
4	Bangladeshi	7 Bangladeshi	5 Bangladeshi
5	Other other	8 Other ethnic group	6 Other ethnic group
6	Black African	9 African; 10 African/White	7 African and *
7	Pakistani	11 Pakistani	8 Pakistani
8	Black Caribbean	12 Caribbean	9 Caribbean
9	Indian	13 Indian	10 Indian
10	White	14 White Briton; 15 Irish; 16 Other White	11-14 White Scottish and Other White groups

Notes: * denotes the Scottish other mixed background group – split into three groups in proportion to the English/Welsh mixed splits.

[a] Northern Ireland did not provide adequate data in 1991; in 2001 the Irish Traveller category was assigned to White.

Table 3.6: Indices of dispersal of ethnic group for England and Wales, 2001

2001	White (%)	Caribbean (%)	African (%)	Black other (%)	Indian (%)	Pakistani (%)	Bangladeshi (%)	Chinese (%)	Asian other (%)	Other other (%)
1	5	62	62	42	55	61	61	32	39	39
2	93	5	7	2	9	6	10	1	2	2
3	16	4	6	1	7	5	9	0	1	1

Table 3.7: Changes in indices of dispersal of ethnic group for England and Wales, 1991-2001

Change	White (%)	Caribbean (%)	African (%)	Black other (%)	Indian (%)	Pakistani (%)	Bangladeshi (%)	Chinese (%)	Asian other (%)	Other other (%)
1	1	0	-4	-6	-2	0	0	-1	-1	1
2	-2	0	3	0	1	2	3	0	1	0
3	4	0	3	0	1	2	3	0	0	0

Table 3.8: Indices of dispersal of ethnic group for Scotland, 2001

2001	White (%)	Caribbean (%)	African (%)	Black other (%)	Indian (%)	Pakistani (%)	Bangladeshi (%)	Chinese (%)	Asian other (%)	Other other (%)
1	0	25	38	24	41	49	47	30	34	26
2	99	0	0	0	0	1	0	0	0	0
3	1	0	0	0	0	0	0	0	0	0

Birthplace and migration

Maps in this section include:

Migration is the main mechanism through which the human geography of the UK changes. It is also the main mechanism through which areas remain similar over time. If people did not migrate into or out of a place they would age *in situ*, their children age, many would purchase their property outright, the tenure structure would change, they would retire, and the employment structure would change, reverting back only when a generation had passed. However, as people age, most of them move home to be replaced by younger people often quite like them when they were young, and thus the social profile of areas are maintained through time by the movement of people in selective ways.

It is the opposite form of selective migration, differential selective migration, that causes the human geography of the UK to change most over time: when like people are not replaced by like of a few years younger than themselves through migration. Such migration was necessary for most of the maps of change in this atlas to be of interest. For the maps of birthplace in 2001 shown here simply to exist such migration was necessary. The maps of change in birthplace are the second derivative of that population movement. There are changes to the human geography of the UK that do not require the population to move – the decline of an industry, or the increased ownership of cars occurring, for example. But such changes often result in population migration or movement, even if not caused by those movements. It is the flows of people over the space of the UK that forms the shape of that space. Nowhere is this better illustrated than through the multiple geographies of birthplace.

Although the majority of the UK population were born in the Kingdom, that majority is falling. The proportion of people who have a parent or grandparent who was born abroad is also rising rapidly. People are moving around the globe at rates never seen before. They meet people abroad and (more for women than men) return to the UK with partners or children born overseas. Other people travel to the UK and settle here, others yet may be here for just a little while, but some of them may meet someone and stay for longer than they had planned, and others are returning to the UK after their parents emigrated decades ago. The geography of birthplace captures and amalgamates all these international flows to depict their average, a snapshot, holding everyone constant for a day and comparing where they are now with where they were on their day of birth.

Between the constituent countries of the UK the flows of people have increased. More and more people born in England are living in Scotland, Wales or Northern Ireland than ever before. More Scottish people have moved south of the border, more to Wales and more to the Province than have for many decades. Welsh people are more populous in England but also in parts of the Province and Scotland than a decade ago. The numbers born in Northern Ireland have risen in the North of England and Scotland, but not South, as rates of emigration from Ireland slow while economic conditions improve in Ireland as a whole. The next largest birthplace group living in the UK are people born in a myriad of largely unfamiliar places, termed 'elsewhere' here: an amalgam of dozens of countries without strong ties to the UK which, in total, provide more immigrants than any traditional migration stream can alone. They, as much as any group of international migrants before them, are increasingly attracted to the UK world city, and central London in particular.

The largest traditional migration stream is from what will soon be the most populous country on earth and which already is when amalgamated with its pre-division neighbours. Empire India is the birthplace of almost a million people now living in the UK. Not only London, but also the Midland cities and Pennine towns continue to draw in people from what were the Empire's borders of India. The declines in their proportions of the local populations are largely in places settled by the returning colonial administration in their retirement, a generation that has now almost totally died out. Just as we have amalgamated the countries of India, Pakistan and Bangladesh to draw one set of maps, so too have we paired up or combined more sets of many other neighbouring countries to show the patterns to their combined populations of birth. The footnotes and text of the following commentaries give greater details of the separate populations. We could have dedicated an entire atlas to birthplace patterns in the UK, such is the variety of origins people living in the Kingdom now have. The next largest flow of migrants is from a single country and that with which the UK has had its longest relationship. Like India it too was part of the Empire, but incorporated in the former nation-state although treated as a colony. The lands of what is now the Irish Republic have provided the longest running and most consistent sources of émigrés to the UK over many centuries. However, by 2001, and for the first time for many decades, fewer and fewer people were making that particular move, save to the Province. The push to leave has declined, as has the pull to come. People born in other countries now come to where the Irish once clustered most in Britain. Most obviously they have been replaced by immigrants from the next most populous source mapped here: the countries that formed the original heart of the European Union, the UK's immediate neighbours to the East.

Travel within Europe has become simpler as the Union has freed up restrictions. As the political boundaries of Empire decline, the restriction on entry is raised, and as the European Union widens, so too are the flows of people diverted. Former flows dry up and new ones start. The number of people living in the UK born in the Caribbean are now falling, as are the numbers of people from that former British colony, the US, who had settled here in many military bases in the 1980s. Thus, the numbers of US military personnel in Britain has declined, although many of their weapons remain and their numbers are revealed to be increasing most in areas near their secret spying bases. Coupled here with that other ancient colony, Canada, and despite the military withdrawal, increased international business flows and other sources have caused the North American presence to rise overall in the UK, especially in the financial districts of the capital.

Similarly, as we move round the globe to the next largest source of migrants to the UK, the numbers born in South Africa and Zimbabwe have risen mostly in London and in the financial districts for the first of those two former colonies. Yet another former colony, Cyprus, accounts for the combined amalgamation of Greece, Cyprus and Turkey being the next largest source of migrants to the Kingdom. Here, however, the abatement of a refugee stream has reduced some concentrations of peoples in particular parts of London.

A final pair of former colonies, Australia and New Zealand, account for the next largest flow, southern-bound again, and increasing in size. Our series of maps ends with two areas of migration to Britain where, for a change, the links are not clearly colonial although where, at least until recently, Britain owned or leased colonial outposts (Gibraltar and Hong Kong). The countries of the Iberian peninsula, and China provide the fourteenth and fifteenth largest sources of immigrants to the UK.

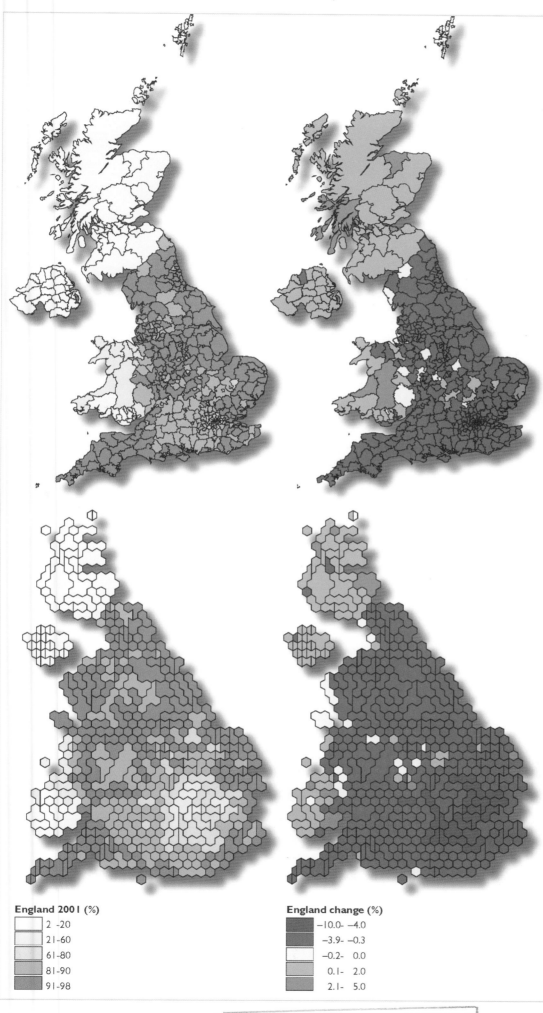

BORN IN ENGLAND

The census records the countries people now living in the UK were born in. Of these by far the largest group is people who were born in England, 44.0 million in 2001, 74.9% of the population, 1.2% less than in 1991.

The English born are most prevalent, unsurprisingly, in England. However, they constitute more than nine tenths of the population only in Northern England and in areas near the coast where the population tends to be older[1]. In the following London boroughs less than two thirds, but more than half, of the people living there were born in England: City of London, Barnet, Brent, Camden, Ealing, Hackney, Hammersmith & Fulham, Haringey, Harrow, Islington, Kensington & Chelsea, Lambeth, Newham, Southwark, Tower Hamlets and Westminster. Nowhere else in England are the proportions of English born living in a district below two thirds of the population.

The fastest increases in the share of local populations being England born are not all found outside of England. The English born share of the local population has risen by two percentage points or more in Corby (as Scottish born immigrants to the steel works there have left or died) and in Cherwell (Oxfordshire) and Suffolk Coastal, both places that have seen significant reductions in the US armed forces. Outside of England rises have been above 2% in Cardiff, Ceredigion (the largest rise of 5%), Powys, Argyll & Bute, Edinburgh, Moray and Antrim – places attracting the English for work, study and retirement.

England 2001 (%)
- 2 -20
- 21-60
- 61-80
- 81-90
- 91-98

England change (%)
- −10.0- −4.0
- −3.9- −0.3
- −0.2- 0.0
- 0.1- 2.0
- 2.1- 5.0

BORN IN SCOTLAND

After England, the most populous country in the UK is Scotland, similarly too for country of birth. A total of 5.2 million people living in the UK in 2001 were born in Scotland, 8.9% of the population, down 0.3% on a decade ago. The large majority of Scottish born people still live in, or have returned to, Scotland. Outside of Scotland proportions are highest in the Scottish borders and in areas that are just within commuting distance of the capital but still a long distance from its centre. Several decades ago there were many more Scottish people living in London and the decline is still evident from the map and cartogram of change.

Outside of Scotland more than 4% of the population are Scottish born only in Carlisle, Blackpool, Alnwick, Berwick-upon-Tweed, Richmondshire and Corby (the highest at 18.9% down by 3.5%, the greatest decrease, on a decade ago).

Inside of Scotland the Scottish born proportion has fallen most where the English born proportion has risen most. However, the fall has often been twice as large as the rise, as the English moving in consume more housing, per person, than the Scottish people they are displacing (other than in Argyll & Bute where the English born rise has helped replace a small exodus of Americans[2]). The least Scottish place in Scotland is now Edinburgh, the most is North Lanarkshire where 95.0% of the population were born in Scotland.

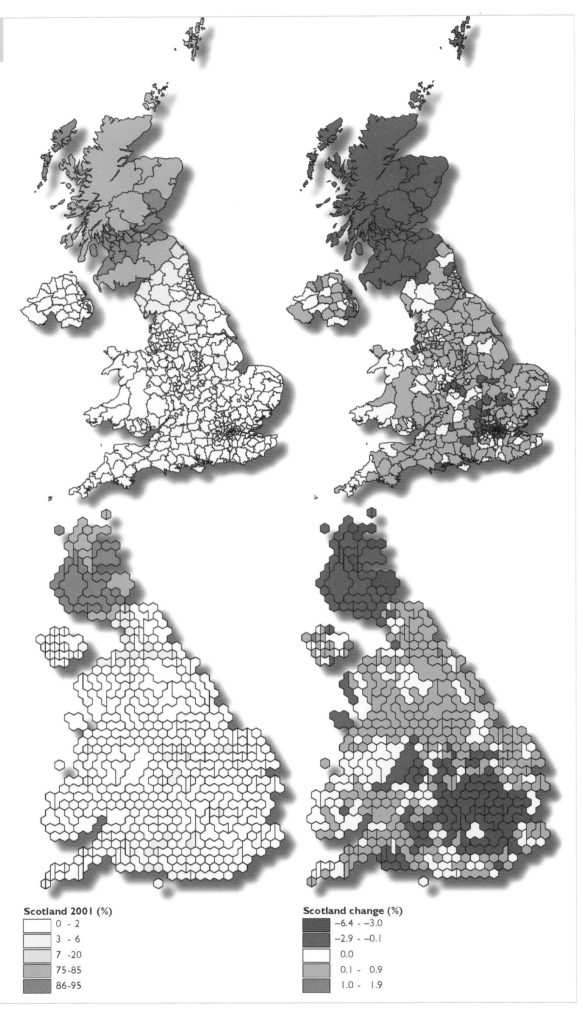

Scotland 2001 (%)

- 0 - 2
- 3 - 6
- 7 - 20
- 75 - 85
- 86 - 95

Scotland change (%)

- −6.4 - −3.0
- −2.9 - −0.1
- 0.0
- 0.1 - 0.9
- 1.0 - 1.9

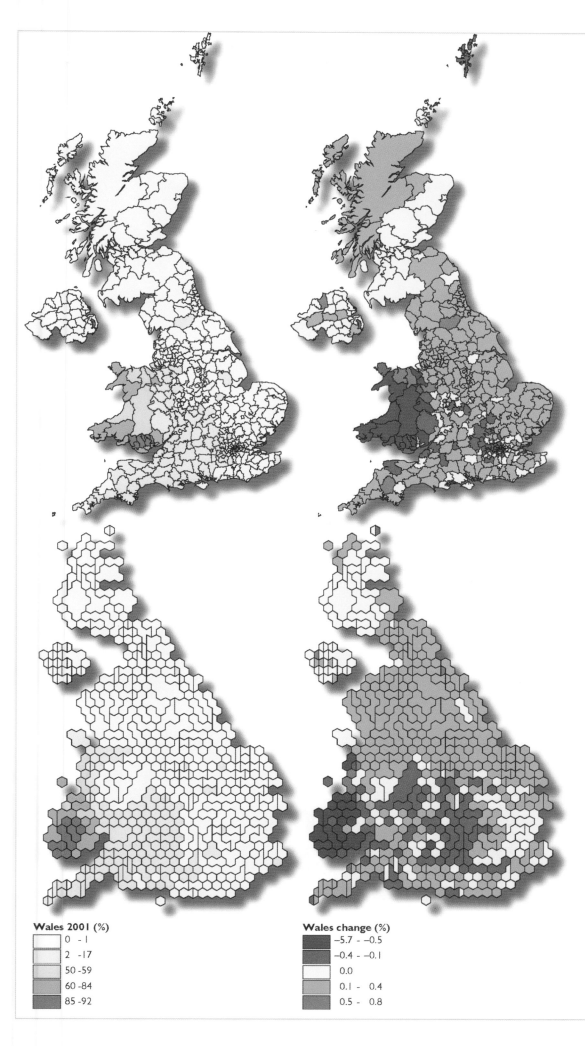

BORN IN WALES

The third largest group by country of birth in the UK are the Welsh born, constituting 2.8 million people in 2001, 4.8% of the population, 0.1% less than in 1991. Welsh people are a little more diffuse than Scottish people, many more having trickled over the border over time, particularly down to the South West of England, and many more having not (at least yet) returned to Wales. The most Welsh part of Wales remains the Valleys, Blaenau Gwent having the highest share at 92.1%. However, across almost all of Wales, the proportion of people who are Welsh born is falling. It is falling most where the proportion of English born is rising by a percentage point or more and, as in Scotland, it is in general falling faster than the proportions of the English are rising[3]. Fewer English born people are replacing Welsh born people as these places change (other than in Pembrokeshire).

Outside of Wales the English share of the population is falling by at least one percentage point, while the Welsh proportion is rising or static in the following districts: Chester, Cheltenham, Forest of Dean, North Shropshire and the Malvern Hills. Within Wales the proportions who are Welsh born have also risen in Conwy, Denbighshire and Torfaen. In all three districts the proportions of the population born in England have fallen. The largest falls in England have been in Slough (−0.5% with rising numbers born overseas) and in South Shropshire (−0.8% with rising numbers of English born). The declines, due to deaths, of people who left Wales for work in the 1930s can also be seen across England.

Wales 2001 (%)

- 0 - 1
- 2 - 17
- 50 - 59
- 60 - 84
- 85 - 92

Wales change (%)

- −5.7 - −0.5
- −0.4 - −0.1
- 0.0
- 0.1 - 0.4
- 0.5 - 0.8

BORN IN NORTHERN IRELAND

A total of 1.8 million people living in the UK in 2001 were born in Northern Ireland, the fourth largest group by birthplace in the country, 3.0% of the population, unchanged in share on a decade ago. Northern Ireland is also the last country of birth group recorded in sufficient detail for us to be able to measure change in its size within the Province.

The share of the population born in the Province has fallen most in the Province. Again, where the share of English born has risen most, the decline in Northern Irish born has been greatest. However, in the Province it is rises in English born of three quarters of a percentage point or more that correlate best to the falls[4]. Only in Down has the rise in the proportion of English born been greater than the fall in the share of Northern Irish born, and there that was due to Scottish born falling by 0.9% (and changing military postings).

Within Britain the highest proportions of people born in Northern Ireland, between 1.0% and 1.3%, are found in: City of London, Corby, Richmondshire, Dumfries & Galloway, Dundee, Edinburgh and Stirling. The 10 areas with the lowest proportions are mainly areas that have attracted little immigration for decades: Rotherham, North East Derbyshire, Chester-le-Street, Easington, Wansbeck, Blaenau Gwent, Caerphilly, Merthyr Tydfil, Neath Port Talbot and Rhondda Cynon Taf.

Northern Ireland 2001 (%)

	0.1 - 0.5
	0.6 - 1
	1.1 - 2
	85 - 92.9
	93 - 95.1

Northern Ireland change (%)

	−3.0 - −2.2
	−2.1 - −1.3
	−1.2 - −0.1
	0.0
	0.1 - 0.8

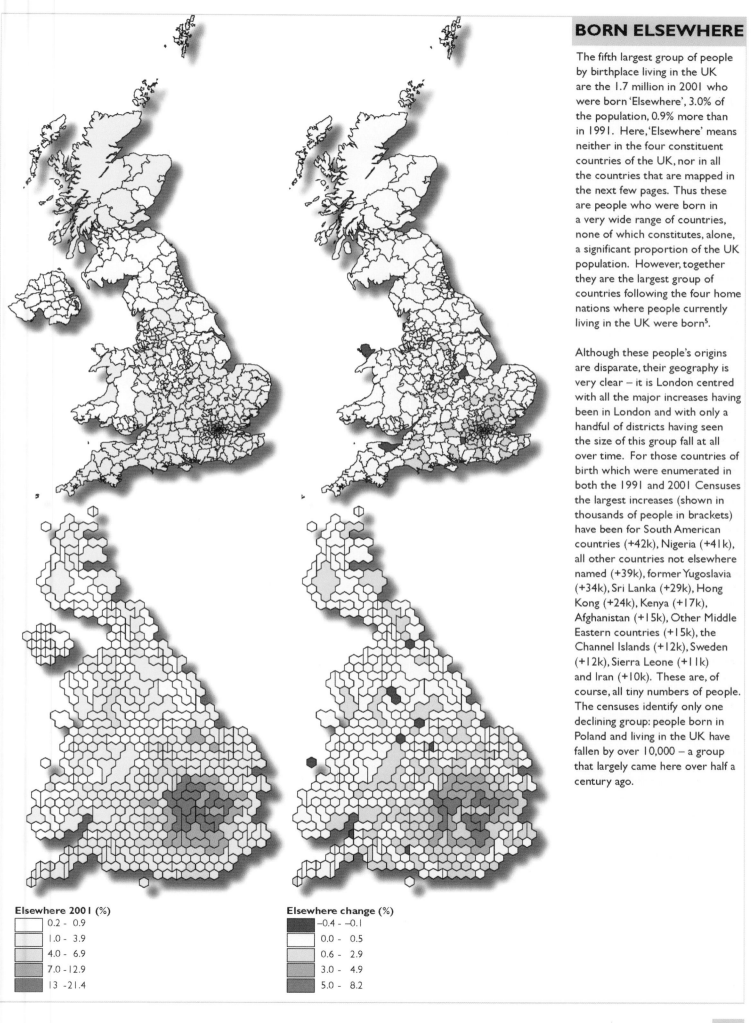

BORN ELSEWHERE

The fifth largest group of people by birthplace living in the UK are the 1.7 million in 2001 who were born 'Elsewhere', 3.0% of the population, 0.9% more than in 1991. Here, 'Elsewhere' means neither in the four constituent countries of the UK, nor in all the countries that are mapped in the next few pages. Thus these are people who were born in a very wide range of countries, none of which constitutes, alone, a significant proportion of the UK population. However, together they are the largest group of countries following the four home nations where people currently living in the UK were born[5].

Although these people's origins are disparate, their geography is very clear – it is London centred with all the major increases having been in London and with only a handful of districts having seen the size of this group fall at all over time. For those countries of birth which were enumerated in both the 1991 and 2001 Censuses the largest increases (shown in thousands of people in brackets) have been for South American countries (+42k), Nigeria (+41k), all other countries not elsewhere named (+39k), former Yugoslavia (+34k), Sri Lanka (+29k), Hong Kong (+24k), Kenya (+17k), Afghanistan (+15k), Other Middle Eastern countries (+15k), the Channel Islands (+12k), Sweden (+12k), Sierra Leone (+11k) and Iran (+10k). These are, of course, all tiny numbers of people. The censuses identify only one declining group: people born in Poland and living in the UK have fallen by over 10,000 – a group that largely came here over half a century ago.

Elsewhere 2001 (%)

- 0.2 - 0.9
- 1.0 - 3.9
- 4.0 - 6.9
- 7.0 - 12.9
- 13 - 21.4

Elsewhere change (%)

- −0.4 - −0.1
- 0.0 - 0.5
- 0.6 - 2.9
- 3.0 - 4.9
- 5.0 - 8.2

BORN IN EMPIRE INDIA

The sixth largest group of people living in the UK by country of birth are those born in what was India by its boundaries as they existed when it was part of the British Empire (India and Pakistan gained independence in 1947, Bangladesh was established in 1971). Depending on when they are born, two people born in the same place can be born in different countries and so we have amalgamated these three nations. A total of 0.94 million people living in the UK in 2001 were born within the boundaries of Empire India, 1.6% of the population, 0.3% more than a decade ago.

The population has fallen in many costal districts, particularly along the south coast[6]. These falls are mainly due to the deaths of former colonial officers born in India and their children, who left around the time of independence and before.

The population born in Empire India, has risen mainly in cities[7], and by more than 2% only in Newham (mainly Bangladesh born increase), Redbridge (largest proportionate increase is of Pakistani born) and Tower Hamlets (mainly Bangladeshi born rise).

In 1991, 54.7% of all people born in Empire India living in Britain said they were born in what is now India; by 2001 that proportion had fallen to 49.6%. A majority of people now living in Britain born in what was India before 1947 were born in Pakistan or Bangladesh. The deaths of older people born in India have contributed to that change as much as has the increase of 49,000 people born in Bangladesh and 87,000 people born in Pakistan since 1991.

Empire India 2001 (%)

	0.0- 0.9
	0.1- 2.5
	2.6- 5.9
	6.0- 11.9
	12 - 19.2

Empire India change (%)

	−0.7 - −0.1
	0.0
	0.1- 0.5
	0.6- 1.5
	1.6- 3.7

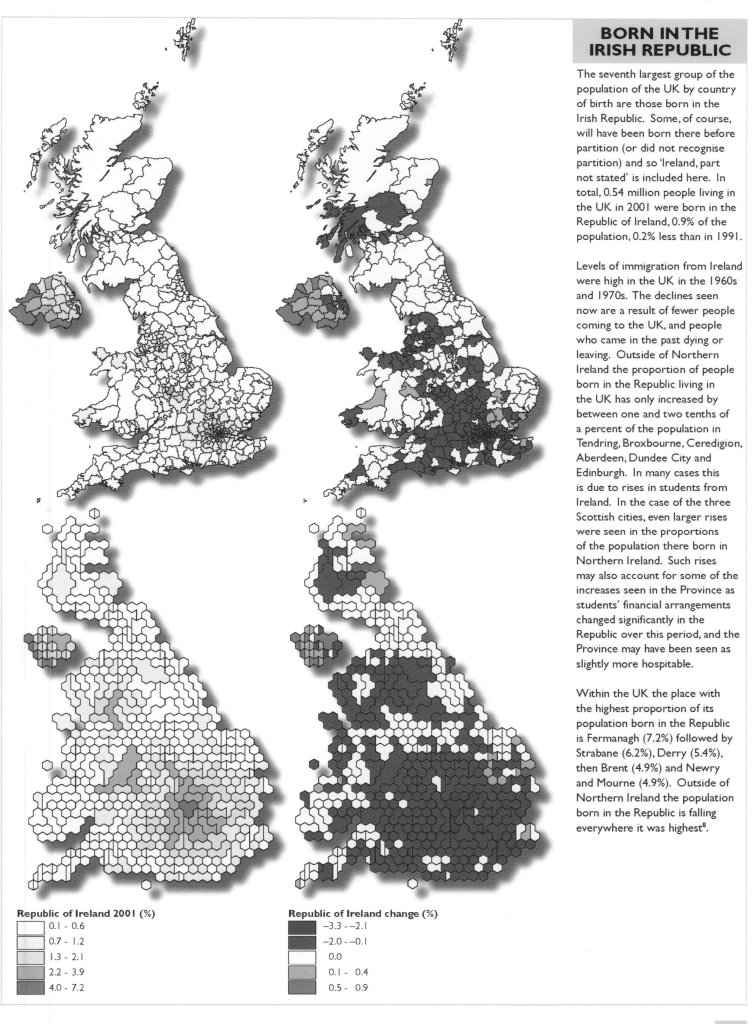

BORN IN THE IRISH REPUBLIC

The seventh largest group of the population of the UK by country of birth are those born in the Irish Republic. Some, of course, will have been born there before partition (or did not recognise partition) and so 'Ireland, part not stated' is included here. In total, 0.54 million people living in the UK in 2001 were born in the Republic of Ireland, 0.9% of the population, 0.2% less than in 1991.

Levels of immigration from Ireland were high in the UK in the 1960s and 1970s. The declines seen now are a result of fewer people coming to the UK, and people who came in the past dying or leaving. Outside of Northern Ireland the proportion of people born in the Republic living in the UK has only increased by between one and two tenths of a percent of the population in Tendring, Broxbourne, Ceredigion, Aberdeen, Dundee City and Edinburgh. In many cases this is due to rises in students from Ireland. In the case of the three Scottish cities, even larger rises were seen in the proportions of the population there born in Northern Ireland. Such rises may also account for some of the increases seen in the Province as students' financial arrangements changed significantly in the Republic over this period, and the Province may have been seen as slightly more hospitable.

Within the UK the place with the highest proportion of its population born in the Republic is Fermanagh (7.2%) followed by Strabane (6.2%), Derry (5.4%), then Brent (4.9%) and Newry and Mourne (4.9%). Outside of Northern Ireland the population born in the Republic is falling everywhere it was highest[8].

Republic of Ireland 2001 (%)

	0.1 - 0.6
	0.7 - 1.2
	1.3 - 2.1
	2.2 - 3.9
	4.0 - 7.2

Republic of Ireland change (%)

	-3.3 - -2.1
	-2.0 - -0.1
	0.0
	0.1 - 0.4
	0.5 - 0.9

BORN IN THE EUROPEAN COAL AND STEEL COMMUNITY (ECSC)

The eighth largest group by birthplace in the UK are those born in the original European Union (EU). We do not have space to map every single country of birth group and so we have amalgamated geographically proximate countries or those with connections such as these six. In 1951 Belgium, France, Germany, Italy, Luxembourg and the Netherlands formed the European Coal and Steel Community (ECSC), the precursor of the EEC (European Economic Community), EC (European Community) and the current EU. A total of 0.53 million people living in the UK in 2001 were born in the six ECSC countries, comprising 0.9% of the population, 0.2% more than in 1991. Of these, almost half were born in Germany (266,000), 107,000 in Italy, 95,000 in France, 40,000 in the Netherlands, 22,000 in Belgium and just over 1,000 in Luxembourg.

People born in the ECSC mainly live in southern England, but also along the east coast of Scotland. In fact it is just possible to discern the routes of the east and west coast mainline railways on the 2001 map. Increases have been concentrated in university cities and London. The largest increase, of 1.6% of the population, has been in Kensington & Chelsea, which also has the largest share, 7.2%, and which houses many embassies among other relevant institutions[9]. A scattering of areas have experienced falls in these proportions. The largest fall, of −0.6%, being in Richmondshire in North Yorkshire, is associated with the military base there (many British troops had children born in Germany).

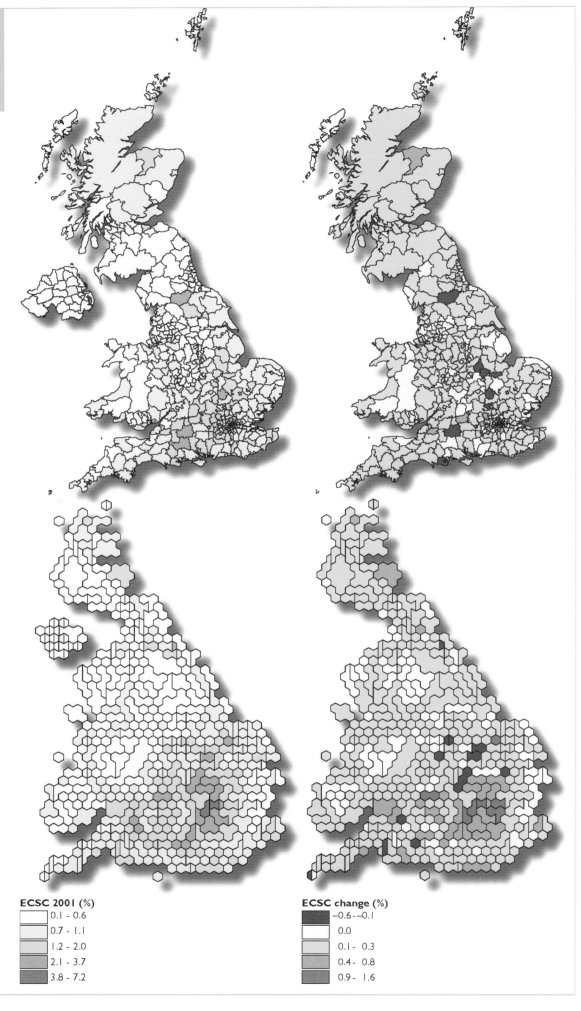

ECSC 2001 (%)

	0.1 - 0.6
	0.7 - 1.1
	1.2 - 2.0
	2.1 - 3.7
	3.8 - 7.2

ECSC change (%)

	−0.6 - −0.1
	0.0
	0.1 - 0.3
	0.4 - 0.8
	0.9 - 1.6

BORN IN THE CARIBBEAN

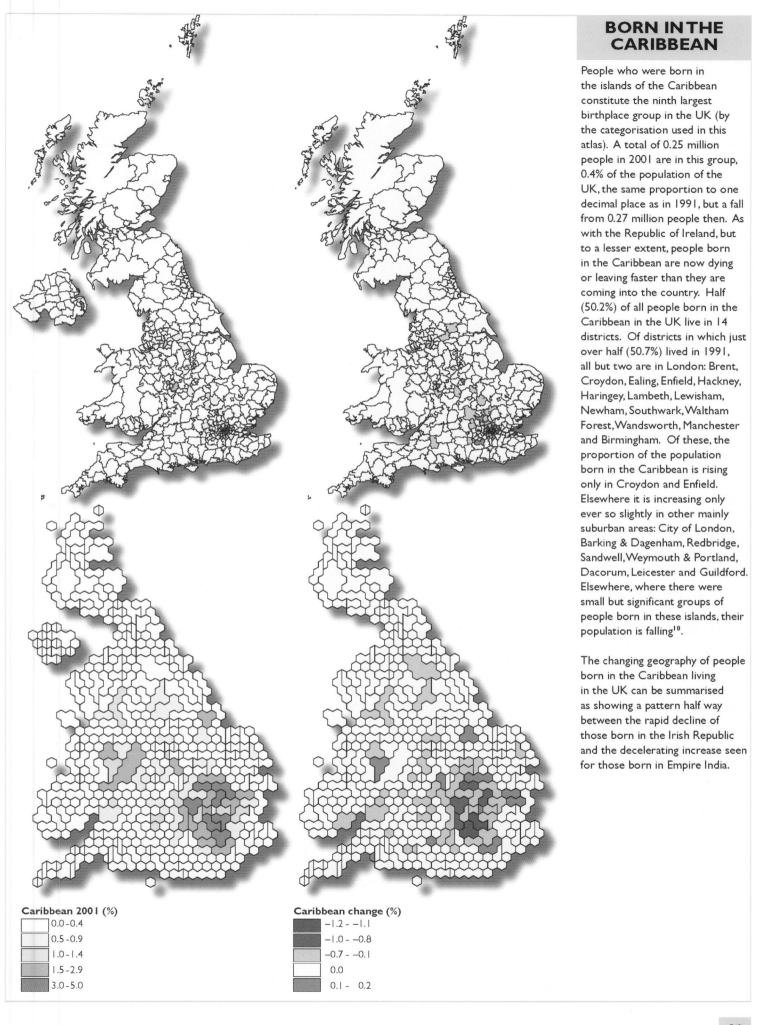

People who were born in the islands of the Caribbean constitute the ninth largest birthplace group in the UK (by the categorisation used in this atlas). A total of 0.25 million people in 2001 are in this group, 0.4% of the population of the UK, the same proportion to one decimal place as in 1991, but a fall from 0.27 million people then. As with the Republic of Ireland, but to a lesser extent, people born in the Caribbean are now dying or leaving faster than they are coming into the country. Half (50.2%) of all people born in the Caribbean in the UK live in 14 districts. Of districts in which just over half (50.7%) lived in 1991, all but two are in London: Brent, Croydon, Ealing, Enfield, Hackney, Haringey, Lambeth, Lewisham, Newham, Southwark, Waltham Forest, Wandsworth, Manchester and Birmingham. Of these, the proportion of the population born in the Caribbean is rising only in Croydon and Enfield. Elsewhere it is increasing only ever so slightly in other mainly suburban areas: City of London, Barking & Dagenham, Redbridge, Sandwell, Weymouth & Portland, Dacorum, Leicester and Guildford. Elsewhere, where there were small but significant groups of people born in these islands, their population is falling[10].

The changing geography of people born in the Caribbean living in the UK can be summarised as showing a pattern half way between the rapid decline of those born in the Irish Republic and the decelerating increase seen for those born in Empire India.

Caribbean 2001 (%)
- 0.0 - 0.4
- 0.5 - 0.9
- 1.0 - 1.4
- 1.5 - 2.9
- 3.0 - 5.0

Caribbean change (%)
- −1.2 - −1.1
- −1.0 - −0.8
- −0.7 - −0.1
- 0.0
- 0.1 - 0.2

BORN IN CANADA AND THE USA

The tenth largest birthplace group shown here are those people born in Canada and the USA living in the UK, 0.23 million in 2001, 0.4% of the population, a percentage unchanged on a decade ago. Of these people, 158,000 were born in the US and 73,000 in Canada.

Although London is one centre of attraction, as with almost all people born overseas, North Americans are also found clustered in very remote areas of the country. These are places often associated with military bases. Where there have been declines in the proportions of the local populations born in North America, such declines are very often due to the closure or reduction in size of such facilities[11]. In contrast to these falls the number of people born in the US living in Harrogate (located near secret US military bases) has risen by 947, to now stand at over 3,000. The highest number of people born in the US living in any district in the UK are the almost 10,000 mainly armed forces personnel (and their families) still based in Forest Heath.

Canadians do not have military interests in the UK. In contrast to their US neighbours, Canadian born people are found in their highest absolute numbers in university towns, business centres and perhaps where emigrants returned to with their children: Edinburgh, Westminster, Kensington & Chelsea, Camden, Wandsworth, Glasgow City, Hammersmith & Fulham, Richmond upon Thames, Lambeth and Oxford. Canadians are also not always the smaller group[12].

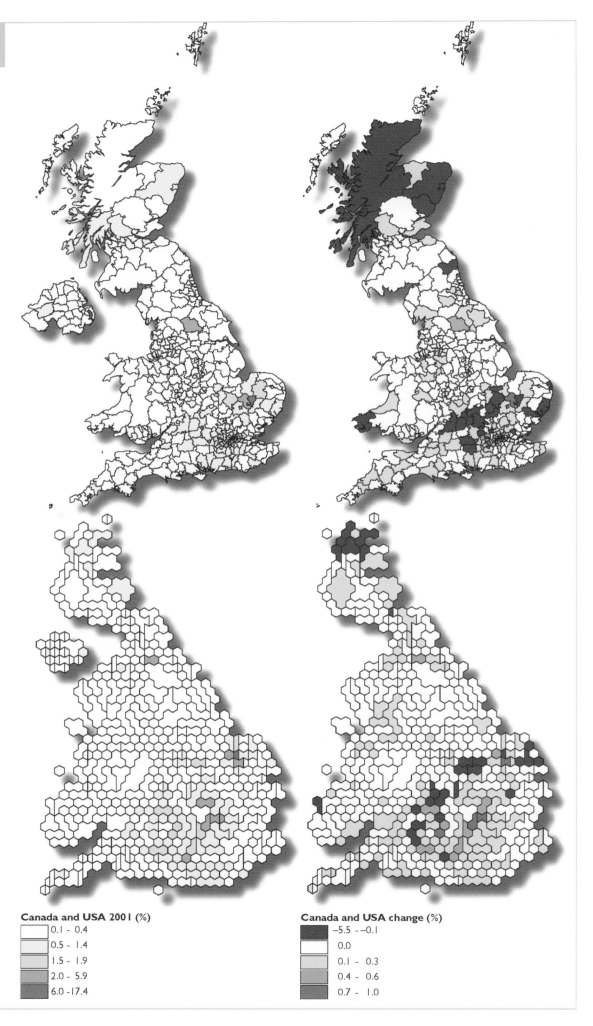

Canada and USA 2001 (%)

	0.1 - 0.4
	0.5 - 1.4
	1.5 - 1.9
	2.0 - 5.9
	6.0 - 17.4

Canada and USA change (%)

	−5.5 - −0.1
	0.0
	0.1 - 0.3
	0.4 - 0.6
	0.7 - 1.0

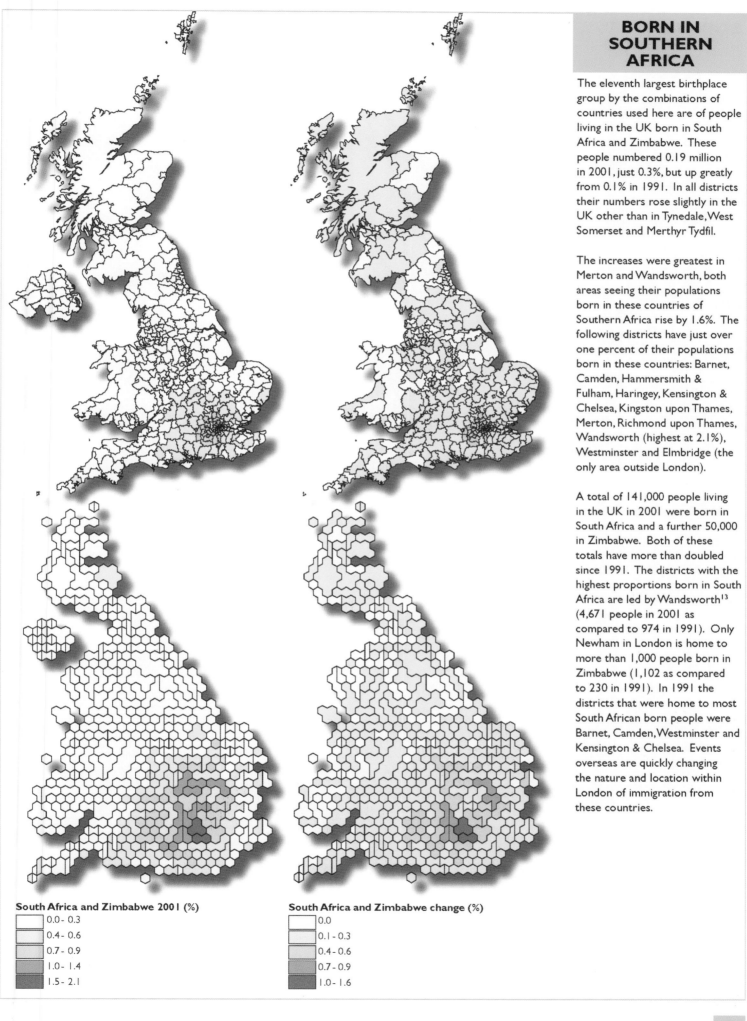

BORN IN SOUTHERN AFRICA

The eleventh largest birthplace group by the combinations of countries used here are of people living in the UK born in South Africa and Zimbabwe. These people numbered 0.19 million in 2001, just 0.3%, but up greatly from 0.1% in 1991. In all districts their numbers rose slightly in the UK other than in Tynedale, West Somerset and Merthyr Tydfil.

The increases were greatest in Merton and Wandsworth, both areas seeing their populations born in these countries of Southern Africa rise by 1.6%. The following districts have just over one percent of their populations born in these countries: Barnet, Camden, Hammersmith & Fulham, Haringey, Kensington & Chelsea, Kingston upon Thames, Merton, Richmond upon Thames, Wandsworth (highest at 2.1%), Westminster and Elmbridge (the only area outside London).

A total of 141,000 people living in the UK in 2001 were born in South Africa and a further 50,000 in Zimbabwe. Both of these totals have more than doubled since 1991. The districts with the highest proportions born in South Africa are led by Wandsworth[13] (4,671 people in 2001 as compared to 974 in 1991). Only Newham in London is home to more than 1,000 people born in Zimbabwe (1,102 as compared to 230 in 1991). In 1991 the districts that were home to most South African born people were Barnet, Camden, Westminster and Kensington & Chelsea. Events overseas are quickly changing the nature and location within London of immigration from these countries.

South Africa and Zimbabwe 2001 (%)

- 0.0 - 0.3
- 0.4 - 0.6
- 0.7 - 0.9
- 1.0 - 1.4
- 1.5 - 2.1

South Africa and Zimbabwe change (%)

- 0.0
- 0.1 - 0.3
- 0.4 - 0.6
- 0.7 - 0.9
- 1.0 - 1.6

BORN IN CYPRUS, GREECE AND TURKEY

The twelfth largest birthplace group shown here are of those people living in the UK who were born in Greece or Turkey. Cyprus has also been included in this group due to its disputed affiliation with both countries. Its addition has a great influence on the maps. In total, 0.17 million people living in the UK in 2001 were born in these countries, 0.3% of the population, a rise of 0.1% from 1991. Cypriot born is the largest group making up this amalgam, including 78,000 people in 2001, a total almost unchanged on a decade ago. Almost 12,000 of these people live in the borough of Enfield, which is home to a further 6,000 Turkish born people, but less than a 1,000 Greek born. The only higher numbers of Turkish born people are found in Haringey (8,500) and Hackney (7,700). Over half of all Turkish born people living in the UK live in these three boroughs and Islington, Waltham Forest and Barnet. In contrast the Greek born population is more spread out across the country with the two highest numbers found in Westminster (1,700) and Manchester (900). The areas of declining population share on the cartogram of change are all due to slightly falling numbers of Cypriot born people living in Brent, Camden, Kensington & Chelsea, Lambeth and Newham, as this group becomes more spread out across the country. The spreading out has tended to be concentrated in larger towns and cities across Britain, as the speckled cartogram of change highlights[14].

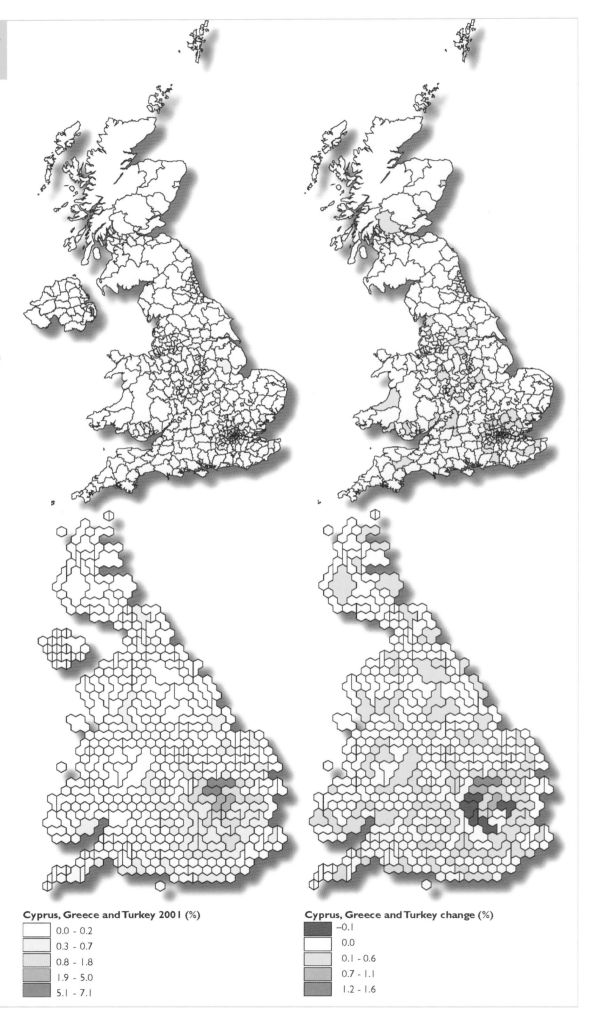

Cyprus, Greece and Turkey 2001 (%)

- 0.0 - 0.2
- 0.3 - 0.7
- 0.8 - 1.8
- 1.9 - 5.0
- 5.1 - 7.1

Cyprus, Greece and Turkey change (%)

- −0.1
- 0.0
- 0.1 - 0.6
- 0.7 - 1.1
- 1.2 - 1.6

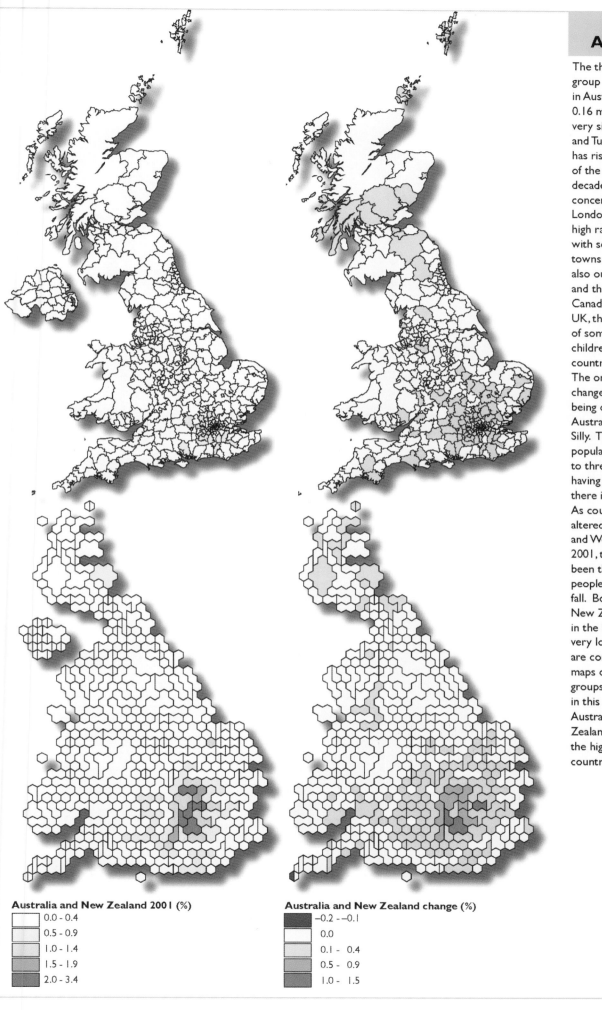

BORN IN AUSTRALASIA

The thirteenth largest birthplace group in the UK is of those born in Australia and New Zealand. At 0.16 million in 2001 this group is very similar in size to the Greek and Turkish born population, and has risen similarly in size to 0.3% of the population, up 0.1% on a decade ago. Again the group is concentrated in particular parts of London and again, in some areas, high rates of increase are found with some diffusion to the larger towns and cities of the UK but also out into suburban London and the Home Counties. As with Canadian born people living in the UK, there may be an indication of some return migration of the children of emigrants to these countries, particularly in Scotland. The one anomaly on the map of change is the only recorded fall, being of the proportion born in Australasia living in the Isles of Silly. The Isles of Scilly have a tiny population. This fall is entirely due to three Australian born people having been recorded as living there in 1991 and none in 2001. As counts of three or less were altered at random by the English and Welsh census authorities in 2001, there may have actually been three Australian born people living there and hence no fall. Both censuses counted four New Zealand born people living in the Isles. This illustrates the very low numbers of people we are considering as we draw these maps of the smaller birthplace groups. In total 108,000 people in this group were born in Australia and 58,000 in New Zealand. Wandsworth is home to the highest numbers from both countries[15].

Australia and New Zealand 2001 (%)

	0.0 - 0.4
	0.5 - 0.9
	1.0 - 1.4
	1.5 - 1.9
	2.0 - 3.4

Australia and New Zealand change (%)

	−0.2 - −0.1
	0.0
	0.1 - 0.4
	0.5 - 0.9
	1.0 - 1.5

BORN IN IBERIA

The penultimate and fourteenth largest birthplace group living in the UK are those people born in Spain and Portugal, 0.09 million people in 2001, 0.2% of the population, 0.1% more than in 1991. Again we see what is becoming a familiar pattern, concentration in London, but that concentration diminishing over the 1990s in some of the most concentrated boroughs and a spreading out occurring across space, generally into the rest of the South East but also to some of the larger towns and cities of Britain. By 2001 more than 2,000 people born in these two countries lived in each of the London boroughs of Brent, Camden, Hammersmith & Fulham, Kensington & Chelsea, Lambeth and Westminster. People travel to live in the UK from abroad for a wide variety of reasons. Some are students here to study for a few years, others are young people spending some time travelling and working in the country before returning, others have lived here for many years and are settled (often the partners of UK born people), while others still are the children of UK born people born overseas whose parents have returned with them to the country. This wide variety of reasons results in quite a simple overall map both of distribution[16] and of change[17].

Of the 91,000 people in this group in 2001, 54,000 were born in Spain and 37,000 in Portugal, up from 39,000 and 20,000 respectively a decade ago. Increasing levels of international migration are slowly increasing the variety of places in which people living in the UK were born.

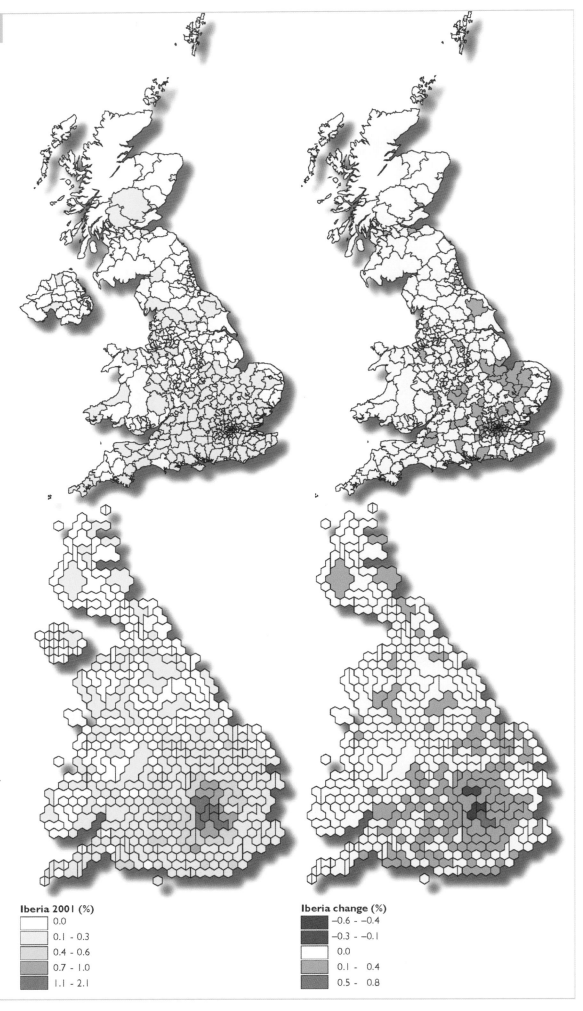

Iberia 2001 (%)
- 0.0
- 0.1 - 0.3
- 0.4 - 0.6
- 0.7 - 1.0
- 1.1 - 2.1

Iberia change (%)
- −0.6 - −0.4
- −0.3 - −0.1
- 0.0
- 0.1 - 0.4
- 0.5 - 0.8

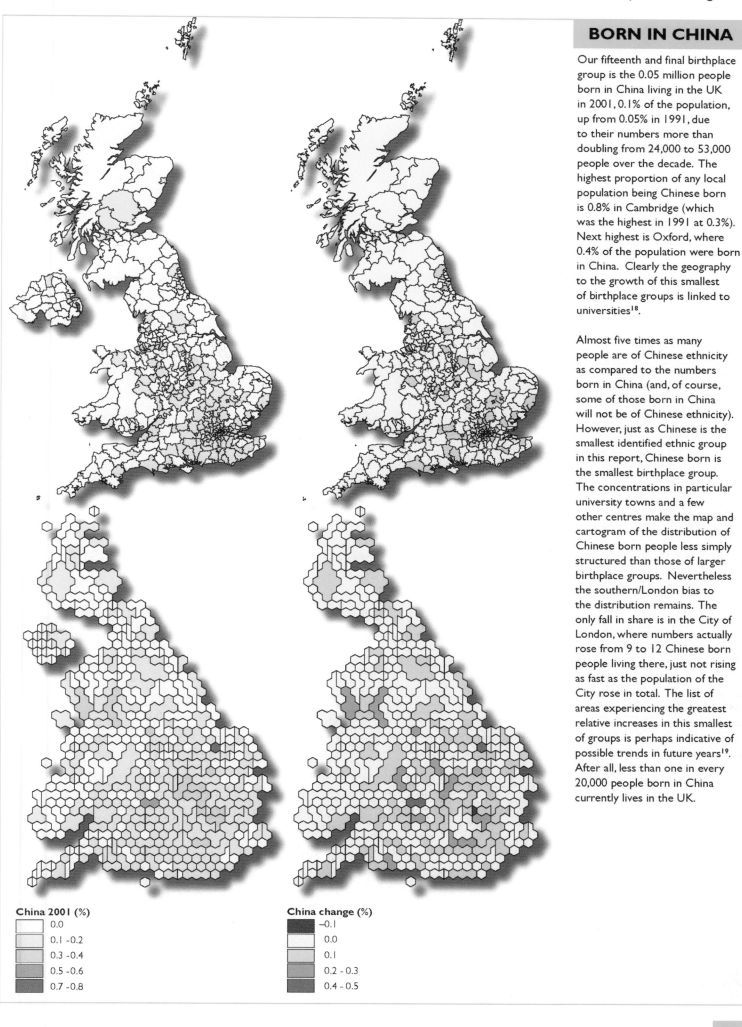

BORN IN CHINA

Our fifteenth and final birthplace group is the 0.05 million people born in China living in the UK in 2001, 0.1% of the population, up from 0.05% in 1991, due to their numbers more than doubling from 24,000 to 53,000 people over the decade. The highest proportion of any local population being Chinese born is 0.8% in Cambridge (which was the highest in 1991 at 0.3%). Next highest is Oxford, where 0.4% of the population were born in China. Clearly the geography to the growth of this smallest of birthplace groups is linked to universities[18].

Almost five times as many people are of Chinese ethnicity as compared to the numbers born in China (and, of course, some of those born in China will not be of Chinese ethnicity). However, just as Chinese is the smallest identified ethnic group in this report, Chinese born is the smallest birthplace group. The concentrations in particular university towns and a few other centres make the map and cartogram of the distribution of Chinese born people less simply structured than those of larger birthplace groups. Nevertheless the southern/London bias to the distribution remains. The only fall in share is in the City of London, where numbers actually rose from 9 to 12 Chinese born people living there, just not rising as fast as the population of the City rose in total. The list of areas experiencing the greatest relative increases in this smallest of groups is perhaps indicative of possible trends in future years[19]. After all, less than one in every 20,000 people born in China currently lives in the UK.

China 2001 (%)

- 0.0
- 0.1 - 0.2
- 0.3 - 0.4
- 0.5 - 0.6
- 0.7 - 0.8

China change (%)

- −0.1
- 0.0
- 0.1
- 0.2 - 0.3
- 0.4 - 0.5

INTERNATIONAL MIGRATION

The national census asks people where they were living a year before the census was taken. A total of 0.4 million people living in the UK in 2001 were living abroad at the same time in the year 2000. Many of these people will have lived in the UK before, and a proportion of these will have been born in the UK, so this is not a count of the number of people immigrating to the UK. At 0.7% of the total population, the proportion is 0.1% higher than that recorded in 1991, mainly reflecting higher rates of international travel over time. However, changes in the national and international housing markets over the decade will have also increased mobility. A similar proportion of the population counted in the 2001 Census as living in the UK was probably living overseas a year later in 2002.

London, the Home Counties and university towns and cities attract the bulk of international migrants. They will also include UK armed forces who were stationed overseas a year before the censuses were taken, and their locations explain some of the areas which have experienced a decline in international migrants over time. The three largest declines in the UK of the decade are all associated with areas where large numbers of US armed forces travelled to the UK between 1990 and 1991[20]. The largest rises in the proportions of the population who were international migrants were recorded almost exclusively in areas with large universities, but also in three of the parts of central London traditionally associated with international migration[21].

International migrant 2001 (%)

- 0.0 - 0.1
- 0.2 - 0.3
- 0.4 - 0.5
- 0.7 - 1.0
- 1.1 - 5.8

International migrant change (%)

- −1.8 - −0.6
- −0.5 - −0.1
- 0.0 - 0.1
- 0.2 - 0.4
- 0.5 - 1.7

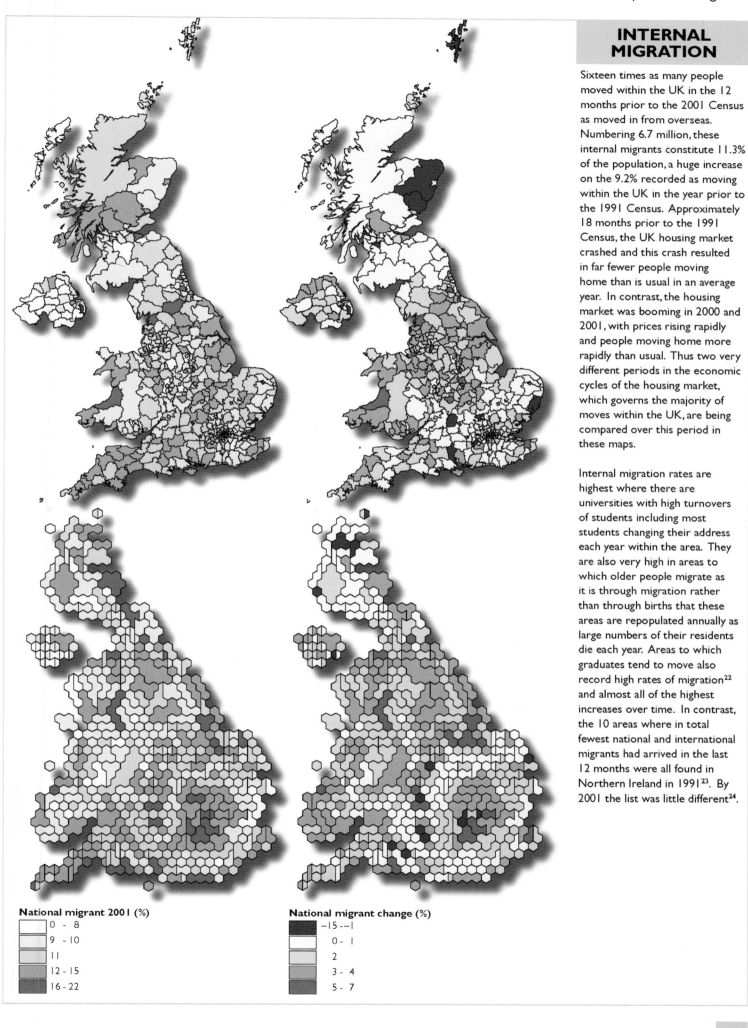

INTERNAL MIGRATION

Sixteen times as many people moved within the UK in the 12 months prior to the 2001 Census as moved in from overseas. Numbering 6.7 million, these internal migrants constitute 11.3% of the population, a huge increase on the 9.2% recorded as moving within the UK in the year prior to the 1991 Census. Approximately 18 months prior to the 1991 Census, the UK housing market crashed and this crash resulted in far fewer people moving home than is usual in an average year. In contrast, the housing market was booming in 2000 and 2001, with prices rising rapidly and people moving home more rapidly than usual. Thus two very different periods in the economic cycles of the housing market, which governs the majority of moves within the UK, are being compared over this period in these maps.

Internal migration rates are highest where there are universities with high turnovers of students including most students changing their address each year within the area. They are also very high in areas to which older people migrate as it is through migration rather than through births that these areas are repopulated annually as large numbers of their residents die each year. Areas to which graduates tend to move also record high rates of migration[22] and almost all of the highest increases over time. In contrast, the 10 areas where in total fewest national and international migrants had arrived in the last 12 months were all found in Northern Ireland in 1991[23]. By 2001 the list was little different[24].

National migrant 2001 (%)

	0 - 8
	9 - 10
	11
	12 - 15
	16 - 22

National migrant change (%)

	−15 −−1
	0 - 1
	2
	3 - 4
	5 - 7

NOTES

[1] More than 95% of the populations of the following boroughs were born in England. These are places which have attracted relatively few migrants in recent decades, particularly from overseas: Wigan, Knowsley, St Helens, Barnsley, Rotherham, Gateshead, South Tyneside, Sunderland and Wakefield. Outside of the metropolitan boroughs similarly high proportions of the population being English born are found in Halton, Amber Valley, Bolsover, Chesterfield, North East Derbyshire, Chester-le-Street, Derwentside, Easington (the highest with 97.5% of its population born in England), Hartlepool, Sedgefield, Wear Valley, Kingston upon Hull, Castle Point, Rochford, North East Lincolnshire, Blyth Valley, Wansbeck, Redcar & Cleveland, Ashfield, Cannock Chase, South Staffordshire, Staffordshire Moorlands and North Warwickshire.

[2] See Table 4.1.

[3] See Table 4.2.

[4] See Table 4.3.

[5] In descending order of the populations born in these countries (with those populations shown in brackets) these countries are: Other South and Eastern Africans countries not otherwise listed (197,277), Kenya (129,633), Other Far East (119,542), Hong Kong (96,446), Nigeria (88,378), Other Central and Western Africa (86,431), South America (76,778), Non-EU countries in Western Europe (73,926), North Africa (72,323), Other Middle East (72,045), Sri Lanka (67,947), Poland (60,709), Malaysia (49,893), Former Yugoslavia (47,406), Somalia (43,533), Iran (42,499), all other countries not listed (42,219), Singapore (40,474), Japan (37,536), Iraq (32,230), Channel Islands (31,023), Other European countries in former USSR (29,150), Other Eastern Europe (23,814), Sweden (22,523), Austria (19,498), Denmark (18,644), Sierra Leone (17,058), Afghanistan (14,873), Czech Republic (12,215), Finland (11,329), Baltic States (10,661), Other North America (8,943), UK part not specified (8,626), Democratic Republic of Congo (8,546), Romania (7,627), Other South Asia (6,401), Other Oceania (5,748), Asian countries in former USSR (3,397) and Albania (2,317).

[6] In London the proportion of the population born in Empire India fell in Bexley, Haringey and Lambeth. Outside of London they fell mainly in areas where people who write letters to the *Daily Telegraph* are renowned to live, particularly those who refer to their days in colonial service: North Dorset, West Dorset, Rother, Braintree, North Hertfordshire, Medway, Shepway, Tonbridge & Malling, Tunbridge Wells, North Norfolk, Harrogate, Richmondshire, Rugby, Warwick, Ceredigion and Clackmannanshire.

[7] Over 8% of the populations of the following areas were born in Empire India: Brent, Ealing, Hounslow, Newham, Redbridge, Tower Hamlets (highest at 19.2%), Luton, Slough and Leicester.

[8] In areas where more than 2% of the population were born in the Republic of Ireland in 1991 all have seen that proportion fall by the percentage share shown in brackets as follows: Barnet (−1.0), Brent (−3.3), Camden (−2.1), Croydon (−0.5), Ealing (−1.7), Enfield (−0.6), Greenwich (−0.6), Hackney (−1.2), Hammersmith & Fulham (−2.1), Haringey (−1.6), Harrow (−1.4), Hillingdon (−0.3), Hounslow (−0.9), Islington (−2.2), Kensington & Chelsea (−0.9), Kingston upon Thames (−0.5), Lambeth (−1.7), Lewisham (−0.8), Merton (−0.8), Redbridge (−0.8), Richmond upon Thames (−0.3), Southwark (−1.5), Tower Hamlets (−0.6), Waltham Forest (−0.8), Wandsworth (−1.1), Westminster (−1.7), Manchester (−0.9), Trafford (−0.4), Birmingham (−0.8), Coventry (−0.9), Luton (−1.1), Reading (−0.7), Slough (−1.0), Watford (−0.5), Corby (−0.4), Oxford (−0.6) and Warwick (−0.4).

[9] Outside of London the highest numbers of Belgium born people living in the UK are found in Edinburgh, Brighton & Hove, Birmingham, Elmbridge, Oxford and Bristol. The French are most populous in Edinburgh, Brighton & Hove, Birmingham, Bristol, Oxford and Cambridge. The Germans are most numerous in Edinburgh, Leeds, Birmingham, Salisbury and Colchester (the latter two being part military towns possibly housing many army children born in Germany when the army of the Rhine was based there or who have moved from Richmondshire). The largest Italian born groups by district are in Bedford, Broxbourne, Edinburgh, Peterborough and Bradford. Outside of London more than two dozen people born in Luxembourg are found only in Bristol, Brighton & Hove, Canterbury, Oxford and Edinburgh. Outside London there are more than 400 people born in the Netherlands only in Birmingham, Elmbridge, Woking, Aberdeen City and Edinburgh.

[10] All the following areas have seen the proportion of their populations who were born in the Caribbean fall by at least a tenth of a percent. The change in percentage share is shown in brackets as follows: Brent (−0.8), Camden (−0.3), Ealing (−0.5), Hackney (−0.9), Hammersmith & Fulham (−0.9), Haringey (−0.8), Harrow (−0.1), Hounslow (−0.1), Islington (−0.4), Kensington & Chelsea (−0.2), Lambeth (−1.1), Merton (−0.3), Newham (−0.5), Southwark (−0.6), Tower Hamlets (−0.4), Waltham Forest (−0.1), Wandsworth (−1.2), Westminster (−0.5), Wolverhampton (−0.1), Kirklees (−0.1), Bedford (−0.1), Reading (−0.3), Bristol, City of (−0.1), Wycombe (−0.2), Gloucester (−0.1), Northampton (−0.1), Oxford (−0.2), Epsom & Ewell (−0.1) and Rugby (−0.1).

[11] The following district has seen the numbers of people born in the US living there fall by 200 people or more between 1991 and 2001 (falls shown in brackets): Suffolk coastal (−5,893), Cherwell (−4,422), Huntingdonshire (−2,229), Argyll & Bute (−2,125), Mid Bedfordshire (−1,716), South Northamptonshire (−1,412), West Berkshire (−896), Aberdeenshire (−764), Angus (−573), Forest Heath (−532), Pembrokeshire (−517), Cotswold (−440), Peterborough (−384), Ipswich (−347), Three Rivers (−324), Highland (−305), West Oxfordshire (−273) and Wycombe (−202).

[12] The following districts have at least two dozen more Canadian born than US born. These places are perhaps typical of the destinations of returning emigrants' children: Barrow-in-Furness, Ards, Highland, North Down, Torbay, Castlereagh, Sefton, Carrickfergus, South Lanarkshire, Conwy, Oldham, East Ayrshire, North Tyneside, Clackmannanshire and Midlothian.

[13] The following districts contained more than 1,000 people born in South Africa living there in 2001: Wandsworth (4,671), Barnet (3,144), Merton (3,041), Camden (2,324), Ealing (2,148), Hammersmith & Fulham (1,913), Richmond upon Thames (1,876), Brent (1,836), Westminster (1,738), Haringey (1,722), Kensington & Chelsea (1,695), Lambeth (1,599), Waltham Forest (1,543), Edinburgh (1,331), Southwark (1,258), Elmbridge (1,248), Croydon (1,167), Kingston upon Thames (1,148), Tower Hamlets (1,146), Bromley (1,135), Birmingham MB (1,076), Hounslow (1,075), Newham (1,030), Harrow (1,029) and Windsor & Maidenhead (1,016).

[14] The following areas have seen the share of their population who were born in these countries rise by a fifth of a percentage point or more: City of London, Barking & Dagenham, Enfield, Greenwich, Hackney, Haringey, Islington, Kingston upon Thames, Waltham Forest, Westminster, Manchester, Newcastle upon Tyne, Coventry, Reading, Cambridge, Brighton & Hove, Colchester, Portsmouth, Broxbourne, Welwyn Hatfield, Canterbury, Oxford, Guildford and Runnymede.

[15] The proportion of the population born in these two countries has risen by over a fifth of a percentage point in the following areas (which include non-metropolitan boroughs outside of London): City of London, Brent, Camden, Ealing, Greenwich, Hackney, Hammersmith & Fulham, Haringey, Hounslow, Islington, Kingston upon Thames, Lambeth, Merton, Newham, Richmond upon Thames, Southwark, Tower Hamlets, Waltham Forest, Wandsworth, Westminster, Windsor & Maidenhead, Cambridge, St Albans, Oxford, Elmbridge and Edinburgh.

[16] More than a tenth (3,900) of Portuguese born people living in the UK live in Lambeth, by far the highest concentration, up from 1,800 people in 1991. Conversely, less than a tenth of the Spanish born population lives in the two boroughs with their highest numbers, Kensington & Chelsea (2,100) and Westminster (2,000). In both these places the Spanish born population is declining over time. The Spanish born population is rising most in absolute numbers in Edinburgh and Manchester.

[17] The share of the population born in these two countries has risen by a fifth of a percentage point or more only in: Brent, Haringey, Hounslow, Lambeth, Newham, Southwark, Waltham Forest, Cambridge, Bournemouth, Breckland, Oxford and Crawley.

[18] The 10 districts containing the highest proportions of Chinese born people in 2001 were: Barnet, Haringey, Islington, Southwark, Westminster, Manchester, Liverpool, Cambridge, Broxtowe and Oxford.

[19] The local proportion of the population born in China has risen by 0.1% or more in: Barnet, Ealing, Greenwich, Haringey, Harrow, Kingston upon Thames, Lewisham, Merton, Southwark, Tower Hamlets, Waltham Forest, Manchester, Salford, Liverpool, Coventry, Luton, Reading, Wokingham, Milton Keynes, Cambridge, East Cambridgeshire, Purbeck, Durham, Colchester, Southampton, Welwyn Hatfield, Lancaster, Preston, Charnwood, Boston, Norwich, Northampton, Broxtowe, Nottingham, Oxford, Dundee and Edinburgh.

[20] The populations of the local authority districts of Suffolk Coastal, Forest Heath and Cherwell who were international migrants fell by 1.8%, 1.6% and 1.5% respectively over the course of the decade.

[21] The 10 local authorities with the highest increases in their local populations travelling from overseas a year before were as follows: the City of London and the boroughs of Southwark and Tower Hamlets, Reading, Windsor & Maidenhead, Durham, Nottingham, Oxford, Runnymede and Edinburgh. Many university students live in the two London boroughs outside of the City and in the remaining seven districts. A large part of this increase is probably due as much to the increased popularity of gap years among more affluent undergraduates as to the universities based in or near these areas attracting more overseas students.

[22] The highest three rates of internal in-migration recorded in the UK in 2001 were in the City of London, Cambridge and Oxford at 18.7%, 20.8% and 21.6% respectively. A further 4.3%, 4.1% and 3.8% of their populations were migrants from overseas and thus only around three quarters of the residents of these three areas were resident there in the same house or flat a year ago. A decade ago four fifths of the population of the two university towns had been residents there a year ago.

[23] In 1991 more than 94% of people had not moved in the last year in: Armagh, Ballymoney, Banbridge, Cookstown, Dungannon, Fermanagh, Magherafelt, Moyle, Newry & Mourne and Strabane.

[24] By 2001 the 10 areas with the lowest proportion of in-migrants were: Havering, East Dunbartonshire, Armagh, Castlereagh, Cookstown, Dungannon, Fermanagh, Magherafelt, Newry & Mourne and Strabane.

Table 4.1: Increase of English born living in Scotland

Districts where English born has risen by 1%+ in Scotland 1991-2001	English change 1991-2001 (%)	Scottish change 1991-2001 (%)	English 2001 (%)	Scottish 2001 (%)
Aberdeen City	1.1	−3.2	8.4	84.4
Argyll & Bute	3.0	−1.4	17.0	78.1
Dumfries & Galloway	1.6	−2.1	15.6	80.5
Dundee City	1.1	−3.4	5.7	87.8
East Lothian	1.2	−1.9	9.5	86.6
Edinburgh	2.7	−6.4	12.1	77.8
Glasgow City	1.0	−2.8	4.2	89.1
Highland	1.8	−2.2	13.7	82.2
Moray	2.8	−4.1	16.2	78.5
Orkney Islands	1.8	−2.4	13.6	83.4
Perth & Kinross	1.1	−2.0	12.0	83.0
Stirling	1.4	−3.0	11.6	82.5

Table 4.2: Increase of English born living in Wales

Districts where English born has risen by 1%+ in Wales 1991-2001	English change 1991-2001 (%)	Welsh change 1991-2001 (%)	English 2001 (%)	Welsh 2001 (%)
Cardiff	2.6	−4.1	16.3	74.9
Carmarthenshire	1.4	−1.9	16.8	80.1
Ceredigion	5.0	−5.7	36.4	58.6
Flintshire	1.5	−1.9	44.7	51.1
Gwynedd	1.8	−2.0	26.6	69.8
Pembrokeshire	1.3	−1.0	26.3	68.7
Powys	4.5	−4.9	40.6	55.6
Swansea	1.5	−2.0	13.3	82.1
Wrexham	1.0	−1.3	24.5	71.9

Table 4.3: Increase of English born living in Northern Ireland

Districts where English born has risen by 0.75%+ in Northern Ireland 1991-2001	English change 1991-2001 (%)	Northern Irish change 1991-2001 (%)	English 2001 (%)	Northern Irish 2001 (%)
Antrim	2.0	−3.0	7.3	87.0
Ballymoney	0.9	−1.1	2.6	95.0
Banbridge	0.8	−1.7	2.9	93.7
Derry	0.9	−1.9	4.0	88.1
Down	1.2	−0.6	4.5	91.3
Fermanagh	1.3	−2.6	4.1	87.0
Moyle	1.3	−2.0	3.6	91.9
North Down	0.9	−2.4	6.2	86.1

Qualifications and employment

Maps in this section include:

Low qualifications (p 83)	Medium qualifications (p 84)	High qualifications (p 85)	University degrees (p 86)	Not unemployed (p 87)	Youth unemployment (p 88)
Working age unemployment (p 89)	Old age unemployment (p 90)	Unemployed never worked (p 91)	Students (p 92)	Permanently sick (p 93)	Young retired (p 94)
Full time at home (p 95)	Working part-time (p 96)	Full-time employment (p 97)	Self-employed (p 98)	Not working any hours (p 99)	Working under 16 hours (p 100)
Working 16-30 hours (p 101)	Working over 30 hours (p 102)				

Most of the questions asked in the 2001 Census of population had been asked in previous censuses, allowing us to map the changes shown throughout this atlas. Some have been asked for many decades, which is why, for instance, we know so much about the changing geography of migration and birthplace in the UK.

Other questions that were included in the 2001 Census had not been asked for a long time. Religious affiliation was last questioned 150 years ago, and it has also been many decades since a relevant question was asked of the educational qualifications of the population as a whole. Now that a question has been asked, a pattern is revealed of quite remarkable geographical inequalities in qualifications attained across the Kingdom. This pattern has resulted almost exclusively as a result of selective patterns of differential lifetime migration from place of schooling to current place of residence. The result that we see is that in most of the larger towns of the North of England, in South Wales, Central Scotland and almost all of Northern Ireland, up to third of the population hold no educational qualifications. In most of the South less than a sixth of the population are in the same situation, despite the concentration of many retirement areas in the South.

Over the course of the last half century, the population moved around the country, resulting in the fact that those without such skills were increasingly left where they were not educated, while others with no qualifications found themselves moving there as they could not afford to live in the South. People in the South were educated to a slightly higher standard but most importantly were joined, year after year, by migrants with skills from the rest of the UK and increasingly from the rest of the world.

The nation is divided along geographical lines by the skills its universal system of education was supposed to have provided everywhere. Nowhere is this clearer than in the current locations of people with university degrees or their equivalent, who migrated to a place of education to attain them and from which, in the main, they then migrated again. Most of these moves were into London and the South East. What is most remarkable of all is that despite the huge recent increase in graduates, upon graduation people continue to cluster within the capital in increasing concentrations. Our education system serves the world city best and leaves millions behind in places damned for their population's supposed inadequacies. Educational labels can then be used to try to legitimate regional inequalities, inequalities that continue to grow due to the differential flows of people with differing educational qualifications.

The employment profiles of different districts spread across the UK are partly caused by educational inequalities, and partly also the cause of the differential migration flows that create those inequalities. The success and declines of particular industries and occupations also play a part as we see in the next chapter. Here we concentrate on the employment status of the entire working-age population, not just those in work. For everyone of working age the most extreme form of isolation from the labour market, unemployment, has decreased rapidly in recent years. It has decreased the most, often, where it needed to fall the most, and quickest for younger people, partly as increased educational opportunities have helped create a scarcity of cheap young labour. There are very few people who are now unemployed and have never worked, more than four times fewer in 2001 than in 1991; and, in general more of the working-age population are in work than before, but not that many more. The numbers of people of working age who are neither working nor unemployed have increased greatly, but these increases have been very clearly geographically patterned. The million extra students in the UK live only in particular places.

The more than half a million extra adults of working age who are permanently sick and cannot work were mainly added to the cities of the North, while rates of such sickness actually fell in a scattering of places located almost exclusively in the Home Counties. Only differential migration can account for such changes. People who fell ill had to leave the affluent areas in flows not clearly seen before, and those who replaced them are healthier than ever recorded. People left the North in higher numbers the more able they were to travel South; armed with qualifications or a strong constitution, they left behind a population becoming increasingly both sicker and less educated as compared to the country as a whole.

Simultaneously, more than a million additional adults chose to retire early by the end of the 1990s as compared to the beginning. They left the South in their greatest numbers and moved in ever increasing numbers towards the coasts, to which coast depending most on where they were moving from and to where they could afford to move. Thus even in retirement the population is increasingly being sorted through space.

As work grew in both necessity and popularity, the numbers of people looking after the home and caring for their children fell by almost one-and-a-half million, but not within the most densely populated cities, creating a very urban pattern to what has been thought of as traditional family life, one which is surprisingly similar to the geography of the Muslim religion in places.

Part-time work increased everywhere but most where living is most expensive; the proportion of the population engaged in full-time work fell almost everywhere except for Northern Ireland, which experienced a particularly strong boom in employment during this decade. Self-employment rose slightly, especially in London, but not at rates able to dent the fall in full-time work, and it fell abruptly in many rural areas. More people were working in the UK than ever before, but, on average, for fewer hours than the average before, although at the extremes some were commuting and working far longer hours around London.

London also saw a dramatic rise in both employment and average working hours within its core. Work increased most in the capital, sickness was further banished from the surrounding Home Counties, people were encouraged or able to retire earlier and moved further away from the centre more quickly, more worked in general, but worklessness and low-paid part-time work was still concentrated in the North of the country. Pockets of unemployment and non-employment remained in the cities.

More people were educated than ever before but more of them moved away from where they were brought up than ever before. The changes were accelerating. The periphery of the UK as a workplace, with the exception of Northern Ireland, improved the least for its young people, but saw sickness rise and its employment profile become ever more differentiated from that of the South East and London. Northern Ireland moved rapidly from a dire situation to the normality for a peripheral area. The capital and the commuting areas that ring it simply moved further away from the rest.

The primary industry of the world city, banking, grew most rapidly. The customers were increasingly overseas corporations. London had less and less to do with the remainder of the UK economy, but its influence dominated the patterns of change seen through the following pages, as rings of effect ripple out from its centre up and across the entire Kingdom.

There are a few blips. Edinburgh has become established as a mini financial alternative to the capital and so appears like a pebble being washed over by many of the ripples emanating from the core. However, these few exceptions and anomalies aside, the geography of people with qualifications and in work is increasingly creating a geographical image of successful London in contrast to a provincial archipelago of cities to the North that are not reaping the benefits of economic growth.

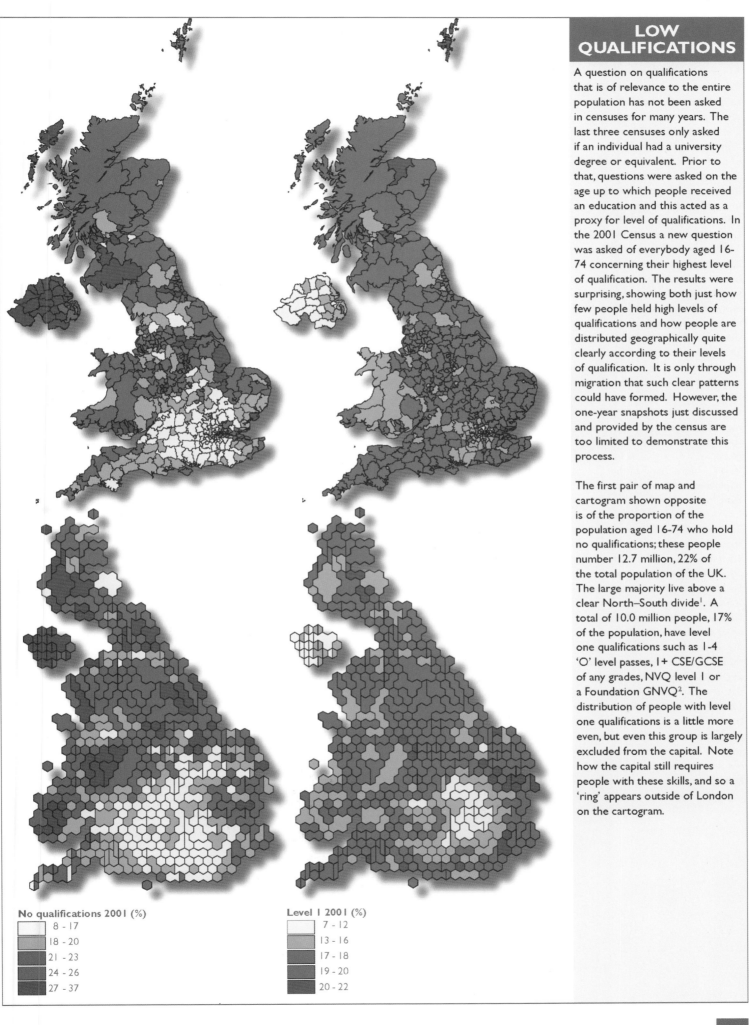

A question on qualifications that is of relevance to the entire population has not been asked in censuses for many years. The last three censuses only asked if an individual had a university degree or equivalent. Prior to that, questions were asked on the age up to which people received an education and this acted as a proxy for level of qualifications. In the 2001 Census a new question was asked of everybody aged 16-74 concerning their highest level of qualification. The results were surprising, showing both just how few people held high levels of qualifications and how people are distributed geographically quite clearly according to their levels of qualification. It is only through migration that such clear patterns could have formed. However, the one-year snapshots just discussed and provided by the census are too limited to demonstrate this process.

The first pair of map and cartogram shown opposite is of the proportion of the population aged 16-74 who hold no qualifications; these people number 12.7 million, 22% of the total population of the UK. The large majority live above a clear North–South divide[1]. A total of 10.0 million people, 17% of the population, have level one qualifications such as 1-4 'O' level passes, 1+ CSE/GCSE of any grades, NVQ level 1 or a Foundation GNVQ[2]. The distribution of people with level one qualifications is a little more even, but even this group is largely excluded from the capital. Note how the capital still requires people with these skills, and so a 'ring' appears outside of London on the cartogram.

No qualifications 2001 (%)

	8 - 17
	18 - 20
	21 - 23
	24 - 26
	27 - 37

Level 1 2001 (%)

	7 - 12
	13 - 16
	17 - 18
	19 - 20
	20 - 22

MEDIUM QUALIFICATIONS

Scotland has a different system for the award of the majority of its qualifications, and the influence of this is most apparent on the first map opposite. The map and cartogram are of the distribution of 8.1 million people in the UK, 14% of the population, holding level two qualifications. These include 5+ 'O' level passes, 5+ CSEs (all at grade 1), 5+ GCSEs (grades A-C), a School Certificate, 1+ 'A' levels/'AS' levels, NVQ level 2, or an intermediate GNVQ[3]. Level two is the basic level to which schools in the UK have attempted, in theory, to educate all children for many years. In the distant past the aim was for all children to receive a school certificate, that was transformed to 5 ordinary level passes when they were introduced, and the current equivalent for the majority of the population going through school is now five or more GCSEs, each of at least level C. More than half the population do not hold these basic qualifications[4].

The second map and cartogram show the distribution of the 3.5 million people, 6% of the population holding level three qualifications: 2+ 'A' levels, 4+ 'AS' levels, a Higher School Certificate, a NVQ level 3, or an advanced GNVQ[5]. Here the university towns feature as these are the qualifications most of their students need to study. But here also we begin to see a concentration forming within London that is not simply the product of its universities. People with yet higher qualifications are not included in these maps and cartograms.

Level 2 2001 (%)

- 9 - 10
- 11 - 12
- 13 - 14
- 15 - 16
- 17 - 20

Level 3 2001 (%)

- 3 - 4
- 5
- 6
- 7 - 8
- 9 - 15

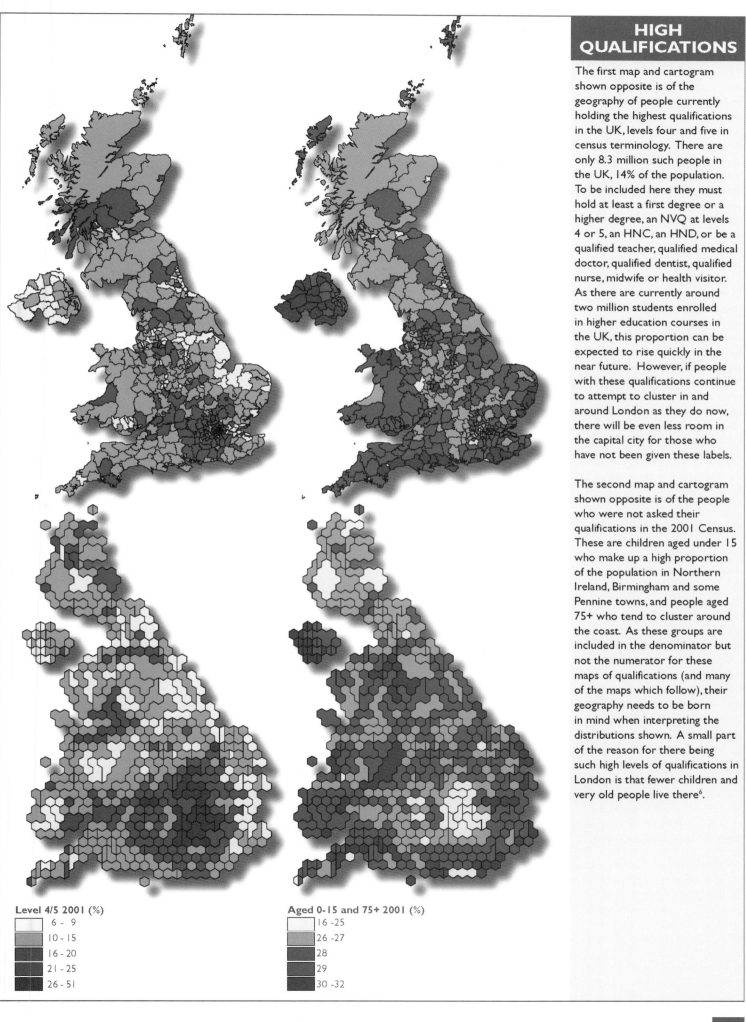

HIGH QUALIFICATIONS

The first map and cartogram shown opposite is of the geography of people currently holding the highest qualifications in the UK, levels four and five in census terminology. There are only 8.3 million such people in the UK, 14% of the population. To be included here they must hold at least a first degree or a higher degree, an NVQ at levels 4 or 5, an HNC, an HND, or be a qualified teacher, qualified medical doctor, qualified dentist, qualified nurse, midwife or health visitor. As there are currently around two million students enrolled in higher education courses in the UK, this proportion can be expected to rise quickly in the near future. However, if people with these qualifications continue to attempt to cluster in and around London as they do now, there will be even less room in the capital city for those who have not been given these labels.

The second map and cartogram shown opposite is of the people who were not asked their qualifications in the 2001 Census. These are children aged under 15 who make up a high proportion of the population in Northern Ireland, Birmingham and some Pennine towns, and people aged 75+ who tend to cluster around the coast. As these groups are included in the denominator but not the numerator for these maps of qualifications (and many of the maps which follow), their geography needs to be born in mind when interpreting the distributions shown. A small part of the reason for there being such high levels of qualifications in London is that fewer children and very old people live there[6].

Level 4/5 2001 (%)

	6 - 9
	10 - 15
	16 - 20
	21 - 25
	26 - 51

Aged 0-15 and 75+ 2001 (%)

	16 - 25
	26 - 27
	28
	29
	30 - 32

UNIVERSITY DEGREES

The holding of a university degree or its equivalent has been recorded at successive censuses, and thus we can measure the extent to which the geographical distribution of people holding this highest general level of qualification has changed over time. The first map and cartogram shown here are identical to the first shown on the last page, of people with level four and five qualifications, except that a slightly different scale has been used to shade these figures[7]. Thus, again, the same 8.3 million people, 14% of the population in 2001, are being shown, but now alongside the change from the 5.8 million people, 10% of the population in 1991, who then held equivalent qualifications at these ages. Note that everyone aged 18+ was asked if they had a degree in 1991 and we are thus including some people then aged 75+.

Although nowhere has seen their proportion of graduates in the population decrease, it has not risen in the retirement areas of Christchurch, Purbeck and Rother, and has hardly risen in many other districts away from the capital and the major cities. In contrast, the proportion in the City of London has risen by thirty percentage points and next fastest in Westminster by twenty-one percentage points, from 18% of the population there in 1991 to 39% in 2001. It was, of course, during the 1990s in Westminster that the local council illegally worked to change the characteristics of the local population through encouraging particular forms of selective migration[8]. However, as we see below, London continues to be home to large numbers of people with poor economic prospects.

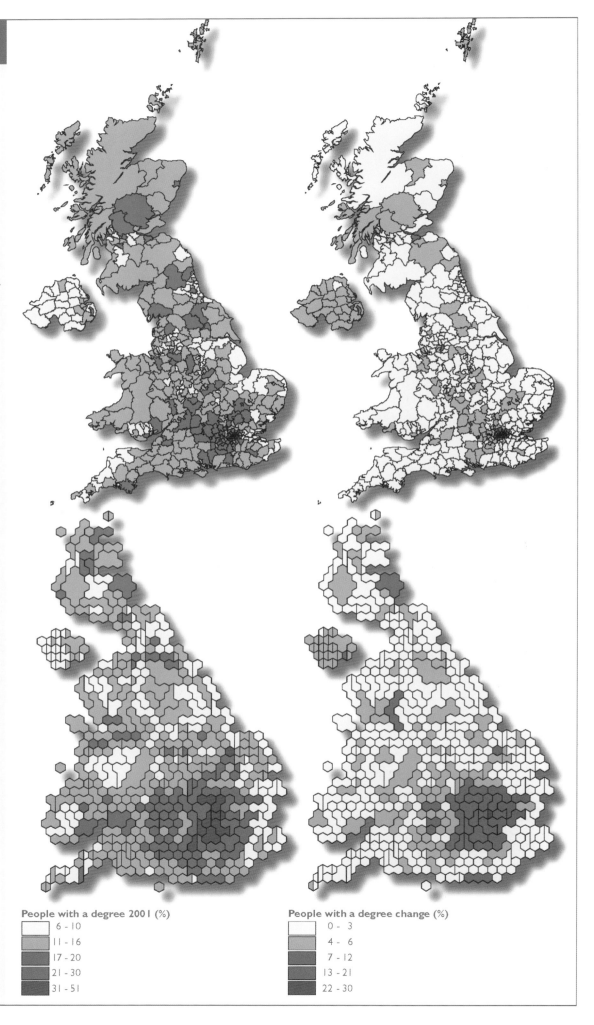

People with a degree 2001 (%)

- 6 - 10
- 11 - 16
- 17 - 20
- 21 - 30
- 31 - 51

People with a degree change (%)

- 0 - 3
- 4 - 6
- 7 - 12
- 13 - 21
- 22 - 30

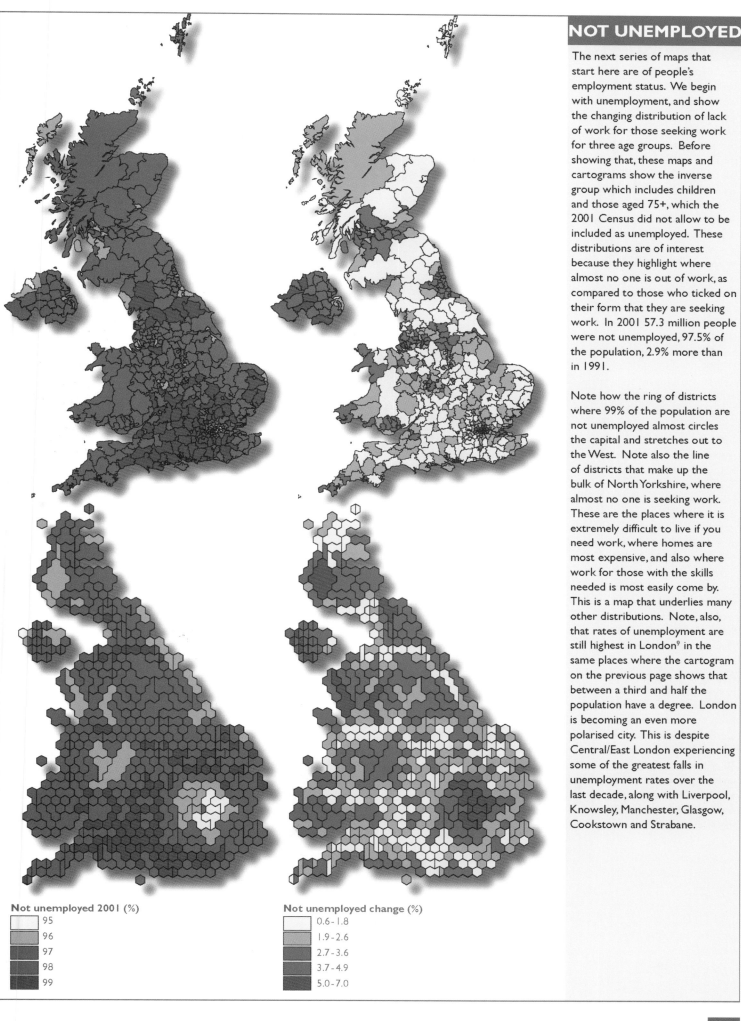

NOT UNEMPLOYED

The next series of maps that start here are of people's employment status. We begin with unemployment, and show the changing distribution of lack of work for those seeking work for three age groups. Before showing that, these maps and cartograms show the inverse group which includes children and those aged 75+, which the 2001 Census did not allow to be included as unemployed. These distributions are of interest because they highlight where almost no one is out of work, as compared to those who ticked on their form that they are seeking work. In 2001 57.3 million people were not unemployed, 97.5% of the population, 2.9% more than in 1991.

Note how the ring of districts where 99% of the population are not unemployed almost circles the capital and stretches out to the West. Note also the line of districts that make up the bulk of North Yorkshire, where almost no one is seeking work. These are the places where it is extremely difficult to live if you need work, where homes are most expensive, and also where work for those with the skills needed is most easily come by. This is a map that underlies many other distributions. Note, also, that rates of unemployment are still highest in London[9] in the same places where the cartogram on the previous page shows that between a third and half the population have a degree. London is becoming an even more polarised city. This is despite Central/East London experiencing some of the greatest falls in unemployment rates over the last decade, along with Liverpool, Knowsley, Manchester, Glasgow, Cookstown and Strabane.

Not unemployed 2001 (%)

- 95
- 96
- 97
- 98
- 99

Not unemployed change (%)

- 0.6 - 1.8
- 1.9 - 2.6
- 2.7 - 3.6
- 3.7 - 4.9
- 5.0 - 7.0

YOUTH UNEMPLOYMENT

In 2001, 0.38 million people aged between 16-24 were seeking work, only 0.6% of the population, remarkably just a third of the 1.8% in 1991, but a significant number nonetheless. Importantly, the places where young people are most likely not to find work are very similar to those places where youth unemployment was highest a decade ago. Youth unemployment has fallen quite evenly across the country, less so in percentage point terms only where it was low to begin with. The 10 areas with the highest rates of youth unemployment in 2001 were: Newham, Tower Hamlets, Knowsley, Liverpool, South Tyneside, Kingston upon Hull, Middlesbrough, Glasgow City, North Ayrshire and Derry. In 1991 Hackney, Manchester, Sunderland and Nottingham were in this list (they all still have 1.0% of their population being unemployed and of these ages). Rates fell a little more slowly in Tower Hamlets, South Tyneside, North Ayrshire and Derry, causing them to enter the top 10.

In the best of the 10 worse-off areas rates of youth unemployment are now four times higher (1.2% of the population as compared to the worst of the best-off 10 areas, 0.3%). The gap was almost identical a decade ago (3.1% compared to 0.8%). Youth unemployment has fallen most in absolute terms where it was highest; in relative terms it has fallen more where it was lowest first[10]. The only recorded rise, in the City of London, is from 30 people to just 40. Youth unemployment remains as much a distinct feature of particular areas as it did a decade ago, just at much lower rates.

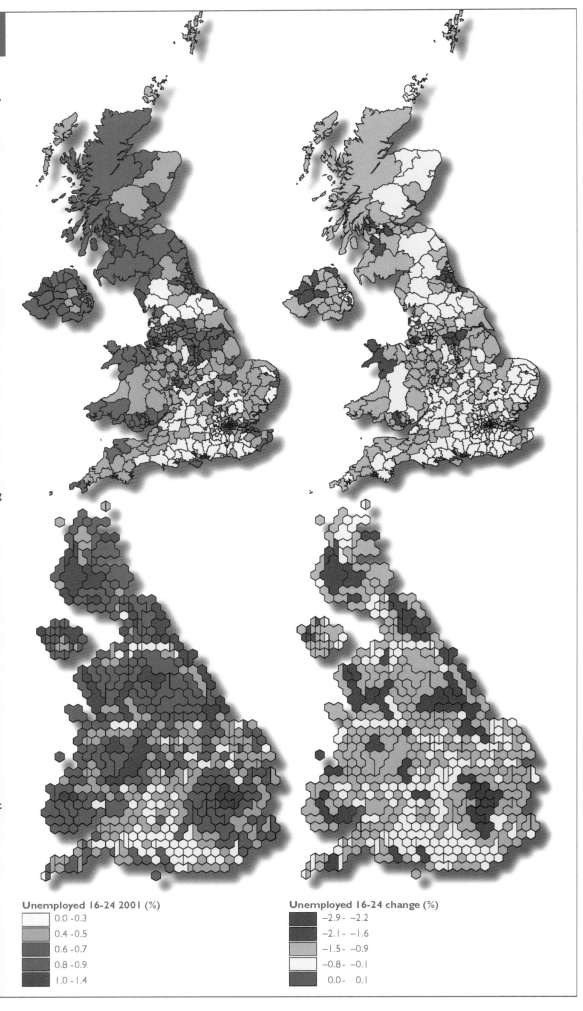

Unemployed 16-24 2001 (%)
0.0 -0.3
0.4 -0.5
0.6 -0.7
0.8 -0.9
1.0 -1.4

Unemployed 16-24 change (%)
−2.9- −2.2
−2.1- −1.6
−1.5- −0.9
−0.8- −0.1
0.0- 0.1

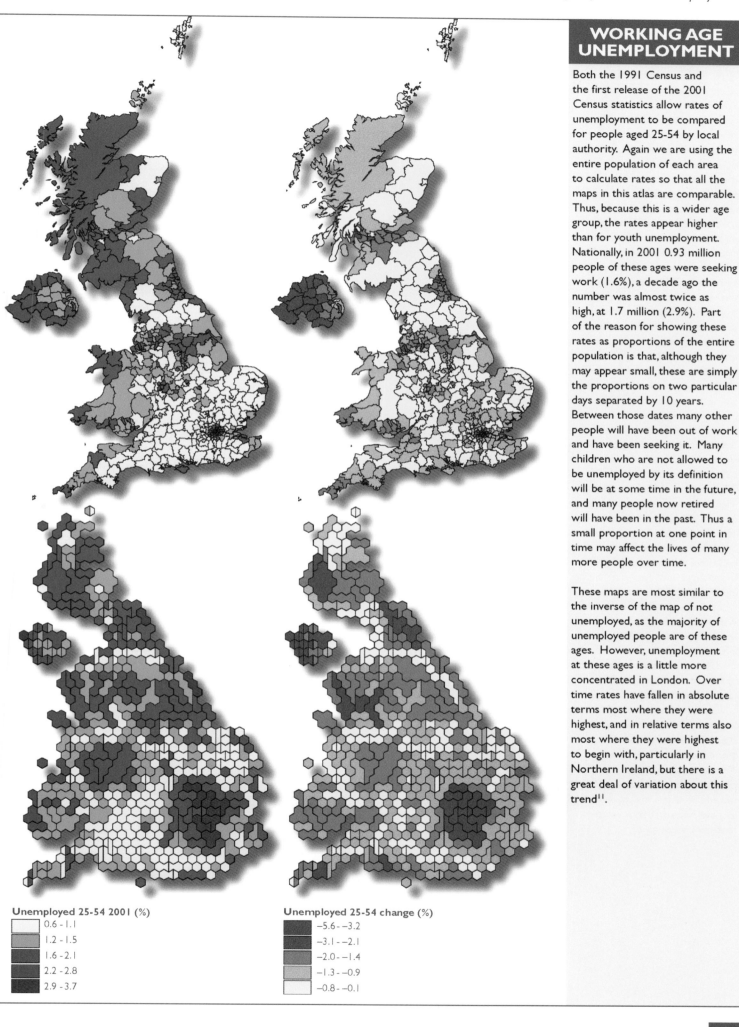

WORKING AGE UNEMPLOYMENT

Both the 1991 Census and the first release of the 2001 Census statistics allow rates of unemployment to be compared for people aged 25-54 by local authority. Again we are using the entire population of each area to calculate rates so that all the maps in this atlas are comparable. Thus, because this is a wider age group, the rates appear higher than for youth unemployment. Nationally, in 2001 0.93 million people of these ages were seeking work (1.6%), a decade ago the number was almost twice as high, at 1.7 million (2.9%). Part of the reason for showing these rates as proportions of the entire population is that, although they may appear small, these are simply the proportions on two particular days separated by 10 years. Between those dates many other people will have been out of work and have been seeking it. Many children who are not allowed to be unemployed by its definition will be at some time in the future, and many people now retired will have been in the past. Thus a small proportion at one point in time may affect the lives of many more people over time.

These maps are most similar to the inverse of the map of not unemployed, as the majority of unemployed people are of these ages. However, unemployment at these ages is a little more concentrated in London. Over time rates have fallen in absolute terms most where they were highest, and in relative terms also most where they were highest to begin with, particularly in Northern Ireland, but there is a great deal of variation about this trend[11].

Unemployed 25-54 2001 (%)

	0.6 - 1.1
	1.2 - 1.5
	1.6 - 2.1
	2.2 - 2.8
	2.9 - 3.7

Unemployed 25-54 change (%)

	−5.6 - −3.2
	−3.1 - −2.1
	−2.0 - −1.4
	−1.3 - −0.9
	−0.8 - −0.1

OLD AGE UNEMPLOYMENT

Here we are comparing the rates of unemployment of people aged 55-74 in 2001 with those aged 55+ in 1991. Although not strictly comparable, very few people aged 75+ would have ticked the boxes to indicate that they were available for work and seeking work in 2001, had that choice been recorded. When considering comparability it is more important to remember that over the course of the 1990s more and more people retired early rather than register as unemployed, more may have said that they were self-employed as compared to a decade earlier (but have been living at both points in time in similar circumstances), and more who lost their jobs at these ages certainly claimed sickness benefits rather than unemployment benefits as the years passed. Thus the rates of unemployment in old age fell slightly faster in relative terms (by 53%) than they did at the main working ages of 25-54 (by 47%). They fell fastest for people aged under 25 (by 65%, see footnote 10). But for that age group other opportunities, such as more university places, opened up and that cohort was also falling in size (see Chapter 2, footnote 11).

Nationally, 0.15 million people aged 55+ were unemployed in 2001, 0.26% of the population of the UK and less than half the 0.31 million counted in 1991. Rates fell most where they were highest to begin with in both absolute and relative terms, reducing the disparities seen across the country slightly[12]. However, if there are always a small proportion of people out of work, moving between jobs, then this may still be polarisation (as the minimum is not zero).

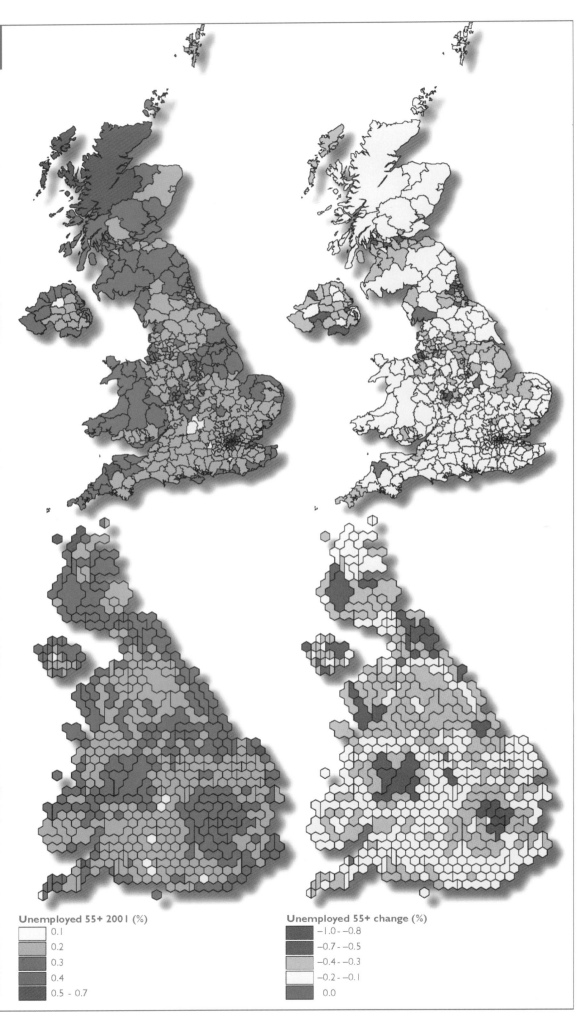

Unemployed 55+ 2001 (%)

	0.1
	0.2
	0.3
	0.4
	0.5 - 0.7

Unemployed 55+ change (%)

	−1.0 - −0.8
	−0.7 - −0.5
	−0.4 - −0.3
	−0.2 - −0.1
	0.0

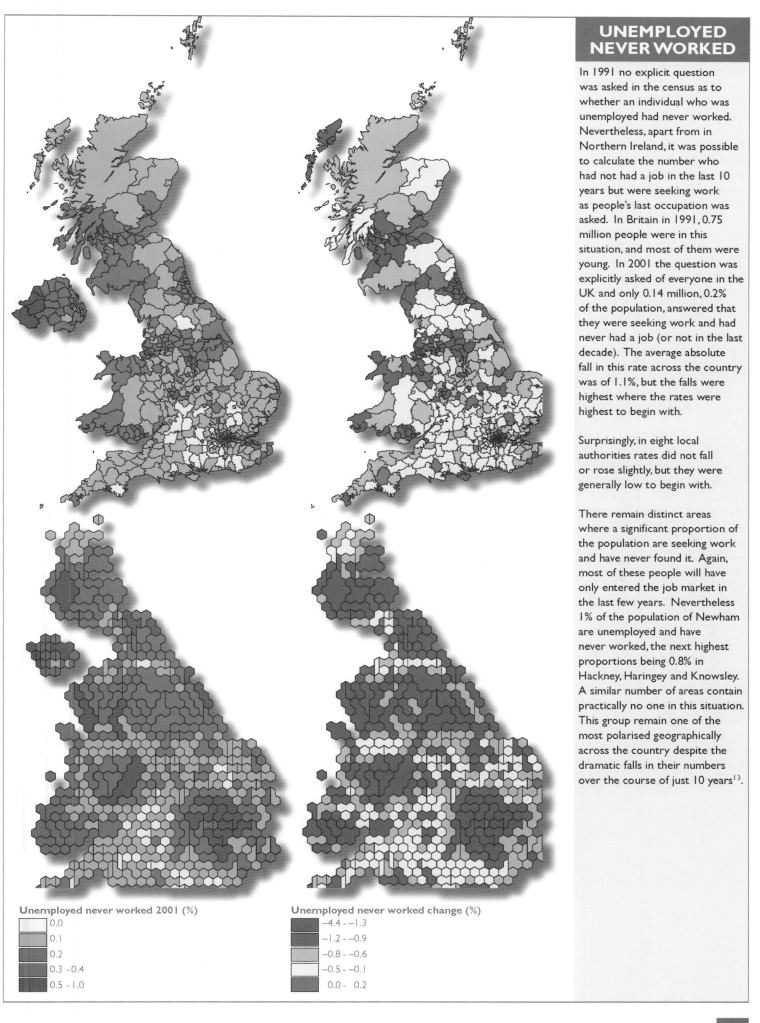

UNEMPLOYED NEVER WORKED

In 1991 no explicit question was asked in the census as to whether an individual who was unemployed had never worked. Nevertheless, apart from in Northern Ireland, it was possible to calculate the number who had not had a job in the last 10 years but were seeking work as people's last occupation was asked. In Britain in 1991, 0.75 million people were in this situation, and most of them were young. In 2001 the question was explicitly asked of everyone in the UK and only 0.14 million, 0.2% of the population, answered that they were seeking work and had never had a job (or not in the last decade). The average absolute fall in this rate across the country was of 1.1%, but the falls were highest where the rates were highest to begin with.

Surprisingly, in eight local authorities rates did not fall or rose slightly, but they were generally low to begin with.

There remain distinct areas where a significant proportion of the population are seeking work and have never found it. Again, most of these people will have only entered the job market in the last few years. Nevertheless 1% of the population of Newham are unemployed and have never worked, the next highest proportions being 0.8% in Hackney, Haringey and Knowsley. A similar number of areas contain practically no one in this situation. This group remain one of the most polarised geographically across the country despite the dramatic falls in their numbers over the course of just 10 years[13].

Unemployed never worked 2001 (%)

- 0.0
- 0.1
- 0.2
- 0.3 - 0.4
- 0.5 - 1.0

Unemployed never worked change (%)

- −4.4 - −1.3
- −1.2 - −0.9
- −0.8 - −0.6
- −0.5 - −0.1
- 0.0 - 0.2

STUDENTS

Part of the reason why youth unemployment has fallen faster than unemployment for people of other ages, and for why there are now so few young people who have never worked, is due to the rise in student places which are almost all taken up by people aged under 25. The cartograms and maps here include everyone aged between 16-74 whose main occupation is as a student. Thus, some will be in sixth form colleges or still at school. The vast bulk of these students are in further or higher education and are concentrated in the university towns, cities and boroughs shaded opposite to show where between 10% and 20% of the entire population of these places are students (on the cartogram and map three areas where 9.5% to 9.9% of the population are students are included in the 10-20 category as we round to the nearest percentage).

In 1991 there were 2.1 million students, 3.6% of the population. By 2001 this proportion had increased by 1.6% as they now numbered 3.1 million people. The list of where students make up the highest proportions of local populations is predictable[14]. The list of where their numbers have been raised the most is very similar[15]. What may be more surprising is the large number of areas where the proportions of students appear to be falling despite their numbers increasing nationally. We are counting students at their term-time address at each point in time so this is not an error of definition; rather it reflects the falling numbers of 16- and 17-year-olds in many areas with no universities (see Chapter 2, footnotes 8-10).

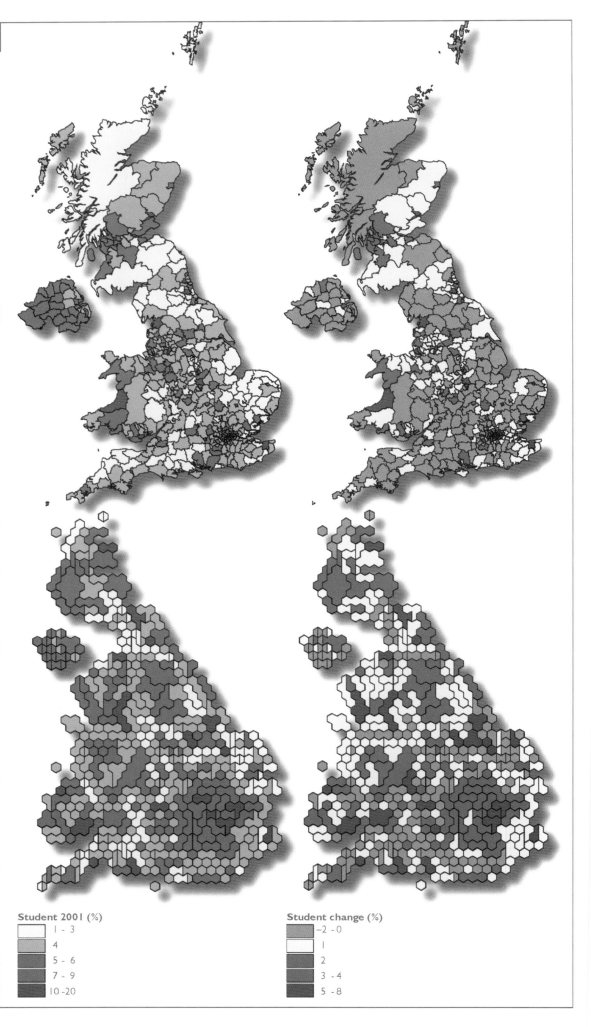

Student 2001 (%)

- 1 - 3
- 4
- 5 - 6
- 7 - 9
- 10 -20

Student change (%)

- −2 - 0
- 1
- 2
- 3 - 4
- 5 - 8

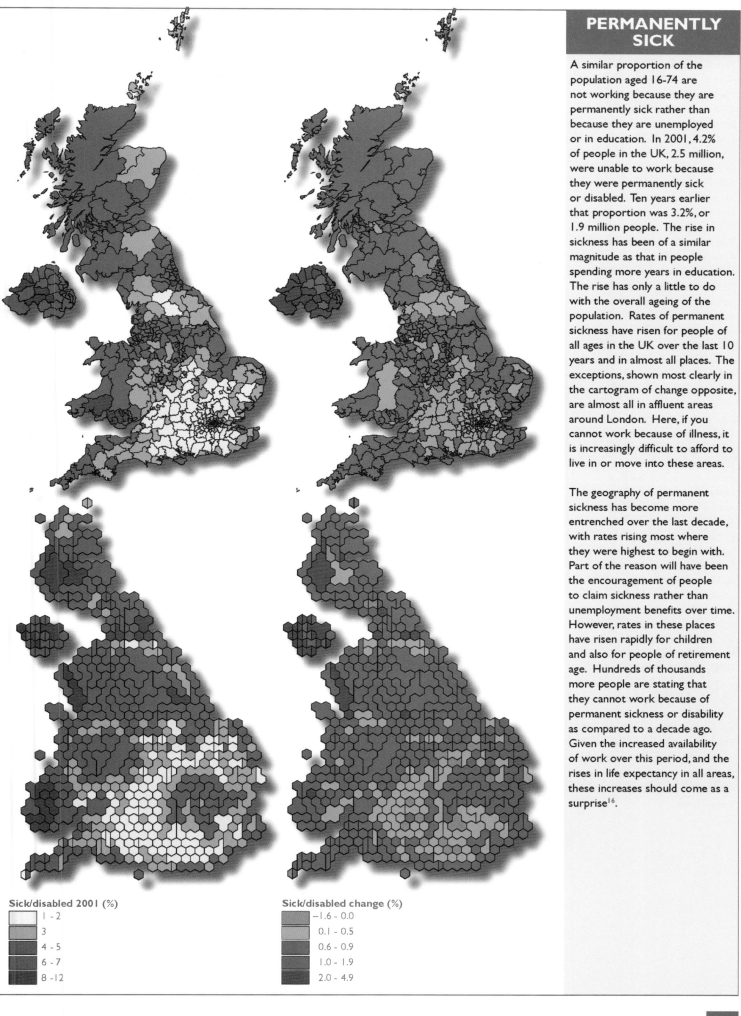

PERMANENTLY SICK

A similar proportion of the population aged 16-74 are not working because they are permanently sick rather than because they are unemployed or in education. In 2001, 4.2% of people in the UK, 2.5 million, were unable to work because they were permanently sick or disabled. Ten years earlier that proportion was 3.2%, or 1.9 million people. The rise in sickness has been of a similar magnitude as that in people spending more years in education. The rise has only a little to do with the overall ageing of the population. Rates of permanent sickness have risen for people of all ages in the UK over the last 10 years and in almost all places. The exceptions, shown most clearly in the cartogram of change opposite, are almost all in affluent areas around London. Here, if you cannot work because of illness, it is increasingly difficult to afford to live in or move into these areas.

The geography of permanent sickness has become more entrenched over the last decade, with rates rising most where they were highest to begin with. Part of the reason will have been the encouragement of people to claim sickness rather than unemployment benefits over time. However, rates in these places have risen rapidly for children and also for people of retirement age. Hundreds of thousands more people are stating that they cannot work because of permanent sickness or disability as compared to a decade ago. Given the increased availability of work over this period, and the rises in life expectancy in all areas, these increases should come as a surprise[16].

Sick/disabled 2001 (%)

	1 - 2
	3
	4 - 5
	6 - 7
	8 - 12

Sick/disabled change (%)

	−1.6 - 0.0
	0.1 - 0.5
	0.6 - 0.9
	1.0 - 1.9
	2.0 - 4.9

YOUNG RETIRED

The number of people aged under 75 who were retired in 2001 in the UK was 5.8 million, 9.8% of the population as compared to 8.0% in 1991 (4.6 million people then). This rise occurred despite a fall in the proportion of the population aged 60-74 (see Chapter 2, footnote 19). The cohort aged around 60 did grow in size over the decade, thus the overall rise in young retirees is not yet due to demographic shifts. Retirement is becoming more common at younger ages than ever seen before. Part of this rise is voluntary. Many affluent people can afford now to retire in their fifties. Another part is forced, people having to retire because they cannot find work. A great deal of the reason for many people may lie somewhere in between these extremes.

The geography of early retirees is inevitably very similar to that of old age, with a tendency for clustering around the coasts[17]. However, it is notable that early retirement (and remaining where you are once you retire) is as rare in the more rural parts of Northern Ireland as it is in London, but for very different reasons. There are also three very distinct contiguous clusters of districts where early retirement has become far less common, as is clear from the cartogram of change, but almost invisible on the map for two of these clusters[18]. It is early retirees leaving the capital quicker which creates one cluster; young people coming into Manchester which creates another; and a mixture of demographic, economic and social changes in the Province that has led to the third clear area of reduction in this population.

Retired 2001 (%)

- 5 - 7
- 8 - 9
- 10 - 11
- 12 - 13
- 14 - 17

Retired change (%)

- −17 - −1
- 0 - 1
- 2
- 3
- 4 - 5

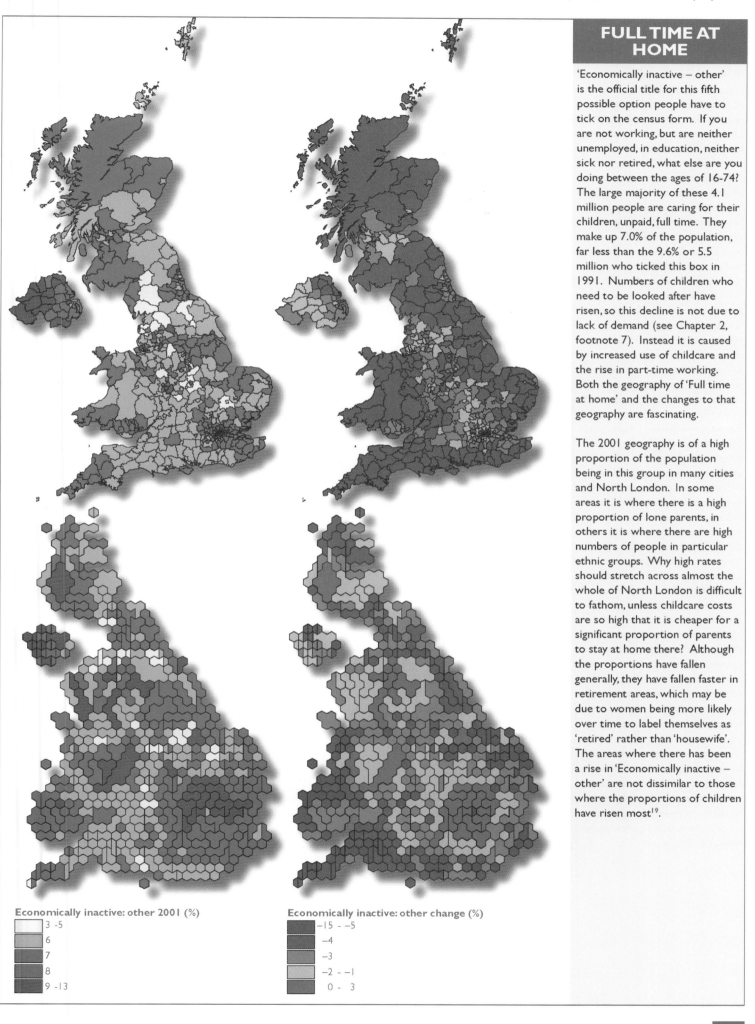

FULL TIME AT HOME

'Economically inactive – other' is the official title for this fifth possible option people have to tick on the census form. If you are not working, but are neither unemployed, in education, neither sick nor retired, what else are you doing between the ages of 16-74? The large majority of these 4.1 million people are caring for their children, unpaid, full time. They make up 7.0% of the population, far less than the 9.6% or 5.5 million who ticked this box in 1991. Numbers of children who need to be looked after have risen, so this decline is not due to lack of demand (see Chapter 2, footnote 7). Instead it is caused by increased use of childcare and the rise in part-time working. Both the geography of 'Full time at home' and the changes to that geography are fascinating.

The 2001 geography is of a high proportion of the population being in this group in many cities and North London. In some areas it is where there is a high proportion of lone parents, in others it is where there are high numbers of people in particular ethnic groups. Why high rates should stretch across almost the whole of North London is difficult to fathom, unless childcare costs are so high that it is cheaper for a significant proportion of parents to stay at home there? Although the proportions have fallen generally, they have fallen faster in retirement areas, which may be due to women being more likely over time to label themselves as 'retired' rather than 'housewife'. The areas where there has been a rise in 'Economically inactive – other' are not dissimilar to those where the proportions of children have risen most[19].

Economically inactive: other 2001 (%)

- 3 -5
- 6
- 7
- 8
- 9 -13

Economically inactive: other change (%)

- −15 - −5
- −4
- −3
- −2 - −1
- 0 - 3

WORKING PART-TIME

People who are in work are grouped together by the census as being 'Economically active', and are classed as either part time employees, working 30 hours or less a week, full time employees or self-employed. Five million people were in part-time employment in the UK in 2001, 8.4% of the population, up from 4.4 million in 1991 or 7.7% of all people in the UK then. A large part of the decline in people being 'Full time at home' is due to this rise in part-time employment.

Part-time employment is most common away from the city centres in areas where there are many people in late middle age, where there are more elderly people who need carers (many of whom are employed part-time), in more rural areas and particularly in places where local industries tend to favour part-time work[20]. It is least common and falling in popularity in London. In Northern Ireland part-time employment is still rare but has increased as early retirement has decreased. Elsewhere part-time employment is on the rise most where the population is ageing the most. A combination of needing to be at home to care for an ageing population, and the employment of more part-time workers to provide this care, may be part of the reason why the rises seen in the cartogram of change look quite similar to areas where the very elderly population has grown most (see Chapter 2, footnote 21), as well as being similar to many other changes occurring to the population structure of the UK and its distribution across space. The geography of part-time employment is becoming more distinct partly as the nation divides more by age.

Part-time 2001 (%)

- 4 - 6
- 7
- 8
- 9
- 10 - 11

Part-time change (%)

- −1.4 - −0.1
- 0.0 - 0.4
- 0.5 - 0.9
- 1.0 - 1.4
- 1.5 - 2.6

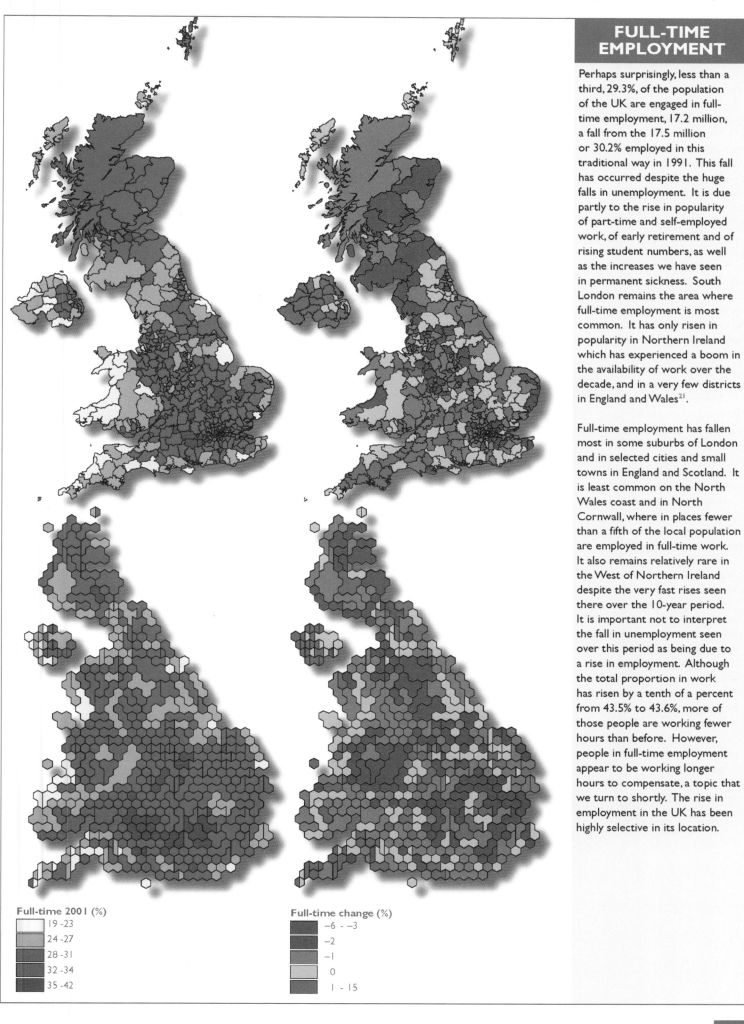

FULL-TIME EMPLOYMENT

Perhaps surprisingly, less than a third, 29.3%, of the population of the UK are engaged in full-time employment, 17.2 million, a fall from the 17.5 million or 30.2% employed in this traditional way in 1991. This fall has occurred despite the huge falls in unemployment. It is due partly to the rise in popularity of part-time and self-employed work, of early retirement and of rising student numbers, as well as the increases we have seen in permanent sickness. South London remains the area where full-time employment is most common. It has only risen in popularity in Northern Ireland which has experienced a boom in the availability of work over the decade, and in a very few districts in England and Wales[21].

Full-time employment has fallen most in some suburbs of London and in selected cities and small towns in England and Scotland. It is least common on the North Wales coast and in North Cornwall, where in places fewer than a fifth of the local population are employed in full-time work. It also remains relatively rare in the West of Northern Ireland despite the very fast rises seen there over the 10-year period. It is important not to interpret the fall in unemployment seen over this period as being due to a rise in employment. Although the total proportion in work has risen by a tenth of a percent from 43.5% to 43.6%, more of those people are working fewer hours than before. However, people in full-time employment appear to be working longer hours to compensate, a topic that we turn to shortly. The rise in employment in the UK has been highly selective in its location.

Full-time 2001 (%)
- 19 -23
- 24 -27
- 28 -31
- 32 -34
- 35 -42

Full-time change (%)
- −6 - −3
- −2
- −1
- 0
- 1 - 15

SELF-EMPLOYED

The eighth and last category into which people aged 16-74 are placed under the label of employment status is self-employment. Self-employment can range from people working from home alone, to those running small businesses, to those compelled to employ themselves on low-paid contracts to free their employers from the obligations that they should have. Self-employment accounts for 5.9% of the UK population, up from 5.6% in 1991 (3.5 million people as compared to 3.2 million in 1991). This rise has occurred despite widespread falls in people working in this way in Wales, the South West, East Anglia and in much of Lancashire. Changes in rural employment patterns may be part of the reason in many of these areas of decline (most farmers are self-employed).

Self-employment has risen most in Northern Ireland as part of the general rise in employment there, and around the Scottish border. It has also risen for very different reasons within central London and in particular London suburbs. In some parts of London there are as many people working for themselves as in the most remote parts of, say, North Yorkshire. These rises reflect the advent of both new industries in which self-employment is the norm, and new business practices in which people are employed on a consultative basis, having to cover their own possible sickness, maternity and retirement costs, but perhaps receiving higher pay while they are young, fit and childless. The geography of self-employment is changing quickly too[22], switching from rural to urban occupations.

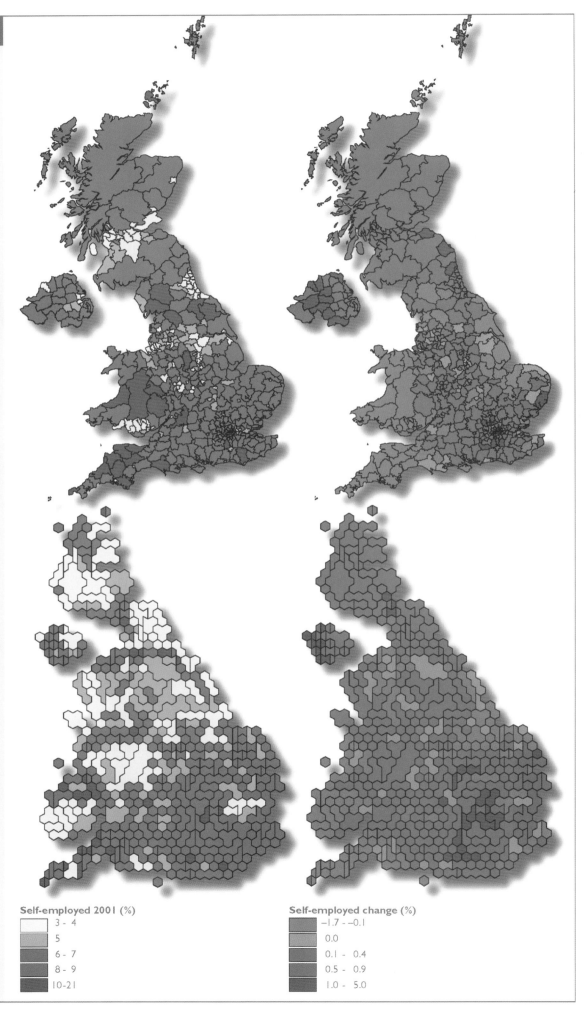

Self-employed 2001 (%)

- 3 - 4
- 5
- 6 - 7
- 8 - 9
- 10-21

Self-employed change (%)

- −1.7 - −0.1
- 0.0
- 0.1 - 0.4
- 0.5 - 0.9
- 1.0 - 5.0

NOT WORKING ANY HOURS

The majority of the population are not in work. Here, unlike in the previous eight pages, we have included people aged under 16 and over 74 to illustrate this. Another change we have made here is to include students who also work as being in work. If we had not included students working, the overall change would be seen as static[23]. Instead, in 1991, 34.0 million people were not working any hours in paid employment; by 2001 that number had fallen to 32.3 million. This is a decline from 58.8% of the population to 54.8%. People are most likely not to be in work in a few parts of East London, much of Wales, and in urban centres from the Midlands northwards. The highest proportions are of between 64% and 66% of the population working no hours a week in Newham, Liverpool, Easington, Blaenau Gwent, Merthyr Tydfil, Derry and Strabane. The lowest proportions are of only between 40% and 46% of the population working no hours in the City of London, Wandsworth, Bracknell Forest, Wokingham, Isles of Scilly, Basingstoke & Deane, Hart and Rushmoor.

The proportion of people working no hours has fallen most in Northern Ireland, London and in two of the island districts of Scotland. It has risen only in Barrow-in-Furness, Oadby & Wigston (see Chapter 3, text above, footnote 6), Rutland and Stoke-on-Trent. When everyone who works at least one hour a week is classed as employed, employment has risen everywhere. But only in a few places is paid work done by a majority of the local population.

Not in work 2001 (%)

	40 - 49
	50 - 53
	54 - 56
	57 - 59
	60 - 66

Not in work change (%)

	−13 - −7
	−6 - −5
	−4
	−3 - −1
	0 - 1

WORKING UNDER 16 HOURS

A total of 2.2 million people work between 1-15 hours a week, up from 1.9 million in 1991, a rise of 0.5% on 3.2% of the population then living in the UK and working these hours. Working this low number of hours does not bring in a great deal of money. That may be one of the major reasons why such work is concentrated in the more affluent parts of the UK[24]. It could be the partners of well-paid people in full-time employment being engaged in a few hours work a week. More likely it is the cleaners and gardeners who they are employing who help contribute towards this pattern. In addition, in these places, where there is a shortage of labour, shops may be disproportionately staffed by older teenagers at weekends, and cafes may rely on a series of people to staff them rather than on a smaller number of people working longer hours. There are also large numbers of people nearing retirement or who are just over retirement age in these places who may be working only a few hours a week. There are many possibilities to explain this pattern.

The possible reasons for the changes seen in the geography of people working only a few hours a week are more difficult to speculate over. The general rise in the South of England in the proportion of people working these hours may reflect the higher demand for labour there as opposed to the North, or the cost of living there forcing more young mothers now to work. Where such part-time employment has fallen most in the North, it may have been in places where much part-time work has been replaced by an increase in more full-time employment, as the maps on the next two pages suggest.

15 hours or fewer 2001 (%)
- 1.9 - 2.6
- 2.7 - 3.2
- 3.3 - 3.9
- 4.0 - 4.5
- 4.6 - 5.3

15 hours or fewer change (%)
- −0.7 - −0.1
- 0.0 - 0.2
- 0.3 - 0.5
- 0.6 - 0.9
- 1.0 - 1.4

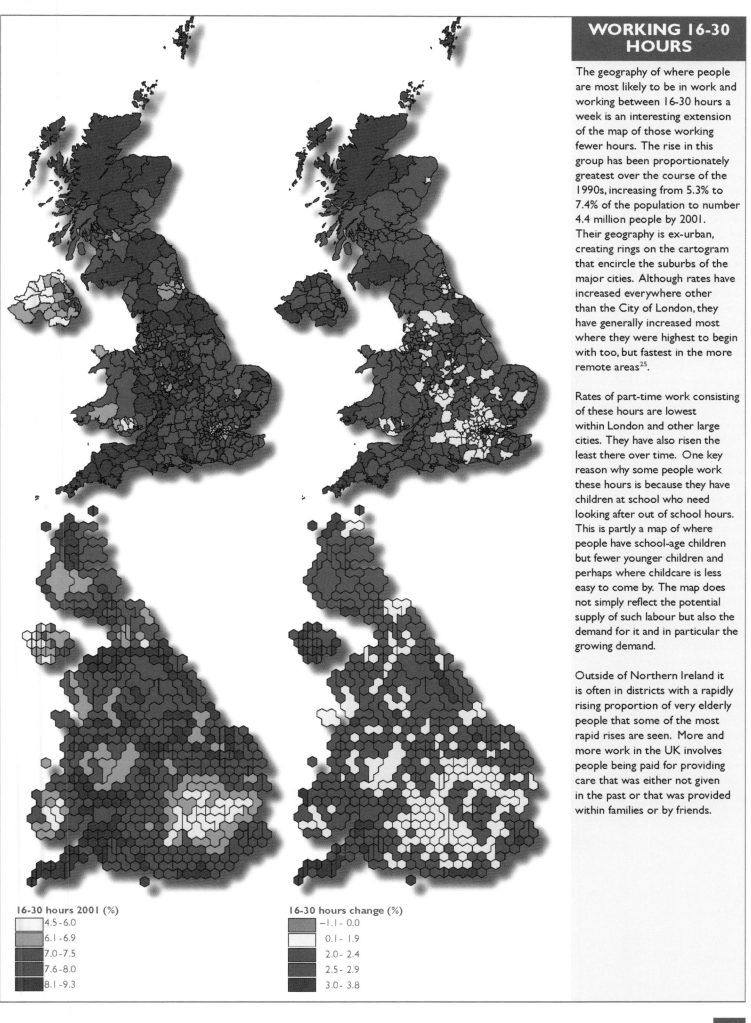

WORKING 16-30 HOURS

The geography of where people are most likely to be in work and working between 16-30 hours a week is an interesting extension of the map of those working fewer hours. The rise in this group has been proportionately greatest over the course of the 1990s, increasing from 5.3% to 7.4% of the population to number 4.4 million people by 2001. Their geography is ex-urban, creating rings on the cartogram that encircle the suburbs of the major cities. Although rates have increased everywhere other than the City of London, they have generally increased most where they were highest to begin with too, but fastest in the more remote areas[25].

Rates of part-time work consisting of these hours are lowest within London and other large cities. They have also risen the least there over time. One key reason why some people work these hours is because they have children at school who need looking after out of school hours. This is partly a map of where people have school-age children but fewer younger children and perhaps where childcare is less easy to come by. The map does not simply reflect the potential supply of such labour but also the demand for it and in particular the growing demand.

Outside of Northern Ireland it is often in districts with a rapidly rising proportion of very elderly people that some of the most rapid rises are seen. More and more work in the UK involves people being paid for providing care that was either not given in the past or that was provided within families or by friends.

16-30 hours 2001 (%)

	4.5 - 6.0
	6.1 - 6.9
	7.0 - 7.5
	7.6 - 8.0
	8.1 - 9.3

16-30 hours change (%)

	-1.1 - 0.0
	0.1 - 1.9
	2.0 - 2.4
	2.5 - 2.9
	3.0 - 3.8

WORKING OVER 30 HOURS

The majority of people in full-time employment work between 35-40 hours a week. Because the last two censuses tabulated the number of hours people worked using different categories, the only group we can consistently compare over time working a relatively high number of hours in paid employment are those employed for 31 or more hours per week. They numbered 20 million people in 2001, 34.1% of the population as compared to 18.9 million, or 32.7% of the population in 1991. Thus while the proportions working full-time shown previously have fallen, the proportions of the population working these hours has risen. There has thus been a disproportionate rise in the number of people working in two part-time jobs a week, and some students, not actually classified as employed, also do 31 hours or more paid hours a week to get by (see footnote 23).

Working longer hours is most closely associated with living in London or in some of the commuter towns that surround the capital. People may have included their commuting time as work[26]. In contrast, relatively few people in parts of West and South Wales can secure employment for so many hours a week. Only 26% of people in Liverpool, 27% of the people of Manchester and 28.5% of Glasgow's population secure more than 30 hours of paid employment a week. In parts of the South (where we speculate that more people may have to hold down two jobs now), many will resent the hours they have to work, while in the North finding one full-time job is still often difficult.

31+ hours 2001 (%)
- 25 - 29
- 30 - 33
- 34 - 36
- 37 - 40
- 41 - 53

31+ hours change (%)
- −3.5 - −0.1
- 0.0 - 1.0
- 1.1 - 2.3
- 2.4 - 4.6
- 4.7 - 9.7

NOTES

[1] More than 30% of the people of the following areas have no qualifications: Knowsley, Sandwell, Walsall, Easington, Stoke-on-Trent, Blaenau Gwent, Merthyr Tydfil, East Ayrshire, Glasgow City, Armagh, Ballymena, Ballymoney, Cookstown, Craigavon, Derry, Dungannon, Fermanagh, Larne, Limavady, Magherafelt, Moyle, Newry & Mourne and Strabane. In contrast, less than 15% of people in these areas have none: City of London, Barnet, Camden, Hammersmith & Fulham, Kensington & Chelsea, Kingston upon Thames, Merton, Richmond upon Thames, Wandsworth, Westminster, Bracknell Forest, Windsor & Maidenhead, Wokingham, Chiltern, South Bucks, Cambridge, South Cambridgeshire, Isles of Scilly, East Hampshire, Hart, Winchester, St Albans, Rushcliffe, Oxford, South Oxfordshire, Elmbridge, Epsom & Ewell, Guildford, Mole Valley, Reigate & Banstead, Surrey Heath, Tandridge, Waverley, Woking, Horsham and Mid Sussex.

[2] Level one qualifications also include standard grades in Scotland, City & Guilds craft qualifications and many similar vocational and academic equivalents.

[3] Or higher grades in Scotland, City & Guilds advanced craft qualifications, RSA advanced diploma, SVQ level 3, CSYS, ONC or OND qualifications.

[4] The first cartogram above shows an almost unbroken swath of districts where more than 15% of the population hold these basic qualifications as their highest qualifications. The swath encircles London within which the population tends to be even better qualified as the second cartogram suggests. It includes most of the South West and stretches up through Mid and North Wales into Cheshire, where it becomes broken up as it generally avoids the metropolitan boroughs of the North, while still stretching up to the Scottish border and across North Yorkshire to the North Sea. These are the places where a high proportion of people have average and just above average qualifications. Elsewhere the population is generally either very highly qualified or holds very few qualifications.

[5] And similar qualifications such as RSA Higher Diploma, or SVQ level 4 or 5.

[6] Part of the reason that fewer children and older people live in London than elsewhere in Britain is because of the demand for people with high qualifications in the capital. These people tend to have children later, and many leave London when they do have children. London is an expensive place to live with a family, as it is for older people, property prices being a major component of the expense. Property prices are higher partly because people with higher qualifications are paid more and thus can afford to pay more for their housing. Thus, although low numbers of children and older people are part of the reason why levels of qualifications are so high in the capital, the demand for high qualifications are a large part of the reason for the capital's unique demographic make-up.

[7] By comparing the map and cartogram of people holding university degrees above, with that of the highest qualifications shown on the previous page, it is possible to see what influence our choice of categories to use for shading in areas has had on these figures. In general the influence is minimal when the underlying patterns are as clear as those being studied here.

[8] Although Westminster stands out as having the second highest increase in its proportion of graduates, it is hardly out of line with neighbouring boroughs encircling the City of London, as the cartogram of change above shows. If the local council had simply let market forces play out rather than have sold homes for votes, the results might have been little different.

[9] In 1991 more than 10% of the entire population of the following eight districts ticked that they were unemployed and seeking work: Hackney (which had the highest rate of unemployment in both 1991 and 2001), Haringey, Lambeth, Southwark, Tower Hamlets, Knowsley, Liverpool and Glasgow City. In 2001 there was no district in which even 5% of the population ticked the boxes to indicate that they were unemployed. It is true that you had to tick more boxes in a more complicated pattern if you wished to indicate that you were unemployed in 2001; it is also true that many more people were 'encouraged' to take low-paid work or sickness benefits in the 1990s. However, even taking these factors into account, the fall in unemployment is staggering over the course of the decade.

[10] Nationally youth unemployment as a proportion of the total population fell by 65% between 1991 and 2001 (from 1.85% to 0.65%). In the 10 local authorities where it fell the most, by 75% or more, all but three had rates near or less than 1% in 1991. They include some very affluent areas and are all in the South of England: Cambridge, Isles of Scilly, Exeter, Brighton & Hove, Cotswold, Portsmouth, Winchester, Oxford, Runnymede and Waverley. Conversely, none of the 10 areas where youth unemployment fell by less than 50% are in the South. The areas that have benefited least from the fall are: Carlisle, Pendle, Rossendale, Corby, Berwick-upon-Tweed, Redditch, Aberdeen City, Aberdeenshire, Derry and North Down.

[11] Across the UK as a whole, unemployment rates at these ages as a proportion of the total population fell by 47% between 1991 (from 2.95%) and 2001 (to 1.58%). In Britain the five highest declines, all of over 60%, were in the City of London, Plymouth, Eastleigh, Southampton and Test Valley. Five similar sized falls were recorded in areas of Northern Ireland, which all had rates of over 4% of the total population in 1991: Ballymoney, Cookstown, Dungannon, Magherafelt and Newry & Mourne. Rates fell by less than 20% in seven areas, all of which had initial rates of less than 3%: Isles of Scilly (from only 13 people to only 12), Copeland, South Lakeland, Ryedale, Waveney, Aberdeenshire and the Orkney Islands. Thus at these ages self-declared unemployment became less spatially concentrated over time.

[12] Rates of unemployment in old age did not fall in only three areas, South Lakeland, Melton and Torridge, but in all three of these areas they were near the national average at both points in time. They fell most where they were highest to begin with. An additional 1% of the entire population of Tower Hamlets was unemployed aged 55+ in 1991 as compared to 2001. Of all local authorities in the UK, Tower Hamlets experienced the largest relative fall in its old age unemployment rate, of 77%, as well as the largest absolute fall. The elderly population of Tower Hamlets was declining at the same time, which contributed to this decrease, but the same cannot be said of other areas of the UK which also experienced the most rapid falls in the North West, in metropolitan boroughs, in Glasgow and in much of Northern Ireland.

[13] Over half a percent (25,803 people) of the population (3.9 million) of the following districts have never found work and are unemployed: Brent, Greenwich, Hackney, Haringey, Islington, Lambeth, Lewisham, Newham, Southwark, Tower Hamlets, Knowsley, Liverpool, Birmingham, Middlesbrough, Glasgow, Belfast, Derry, Omagh and Strabane. In contrast, less than 0.02% of the populations of the following areas are in the same situation: South Cambridgeshire, Isles of Scilly, Cotswold, Hart, Test Valley, Waverley and Horsham. In the districts shaded the lightest category in the 2001 cartogram above, where nearer to 0 than to 0.1% of the population have never worked, their numbers total only 1,259 out of a population of 2.9 million.

[14] More the a tenth of the populations of the following areas were students in 2001: Camden, Manchester, Newcastle upon Tyne, Cambridge, Exeter, Durham, Southampton, Nottingham, Oxford and Ceredigion (containing Aberystwyth University).

[15] The proportion of the local populations of these areas who are students rose by 5% or more in the 1990s: Newham, Southwark, Manchester, Cambridge, Exeter, Durham, Southampton, Lancaster, Charnwood, Nottingham, Runnymede, Cardiff and Ceredigion.

[16] Other than in Barrow-in-Furness, rates have risen most in Northern Ireland. The two areas with the highest proportions of their populations being unable to work due to permanent sickness or disability are Merthyr Tydfil (11.3%) and Easington (11.7%), both areas that were mainly reliant on coal mining in the past. Former mining areas that have not seen many new industries emerge stand out clearly on the map of the situation in 2001, but are not the places that have seen the bulk of the increase in sickness over time. In huge contrast to those parts of the UK where such illness is common, permanent illness is very rare in the Home Counties and is at its minimum, at less than 1.5% of the population in Wokingham, Isles of Scilly, Hart, Elmbridge and Surrey Heath.

[17] However, the greatest increases in the proportion of the local population who are retired before the age of 75 have not all occurred on the coast. The proportion has increased by at least an additional 4.5 people per hundred in the following areas, all of which now have more than a tenth of their populations being retired young: Chiltern, West Devon, West Dorset, North Norfolk, Alnwick, Berwick-upon-Tweed, Castle Morpeth, Hambleton, Ryedale, Suffolk Coastal, Chichester and Argyll & Bute.

[18] The largest fall has been in the City of London (–17%), but that is only due to a decrease of a few hundred people in this category. After the City the largest falls range from between –6.5% (Belfast), to –2.1% (Lisburn), all being in Northern Ireland. The falls in London are all lower still and that in Manchester is of only –0.9%.

[19] The proportion of the local population 'Full time at home' has increased by at least half a percentage point in Camden, Hackney, Hammersmith & Fulham, Haringey, Islington, Newham, Tower Hamlets, Oldham, Blackburn with Darwen, Burnley, Pendle and Leicester. The proportion has fallen most both in traditional retirement areas and in areas where the proportion of young children has fallen or where the proportion of young adults without children has risen greatly; hence it is now lowest in the following 10 areas: Cambridge, Isles of Scilly, South Lakeland, Ribble Valley, South Ribble, Blaby, Oadby & Wigston, Craven, York and Warwick.

[20] Over a tenth of the population are in employment on a part-time basis in the following areas: Barrow-in-Furness, Carlisle, Derbyshire Dales, North East Derbyshire, Purbeck, Weymouth & Portland, Gloucester, South Gloucestershire, Eastleigh, Blaby, Boston, North East Lincolnshire, Broadland, Berwick-upon-Tweed, Selby, York, Shrewsbury & Atcham, Taunton Deane, South Staffordshire, Ipswich, St Edmundsbury, Isle of Wight and the Shetland Islands.

[21] In Britain full-time employment has risen by one percent or more of the population only in: the City of London, Lambeth, Wandsworth, Sunderland, Milton Keynes, East Cambridgeshire, Caradon, Restormel, Isles of Scilly, Torbay, West Devon, North Dorset, Derwentside, North West Leicestershire, South Northamptonshire, Wansbeck, Bridgnorth, Oswestry, Tamworth, Caerphilly and Denbighshire.

[22] Five of the ten quickest increases in self-employment have been in or near London and five in Northern Ireland: City of London, Hackney, Islington, Richmond upon Thames, St Albans, Limavady, Magherafelt, Moyle, Newry & Mourne and Omagh. Rates remain highest in rural, resort and retirement areas, but are also falling fastest there. The 10 areas that have experienced the greatest declines in self-employment over the decades are: North Cornwall, Restormel, Torbay, Torridge, North Dorset, Blackpool, South Holland, Oswestry, Carmarthenshire and Ceredigion.

[23] We have done this so that the maps shown here are consistent with the next set of three which show the proportions of people working particular numbers of hours a week. Many students work as well as study (including many 16- and 17-year-olds who have Saturday jobs). If we had excluded everyone whose main employment status was not working, then our overall figures for change would have been as follows: in 1991 32.7 million people were mainly not in work, by 2001 that number had risen to 33.2 million. This is actually a slight decline from 56.5% of the population to 56.4%, but given that the population is ageing, it implies that slightly fewer people of working age are now working in the UK despite the good economic position of 2001 as compared to 1991. However, the large numbers of students who work, and other factors, means that roughly a million more people are working some hours than are counted as mainly being employed in the UK in 2001.

[24] Over 5% of the populations of the following, generally well-to-do, areas work less than 16 hours a week, all in the South of England: Chiltern, Eden, East Dorset, Wealden, Uttlesford, Hart, New Forest, Winchester, Bath and North East Somerset, Mid Suffolk, Suffolk Coastal and Waverley. Conversely the lowest rate to be found in Britain is of only 2.1% of the population of Tower Hamlets working these hours.

[25] An additional 3% or more of the population is now working these hours of employment in: Doncaster (the only metropolitan borough in this list), Halton, Carrick, Kerrier, North Cornwall, Penwith, Restormel, the Isles of Scilly, Plymouth, South Hams, Torridge, West Dorset, Brighton & Hove, Shepway, Lincoln, Scarborough, North Somerset, Isle of Wight, Eilean Siar, Highland, Orkney Islands, Shetland Islands, Ards, Banbridge, Coleraine, Fermanagh, Limavady, Newry & Mourne and in North Down.

[26] More than 50% of the population of the City of London claim to work at least 31 hours a week. At the extreme elsewhere between 40% and 50% of the population make this claim in 2001, almost all in or around the capital living in: Hammersmith & Fulham, Lambeth, Merton, Richmond upon Thames, Wandsworth, Westminster, Mid Bedfordshire, Bracknell Forest, Reading, Slough, West Berkshire, Wokingham, Aylesbury Vale, Milton Keynes, Huntingdonshire, South Cambridgeshire, Isles of Scilly (hotels), Basingstoke & Deane, Hart, Rushmoor, East Hertfordshire, Watford, South Northamptonshire, Cherwell, Forest Heath, Spelthorne, Surrey Heath, Crawley and Swindon.

Occupation and industry

6

Maps in this section include:

Managers (p 107)	Professionals (p 108)	Associate professionals (p 109)	Administrative and secretarial (p 110)	Sales and customer services (p 111)	Personal services (p 112)
Skilled trades (p 113)	Machine operatives (p 114)	Elementary occupations (p 115)	Mining and quarrying (p 116)	Energy and water (p 117)	Agriculture, forestry and fishing (p 118)
Construction (p 119)	Transport (p 120)	Manufacturing (p 121)	Banking and finance (p 122)	Distribution and catering (p 123)	Other services (p 124)

For most people in the UK it is their job or their partner's or parents' jobs that largely determines their income, wealth and lifestyle. It is their friends and geographical neighbours' jobs that determine the costs of living in their localities and the amenities available to them there; and it is the industries that provide these jobs that most govern their location and fortunes.

The geography to which types of employment people are most occupied in has changed rapidly in the 1990s. This has been determined by and helps determine the changing geographical demography of the country – the patterns to people's ethnic and birthplace origins, their educational qualifications and their activities other than work.

Occupation and industry are also key to many of the patterns shown in the final two chapters of the atlas that follow this chapter, to the differences seen between families and households and in the provision of material goods such as cars and homes. Work now matters more in the UK than ever before. More people are engaged in paid work than at any time in the past. The kind of pay they get depends on the kind of work they do, and that too increasingly depends on where they live or have moved to.

There has been no increase in the overall numbers of people who manage others. A decline in management in small-scale farming has cancelled out a rise in the numbers of corporate managers in the UK, centred, as you may be able to guess, in the gentrifying core of inner London.

In contrast, the rise in university students largely accounts for an increase of almost a million in the numbers of people working in jobs now labelled as 'professional'. Again, growth has been strongest in London. The same is true for the great acceleration in the numbers of associate professionals, now up more than a million-and-a-half

on the count of a decade ago. In contrast, the numbers of people that these groups used to rely on the most, administrative and secretarial staff, fell during the 1990s, most strongly in a ring of districts surrounding the Capital. More of the bosses now type their own memos and do their own filing. Thus the status of these high status jobs may not be quite as high as it once was, although the people who are in these positions may be a little more efficient than before, able at least to type for themselves.

The second greatest growth in work following that in the professions and corporate management has been in jobs that cater to consumption and the movement, sale and provision of routine services and goods. Over a million more people work in elementary occupations – cleaning, washing up, stacking shelves and serving others – at a basic level than a decade ago. Almost half a million more now work in sales and customer services. Many of these people have to commute further to provide these services than was the case in 1991. They have been priced out of the most expensive areas where demand for their labour is highest. Others are providing their services at a distance, through call centres and mail order provision.

In contrast, fewer people are working in personal services, although they are growing still in areas with rapidly rising numbers of older people requiring care. Part of the reason for the decline in this sector of occupations is that it included many of the military in the past whose jobs may now be labelled by the authorities as associate professional and technical, rather than providing a more personal service. Other people working in this sector may now be doing much the same work as 10 years ago, but may have a slightly more upmarket sounding job title and hence have also joined the ranks of the associate professionals.

The occupations that have certainly declined (not due to any re-labelling) have been those working in skilled trades, down half a million in 10 years, almost exclusively in the North. Similarly, the numbers of machine operatives have fallen, also mostly in the North. Fewer people are employed in occupations that involve making something, growing it, or mining it. More are working in selling things, providing services to each other, caring for others (associate professionals), advising others (professionals) or managing others. We now talk more, write more and do less.

The underlying reason why our work has changed in the way that it has is that the demand for various types of work has risen and declined as the demand for various products has changed over time. The changing geography to industries in the UK demonstrates this most clearly. We no longer produce what we consume, but we put much more effort into consumption, into moving goods and people around, but most importantly, into moving money around, especially other people's and other countries' money.

The greatest relative decline of any industry has been the disappearance of what little was left of mining in the UK by 1991. Next, the numbers of people employed to produce our energy and treat our water has more than halved in the decade. We consume more but require fewer people to produce what we consume. Agriculture, forestry and fishing has also declined but, as with the construction industries, only slightly. In contrast, manufacturing has continued its long decline unabated, employing half a million fewer people in 2001 than it did at the low of 1991, with the bulk of the losses being in Northern and Midland towns.

On the growth side more people now work in transport than before, especially near the largest airports. Three quarters of a million more people are working in distribution and catering than before, selling goods and serving food to others. A similar additional number are employed in the 'other service' category that is largely the state sectors of health, education and government. However, the largest rise of all has been of an additional 1.7 million people being employed in banking and finance during the course of the 1990s. This huge growth in a single industry has been strongest where it was already best established, in London.

Almost five million people work in the financial industries selling products to the remaining 58.8 million of us, looking after our money and checking that we make our mortgage payments or encouraging us into further debt. A further 5.7 million work in shops and cafes, selling goods and serving food. Almost 8 million people provide other, mainly state, services; almost 2 million more move us and our goods around the country. These 20 million people represent the large majority of the workforce and all the workforce of the sectors that are growing.

How is the UK becoming wealthier when we are producing less and consuming more? A small part of the reasons for this is that we cater, sell to and move around more international visitors than we did before, bringing more money in from overseas. The bulk of the reason is that our banking sector extracts huge and rising profits from its overseas operations; these are the profits that run London. We see these ripple out through the Home Counties, and their huge volume casts a shadow across the rest of the nation. Thus, it should not be so surprising to find services growing around the London airports, and millions of people entering one of the last sectors through which the UK can make money out of the rest of the world. The growth is simply so fast because there is so little else that is growing. If it were not for banking and its associated financial services, there would be little economic need for the UK in the 21st century.

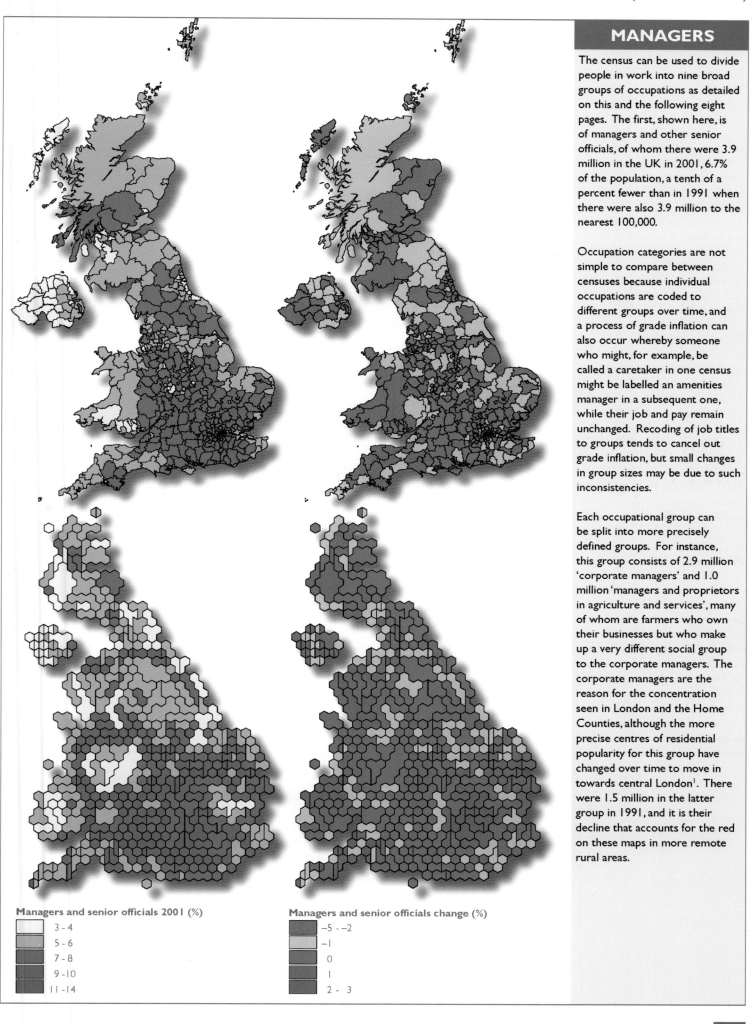

MANAGERS

The census can be used to divide people in work into nine broad groups of occupations as detailed on this and the following eight pages. The first, shown here, is of managers and other senior officials, of whom there were 3.9 million in the UK in 2001, 6.7% of the population, a tenth of a percent fewer than in 1991 when there were also 3.9 million to the nearest 100,000.

Occupation categories are not simple to compare between censuses because individual occupations are coded to different groups over time, and a process of grade inflation can also occur whereby someone who might, for example, be called a caretaker in one census might be labelled an amenities manager in a subsequent one, while their job and pay remain unchanged. Recoding of job titles to groups tends to cancel out grade inflation, but small changes in group sizes may be due to such inconsistencies.

Each occupational group can be split into more precisely defined groups. For instance, this group consists of 2.9 million 'corporate managers' and 1.0 million 'managers and proprietors in agriculture and services', many of whom are farmers who own their businesses but who make up a very different social group to the corporate managers. The corporate managers are the reason for the concentration seen in London and the Home Counties, although the more precise centres of residential popularity for this group have changed over time to move in towards central London[1]. There were 1.5 million in the latter group in 1991, and it is their decline that accounts for the red on these maps in more remote rural areas.

Managers and senior officials 2001 (%)

- 3 - 4
- 5 - 6
- 7 - 8
- 9 -10
- 11 -14

Managers and senior officials change (%)

- −5 - −2
- −1
- 0
- 1
- 2 - 3

PROFESSIONALS

In the UK in 2001 3 million people worked in professional occupations, 5.0% of the population as compared to 3.7% or 2.1 million people in 1991. This group can be split into four sub-groups of 0.8 million 'science and technology' professionals, 0.2 million 'health' professionals, 1.2 million 'teaching and research' professionals and 0.7 million 'business and public service' professionals. The number for health is so low because most nurses are labelled as associate professionals by the census authorities (see next page for their distribution).

There is nowhere where professionals have fallen in number, and, again, like managers, they are concentrated towards London and becoming more concentrated within the centre of the Capital. However, that is only partly due to the clustering of business people there[2]. Science and technology professionals moved nearer to the Capital over the decade, and the health sector employs many people in London.

It is in many of the cities of the North, Scotland, Wales and in a ring of districts further out from the Home Counties that the proportions of professionals are not rising as much as they are increasing across the country as a whole. Although the peripheral areas are not seeing falls, as is the case for managers, the country is becoming increasingly split by what occupations people living in particular places are most likely to be doing, and their consequent pay, conditions and lifestyles.

Professional occupations 2001 (%)
- 2 - 3
- 4 - 5
- 6 - 7
- 8 - 9
- 10 - 19

Professional occupations change (%)
- 0.1 - 0.9
- 1.0 - 1.4
- 1.5 - 1.9
- 2.0 - 3.0
- 3.1 - 6.4

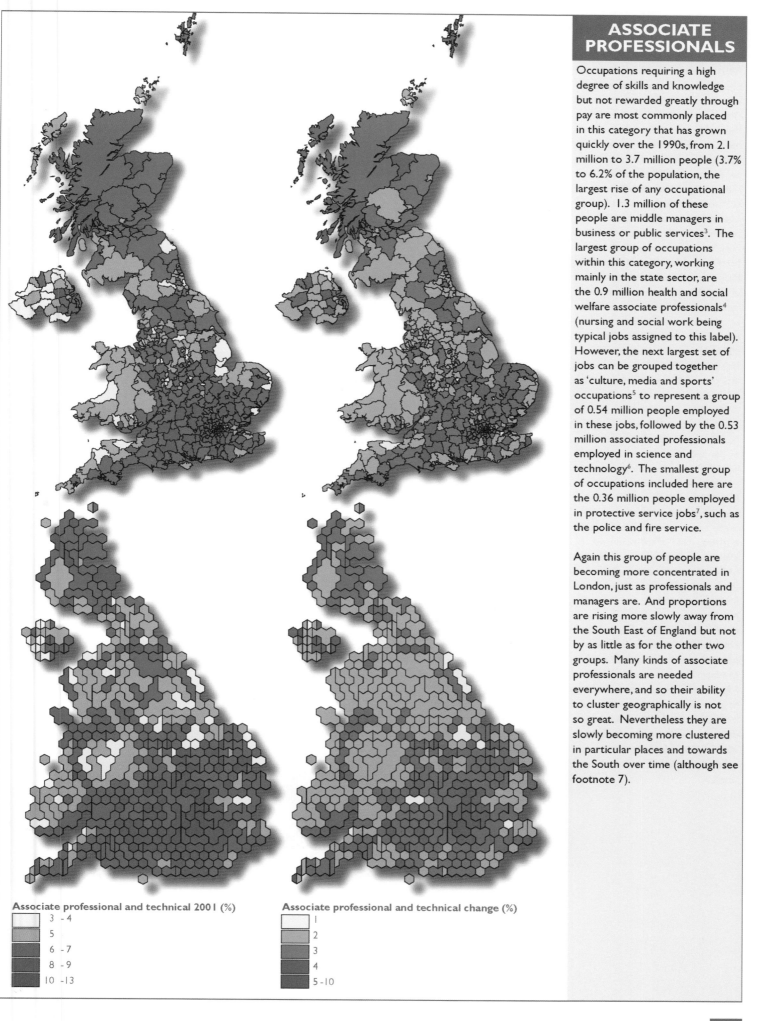

ASSOCIATE PROFESSIONALS

Occupations requiring a high degree of skills and knowledge but not rewarded greatly through pay are most commonly placed in this category that has grown quickly over the 1990s, from 2.1 million to 3.7 million people (3.7% to 6.2% of the population, the largest rise of any occupational group). 1.3 million of these people are middle managers in business or public services[3]. The largest group of occupations within this category, working mainly in the state sector, are the 0.9 million health and social welfare associate professionals[4] (nursing and social work being typical jobs assigned to this label). However, the next largest set of jobs can be grouped together as 'culture, media and sports' occupations[5] to represent a group of 0.54 million people employed in these jobs, followed by the 0.53 million associated professionals employed in science and technology[6]. The smallest group of occupations included here are the 0.36 million people employed in protective service jobs[7], such as the police and fire service.

Again this group of people are becoming more concentrated in London, just as professionals and managers are. And proportions are rising more slowly away from the South East of England but not by as little as for the other two groups. Many kinds of associate professionals are needed everywhere, and so their ability to cluster geographically is not so great. Nevertheless they are slowly becoming more clustered in particular places and towards the South over time (although see footnote 7).

Associate professional and technical 2001 (%)

	3 - 4
	5
	6 - 7
	8 - 9
	10 - 13

Associate professional and technical change (%)

	1
	2
	3
	4
	5 - 10

ADMINISTRATIVE AND SECRETARIAL

Next come administrative and secretarial staff. These are people whose job titles do not elevate them to one of the previous three categories. There are now fewer people in these posts (3.5 million) than there are associate professionals, a fall from 3.9 million in 1991, or of 0.8%, to 6.0% of the population. Part of that fall may be due to the renaming of job titles over time, but the distinct geographical patterns to the changes suggest that most of this change is real. In particular the number of secretaries fell from 1.1 million to 0.9 million, and administrators from 2.7 million to 2.6 million by 2001. There may simply be both less demand for these jobs and less people, mainly women, willing to do them.

South East London remains the home of the highest proportions of the population in this line of work[8]. Rates of employment in these jobs have only risen in Northern Ireland as part of the general economic boom seen there and in a few, generally more outlying, areas of the mainland. We may be seeing more mangers and professionals, but each of these has, on average, access to fewer secretaries or clerical staff. More of what was being done in the past by the latter has to be done by the former, or simply not done at all. In early British censuses these were some of the highest status occupations, held largely by men and concentrated in the Capital. Now we are seeing them decline in number, and most quickly, geographically, in more affluent places that surround London.

Administrative and secretarial 2001 (%)

- 4 - 5
- 6
- 7
- 8
- 9 - 10

Administrative and secretarial change (%)

- −3.0 - −1.8
- −1.7 - −1.1
- −1.0 - −0.6
- −0.5 - 0.0
- 0.1 - 1.7

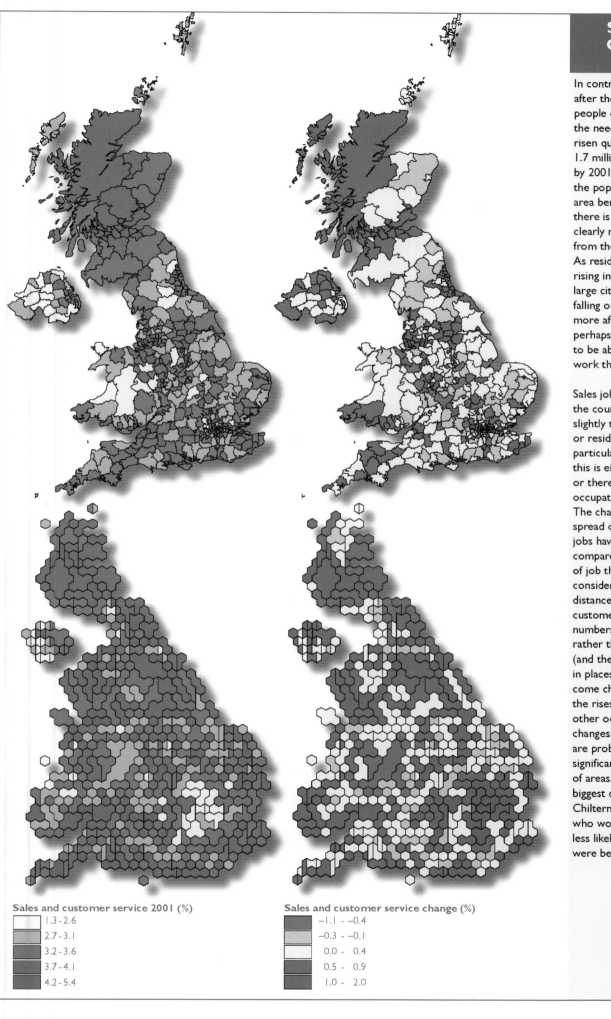

SALES AND CUSTOMER SERVICES

In contrast to people looking after the needs of their bosses, people charged with looking after the needs of consumers have risen quickly in number, from 1.7 million in 1991 to 2.1 million by 2001 (from 3.0% to 3.5% of the population). The only large area bereft of sales people living there is Central London, although clearly many thousands travel in from the suburbs to staff shops. As residents, their numbers are rising in London and all the other large cities of Britain. They are falling only in small and often more affluent southern districts, perhaps as people are less likely to be able to live where they work than before[9].

Sales jobs are located across the country, concentrated slightly towards particular towns or residential suburbs and in particular in a few areas where this is either a major occupation or there are fewer other occupations to compete with[10]. The changes to the geographical spread of people working in these jobs have been less dramatic as compared to the four categories of job that we have already considered. If anything, the distance from sales person to customer is rising slightly as the numbers working by telephone rather than face-to-face increase (and they can be employed in places where employees come cheaper). Conversely, the rises in the popularity of other occupations and local changes in relative house prices are probably major reasons for significant declines in a number of areas. On mainland Britain the biggest declines have been in the Chilterns and in Rutland. People who work in the shops there are less likely to live there than they were before.

Sales and customer service 2001 (%)

- 1.3 - 2.6
- 2.7 - 3.1
- 3.2 - 3.6
- 3.7 - 4.1
- 4.2 - 5.4

Sales and customer service change (%)

- −1.1 - −0.4
- −0.3 - −0.1
- 0.0 - 0.4
- 0.5 - 0.9
- 1.0 - 2.0

PERSONAL SERVICES

An all-embracing category, personal services, range from hairdressing and childcare, to other forms of relatively routine service work such as nightclub security. Personal services employ 1.8 million people, 3.1%, 0.8% fewer than the 2.3 million in 1991. Like secretarial and administrative occupations, part of the reason for this decline will be the regrading of jobs or their titles. Most importantly, many jobs which are now labelled as 'associate professional, protective services' would have been labelled as personal services in 1991. This artefactual explanation accounts for the some of the areas of greatest decline in this category of employment[11]. Nevertheless, the geographical patterns seen in the changes in areas without a large military presence (such as outside of Hampshire and Northern Ireland) suggest that a general decline is happening that is more acute in the South than the North, particularly outside of northern cities. There are also a few places that have seen the proportions of people working in these jobs increase. This is particularly true in remote areas where there are growing numbers or proportions of older people to support[12]. Because of the plethora of occupations that fall into this category, it is difficult to comment in general over why the patterns should be as they are[13]. Rates are higher along the south coast and in a few other places with many older people, but are falling also along much of the coastline. They are falling too in similar places such as those where the proportions of sales people are falling, in areas where it is now often too expensive to live, if you work in these generally low-paid occupations.

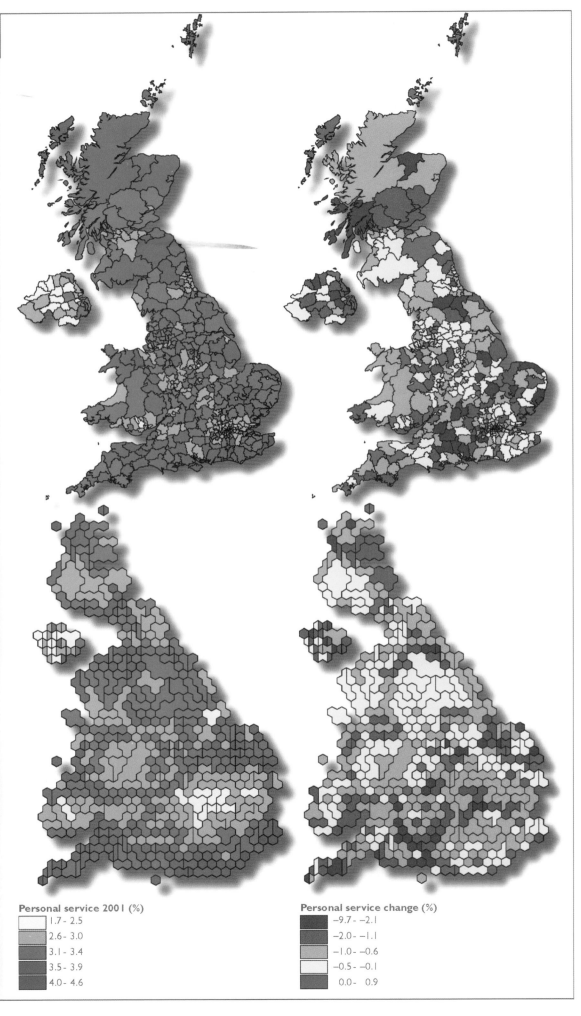

Personal service 2001 (%)
- 1.7 - 2.5
- 2.6 - 3.0
- 3.1 - 3.4
- 3.5 - 3.9
- 4.0 - 4.6

Personal service change (%)
- −9.7 - −2.1
- −2.0 - −1.1
- −1.0 - −0.6
- −0.5 - −0.1
- 0.0 - 0.9

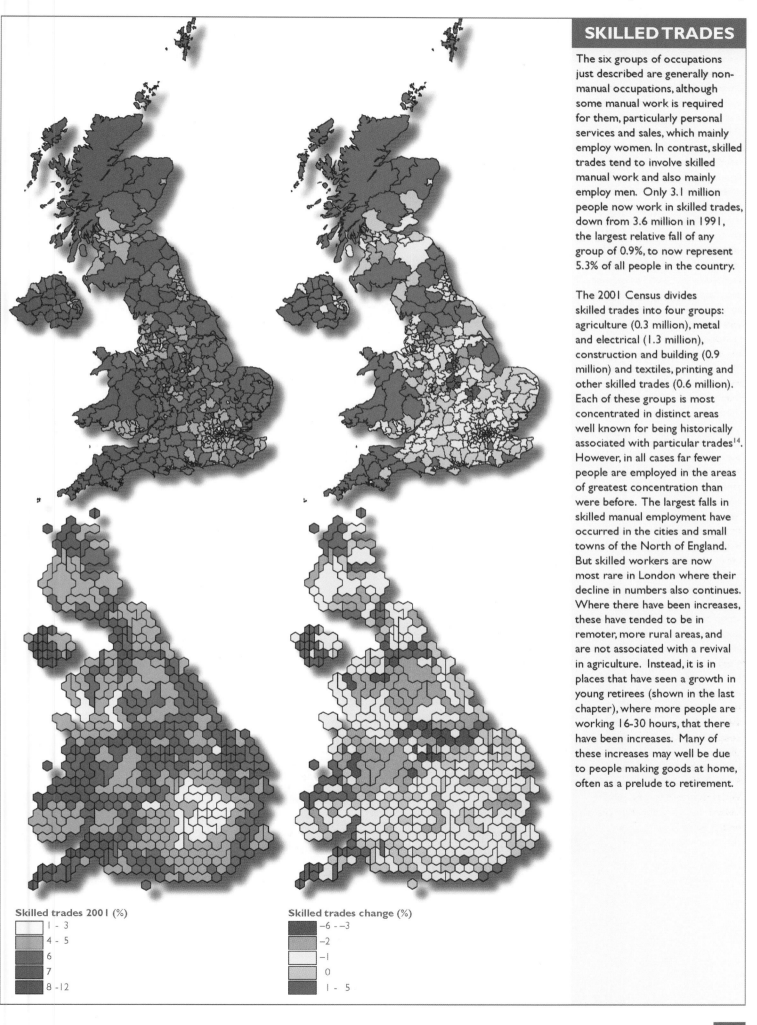

SKILLED TRADES

The six groups of occupations just described are generally non-manual occupations, although some manual work is required for them, particularly personal services and sales, which mainly employ women. In contrast, skilled trades tend to involve skilled manual work and also mainly employ men. Only 3.1 million people now work in skilled trades, down from 3.6 million in 1991, the largest relative fall of any group of 0.9%, to now represent 5.3% of all people in the country.

The 2001 Census divides skilled trades into four groups: agriculture (0.3 million), metal and electrical (1.3 million), construction and building (0.9 million) and textiles, printing and other skilled trades (0.6 million). Each of these groups is most concentrated in distinct areas well known for being historically associated with particular trades[14]. However, in all cases far fewer people are employed in the areas of greatest concentration than were before. The largest falls in skilled manual employment have occurred in the cities and small towns of the North of England. But skilled workers are now most rare in London where their decline in numbers also continues. Where there have been increases, these have tended to be in remoter, more rural areas, and are not associated with a revival in agriculture. Instead, it is in places that have seen a growth in young retirees (shown in the last chapter), where more people are working 16-30 hours, that there have been increases. Many of these increases may well be due to people making goods at home, often as a prelude to retirement.

Skilled trades 2001 (%)
- 1 - 3
- 4 - 5
- 6
- 7
- 8 - 12

Skilled trades change (%)
- −6 - −3
- −2
- −1
- 0
- 1 - 5

MACHINE OPERATIVES

Our eighth group of occupations are entirely manual, and consist of jobs that require semi-skilled and often routine work. In 2001, 2.3 million people worked as process, plant and machine operatives, half a percent of the population fewer than in 1991, when 2.5 million or 4.4% of the population were engaged in what is generally factory work. This work is divided into two sets of jobs, those who work directly on processes, with plant or machinery[15] (1.3 million people), and those working in transport including mobile machine drivers and operatives in factories[16] (1 million people). The decline has only been in the former group. More people drive goods around the country and in warehouses than before, while fewer make them here than ever before.

There have been increases, but outside of Northern Ireland these are probably occurring for the same reasons as the increases seen in skilled trades. In place of retirement, along with retirement, or as the start of an alternative lifestyle, people are trying out new types of occupation in areas such as Cornwall and the West coast of Scotland. They are making pots, weaving wool, screen printing or doing similar manual work on pre-industrial production scales that are hardly a replacement for what was being produced in the UK before, especially where there have been the greatest falls in the East and West Midlands and parts of South Wales. Machine operation and factory work is largely an occupation of the North of England, of particular parts of Wales, Scotland and Northern Ireland, and an occupation that is on the wane.

Process, plant and machine operatives 2001 (%)

- 1 - 2
- 3
- 4
- 5
- 6 - 9

Process, plant and machine operatives change (%)

- −4.2 - −1.4
- −1.3 - −0.7
- −0.6 - −0.1
- 0.0 - 0.5
- 0.6 - 2.4

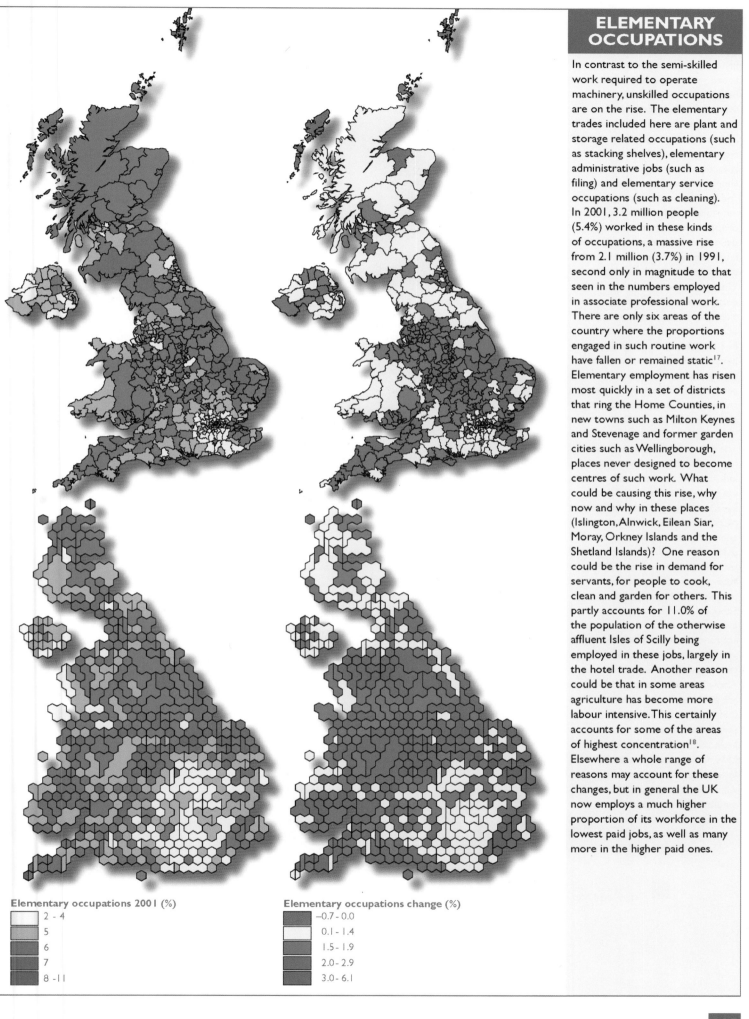

ELEMENTARY OCCUPATIONS

In contrast to the semi-skilled work required to operate machinery, unskilled occupations are on the rise. The elementary trades included here are plant and storage related occupations (such as stacking shelves), elementary administrative jobs (such as filing) and elementary service occupations (such as cleaning). In 2001, 3.2 million people (5.4%) worked in these kinds of occupations, a massive rise from 2.1 million (3.7%) in 1991, second only in magnitude to that seen in the numbers employed in associate professional work. There are only six areas of the country where the proportions engaged in such routine work have fallen or remained static[17]. Elementary employment has risen most quickly in a set of districts that ring the Home Counties, in new towns such as Milton Keynes and Stevenage and former garden cities such as Wellingborough, places never designed to become centres of such work. What could be causing this rise, why now and why in these places (Islington, Alnwick, Eilean Siar, Moray, Orkney Islands and the Shetland Islands)? One reason could be the rise in demand for servants, for people to cook, clean and garden for others. This partly accounts for 11.0% of the population of the otherwise affluent Isles of Scilly being employed in these jobs, largely in the hotel trade. Another reason could be that in some areas agriculture has become more labour intensive. This certainly accounts for some of the areas of highest concentration[18]. Elsewhere a whole range of reasons may account for these changes, but in general the UK now employs a much higher proportion of its workforce in the lowest paid jobs, as well as many more in the higher paid ones.

Elementary occupations 2001 (%)

- 2 - 4
- 5
- 6
- 7
- 8 - 11

Elementary occupations change (%)

- −0.7 - 0.0
- 0.1 - 1.4
- 1.5 - 1.9
- 2.0 - 2.9
- 3.0 - 6.1

MINING AND QUARRYING

Just as the census defines nine broad groups of occupations people may have, it categorises the industry they may work in into another nine broad groups. People in every occupation work in every industry. Every industry has managers and filing clerks, employs plumbers and accountants, but different industries employ different proportions of people from differing occupations and thus the following set of maps complement those nine we have just described. The fortunes of particular occupations are also often closely linked to the fortunes of particular industries, and so by seeing how the geography of people working by industry has changed, we can begin to see partly why occupational patterns and all associated with them have altered during the 1990s.

The first industry we consider here is one of the oldest primary industries concerned with extracting value from the land. By 2001 only 0.1 million people (0.2%) worked in mining and quarrying as compared to 0.7 million in 1991 (1.2%) and the many millions before that. The largest cluster is now found of people living in the North of Scotland associated with the oil extraction industry[19] (bankers and accountants with mining and oil interests account for the rise in the financial centre of London). There is now no discernable trace left of the coal mining industry that so marked past census maps, save in the pattern of decline from the little that was left by 1991[20]. It is doubtful whether future maps of industry in the UK will include a category that now employs so few people.

Mining and quarrying 2001 (%)
- 0.0
- 0.1
- 0.2 - 0.3
- 0.4 - 0.9
- 1.0 - 4.3

Mining and quarrying change (%)
- −9.6 - −3.1
- −3.0 - −1.1
- −1.0 - −0.6
- −0.5 - −0.1
- 0.0 - 3.6

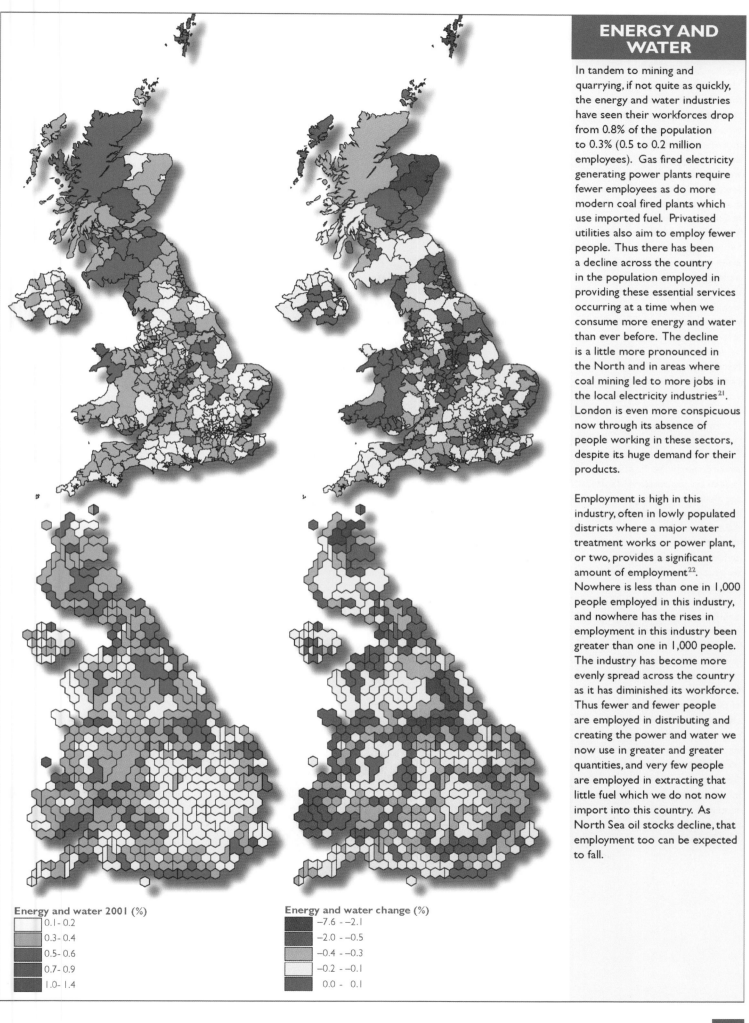

ENERGY AND WATER

In tandem to mining and quarrying, if not quite as quickly, the energy and water industries have seen their workforces drop from 0.8% of the population to 0.3% (0.5 to 0.2 million employees). Gas fired electricity generating power plants require fewer employees as do more modern coal fired plants which use imported fuel. Privatised utilities also aim to employ fewer people. Thus there has been a decline across the country in the population employed in providing these essential services occurring at a time when we consume more energy and water than ever before. The decline is a little more pronounced in the North and in areas where coal mining led to more jobs in the local electricity industries[21]. London is even more conspicuous now through its absence of people working in these sectors, despite its huge demand for their products.

Employment is high in this industry, often in lowly populated districts where a major water treatment works or power plant, or two, provides a significant amount of employment[22]. Nowhere is less than one in 1,000 people employed in this industry, and nowhere has the rises in employment in this industry been greater than one in 1,000 people. The industry has become more evenly spread across the country as it has diminished its workforce. Thus fewer and fewer people are employed in distributing and creating the power and water we now use in greater and greater quantities, and very few people are employed in extracting that little fuel which we do not now import into this country. As North Sea oil stocks decline, that employment too can be expected to fall.

Energy and water 2001 (%)
- 0.1- 0.2
- 0.3- 0.4
- 0.5- 0.6
- 0.7- 0.9
- 1.0- 1.4

Energy and water change (%)
- −7.6 - −2.1
- −2.0 - −0.5
- −0.4 - −0.3
- −0.2 - −0.1
- 0.0 - 0.1

AGRICULTURE, FORESTRY AND FISHING

The third primary industry that the census allows us to measure changes in is agriculture and its associated extractive partners of forestry and fishing. Just as with mining, quarrying, energy and water, these industries too have seen a decline in employment, but now much slower, from 0.8% to 0.7% of all people in the UK, from 0.5 to 0.4 million employees. While employment has fallen in many rural areas[23] it has risen in most towns and cities. Put most simply, more and more people are employed in agriculture in ways in which they do not get their hands dirty, as middle-men[24].

Rural UK is still solidly the home of agriculture, but at its height it only employs 6.8% of the local population in the Orkneys (fishing plays a large part), the next highest concentration being 5.1% of the population of Eden. Unsurprisingly, the 10 areas with the lowest proportions employed are all London boroughs apart from Liverpool. With the exception of the odd urban allotment or city farm, urban agricultural employment has to be people in the businesses but not on the farms. On the farms employment continues to fall, but only relatively slowly as compared to the other primary industries of Britain that have been decimated in places. In some farming areas employment is actually rising, particularly where large numbers of people are being used in elementary jobs as fruit and vegetable pickers to ensure that discerning consumers receive the perfect looking product (see footnote 18). The decline in agriculture may be coming to an end as the industry slowly transforms itself.

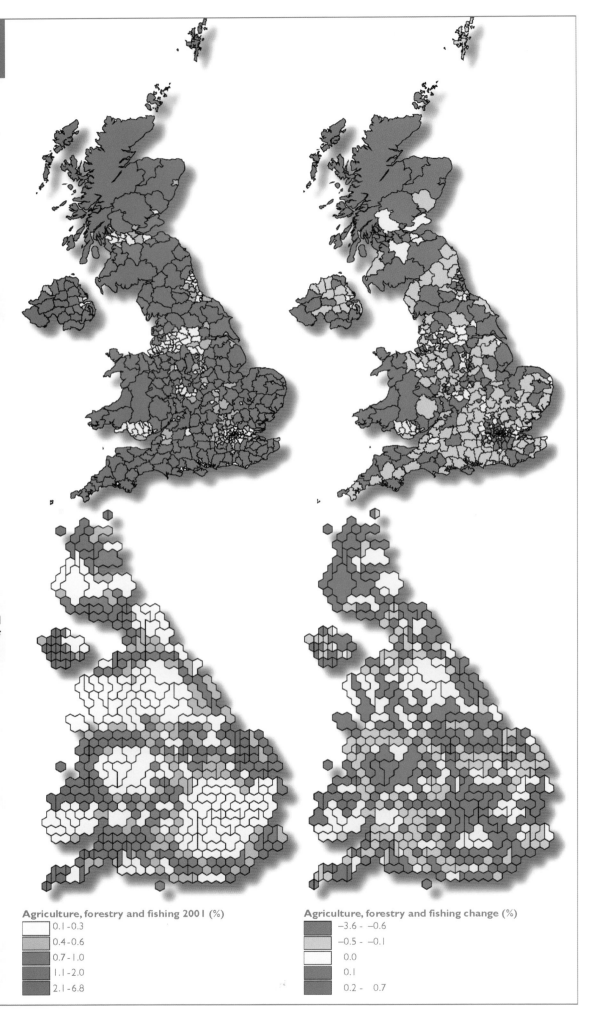

Agriculture, forestry and fishing 2001 (%)

- 0.1 - 0.3
- 0.4 - 0.6
- 0.7 - 1.0
- 1.1 - 2.0
- 2.1 - 6.8

Agriculture, forestry and fishing change (%)

- −3.6 - −0.6
- −0.5 - −0.1
- 0.0
- 0.1
- 0.2 - 0.7

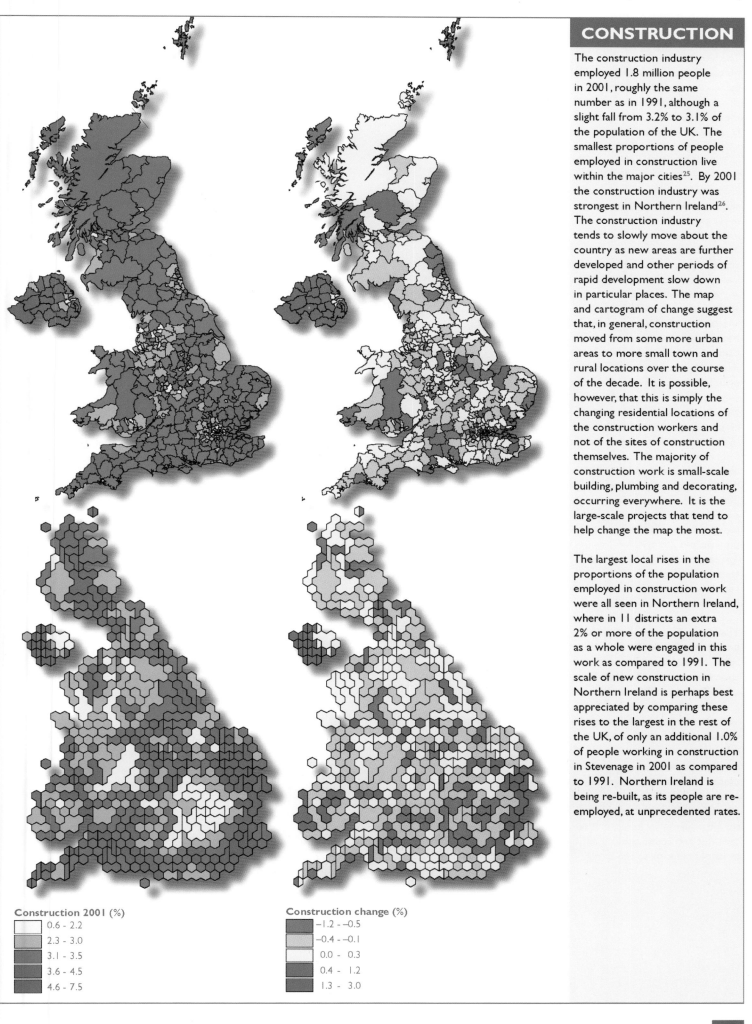

CONSTRUCTION

The construction industry employed 1.8 million people in 2001, roughly the same number as in 1991, although a slight fall from 3.2% to 3.1% of the population of the UK. The smallest proportions of people employed in construction live within the major cities[25]. By 2001 the construction industry was strongest in Northern Ireland[26]. The construction industry tends to slowly move about the country as new areas are further developed and other periods of rapid development slow down in particular places. The map and cartogram of change suggest that, in general, construction moved from some more urban areas to more small town and rural locations over the course of the decade. It is possible, however, that this is simply the changing residential locations of the construction workers and not of the sites of construction themselves. The majority of construction work is small-scale building, plumbing and decorating, occurring everywhere. It is the large-scale projects that tend to help change the map the most.

The largest local rises in the proportions of the population employed in construction work were all seen in Northern Ireland, where in 11 districts an extra 2% or more of the population as a whole were engaged in this work as compared to 1991. The scale of new construction in Northern Ireland is perhaps best appreciated by comparing these rises to the largest in the rest of the UK, of only an additional 1.0% of people working in construction in Stevenage in 2001 as compared to 1991. Northern Ireland is being re-built, as its people are re-employed, at unprecedented rates.

Construction 2001 (%)

	0.6 - 2.2
	2.3 - 3.0
	3.1 - 3.5
	3.6 - 4.5
	4.6 - 7.5

Construction change (%)

	−1.2 - −0.5
	−0.4 - −0.1
	0.0 - 0.3
	0.4 - 1.2
	1.3 - 3.0

TRANSPORT

The fifth industry we consider here is of those employed in the business of moving goods and people around, and in and out of the country. This is the second fastest growing industry in the UK, employing 3.1% of all people in 2001 (1.8 million) as compared to 2.7% in 1991 (1.6 million). From taxis, to lorries, trains, buses, ships and aircraft, nowhere are fewer than 1.2% of the population involved in work in transport. Near the major international airports over a tenth of the entire local population are working in the transport industries, 10.9% in Crawley (Gatwick) and 10.0% in Spelthorne (near Heathrow). Heathrow and Gatwick are clear from the map of highest concentrations in 2001 and of growth in this sector. Concentrations of people working in transport are also evident in the ports of Dover (6.9% working in transport) and Felixstowe in Suffolk Coastal district[27]. However, it is ports that have experienced some of the sharpest declines in employment in this sector over the decade, as is also evident from the map and cartogram of change. The largest reduction of all has been in Dover, where 1.6% fewer people are now employed in this industry.

The starkest large area of decline on the map is East, North and South London, and an area stretching out along both banks of the Thames estuary to the East. The falls here are slight and easily outweighed by the growth in nearby inland employment associated with transport by air rather than sea. As primary modes of transport change, so too do the locations of its employees. London is now clearly served primarily by its airports to the West and South rather than by its old seaports to the East.

Transport 2001 (%)
1 - 2
3
4
5
6 - 11

Transport change (%)
−1.6 - 0.0
0.1 - 0.4
0.5 - 0.9
1.0 - 1.2
1.3 - 3.1

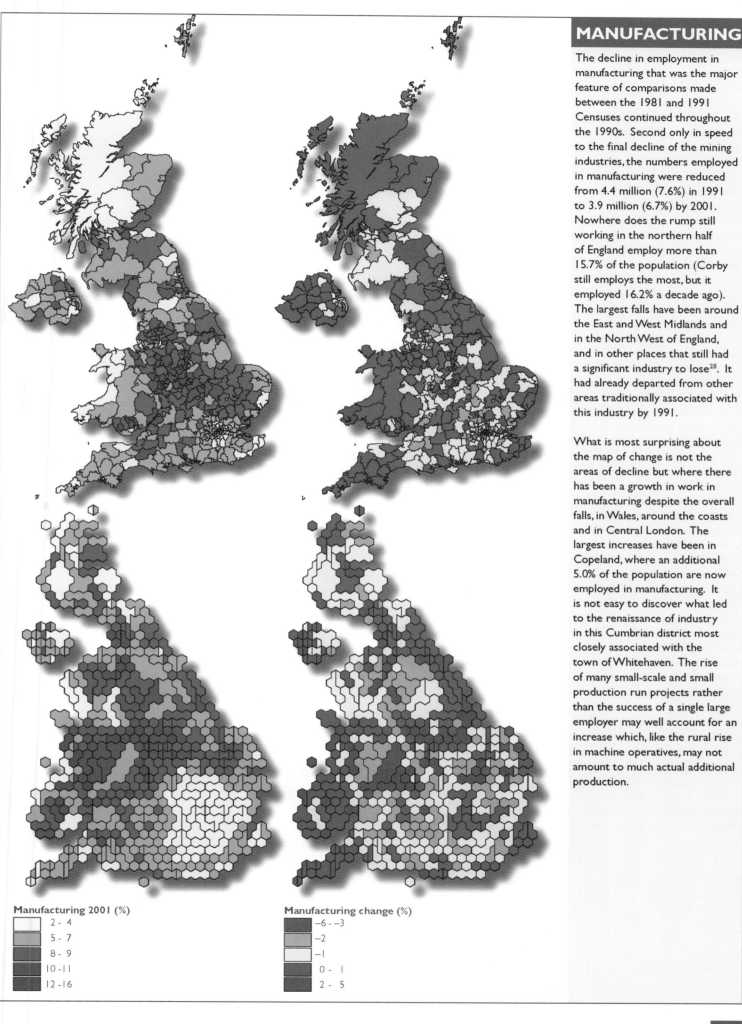

The decline in employment in manufacturing that was the major feature of comparisons made between the 1981 and 1991 Censuses continued throughout the 1990s. Second only in speed to the final decline of the mining industries, the numbers employed in manufacturing were reduced from 4.4 million (7.6%) in 1991 to 3.9 million (6.7%) by 2001. Nowhere does the rump still working in the northern half of England employ more than 15.7% of the population (Corby still employs the most, but it employed 16.2% a decade ago). The largest falls have been around the East and West Midlands and in the North West of England, and in other places that still had a significant industry to lose[28]. It had already departed from other areas traditionally associated with this industry by 1991.

What is most surprising about the map of change is not the areas of decline but where there has been a growth in work in manufacturing despite the overall falls, in Wales, around the coasts and in Central London. The largest increases have been in Copeland, where an additional 5.0% of the population are now employed in manufacturing. It is not easy to discover what led to the renaissance of industry in this Cumbrian district most closely associated with the town of Whitehaven. The rise of many small-scale and small production run projects rather than the success of a single large employer may well account for an increase which, like the rural rise in machine operatives, may not amount to much actual additional production.

Manufacturing 2001 (%)
- 2 - 4
- 5 - 7
- 8 - 9
- 10 - 11
- 12 - 16

Manufacturing change (%)
- −6 - −3
- −2
- −1
- 0 - 1
- 2 - 5

BANKING AND FINANCE

If there is a single success story to the UK economy over the course of the 1990s, it is the growth of this sector, moving money rather than goods or people around, and certainly not involved in making or extracting anything other than profit. A total of 2.9 million people were employed in banking and finance in the UK in 1991 (5.1%); by 2001 that had soared to 4.6 million (7.8%). Only in the Isles of Scilly had there been a decline in employment in this sector (and there only of 25 fewer people being bankers). Centred on London and dominating the South East[29], banking is now the UK's second largest industry, having overtaken manufacturing in the 1990s. Over a fifth of the populations of the City of London, Kensington & Chelsea, Wandsworth and Westminster are bankers or financiers.

The fastest growth in banking has generally been seen where it was strongest as an industry to begin with. Employment has risen between an additional 6.7% and 10.5% only within London, rising most, unsurprisingly, in the City. Outside of London growth has been strongest in neighbouring districts, an additional 6.5% in Bracknell, and by more than an additional 5.0% in Reading, Wokingham, South Cambridgeshire, St Albans, South Oxfordshire and in the Vale of White Horse. Note that these are the areas that have seen the largest rises in the residential population who are bankers. Many people from these districts will commute to the City to work. Outside of South East England the only area to see a rise of 4.8% or more was in Edinburgh, which is also experiencing a boom in this industry.

Banking and finance 2001 (%)

- 2 - 4
- 5 - 6
- 7 - 10
- 11 - 13
- 14 - 31

Banking and finance change (%)

- −1 - 0
- 1
- 2
- 3
- 4 - 11

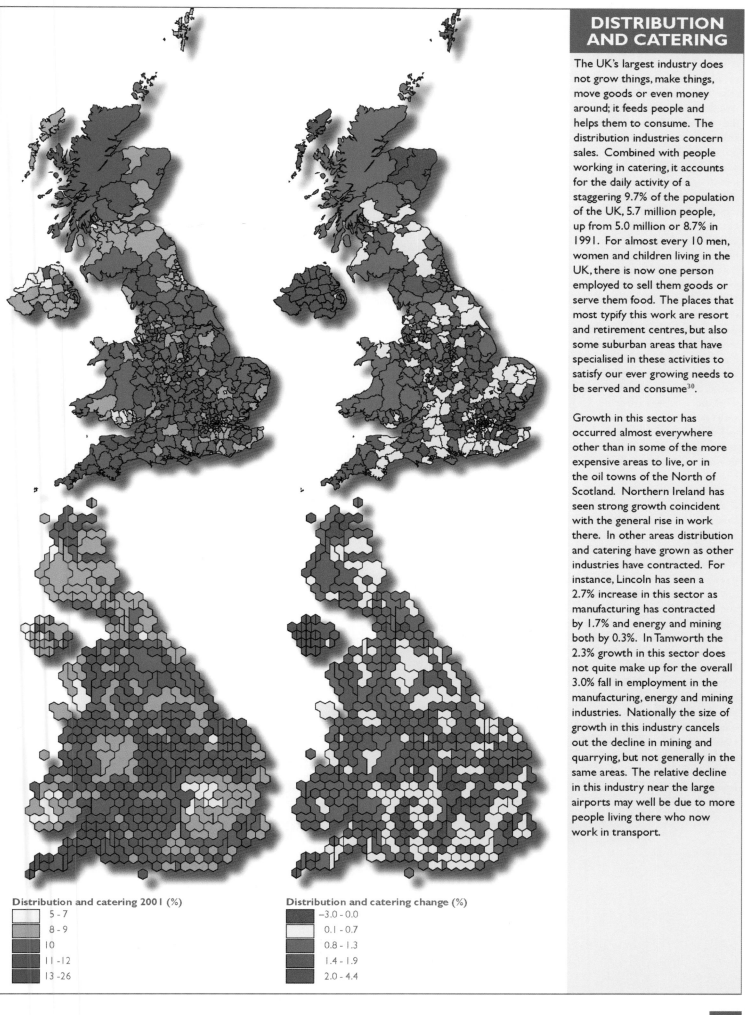

DISTRIBUTION AND CATERING

The UK's largest industry does not grow things, make things, move goods or even money around; it feeds people and helps them to consume. The distribution industries concern sales. Combined with people working in catering, it accounts for the daily activity of a staggering 9.7% of the population of the UK, 5.7 million people, up from 5.0 million or 8.7% in 1991. For almost every 10 men, women and children living in the UK, there is now one person employed to sell them goods or serve them food. The places that most typify this work are resort and retirement centres, but also some suburban areas that have specialised in these activities to satisfy our ever growing needs to be served and consume[30].

Growth in this sector has occurred almost everywhere other than in some of the more expensive areas to live, or in the oil towns of the North of Scotland. Northern Ireland has seen strong growth coincident with the general rise in work there. In other areas distribution and catering have grown as other industries have contracted. For instance, Lincoln has seen a 2.7% increase in this sector as manufacturing has contracted by 1.7% and energy and mining both by 0.3%. In Tamworth the 2.3% growth in this sector does not quite make up for the overall 3.0% fall in employment in the manufacturing, energy and mining industries. Nationally the size of growth in this industry cancels out the decline in mining and quarrying, but not generally in the same areas. The relative decline in this industry near the large airports may well be due to more people living there who now work in transport.

Distribution and catering 2001 (%)

- 5 - 7
- 8 - 9
- 10
- 11 -12
- 13 -26

Distribution and catering change (%)

- −3.0 - 0.0
- 0.1 - 0.7
- 0.8 - 1.3
- 1.4 - 1.9
- 2.0 - 4.4

OTHER SERVICES

This catch-all category is the largest of the nine sets of industries considered in this atlas. All service industries are included in this category, other than those involving banking and finance, transport, distribution or catering. Thus a majority of people employed in these industries work in areas such as health, education, the armed forces and government, and most of them are employed in the state sector. In total, all these other service industries employ 7.9 million people (13.5%), up from 7.2 million in 1991 (12.5%). Only banking and finance and distribution have experienced greater proportional rises. 'Other services' are spread quite evenly across the country as there are similar needs for them in all places. However, they employ disproportionate numbers in cities that act as service centres and that have large universities and hospitals, and also in areas that contain large army bases[31].

The numbers of people working in the other service industries have risen most where the population is ageing. They have declined most in places which have become too expensive for people employed on relatively low state sector wages to live in, and in parts of Northern Ireland where the proportion of people working in the security and other state services have declined[32]. The largest single decline has been in the district of Rushmoor, in Hampshire, of –4.4%. Areas like Hampshire still require large numbers of people to work in the state sector, and many commute into work from cheaper districts either from within the county or from outside.

Other services 2001 (%)

- 8 -10
- 11 -12
- 13 -14
- 15 -16
- 17 -24

Other services change (%)

- –4.4 - –0.1
- 0.0 - 0.9
- 1.0 - 1.4
- 1.5 - 1.9
- 2.0 - 6.9

NOTES

[1] In this footnote and the following seven pages of footnotes we have excluded the Isles of Scilly and the City of London due to their low population numbers, and Northern Ireland, as we were unable to access detailed figures for the province for 1991. In 2001 the highest proportions of corporate managers were found in Richmond upon Thames (10.8%) and the next highest in Kensington & Chelsea (10.7%); the fewest were in Easington (2.3%). A decade earlier corporate bosses were most likely to live in Wokingham (9.8%) then Hart (9.7%), and least found in Blaenau Gwent (1.4%).

[2] In 2001 the district with the highest proportion of science and technology professionals was Wokingham (3.9%), followed by Hart (3.7%; in 1991 Hart had been in first place and Cambridge in second); they were least prevalent in Penwith (0.5%). Health professionals were found in their highest proportions in Camden (1.1%; also highest in 1991 but then only 0.9%) and Newcastle upon Tyne (1.1%), and rarest in Corby where there were ten times fewer (0.1%). Teaching and research professionals were also least likely to live in Corby and most concentrated in Cambridge (6.8%) and Oxford (6.0%). Business and public service professionals made up the highest proportions of the local populations of Westminster and Wandsworth (both 4.7%), and were least seen in Blaenau Gwent (0.3%).

[3] Most common in Wandsworth (5.6%) and Hammersmith & Fulham (5.1%), most rare in Blaenau Gwent (1.0%).

[4] Most common in East Dunbartonshire (2.6%) and Angus (2.4%), most rare in Corby (0.8%).

[5] Most common in Camden (5.2%) and Islington (4.7%), most rare in Easington (0.2%).

[6] Most common in Moray and Aberdeen City (both 1.7%), most rare in Kensington & Chelsea (0.4%).

[7] Most common in Richmondshire (7.6%) and Bridgnorth (3.8%), most rare in Kensington & Chelsea (0.1%). Note that some groups of armed service personnel have been reallocated to this group, which results in some of the increases seen in some isolated spots in the more rural areas on the map and cartogram of change being more an artefact of the classification system than a real change in the work people are doing there.

[8] In 2001 the two areas with the highest proportions working in administrative occupations were Havering and Spelthorne, both with 6.8% of their people employed at these grades. In 1991 the same two places also topped the table but then with 8.1% and 8.4% of their populations engaged in this work. Such work was rarest then in the Orkney Islands and is now rarest in Berwick-upon-Tweed (employing 2.4% of the population at both times in both places). Similarly, in both 2001 and 1991, the districts with the most and least secretaries were Bexley (3.1%, was 3.8%) and Blaenau Gwent (0.7%, unchanged).

[9] The two areas with the highest numbers employed in sales occupations and customer service occupations are areas associated with large shopping centres and/or call centres: Crawley (5.4%) and Thurrock (5.0%). The lowest proportions are found in a similar area, but not one in which the people working in the shops could expect to live: Kensington & Chelsea (2.0%).

[10] The 10 areas where the proportions of people working in these occupations has risen most between 1991 and 2001 include many places a long way, physically and socially, from their customers: Brent, Sunderland, Halton, Plymouth, Easington, Hartlepool, Crawley, Inverclyde, West Dunbartonshire and West Lothian.

[11] The largest declines seen in the country, of over 4% of the populations of Gosport, Rushmoor, Richmondshire, Rutland and Forest Heath, are due to this re-labelling of military occupations.

[12] Rates have risen by a quarter of a percent or more in East Cambridgeshire, Mid Devon, Torridge, Maldon, Stroud, Hyndburn, North West Leicestershire, Kettering, Oswestry, Adur, Eilean Siar, Orkney Islands and in the Shetland Islands.

[13] The highest proportions working in these jobs, the full label for which is 'caring personal services and leisure and other', are to be found in Dover (4.6%) and Crawley (4.5%), the fewest in Tower Hamlets (2.0%).

[14] Agriculture now best typifies skilled occupations in the Orkney Islands (4.9%) and Powys (4.1%), metal and electrical trades employ the highest proportions in Barrow-in-Furness (4.4%) and Redditch (4.0%), construction and building trades employ most in Castle Point (2.6%) and the Orkney Islands (2.5%), and textiles, printing and other skilled trades are most concentrated in Stoke-on-Trent (3.3%, a fall from 8.2%, although under a wider definition, in 1991) and in Eilean Siar (2.3%). Comparisons over time are difficult to make for these sub-categories due to differing occupational categories being used in 1991.

[15] The highest proportions employed in 2001 in process, plant and machine operative jobs are found in Corby (6.3%, 10.3% in 1991) and Sedgefield (5.0%, the area with the second highest proportion in 1991 was Redditch at 7.0%), the fewest in Kensington & Chelsea (0.3%, lowest also in 1991 at 0.2%).

[16] The highest proportions employed in transport and as mobile machine drivers and operatives in 2001 are found in Eden (3.1%, 3.3% in 1991) and Boston (3.0%, North Lincolnshire was second in 1991 at 3.0%), the lowest in Kensington & Chelsea (0.5% in both years).

[17] The highest concentrations of people who work in elementary occupations are found in Corby (9.8%) and Boston (8.4%), the lowest in expensive Richmond upon Thames (2.5%).

[18] We include the Isles of Scilly here despite excluding it from most of the footnotes of the last few pages because now we are considering a major occupation category rather than subdivisions of that category, so our statistics are more robust. After the Isles of Scilly the 10 areas in which the highest proportions are employed in these occupations are: Eden, Boston, Lincoln, South Holland, Corby, Wellingborough, Berwick-upon-Tweed, Tamworth, Orkney Islands and the Shetland Islands.

[19] Only the following districts recorded more than 1% of their population engaged in work in these industries: Restormel (clay), Great Yarmouth (marine services for oil and gas), Selby (coal); and oil and gas being serviced from people living in highest numbers in: Aberdeen City, Aberdeenshire, Angus, Moray and the Shetland Islands.

[20] Even the majority of the areas that saw the greatest falls in employment in these industries in the 1990s were not associated with coal. Five percent or more of the population ceased being employed by these industries in Halton (coal), Teesdale (coal), North Lincolnshire (chalk), Corby (steel), Redcar and Cleveland (steel) and Stoke-on-Trent (clay).

[21] The largest declines in employment in these industries have been in: Copeland, Bolsover, Easington, Selby, Bassetlaw, Mansfield, Newark & Sherwood, Aberdeen City, Aberdeenshire and the Shetland Islands.

[22] However, one large suburb and three large towns still see relatively high numbers working in these industries. The 10 areas employing the highest shares of their local populations in these industries, all between 1.0% and 1.2%, are: Solihull, Warrington, Copeland, Shepway, Lancaster, Selby, Swndon, Isle of Anglesey, East Lothian and Perth & Kinross.

[23] More than an additional 1% of the local populations of the following areas are now not engaged in agriculture as compared to 1991: East Cambridgeshire, Isles of Scilly, Eden, Mid Devon, Torridge, North Dorset, Ribble Valley, South Holland, Hambleton, Ryedale, Selby, Bridgnorth, South Shropshire, West Somerset, Mid Suffolk, Kennet, Wychavon, Carmarthenshire, Ceredigion, Powys, Aberdeenshire, Moray, Orkney Islands, Fermanagh and Moyle.

[24] Market towns like Ipswich and Lincoln have seen rises in employment in agriculture despite having little agricultural land within their borders. Note that the 2001 Census was taken during the foot and mouth outbreak and before it could have been expected to have influenced numbers employed in this industry.

[25] The 10 areas with the lowest proportions of people working in these industries live in the following places and all are in London boroughs: City of London, Camden, Hackney, Hammersmith & Fulham, Haringey, Islington, Kensington & Chelsea, Lambeth, Tower Hamlets and Westminster.

[26] The 10 areas with the highest proportions of people working in these industries who live in these places are all, bar one, in Northern Ireland: Castle Point (Essex), Ballymoney, Banbridge, Cookstown, Down, Limavady, Magherafelt, Moyle, Newry & Mourne and Omagh.

[27] More than 5% of the local population are transport employees in the following areas: Ealing, Hillingdon, Hounslow, Bracknell Forest, Slough, West Berkshire, Windsor & Maidenhead, Milton Keynes, Isles of Scilly, Thurrock, Dover, Ipswich, Suffolk Coastal, Reigate & Barnstead, Runnymede, Spelthorne, Surrey Heath, North Warwickshire, Crawley, Horsham, Mid Sussex, Swindon and the Shetland Islands.

[28] An additional 3% or more of the local population were no longer employed in the manufacturing industries in the following areas by 2001: Coventry (the only metropolitan borough to still contain enough to have enough to lose), Luton, Barrow-in-Furness, Derby, Stevenage, Welwyn Hatfield, Chorley, Hyndburn, Pendle, Rossendale, Blaby, Charnwood, Hinckley & Bosworth, Leicester, Oadby & Wigston, Wellingborough, Ashfield, Broxtowe, Nuneaton & Bedworth, Rugby, and the only place in Scotland to still have enough to lose this much – Clackmannanshire.

[29] Banking and finance employs over a tenth of the populations of the following areas: City of London, Barnet, Bexley, Brent, Bromley, Camden, Croydon, Ealing, Enfield, Greenwich, Hackney, Hammersmith & Fulham, Haringey, Harrow, Havering, Hounslow, Islington, Kensington & Chelsea, Kingston upon Thames, Lambeth, Lewisham, Merton, Redbridge, Richmond upon Thames, Southwark, Sutton, Tower Hamlets, Waltham Forest, Wandsworth, Westminster, Trafford (the only metropolitan borough), Bracknell Forest, Reading, West Berkshire, Windsor & Maidenhead, Wokingham, Bristol, Aylesbury Vale, Chiltern, Milton Keynes, South Bucks, Wycombe, Cambridge, South Cambridgeshire, Macclesfield, Brighton & Hove, Basildon, Brentwood, Castle Point, Chelmsford, Epping Forest, Rochford, Southend-on-Sea, Uttlesford, South Gloucestershire, Basingstoke & Deane, East Hampshire, Hart, Rushmoor, Test Valley, Winchester, Broxbourne, Dacorum, East Hertfordshire, Hertsmere, North Hertfordshire, St Albans, Three Rivers, Watford, Sevenoaks, Tonbridge & Malling, Tunbridge Wells, South Oxfordshire, Vale of White Horse, Elmbridge, Epsom & Ewell, Guildford, Mole Valley, Reigate & Barnstead, Runnymede, Spelthorne, Surrey Heath, Tandridge, Waverley, Woking, Stratford-upon-Avon, Warwick, Horsham, Mid Sussex, Swindon, and only one area outside of England – Edinburgh.

[30] More than 12% of the populations of the following areas are engaged in distribution or catering work: Milton Keynes, Restormel, Isles of Scilly (the highest at 26%), Carlisle, Eden, South Lakeland, North Devon, Harlow, Thurrock, Broxbourne, Blackpool, Boston, South Holland, Berwick-upon-Tweed, West Somerset, Tamworth, Crawley and Worcester.

[31] More than 17% of the local populations of the following areas are engaged in work in these industries: Lambeth, Lewisham, Cambridge, South Cambridgeshire, Durham, Gosport, Winchester, Hambleton, Richmondshire, Oxford, West Oxfordshire, Taunton Deane, Forest Heath, Kennet, Salisbury, Argyll & Bute, East Dunbartonshire, Moray, Antrim, Castlereagh and North Down.

[32] The proportion of people working in these industries has fallen by 1% or more in: City of London, Kensington & Chelsea, Westminster, West Berkshire, Cambridge, Weymouth & Portland, Basingstoke & Deane, Rushmoor, Test Valley, St Albans, Cherwell, South Oxfordshire, Vale of White Horse, Rutland and Suffolk Coastal.

Families and households

Maps in this section include:

One parent, no work (p 129)	Two parents, one working (p 130)	Two parents, both working (p 131)	Part-time care (p 132)	Full-time care (p 133)	Poor health (p 134)
Good health (p 135)	Illness, disability and children (p 136)	Illness, disability and adults (p 137)	Households without families (p 138)	Young and single households (p 139)	Cohabiting with no children (p 140)
Lone-parent households (p 141)	Cohabiting couples with children (p 142)	Married with children (p 143)	Married without children (p 144)	Pensioner families (p 145)	Other pensioner households (p 146)
Single pensioner households (p 146)	Pensioners (p 147)	Pensioners in communal homes (p 148)	Rooms (p 149)	Language (p 150)	

In this chapter we consider where different groups of families and households live in the UK, and how those distributions are changing. We also look at one particular attribute of people that can have an important impact on their families: their state of health.

The census has particular definitions of what constitutes a household and a family which we blur here as, in the vast majority of cases, most homes contain a single household which is also either a single family, a single person or a collection of unrelated individuals. Because we count people, rather than households or families, the differences in definition have little impact on our maps. We show the distributions of people not living in families here and of households who share dwellings in the next chapter.

We begin by considering the changing distributions of three groups of families with dependent children – 40.7% of all people live in such families. Of these, half (20.8%) now live in families where there are two adults and both are working, a quarter (9.7%) where one of two adults is working, and a sixteenth (2.5%) where neither parent is working. The remaining fifth of people living in families with dependent children are lone-parent households, the majority of which have no earnings. Both types of lone-parent households (earning and not earning), and two-parent households where both adults are working, are growing in number. We map the changing geography of three of these five groups: lone parents are becoming more common in particular cities, traditional two-parent one-earner families are reducing in number almost everywhere, and the proportions of two-earner families is rising most in the South, outside of the major cities.

Turning from people who care for their children, we next consider those who care for family and friends who are ill, and thus mainly for older people. One in ten people provide such care, a fifth of them for over 50 hours a week. The more hours of unpaid care a person provides for ill people in need, the more likely they are to live outside the South. The highest proportions of people who have neither childcare, nor responsibilities caring for older people, live in London.

The pattern of unpaid care almost perfectly reflects the distribution of need for that care as reported in the census. Very few people in most of the South of England said that their health had not been good when asked in 2001. More children in the North and Wales are suffering from a limiting long-term illness, and the rise in illness in the South of England has been slowest, but reported illness rates are rising everywhere. The cartogram and map of the changing geography of adults suffering such illness is one of the most clearly patterned of such images shown in this atlas. In and around London, stretching out across southern England, are a mass of districts where limiting illness is both rare and rising most slowly. Only where the population is very old do underlying demographic factors appear to be more important than geography.

Households, families and people are becoming sorted out over space through selective migration over time that depends on the health of their household members, their family composition, whether they have work, and underlying all of this, their recourse to money. Being ill or needing to care for an elderly relative, having childcare responsibilities, living only on a single wage or no wage at all, alters where people in the UK can now afford to live far more than it did just 10 years ago.

Where living is expensive lone parents tend not to be found, and when people become lone parents many leave the area. In these areas are found increasing numbers of two-parent couples both having to work. People cannot afford to become ill; when they become old most leave. Two decades ago people were warned not to be ordinary, to be young, fall ill or grow old. Fewer people are now ordinary. If they are young then their location and probable future fortunes will depend more on their parents' circumstances than they have for many decades. For most who are ill or old, their choices over where to live have been curtailed over time and depend again on their family or recent good or bad fortune. That good or bad fortune too is influenced by what was happening to where they lived in recent decades. The last chapter illustrated that good fortune generally rose for those who were living in the South, where financial and other services have boomed. The households and families of the UK in the 21st century are a product of that recent past, made how they are greatly by where they were, and living where and how they now do more and more according to the needs or ambivalence of the markets which drive their location, education and employment.

In this chapter we divide households into 10 types, and map how each type is changing according to the proportions of the population who live in each type. We begin with people sharing accommodation, now 12.1% of all people (up 4.9%), ever more clustered in London. So too are the 6.6% of people who are younger and now living alone (up 2.2%); and the 4.2% of people in cohabiting couples without children, also most densely found in London (up 1.2%).

The 7.6% of the population who now live in lone-parent households are falling in number in the centre of the Capital, despite rising also in number nationally (up 1.6%). Unmarried couples with children now make up 5.0% (up 2.3%) of the population and increasingly cannot afford to live in the South. It is not until we turn to the largest group, the 29.8% of married people living with their children, that we find an 'ordinary' group in rapid decline (down 6.1%). However, this is the group who still can afford to live in the Home Counties, although even there they are declining in numbers and declining there and in London fastest when their children leave, and they join the 19.1% of people in the second largest household group of married couples with no children (down in size by 2.6%). As they age they become members of another household type: the 7.3% (down 1.5%) of pensioner couples, they are even more likely to have left the Capital if they were still there. The smallest group we consider, of 0.4% of people, are unrelated pensioners living together; these have behaved similarly, and are declining rapidly (down 2.5%). Of all these conventional types of household, only the 6.0% of people who are single pensioners living alone have grown in number (up 0.1%).

We next look in more detail at the changing geography of pensioners and those who live in communal establishments, and at the household space people live in: the changing number of rooms in the UK. The chapter ends by considering some of the non-English national languages understood by people at the periphery of the UK and estimates of the range of possible understanding of languages other than English in England.

It is through families and households that people arrange their lives, pool their collective resources, support each other and depend on one another. Types of family that were common are becoming rarer, and those which were rare in the past are almost all becoming more numerous. However, this is not leading to any greater heterogeneity of community in the UK. The type of household and family each individual lives in determines more and more where they live; and where they live is increasingly influencing the types of families and households they are likely to help form in the future, for whom they will need to care, how likely they are to be ill, and how much they may need, or be able, to work.

Who you live with, what you can depend on them for, and what they are most likely to need from you, depends increasingly on where you are, and is increasingly influencing where you are likely to be in the future.

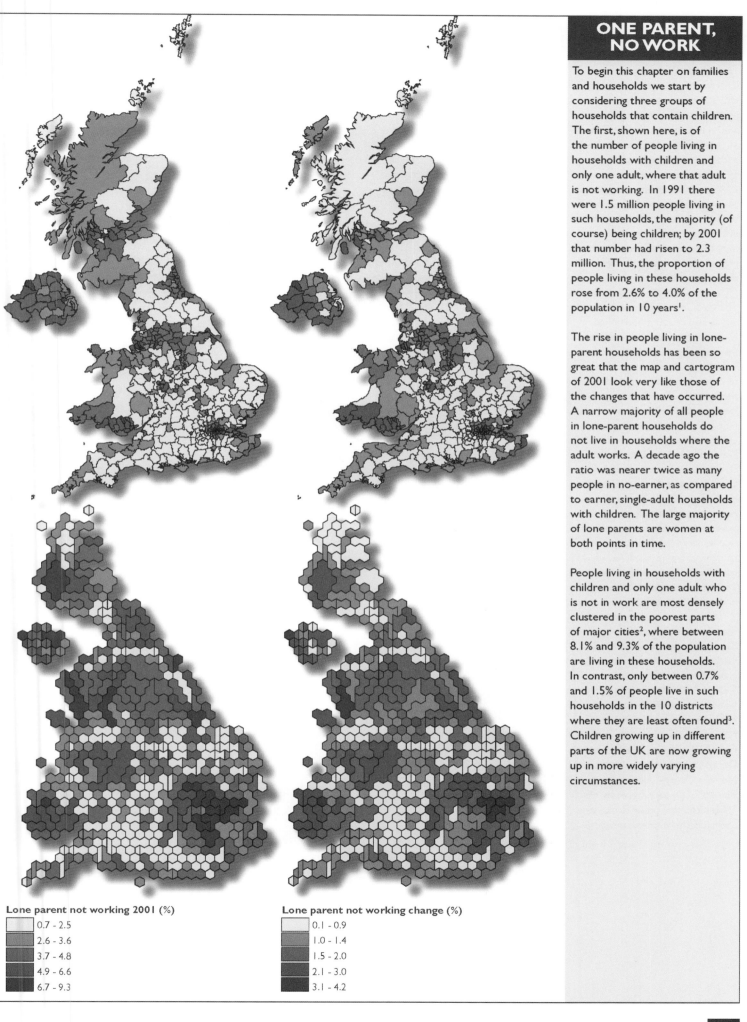

ONE PARENT, NO WORK

To begin this chapter on families and households we start by considering three groups of households that contain children. The first, shown here, is of the number of people living in households with children and only one adult, where that adult is not working. In 1991 there were 1.5 million people living in such households, the majority (of course) being children; by 2001 that number had risen to 2.3 million. Thus, the proportion of people living in these households rose from 2.6% to 4.0% of the population in 10 years[1].

The rise in people living in lone-parent households has been so great that the map and cartogram of 2001 look very like those of the changes that have occurred. A narrow majority of all people in lone-parent households do not live in households where the adult works. A decade ago the ratio was nearer twice as many people in no-earner, as compared to earner, single-adult households with children. The large majority of lone parents are women at both points in time.

People living in households with children and only one adult who is not in work are most densely clustered in the poorest parts of major cities[2], where between 8.1% and 9.3% of the population are living in these households. In contrast, only between 0.7% and 1.5% of people live in such households in the 10 districts where they are least often found[3]. Children growing up in different parts of the UK are now growing up in more widely varying circumstances.

Lone parent not working 2001 (%)

- 0.7 - 2.5
- 2.6 - 3.6
- 3.7 - 4.8
- 4.9 - 6.6
- 6.7 - 9.3

Lone parent not working change (%)

- 0.1 - 0.9
- 1.0 - 1.4
- 1.5 - 2.0
- 2.1 - 3.0
- 3.1 - 4.2

TWO PARENTS, ONE WORKING

The traditional form of family structure for children in the UK is of there being two parents in a household, one of whom is working. Only 9.7% of people in the UK now live in such households with children, 5.7 million people, down from 12.4% in 1991 (then 7.2 million people). This form of household has become more rare almost everywhere despite there now being fewer two-parent households in which neither parent works[4].

The traditional one earner, two adults and children household is most commonly found in the more rural parts of Northern Ireland, and in some suburbs of London, as well as in former mining areas. The 10 highest rates are in: Chiltern, Forest Heath, Elmbridge, Cookstown, Dungannon, Limavady, Magherafelt, Newry & Mourne, Omagh and Strabane. This is an eclectic group of areas. It is where work is scarce or childcare costs are high, as well as where people still believe that one parent should stay at home, perhaps, that the traditional family is still found to make up between 13.7% and 16.3% of the population as it does in those 10 places.

For Northern Ireland the list of places corresponds closely to those areas which have the highest proportions (between 5.6% and 12.1%) of two-adult families with children in which neither adult works: Hackney, Newham, Tower Hamlets (the highest), Easington, Cookstown, Derry, Dungannon, Newry & Mourne, Omagh and Strabane. The list of places where less than 1% fall into this group is too long to include here (see footnote 6).

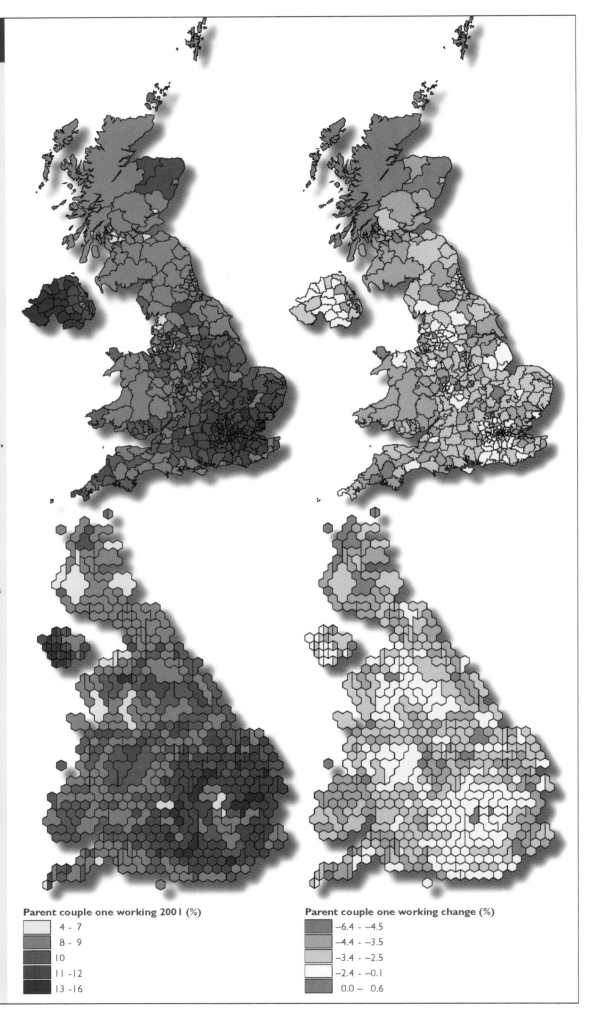

Parent couple one working 2001 (%)

- 4 - 7
- 8 - 9
- 10
- 11 -12
- 13 -16

Parent couple one working change (%)

- −6.4 - −4.5
- −4.4 - −3.5
- −3.4 - −2.5
- −2.4 - −0.1
- 0.0 - 0.6

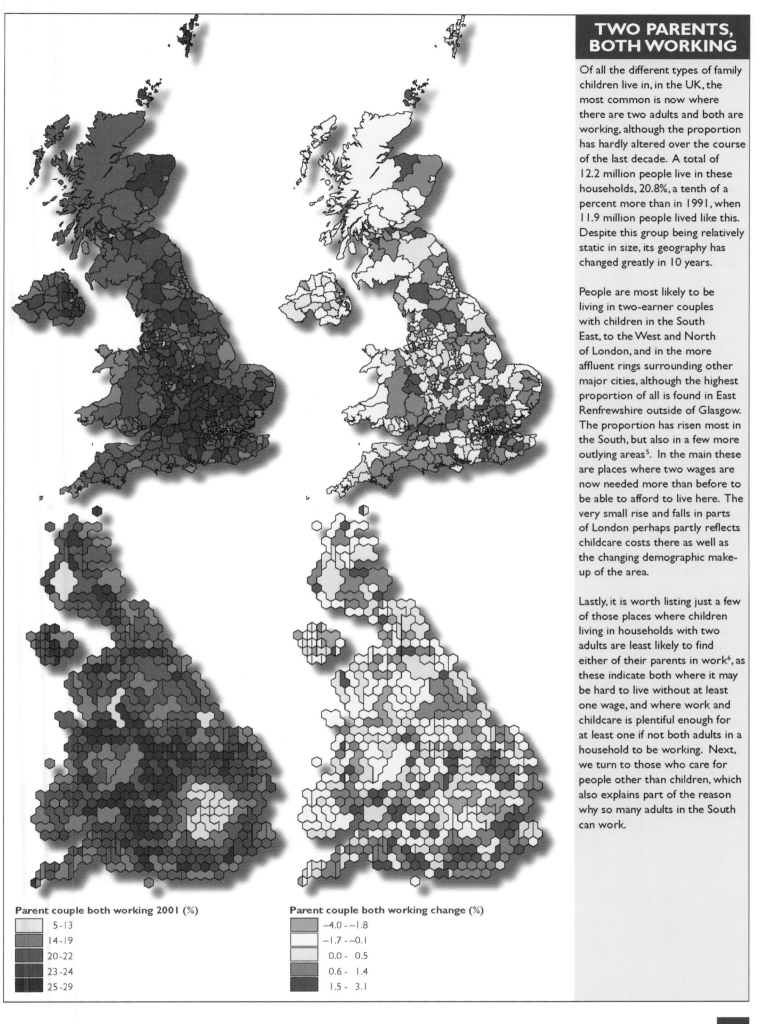

TWO PARENTS, BOTH WORKING

Of all the different types of family children live in, in the UK, the most common is now where there are two adults and both are working, although the proportion has hardly altered over the course of the last decade. A total of 12.2 million people live in these households, 20.8%, a tenth of a percent more than in 1991, when 11.9 million people lived like this. Despite this group being relatively static in size, its geography has changed greatly in 10 years.

People are most likely to be living in two-earner couples with children in the South East, to the West and North of London, and in the more affluent rings surrounding other major cities, although the highest proportion of all is found in East Renfrewshire outside of Glasgow. The proportion has risen most in the South, but also in a few more outlying areas[5]. In the main these are places where two wages are now needed more than before to be able to afford to live here. The very small rise and falls in parts of London perhaps partly reflects childcare costs there as well as the changing demographic make-up of the area.

Lastly, it is worth listing just a few of those places where children living in households with two adults are least likely to find either of their parents in work[6], as these indicate both where it may be hard to live without at least one wage, and where work and childcare is plentiful enough for at least one if not both adults in a household to be working. Next, we turn to those who care for people other than children, which also explains part of the reason why so many adults in the South can work.

Parent couple both working 2001 (%)

	5-13
	14-19
	20-22
	23-24
	25-29

Parent couple both working change (%)

	−4.0 − −1.8
	−1.7 − −0.1
	0.0 − 0.5
	0.6 − 1.4
	1.5 − 3.1

PART-TIME CARE

For the first time in 2001 a question was asked in the census as to how many hours a week each individual spent providing care, free of cost, to members of their family, friends or others who were in need of support because of long-term physical or mental ill-health, or disability, or health problems relating to old age. A total of 5.9 million people, almost a tenth of the population of the UK, said they provided such care. As no similar question was asked in 1991, we only show the current patterns to the provision of that care here, firstly for those providing between 1-19, and 20-49, hours of such care a week. It is perhaps a little disingenuous to call giving up 49 hours of your time a week: 'part-time'. However, many carers have to provide care for others for the majority of their waking hours. If people receive some financial support from the state for providing this care, such as an allowance, they are still included here.

In total, 4.0 million people provide up to 19 hours of unpaid care a week to others with health needs, 6.6% of the population. Such care is least common in parts of the South where fewer people are ill, and in Scotland where more people provide more hours of care[7]. A further 0.7 million people provide between 20-49 hours of unpaid care a week; they are living mostly outside of the South East where provision is lowest, again because need here is lowest[8]. People tend to provide unpaid care in almost direct proportion to the need for that care, which results in fewer adults being available to work in the North.

Unpaid care: 1-19 hours 2001 (%)

	4.6 - 5.5
	5.6 - 6.3
	6.4 - 7.0
	7.1 - 7.6
	7.7 - 9.0

Unpaid care: 20-49 hours 2001 (%)

	0.5 - 0.7
	0.8 - 1.0
	1.1 - 1.2
	1.3 - 1.5
	1.6 - 2.0

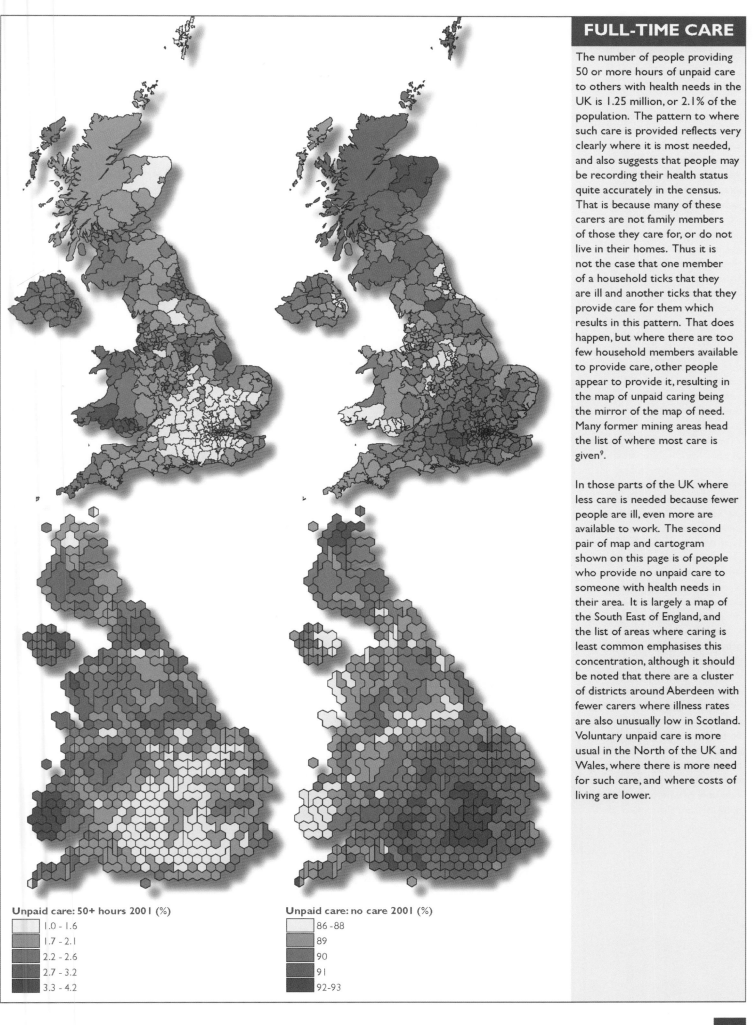

FULL-TIME CARE

The number of people providing 50 or more hours of unpaid care to others with health needs in the UK is 1.25 million, or 2.1% of the population. The pattern to where such care is provided reflects very clearly where it is most needed, and also suggests that people may be recording their health status quite accurately in the census. That is because many of these carers are not family members of those they care for, or do not live in their homes. Thus it is not the case that one member of a household ticks that they are ill and another ticks that they provide care for them which results in this pattern. That does happen, but where there are too few household members available to provide care, other people appear to provide it, resulting in the map of unpaid caring being the mirror of the map of need. Many former mining areas head the list of where most care is given[9].

In those parts of the UK where less care is needed because fewer people are ill, even more are available to work. The second pair of map and cartogram shown on this page is of people who provide no unpaid care to someone with health needs in their area. It is largely a map of the South East of England, and the list of areas where caring is least common emphasises this concentration, although it should be noted that there are a cluster of districts around Aberdeen with fewer carers where illness rates are also unusually low in Scotland. Voluntary unpaid care is more usual in the North of the UK and Wales, where there is more need for such care, and where costs of living are lower.

Unpaid care: 50+ hours 2001 (%)

- 1.0 - 1.6
- 1.7 - 2.1
- 2.2 - 2.6
- 2.7 - 3.2
- 3.3 - 4.2

Unpaid care: no care 2001 (%)

- 86 - 88
- 89
- 90
- 91
- 92 - 93

POOR HEALTH

To reiterate the relationship between health and care, we show here both the proportions of people reporting their health to be poor and those providing unpaid care in total. The 2001 Census included a new question on general health in the previous year which allowed individuals to state whether their health had not been good. A total of 5.5 million people, 9.3% of the population of the UK, said it had not been good. Where people were older, rates tended to be higher, but rates were influenced by geographical location, with poor health being very rare in the South East of England outside of London. Within London it is only in a few of the poorest boroughs that more than a tenth of the population have suffered from poor health within 12 months of the census.

When the maps and cartograms of poor health and unpaid care are compared, they appear almost identical. However, it is possible to subtract one proportion from the other to calculate where there crudely appears to be the least unpaid care being provided, given the number of people with poor health and conversely where more care than usual is provided[10]. In general, it is in the poorer urban boroughs and Welsh Valleys where less care is provided than might be expected given the need. It is in the most affluent areas of the South and in a similar part of Northern Ireland that there are more carers than people who appear to need to be cared for. This comparison does not take into account the number of hours of care provided nor the severity of need, but it is indicative of where there is more need for care than is provided.

Health: not good 2001 (%)

	5 - 7
	8 - 9
	10 - 11
	12 - 13
	14 - 18

Unpaid care 2001 (%)

	6.6 - 8.4
	8.5 - 9.5
	9.6 - 10.5
	10.6 - 11.6
	11.7 - 14.1

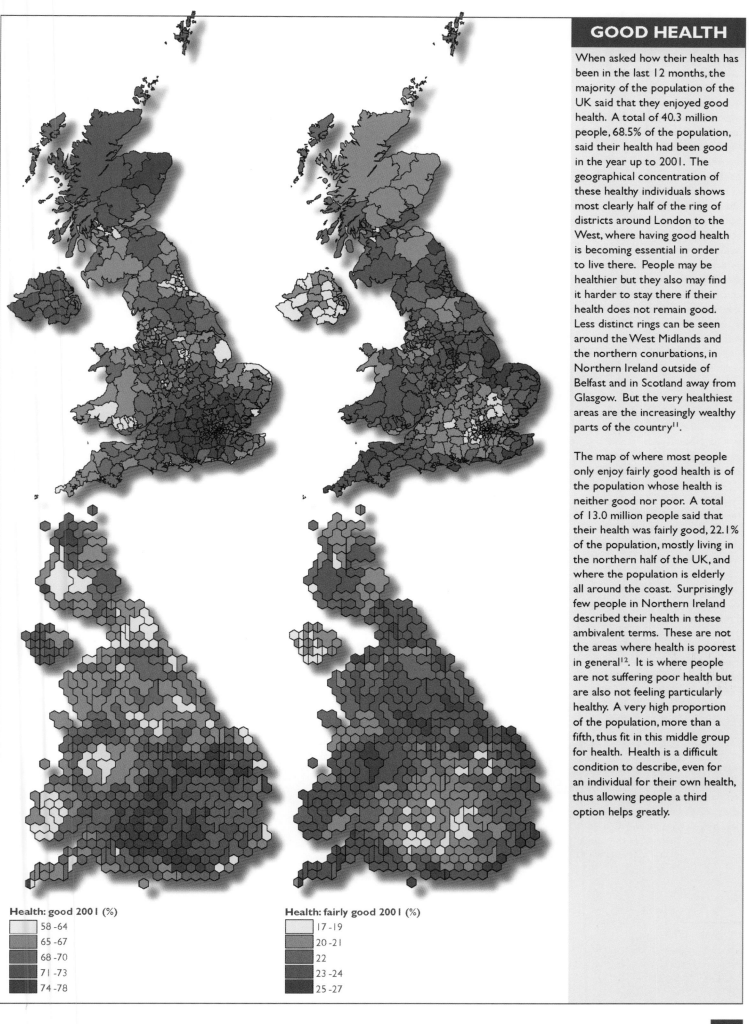

GOOD HEALTH

When asked how their health has been in the last 12 months, the majority of the population of the UK said that they enjoyed good health. A total of 40.3 million people, 68.5% of the population, said their health had been good in the year up to 2001. The geographical concentration of these healthy individuals shows most clearly half of the ring of districts around London to the West, where having good health is becoming essential in order to live there. People may be healthier but they also may find it harder to stay there if their health does not remain good. Less distinct rings can be seen around the West Midlands and the northern conurbations, in Northern Ireland outside of Belfast and in Scotland away from Glasgow. But the very healthiest areas are the increasingly wealthy parts of the country[11].

The map of where most people only enjoy fairly good health is of the population whose health is neither good nor poor. A total of 13.0 million people said that their health was fairly good, 22.1% of the population, mostly living in the northern half of the UK, and where the population is elderly all around the coast. Surprisingly few people in Northern Ireland described their health in these ambivalent terms. These are not the areas where health is poorest in general[12]. It is where people are not suffering poor health but are also not feeling particularly healthy. A very high proportion of the population, more than a fifth, thus fit in this middle group for health. Health is a difficult condition to describe, even for an individual for their own health, thus allowing people a third option helps greatly.

Health: good 2001 (%)

	58 -64
	65 -67
	68 -70
	71 -73
	74 -78

Health: fairly good 2001 (%)

	17 -19
	20 -21
	22
	23 -24
	25 -27

People and places

ILLNESS, DISABILITY AND CHILDREN

The 1991 Census included a question as to whether each individual suffered from a limiting long-term illness, which was repeated in 2001. Using the answers to that question it is possible to compare the share of the population who were children with such a disability at both points in time. Given that the 2001 Census included an additional question on health, it might have been assumed that more people would have used this, and the numbers ticking the limiting long-term illness box would have fallen. That was not the case. For people aged under 16, 0.27 million had such a disability in 1991, 0.5% of the population as a whole, and that number rose to 0.52 million by 2001, 0.9% of all people in the UK. Almost all of these judgements will have been made by the parents, as it is the parents who tend to complete the form[13].

Rates of childhood disability increased everywhere in the UK, but most quickly in Northern Ireland and in other areas away from the Home Counties. Childhood disability is generally most common in poorer northern city centres, in the Province and the Welsh Valleys; but a cluster of London boroughs also report higher than average rates now[14]. Almost all of the areas with the lowest proportions of their populations being children suffering these disabilities are found in southern England[15]. To be more precise as to how unusual these rates are, we would have to use the numbers of children rather than of all people as the denominator in calculating these rates (which would then not be comparable with figures reported in the rest of this atlas).

Illness and disability: age 0-15, 2001 (%)
- 0.3 - 0.6
- 0.7
- 0.8
- 0.9 - 1.0
- 1.1 - 1.7

Illness and disability: age 0-15, change (%)
- 0.1 - 0.3
- 0.4
- 0.5 - 0.6
- 0.7 - 0.8
- 0.9 - 1.0

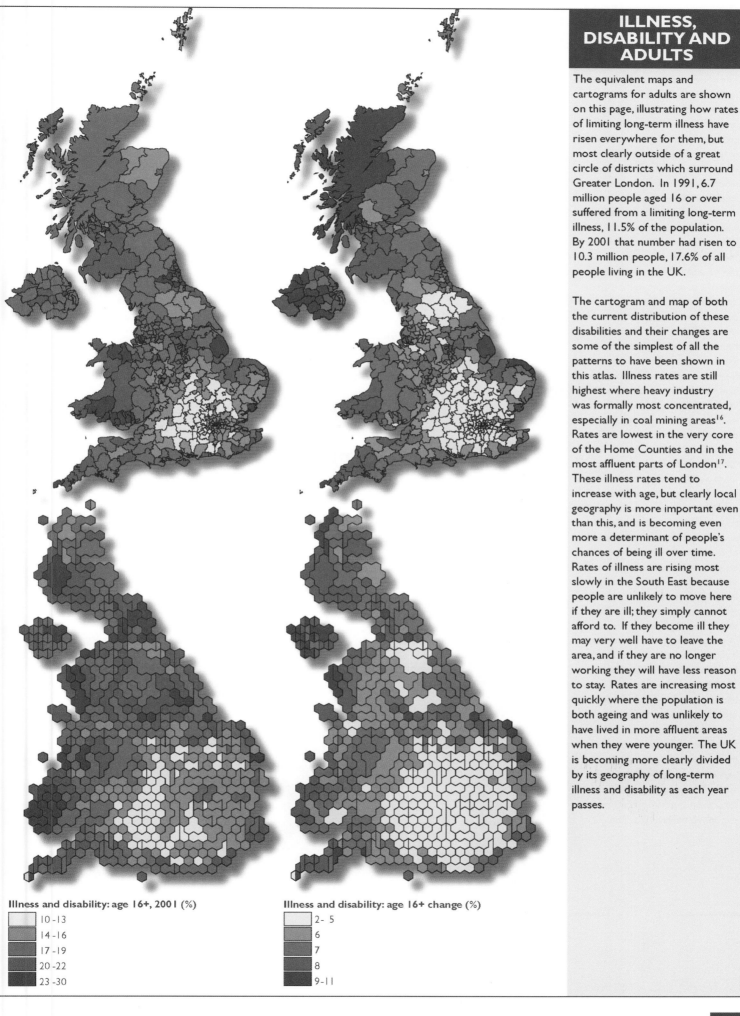

ILLNESS, DISABILITY AND ADULTS

The equivalent maps and cartograms for adults are shown on this page, illustrating how rates of limiting long-term illness have risen everywhere for them, but most clearly outside of a great circle of districts which surround Greater London. In 1991, 6.7 million people aged 16 or over suffered from a limiting long-term illness, 11.5% of the population. By 2001 that number had risen to 10.3 million people, 17.6% of all people living in the UK.

The cartogram and map of both the current distribution of these disabilities and their changes are some of the simplest of all the patterns to have been shown in this atlas. Illness rates are still highest where heavy industry was formally most concentrated, especially in coal mining areas[16]. Rates are lowest in the very core of the Home Counties and in the most affluent parts of London[17]. These illness rates tend to increase with age, but clearly local geography is more important even than this, and is becoming even more a determinant of people's chances of being ill over time. Rates of illness are rising most slowly in the South East because people are unlikely to move here if they are ill; they simply cannot afford to. If they become ill they may very well have to leave the area, and if they are no longer working they will have less reason to stay. Rates are increasing most quickly where the population is both ageing and was unlikely to have lived in more affluent areas when they were younger. The UK is becoming more clearly divided by its geography of long-term illness and disability as each year passes.

Illness and disability: age 16+, 2001 (%)

	10-13
	14-16
	17-19
	20-22
	23-30

Illness and disability: age 16+ change (%)

	2-5
	6
	7
	8
	9-11

HOUSEHOLDS WITHOUT FAMILIES

The geographies of caring, need and illness are related to the types of households found in each area. People can be grouped according to the type of households they live in. This is done here and in the following nine pages primarily according to the relationships between the adults in the household and whether the household includes children or pensioners. Where there is more than one adult in the household but no pair are married or cohabiting, and the household does not include only pensioners, then the household is classed as 'other'. Other households are now the third most common form of household found in the UK. Of all people living in the UK in 2001, 12.1% lived in these households, 7.1 million people and a huge increase of 3 million from 7.2% in 1991.

Other households are mainly made up of younger adults sharing accommodation, most often found in London and university towns. Although increasing numbers of students are part of the reason for the rise in households of this kind, the bulk of the increase is due to adults in their mid twenties and thirties sharing accommodation, often when working in their first job in a city. The 10 areas with the highest rates are all found within London[18]. But only four of these 10 are the same areas that have had the greatest increases[19]. The only decrease has been in the City of London of one tenth of 1%, but the slowest rises elsewhere are in nearby Kensington & Chelsea and Westminster, both of only 1.1%. Sharing may have reached saturation point in the most expensive parts of London.

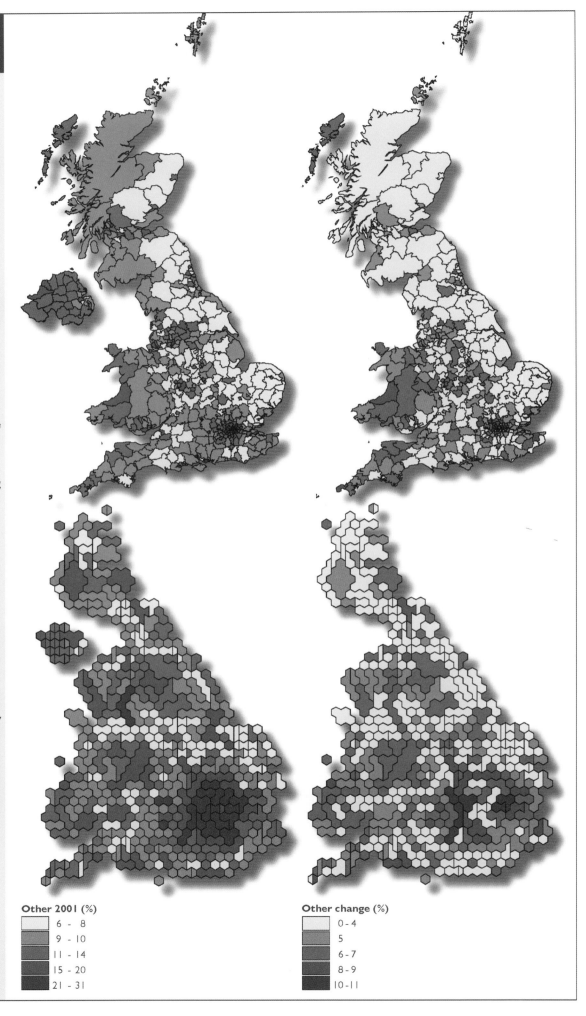

Other 2001 (%)

	6 - 8
	9 - 10
	11 - 14
	15 - 20
	21 - 31

Other change (%)

	0 - 4
	5
	6 - 7
	8 - 9
	10 - 11

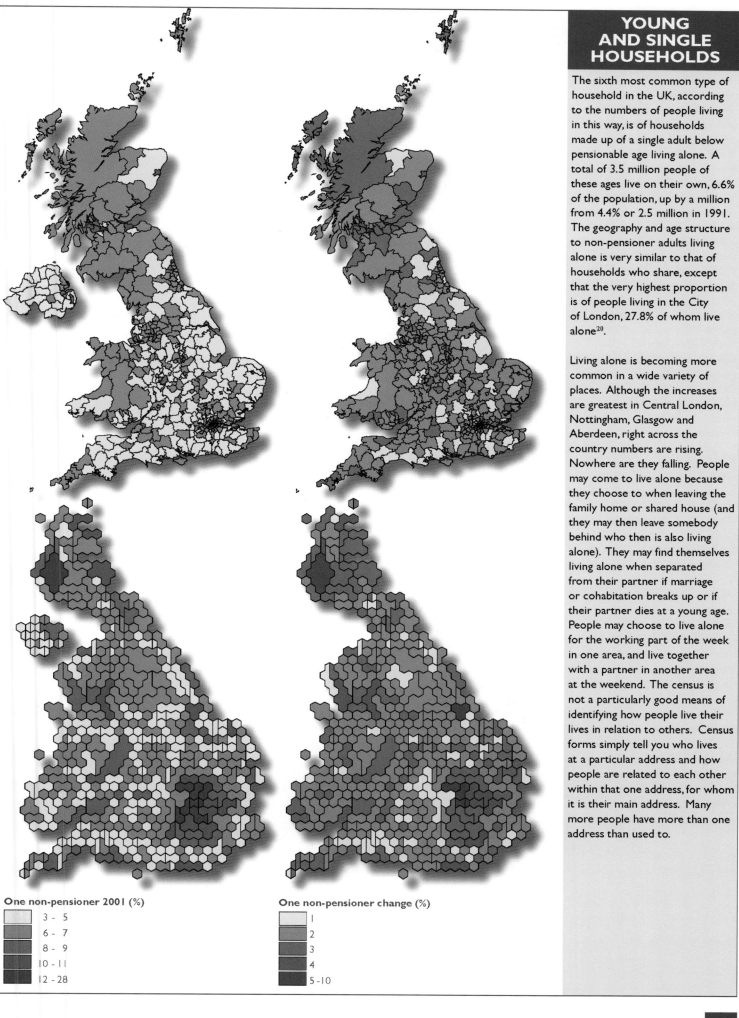

YOUNG AND SINGLE HOUSEHOLDS

The sixth most common type of household in the UK, according to the numbers of people living in this way, is of households made up of a single adult below pensionable age living alone. A total of 3.5 million people of these ages live on their own, 6.6% of the population, up by a million from 4.4% or 2.5 million in 1991. The geography and age structure to non-pensioner adults living alone is very similar to that of households who share, except that the very highest proportion is of people living in the City of London, 27.8% of whom live alone[20].

Living alone is becoming more common in a wide variety of places. Although the increases are greatest in Central London, Nottingham, Glasgow and Aberdeen, right across the country numbers are rising. Nowhere are they falling. People may come to live alone because they choose to when leaving the family home or shared house (and they may then leave somebody behind who then is also living alone). They may find themselves living alone when separated from their partner if marriage or cohabitation breaks up or if their partner dies at a young age. People may choose to live alone for the working part of the week in one area, and live together with a partner in another area at the weekend. The census is not a particularly good means of identifying how people live their lives in relation to others. Census forms simply tell you who lives at a particular address and how people are related to each other within that one address, for whom it is their main address. Many more people have more than one address than used to.

One non-pensioner 2001 (%)

- 3 - 5
- 6 - 7
- 8 - 9
- 10 - 11
- 12 - 28

One non-pensioner change (%)

- 1
- 2
- 3
- 4
- 5 - 10

COHABITING WITH NO CHILDREN

The second smallest of all the 10 types of household considered here consists of a pair of adults under pensionable age who are cohabiting. Coincidentally, the smallest group, ten times fewer in number, is of households consisting of groups of two or more pensioners who are not married or cohabiting. Of people below pensionable age, 2.5 million, 4.2% of the population as a whole, are cohabiting without children in their household. A decade ago the number and proportion were 1.7 million and 3.0% respectively. A significant part of the increase will be due to the census authorities now recognising that some same-sex couples are cohabiting. In 1991 these couples were assigned to the 'other households' group whether they stated they were cohabiting or not.

Cohabiting below pensionable age without children is most common in the City of London (9.1%) and Brighton & Hove (7.8%). Outside of London other high concentrations include Norwich (6.7%), Reading (6.1%) and Watford (6.0%). Cohabiting is generally more common in the South of England, although it has increased most over time across many parts of Britain[21]. We cannot include Northern Ireland in these statistics of change because household type was not tabulated in sufficient detail in 1991 there. Cohabiting without children has become slightly less popular only in a few London boroughs where many more adults below pensionable age are sharing their costs of living without also saying that they cohabit with the people they live with.

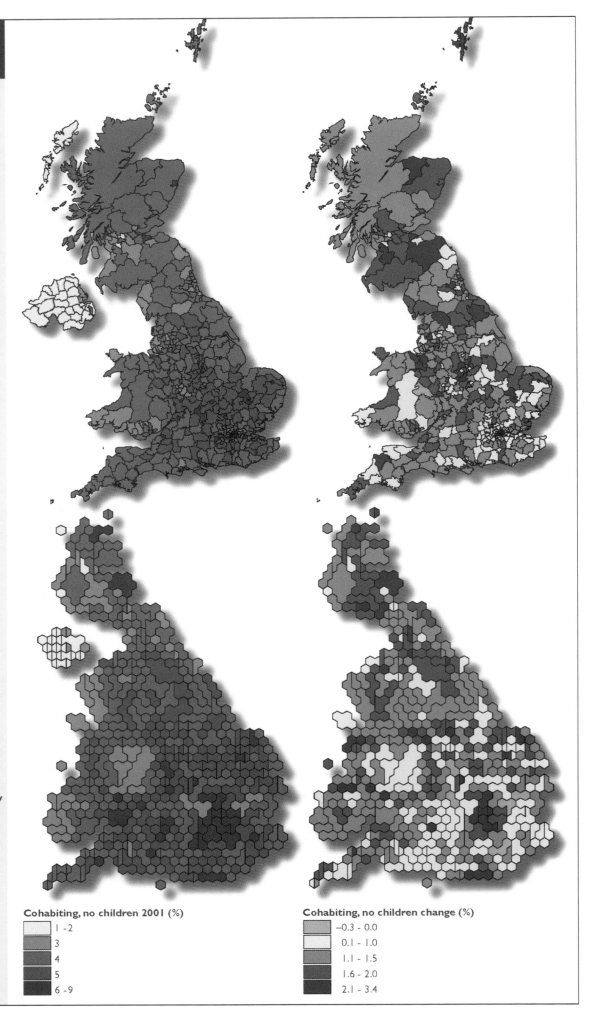

Cohabiting, no children 2001 (%)

- 1 - 2
- 3
- 4
- 5
- 6 - 9

Cohabiting, no children change (%)

- −0.3 - 0.0
- 0.1 - 1.0
- 1.1 - 1.5
- 1.6 - 2.0
- 2.1 - 3.4

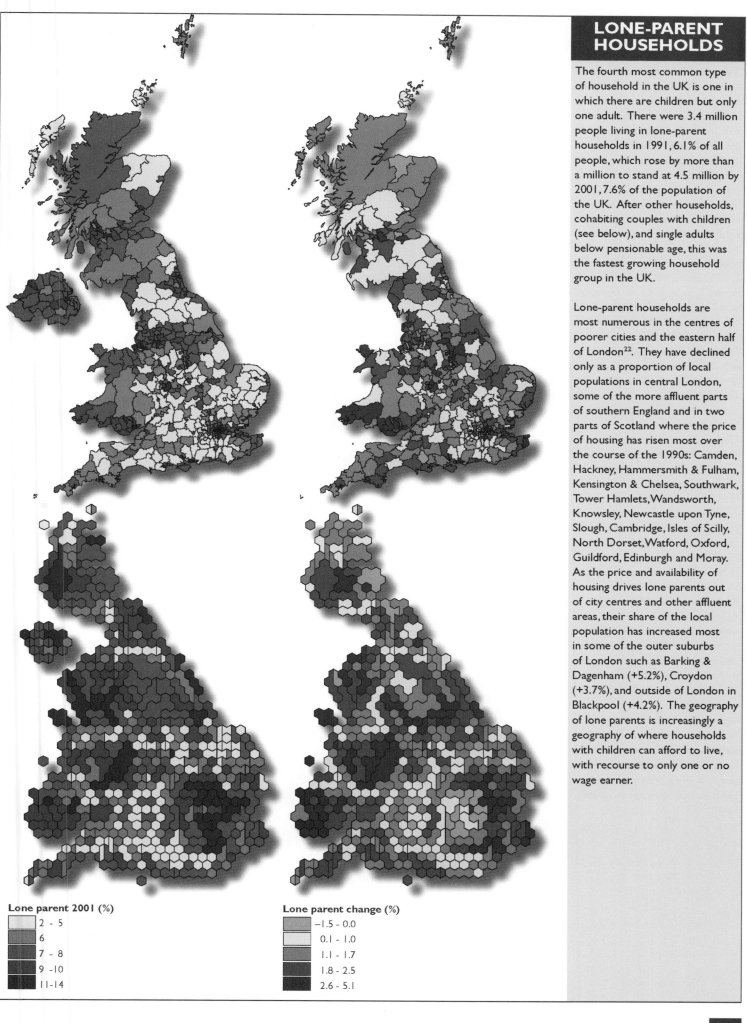

LONE-PARENT HOUSEHOLDS

The fourth most common type of household in the UK is one in which there are children but only one adult. There were 3.4 million people living in lone-parent households in 1991, 6.1% of all people, which rose by more than a million to stand at 4.5 million by 2001, 7.6% of the population of the UK. After other households, cohabiting couples with children (see below), and single adults below pensionable age, this was the fastest growing household group in the UK.

Lone-parent households are most numerous in the centres of poorer cities and the eastern half of London[22]. They have declined only as a proportion of local populations in central London, some of the more affluent parts of southern England and in two parts of Scotland where the price of housing has risen most over the course of the 1990s: Camden, Hackney, Hammersmith & Fulham, Kensington & Chelsea, Southwark, Tower Hamlets, Wandsworth, Knowsley, Newcastle upon Tyne, Slough, Cambridge, Isles of Scilly, North Dorset, Watford, Oxford, Guildford, Edinburgh and Moray. As the price and availability of housing drives lone parents out of city centres and other affluent areas, their share of the local population has increased most in some of the outer suburbs of London such as Barking & Dagenham (+5.2%), Croydon (+3.7%), and outside of London in Blackpool (+4.2%). The geography of lone parents is increasingly a geography of where households with children can afford to live, with recourse to only one or no wage earner.

Lone parent 2001 (%)

- 2 - 5
- 6
- 7 - 8
- 9 -10
- 11-14

Lone parent change (%)

- −1.5 - 0.0
- 0.1 - 1.0
- 1.1 - 1.7
- 1.8 - 2.5
- 2.6 - 5.1

COHABITING COUPLES WITH CHILDREN

By 2001 more people were living in cohabiting couples with children than without them. Of course we include children in our calculations so there will be slightly fewer cohabiting households with children as compared to cohabiting couple households without them. In 2001, 2.9 million people (5.0%) lived in cohabiting couple households with children as compared to only 1.5 million in 1991 (2.6%). The numbers of people living in these households have risen across all of Britain, but most where there are more children and least in London. In the UK as a whole, people are least likely to be living in such households in Northern Ireland, where all 10 areas with the lowest proportions are to be found[23].

The areas where the highest proportions of people in cohabiting couple households with children live are all in the North of England, and generally in the poorer but more traditional parts of the North outside of the main city centres[24]. Of the 10 areas where living in this group of households is most common, six are among the top 10 areas to have seen the fastest growth in this group. These households are most commonly found where they are being established most quickly because this is a relatively new way for millions of people in the UK to live, having almost doubled in popularity in the last decade. It is worth noting that although marriage is most rare in the South and in London in particular, not being married but cohabiting in a couple with children is also rarest, and is increasingly least commonly found there.

Cohabiting with children 2001 (%)

- 1 - 2
- 3 - 4
- 5
- 6
- 7 - 8

Cohabiting with children change (%)

- 0.3 - 1.5
- 1.6 - 2.2
- 2.3 - 2.9
- 3.0 - 3.5
- 3.6 - 4.8

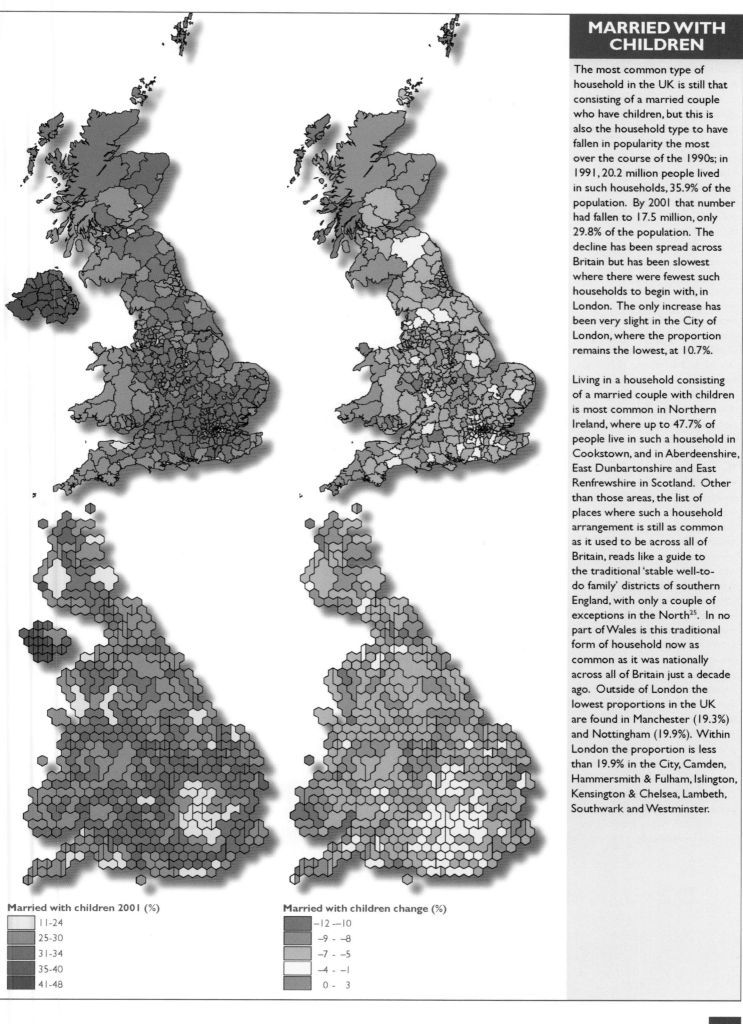

MARRIED WITH CHILDREN

The most common type of household in the UK is still that consisting of a married couple who have children, but this is also the household type to have fallen in popularity the most over the course of the 1990s; in 1991, 20.2 million people lived in such households, 35.9% of the population. By 2001 that number had fallen to 17.5 million, only 29.8% of the population. The decline has been spread across Britain but has been slowest where there were fewest such households to begin with, in London. The only increase has been very slight in the City of London, where the proportion remains the lowest, at 10.7%.

Living in a household consisting of a married couple with children is most common in Northern Ireland, where up to 47.7% of people live in such a household in Cookstown, and in Aberdeenshire, East Dunbartonshire and East Renfrewshire in Scotland. Other than those areas, the list of places where such a household arrangement is still as common as it used to be across all of Britain, reads like a guide to the traditional 'stable well-to-do family' districts of southern England, with only a couple of exceptions in the North[25]. In no part of Wales is this traditional form of household now as common as it was nationally across all of Britain just a decade ago. Outside of London the lowest proportions in the UK are found in Manchester (19.3%) and Nottingham (19.9%). Within London the proportion is less than 19.9% in the City, Camden, Hammersmith & Fulham, Islington, Kensington & Chelsea, Lambeth, Southwark and Westminster.

Married with children 2001 (%)

	11-24
	25-30
	31-34
	35-40
	41-48

Married with children change (%)

	−12 −−10
	−9 - −8
	−7 - −5
	−4 - −1
	0 - 3

MARRIED WITHOUT CHILDREN

In defining these household types we only include children of ages and in circumstances that mean that they are generally dependent on their parents. People who do not have, or no longer have, dependent children living with them are classed as being without children. This can mean, however, that some of the households we include in this category may be headed by a married couple, but still contain non-dependent children in, say, their twenties. Despite these inclusions, this group of households is the second fastest to have declined after married couples with children. It remains the second largest group also with 11.2 million (19.1%), a million fewer than the 12.2 million in 1991 (21.7%). Households that contain only pensioners are included in the categories on the next three pages.

The numbers of adults living in these types of households are highest as a proportion of local populations in the North in areas where people tend to be more elderly, but also where very large numbers are not yet retired[26]. They are least common in much of London, Manchester, Cambridge, Brighton & Hove, Nottingham and Oxford. This group is declining in number the most where there have been increases in the local proportions of student households, of young people often with children, where many older people are now retired, or where a combination of these factors come together[27]. In the future, as fewer households are made up of married couples with children, we can expect this decline to continue. The decline may even accelerate, as many people in this group are soon to become pensioners.

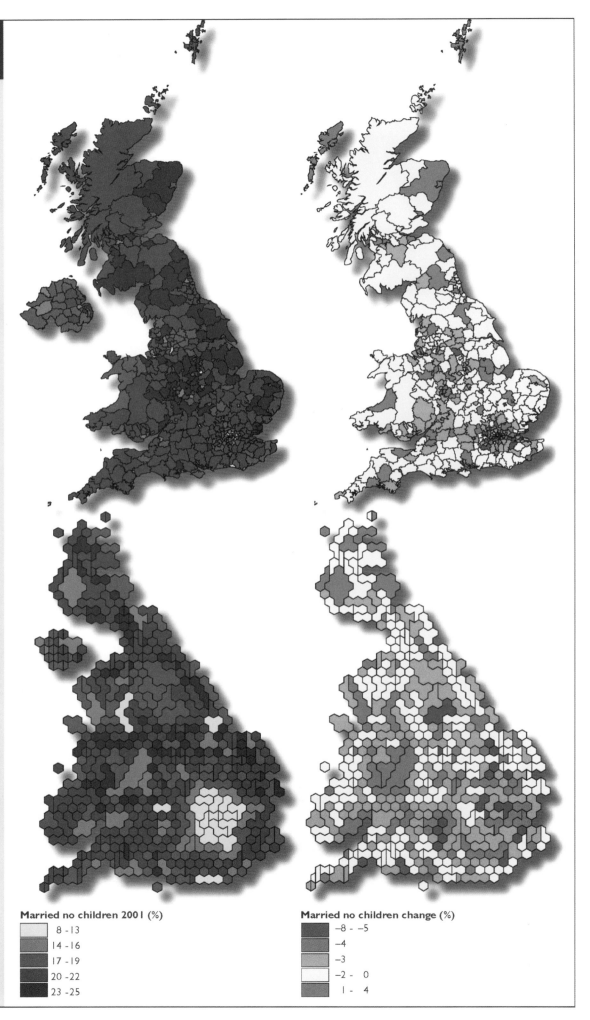

Married no children 2001 (%)

	8 - 13
	14 - 16
	17 - 19
	20 - 22
	23 - 25

Married no children change (%)

	−8 - −5
	−4
	−3
	−2 - 0
	1 - 4

PENSIONER FAMILIES

The 2001 and 1991 Censuses did not release information on pensioner households in identical ways. Here we are comparing the number of people living as a couple who were pensioners in 1991 with all households consisting only of pensioners that contained a family in 2001, people who were related, most commonly by marriage. Our latter definition is a little wider than the former one, and thus all else being equal this group should rise in time. All else is never equal and so across the country we see the proportion of the population who are pensioners living in families with other pensioners to be declining. In 1991 there were 5.0 million people living in pensioner families (8.8%); by 1991 that number had fallen to 4.3 million (7.3%). However, this is still the fifth most common form of household in the UK.

Pensioner families are most commonly found along the coasts of the South of England[28]. Fewer people in couples tend to live long enough for both to be pensioners and still to be together in the North, Scotland, Northern Ireland and Wales. Despite this concentration, pensioner couples are declining in number on the shorelines nearest to London, and are still falling within London despite being found in very low numbers there in 1991. The area where the smallest proportion of the local population consists of pensioner couples is now Hackney (2.1%, from 5.0% in 1991). Pensioner families are only increasing in proportion in a scattering of small districts where local demographics have combined for the age groups associated with this group to be rising rapidly.

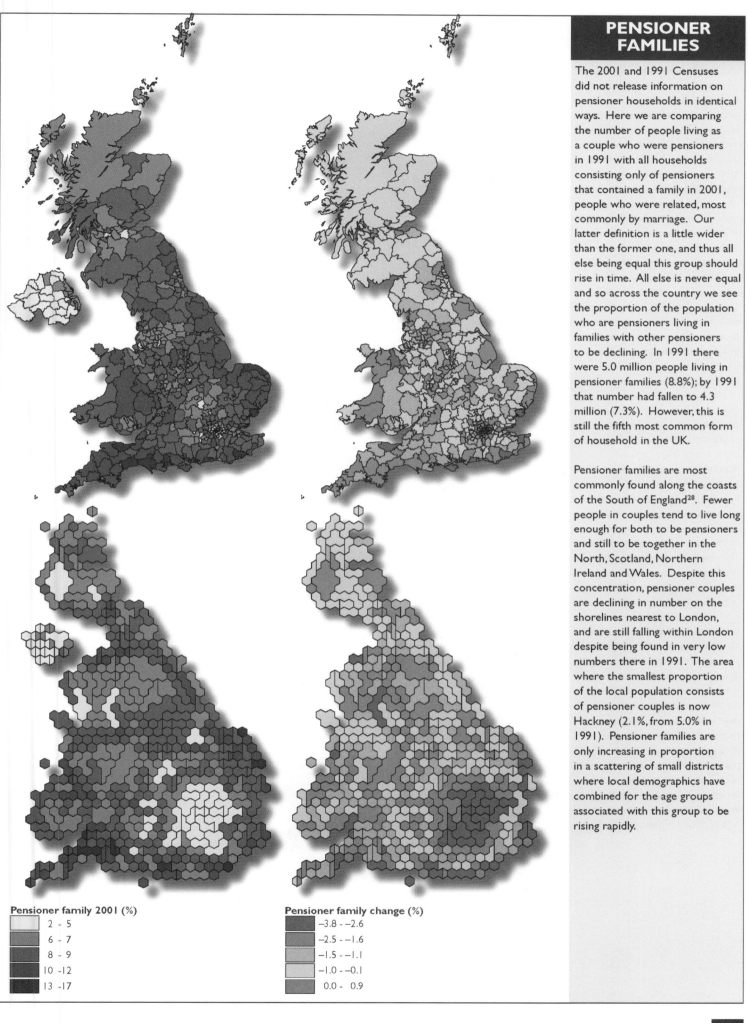

Pensioner family 2001 (%)
- 2 - 5
- 6 - 7
- 8 - 9
- 10 - 12
- 13 - 17

Pensioner family change (%)
- −3.8 - −2.6
- −2.5 - −1.6
- −1.5 - −1.1
- −1.0 - −0.1
- 0.0 - 0.9

145

OTHER PENSIONER HOUSEHOLDS

Our smallest household group in this comparison consists of those made up of only two or more pensioners in which no one is in a couple. This group included 1.6 million people in 1991, but only 0.2 million by 2001, a very large fall from 2.9% to 0.4%. Part of the reason for this fall will be that we included all pensioner households with families in the last category in 2001, and thus one pensioner living in a household with two pensioners who were married would have been included in this group in 1991 but not in 2001. However, the main reason for this fall is that there are now fewer pensioners living in unmarried or not cohabiting couples. The classic 'other pensioner' household would have consisted of two unmarried women in 1991, of which at least one has died or moved into a communal establishment by 2001. There were a very large group of women born roughly 100 years ago who never married following the deaths of young men in the First World War. Many of them lived as a pair in 1991 and most of those pairs are now dissolved. The declines have been highest where there were most such households in the past, the very highest in areas all outside of the South of England[29]. Other pensioner households are now confined more to the coast and similar areas than before[30]. This group may well rise in size in the future as a generation less constrained by the norms of marriage begins to retire in large numbers. Whether they rise in number again to equal the numbers of unmarried pensioners who were living together in the recent past is another matter. What we see here is the passing of a particular generation.

Other pensioner 2001 (%)

- 0.2
- 0.3
- 0.4
- 0.5
- 0.6 - 1.3

Other pensioner change (%)

- −5.8 - −3.5
- −3.4 - −3.0
- −2.9 - −2.6
- −2.5 - −2.0
- −1.9 - −1.3

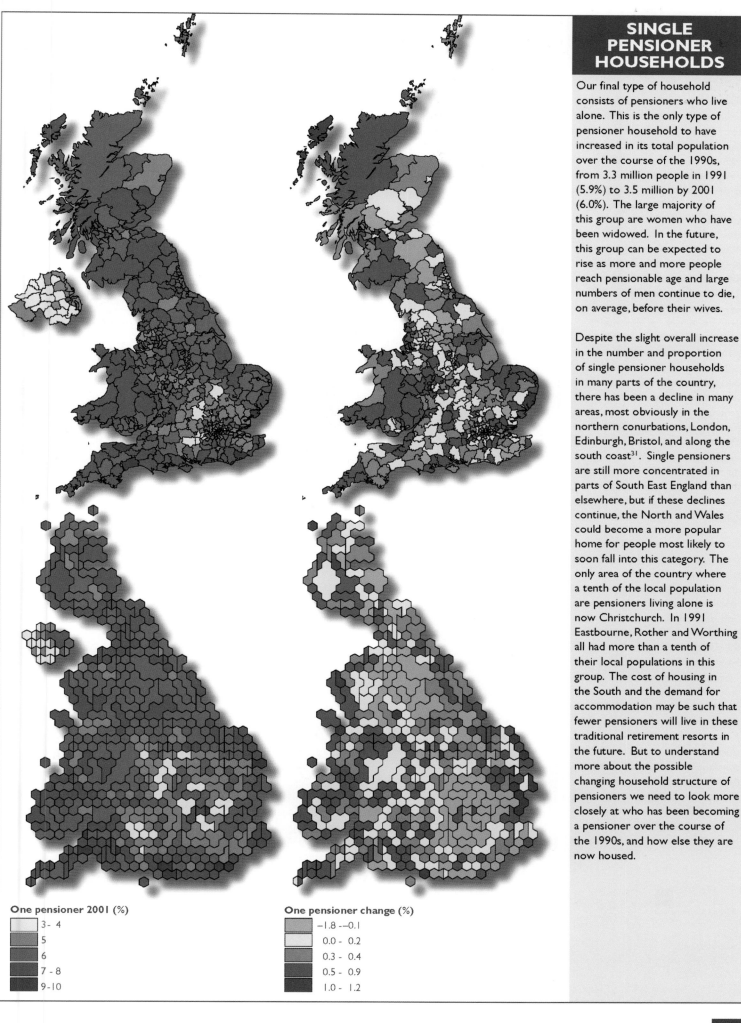

SINGLE PENSIONER HOUSEHOLDS

Our final type of household consists of pensioners who live alone. This is the only type of pensioner household to have increased in its total population over the course of the 1990s, from 3.3 million people in 1991 (5.9%) to 3.5 million by 2001 (6.0%). The large majority of this group are women who have been widowed. In the future, this group can be expected to rise as more and more people reach pensionable age and large numbers of men continue to die, on average, before their wives.

Despite the slight overall increase in the number and proportion of single pensioner households in many parts of the country, there has been a decline in many areas, most obviously in the northern conurbations, London, Edinburgh, Bristol, and along the south coast[31]. Single pensioners are still more concentrated in parts of South East England than elsewhere, but if these declines continue, the North and Wales could become a more popular home for people most likely to soon fall into this category. The only area of the country where a tenth of the local population are pensioners living alone is now Christchurch. In 1991 Eastbourne, Rother and Worthing all had more than a tenth of their local populations in this group. The cost of housing in the South and the demand for accommodation may be such that fewer pensioners will live in these traditional retirement resorts in the future. But to understand more about the possible changing household structure of pensioners we need to look more closely at who has been becoming a pensioner over the course of the 1990s, and how else they are now housed.

One pensioner 2001 (%)
- 3 - 4
- 5
- 6
- 7 - 8
- 9 - 10

One pensioner change (%)
- −1.8 − −0.1
- 0.0 - 0.2
- 0.3 - 0.4
- 0.5 - 0.9
- 1.0 - 1.2

PENSIONERS

To understand why the proportions of people living in the various pensioner households have changed as they have, it is important to understand how the total proportions of pensioners have changed, and are now distributed, across the UK. In 1991 there were 10.6 million pensioners in the UK, 18.3% of the population. This only rose to 10.8 million by 2001, 18.4% of the population. The population of the UK may be ageing but the proportion who have retired remains very similar nationally. This is because the large bulk of the post-war baby boom generation have yet to retire. The numbers of additional young retirees have only just cancelled out the declines in people aged over pensionable age in the UK, which occurred because the generation born in that even earlier baby boom, that followed the First World War, are now beginning to largely die out. For more details of these changes see the footnotes of the 'Age and sex' chapter at the beginning of this atlas.

Pensioners have declined as a proportion of local populations in large numbers in many cities and especially in London and nearby towns[32]. Further away from these areas that are increasingly being populated by the young, their numbers are increasing. Pensioners remain most concentrated in traditional retirement areas although new places are joining that list[33]. To understand how the changing geography of pensioners changes the geography of where pensioners live in households in the UK, it is also important to consider the changing numbers of pensioners who are living in communal establishments.

Pensioners 2001 (%)
- 11 -15
- 16 -18
- 19 -21
- 22 -25
- 26 -33

Pensioners change (%)
- −4.4 - −2.5
- −2.4 - −0.8
- −0.7 - −0.1
- 0.0 - 1.4
- 1.5 - 3.8

PENSIONERS IN COMMUNAL HOMES

As the numbers of very elderly pensioners have fallen, the numbers living in communal homes have also decreased slightly. In 1991, 0.44 million pensioners lived in communal establishments, 0.8% of the population of the UK. By 2001 those numbers had reduced to 0.43 million, or 0.7% of the total population. Thus there are not fewer pensioner families and other pensioner households because more people are now living in retirement and nursing homes. There are fewer of these types of households because more pensioners are now living on their own, in the community, and because there has been hardly any increase in the numbers of pensioners living in the UK over the course of the 1990s. That increase is yet to come.

There are more pensioners living in communal establishments where there are more pensioners in total, and in places where pensioners tend to be a little more affluent than elsewhere[34]. Many communal establishments are privately run and the cost of staying in them can be high. In many traditional areas where retirement homes are clustered, the numbers of pensioners living there has fallen, whereas in many places not usually associated with such accommodation, it is rising[35]. In the future we can expect these communal establishments to fill up again, and more to be built as the rising numbers of pensioners living on their own stop being able to do so, and as more and more of the population age to eventually form the largest ever cohort of people surviving to ages where they will almost certainly need such accommodation in the future.

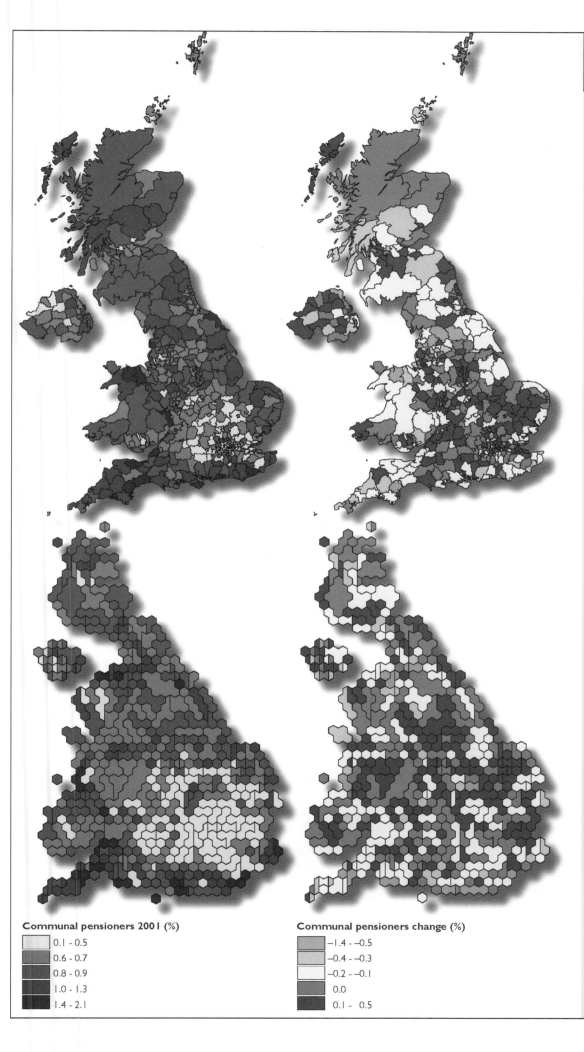

Communal pensioners 2001 (%)

- 0.1 - 0.5
- 0.6 - 0.7
- 0.8 - 0.9
- 1.0 - 1.3
- 1.4 - 2.1

Communal pensioners change (%)

- −1.4 - −0.5
- −0.4 - −0.3
- −0.2 - −0.1
- 0.0
- 0.1 - 0.5

ROOMS

One of the key reasons why slightly fewer older people currently need to be housed in communal establishments than in 1991 is that there is now more space for them to live, particularly in many of the areas where they live in greatest concentrations. In 1991, there were 113.4 million rooms in homes in the UK, 2.0 per person on average. By 2001, that number had risen to 126.9 million rooms, 2.2 per person on average. More rooms were added to dwellings, net, everywhere, but least in London where there was the least room to add them (other than in the City, where the number of rooms available for households doubled in the 10 years, due to redevelopment in particular parts of the City).

The highest number of rooms per person are found in West Somerset, where there are 2.5 times as many rooms in homes as there are people to live there[36]. In contrast, Tower Hamlets has the fewest rooms per person now with two people living there for every three rooms in the borough[37]. The 2001 Census did not report other statistics on people per room in a format comparable with 1991, so we cannot compare rates of overcrowding and under-occupancy in other ways. However, given the general movement of people into the Capital, and given that the fewest rooms have been added there, and that areas there have become more polarised between rich and poor, it would not be foolish to assume that for a growing minority of people in London and maybe elsewhere, more are living in less space. Elsewhere lives a minority who are consuming yet more and more rooms and homes per person[38].

Rooms per person 2001

- 1.6 - 1.9
- 2.0 - 2.1
- 2.2
- 2.3
- 2.4 - 2.5

Rooms per person change

- 0.0
- 0.1
- 0.2
- 0.3
- 0.4

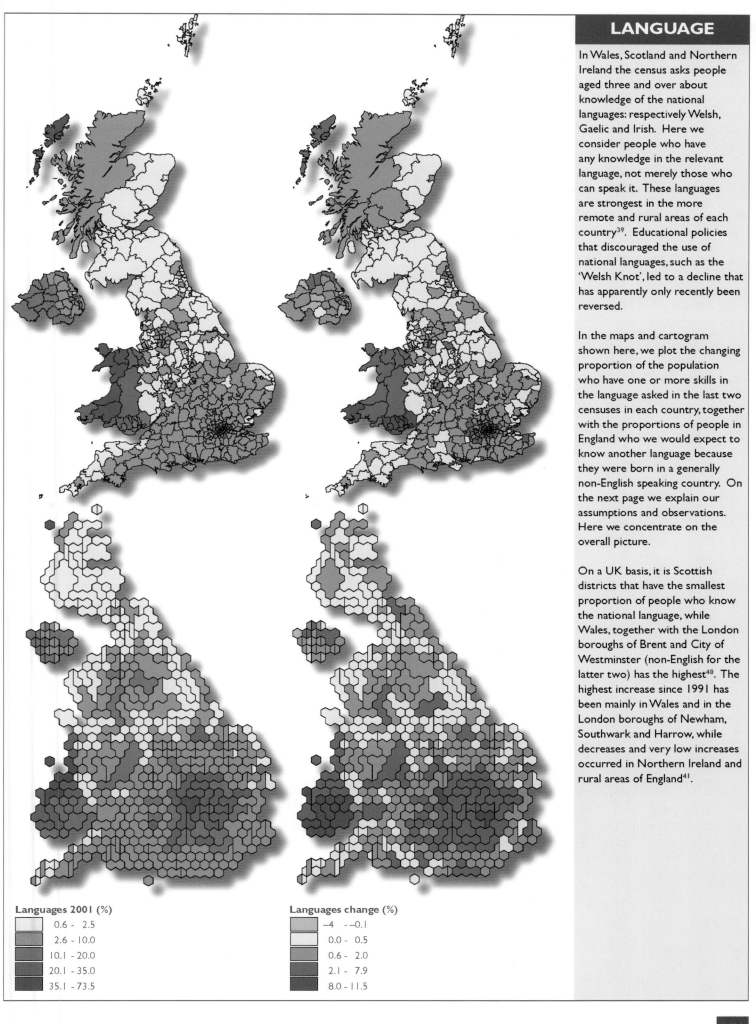

LANGUAGE

In Wales, Scotland and Northern Ireland the census asks people aged three and over about knowledge of the national languages: respectively Welsh, Gaelic and Irish. Here we consider people who have any knowledge in the relevant language, not merely those who can speak it. These languages are strongest in the more remote and rural areas of each country[39]. Educational policies that discouraged the use of national languages, such as the 'Welsh Knot', led to a decline that has apparently only recently been reversed.

In the maps and cartogram shown here, we plot the changing proportion of the population who have one or more skills in the language asked in the last two censuses in each country, together with the proportions of people in England who we would expect to know another language because they were born in a generally non-English speaking country. On the next page we explain our assumptions and observations. Here we concentrate on the overall picture.

On a UK basis, it is Scottish districts that have the smallest proportion of people who know the national language, while Wales, together with the London boroughs of Brent and City of Westminster (non-English for the latter two) has the highest[40]. The highest increase since 1991 has been mainly in Wales and in the London boroughs of Newham, Southwark and Harrow, while decreases and very low increases occurred in Northern Ireland and rural areas of England[41].

Languages 2001 (%)

	0.6 - 2.5
	2.6 - 10.0
	10.1 - 20.0
	20.1 - 35.0
	35.1 - 73.5

Languages change (%)

	−4 - −0.1
	0.0 - 0.5
	0.6 - 2.0
	2.1 - 7.9
	8.0 - 11.5

On this page we treat each constituent country of the UK separately for once. In Wales, 0.8 million people, 27.5% of the population, claimed that they had some ability in the Welsh language in 2001, compared to 0.5 million, 19.2% of the population in 1991, an increase of 8.3%. Note that the wording of one of the language questions in Wales was altered a little between the censuses and this may account for part of that rise. For Scotland, the proportion of people who can read, write or speak Gaelic rose by half a percentage point to 0.1 million in 2001, 1.9% of the total population, compared to 0.07 million, 1.4%, in 1991. The comparable figures for Northern Ireland showed only a slight increase, from 0.14 million users of the Irish language in 1991, to 0.16 million in 2001, from 9.0% to 9.9% of the population living there.

The traditionally Welsh-speaking areas of North and West Wales have shown the lowest increases, while the eastern Anglicised Welsh districts have shown the greatest increase[42]. Welsh has been compulsory for schoolchildren aged up to 14 since 1990, and to age 16 since 1999. Nearly a quarter of secondary schools in Wales are defined as Welsh-speaking schools where the curriculum is delivered through the medium of the Welsh language. The distribution in Wales reflects where children and young adults who have received an education in the Welsh language and older people tend to live.

The only Scottish district where over 10% of the population knows Gaelic is Eilean Siar, with 71.6%, which has also seen the greatest increase of 5%[43]. Knowledge of Gaelic reflects those remote Scottish areas where older people tend to live. It is the older people who are also most likely to actually use these languages in the Celtic fringe. No district in Northern Ireland has more than 20% of their population knowing Irish, and Northern Ireland is the only country to show a decrease in the proportion of national language users in some districts since 1991[44]. The Northern Irish districts with the highest proportions tend to be where young adults live, and may reflect where Irish Medium Education schools have been more recently established.

For England we mapped the proportions of people whose birthplace was in countries where English is not a commonly spoken language. The number of such people rose from 2.4 million, 5.2% of the population of that country in 1991, to 3.5 million, 7.1%, in 2001[45]. As would be expected, these people are found in London and the South East, together with the cities of Birmingham, Manchester, Bradford, Leicester and the university towns of Oxford and Cambridge. Much of the increase has occurred in these same areas, together with Bristol, Coventry, Sheffield and Newcastle. These tend to be areas where young adults live, and thus in England more people may actually be using more languages, especially languages from the rest of Europe.

If this representation is at all a fair picture of the languages understood by people in the UK, then more people can understand a language other than English in the southern half of the country, especially in Wales and London. Almost everywhere there may be slightly more people who understand a language other than English than there were in 1991. However, it is quite possible that fewer people understand languages as well as in the past, can speak them as fluently, write them or read them.

[12] Less than 60% of the population enjoy good health in: Bolsover, Easington, Blaenau Gwent, Merthyr Tydfil and Neath Port Talbot.

[13] The increase may be due partly to increased rates of diagnosis or to the population being less tolerant of conditions now than they were a decade ago. However, if this is the case then it has to account for rates rising in all age groups. The more older people there are the faster their rates have risen. For people providing care of these people if they are being misled, they are being misled in almost direct proportion to the rates at which others declare themselves to be ill. An alternative hypothesis is that more people of all ages really are suffering poorer health than they were in 1991.

[14] Between 1.2% and 1.7% of the local populations of the following areas are children suffering from a limiting long-term illness: Barking & Dagenham, Hackney, Newham, Knowsley, Liverpool, Birmingham, Easington, Stockton-on-Tees, Blackburn with Darwen, Middlesbrough, Redcar & Cleveland, Caerphilly, Merthyr Tydfil, Antrim, Armagh, Ballymoney, Belfast, Cookstown, Craigavon, Derry, Down, Dungannon, Limavady, Lisburn, Magherafelt, Moyle, Newry & Mourne, Omagh and Strabane.

[15] Less than 0.6% of the local populations of the following areas are children suffering from a limiting long-term illness: City of London, Kensington & Chelsea, Richmond upon Thames, Westminster, Windsor & Maidenhead, South Bucks, Cambridge, Isles of Scilly, Derbyshire Dales, Cotswold, Hart, Broadland, Rushcliffe, Elmbridge, Guildford, Runnymede and Warwick.

[16] More than a quarter of the entire population of the following areas are aged 16 or over and suffering such a disability: Easington, Blaenau Gwent, Caerphilly, Carmarthenshire, Merthyr Tydfil, Neath Port Talbot, Rhondda Cynon Taf and Glasgow.

[17] Less than 12.5% of local populations are adults with these disabilities in the following places: Kingston upon Thames, Richmond upon Thames, Mid Bedfordshire, Bracknell Forest, West Berkshire, Windsor & Maidenhead, Wokingham, Aylesbury Vale, Chiltern, Wycombe, Basingstoke & Deane, Hart, Rushmoor, East Hertfordshire, St. Albans, South Northamptonshire, South Oxfordshire, Vale of White Horse, Elmbridge, Guildford, Surrey Heath and Woking.

[18] Between 25% and 31% of all people living in the following London boroughs are living in 'other households' sharing accommodation with usually unrelated adults: Brent, Ealing, Hackney, Hammersmith & Fulham, Kensington & Chelsea, Lambeth, Newham, Southwark, Tower Hamlets and Wandsworth.

[19] The 10 areas which have seen the greatest increases, all of between 8.9% and 10.9% are: Brent, Ealing, Harrow, Hounslow, Newham, Redbridge, Tower Hamlets, Slough, Southampton and Ceredigion. Elsewhere rises have been high where transport routes into London are good or where a university has expanded.

[20] One Scottish city also features in the list of 10 places where the most people live alone below pensionable age. It is possible that in Glasgow significant numbers of these single people are somewhat older than those in London, and more will be single due to being widowed younger than in the Capital. The 10 places where between 11.4% and 27.8% of people live alone and are below pensionable age are: City of London, Camden, Hackney, Hammersmith & Fulham, Islington, Kensington & Chelsea, Lambeth, Wandsworth, Westminster and Glasgow City.

[21] An additional 2% or more people now cohabit without children in: City of London, Islington, Kensington & Chelsea, Lambeth, Westminster, Slough, East Cambridgeshire, Chester, Kerrier, Amber Valley, South Derbyshire, Torridge, Derwentside, Brighton & Hove, Watford, Chorley, North West Leicestershire, Norwich, Craven, Ryedale, Rushcliffe, Worcester, Wyre Forest, Flintshire, Wrexham, East Ayrshire, Edinburgh, Moray, Orkney Islands, Scottish Borders and the Shetland Islands.

[22] More than a tenth of the population of the following areas live in lone-parent households: Barking & Dagenham, Croydon, Greenwich, Hackney, Haringey, Islington, Lambeth, Lewisham, Newham, Southwark, Waltham Forest, Manchester, Salford, Knowsley, Liverpool, Wirral, South Tyneside, Birmingham, Halton, Hartlepool, Kingston upon Hull, Blackpool, Burnley, Leicester, North East Lincolnshire, Corby, Middlesbrough, Nottingham, Blaenau Gwent, Cardiff, Merthyr Tydfil, Newport, Dundee City, Glasgow, Inverclyde, North Ayrshire, West Dunbartonshire, Belfast, Derry and Lisburn.

[23] Only between 1.2% and 2.0% of all people in the following districts are living in such households: Armagh, Banbridge, Cookstown, Dungannon, Fermanagh, Magherafelt, Moyle, Newry & Mourne, Omagh and Strabane.

[24] Between 7.2% and 8.2% of all people in the following areas are living in such households: Bolsover, Easington, Hartlepool, Kingston upon Hull, Swale, Hyndburn, Pendle, Rossendale, North East Lincolnshire and Cannock Chase.

[25] In England and Wales more than 35% of people live in these households in: Mid Bedfordshire, Bracknell Forest, Wokingham, Aylesbury Vale, Chiltern, South Bucks, Huntingdonshire, South Cambridgeshire, Uttlesford, South Gloucestershire, East Hampshire, Eastleigh, Hart, Test Valley, East Hertfordshire, St Albans, Tonbridge & Malling, Harborough, Daventry, South Northamptonshire, Selby, Vale of White Horse, West Oxfordshire, South Staffordshire, Elmbridge, Surrey Heath, Woking, Horsham, Mid Sussex and North Wiltshire.

[26] The highest proportions of between 24.0% and 25.3% are found in: Congleton, Eden, North East Derbyshire, Teesdale, Castle Point, Hinckley & Bosworth, Broadland, Lichfield, South Staffordshire and Staffordshire Moorlands.

[27] The proportion of the local population consisting of people living as married couples without children has fallen by 5% or more in: City of London, Newham, Sheffield, Southampton, Stevenage, Welwyn Hatfield, Dartford, Gravesham, Oadby & Wigston, Runnymede and Spelthorne.

[28] Pensioner families make up more than 10% of the populations of the following areas, all but one in England: Fenland, Carrick, North Cornwall, South Lakeland, East Devon, North Devon, South Hams, Teignbridge, Torbay, Torridge, Christchurch, East Dorset, North Dorset, Poole, Purbeck, West Dorset, Eastbourne, Lewes, Rother, Wealden, Tendring, Cotswold, Havant, New Forest, Fylde, Wyre, Boston, East Lindsey, North Kesteven, South Holland, Breckland, Broadland, King's Lynn & West Norfolk, North Norfolk, South Norfolk, Alnwick, Berwick-upon-Tweed, Castle Morpeth, Craven, Ryedale, Scarborough, South Shropshire, Sedgemoor, South Somerset, West Somerset, Suffolk Coastal, Waveney, Adur, Arun, Chichester, Worthing, Isle of Wight, Malvern Hills and Conwy.

[29] Falls have been of 3.5% of the local population or more in: Liverpool, Carmarthenshire, Gwynedd, Neath Port Talbot, Eilean Siar and the Orkney Islands.

[30] More than 0.7% of the population now live in these households only in: Isles of Scilly, East Devon, Torbay, Christchurch, Eastbourne, Rother, Tendring, Ashford, North Norfolk, Arun, Worthing, Powys, Dumfries & Galloway, Eilean Siar, Ballymena, Ballymoney, Fermanagh, Magherafelt and Moyle.

[31] The proportion of the local population living as a pensioner alone has declined by 0.5% or more in: Barking & Dagenham, Camden, Haringey, Hounslow, Islington, Kingston upon Thames, Lambeth, Lewisham, Merton, Newham, Richmond upon Thames, Southwark, Tower Hamlets, Waltham Forest, Wandsworth, Westminster, Sheffield, Brighton & Hove, Pendle and Worthing.

[32] Three percent fewer people are now pensioners in: Barking & Dagenham, Camden, Lambeth, Lewisham, Richmond upon Thames, Southwark, Tower Hamlets, Wandsworth, Bournemouth, Brighton & Hove, Eastbourne and Worthing.

[33] More than a quarter of the people of the following areas were pensioners in 2001: East Devon, Torbay, Christchurch, East Dorset, West Dorset, Eastbourne, Lewes, Rother, Tendring, New Forest, Fylde, Wyre, East Lindsey, North Norfolk, Berwick-upon-Tweed, South Shropshire, West Somerset, Arun, Chichester, Worthing, Isle of Wight and Conwy.

34 Between 1.5% and 2.1% of all people living in the following areas people are pensioners living in communal establishments: Torbay, Bournemouth, Eastbourne, Hastings, Rother, Fylde, Arun and Worthing.

35 An additional 0.3% of local people are pensioners living in communal establishments in: Bolsover, Castle Point, Watford, Welwyn Hatfield, Oadby & Wigston, Breckland, Berwick-upon-Tweed, Ashfield and Ballymena.

36 There are more than 2.4 rooms per person in: Macclesfield, Eden, East Devon, West Dorset, Cotswold, South Holland, North Norfolk, South Shropshire, West Somerset, Suffolk Coastal, Stratford-upon-Avon and Powys.

37 The following areas have less than 1.9 rooms per person: Barking & Dagenham, Brent, Camden, Ealing, Hackney, Haringey, Hounslow, Islington, Newham, Southwark, Tower Hamlets, Slough, Glasgow, North Lanarkshire, West Dunbartonshire, Derry, Limavady, Magherafelt and Strabane.

38 Unfortunately the 2001 Census did not report numbers of people living in second homes in a way that would allow us to compare changes over time in that form of accommodation.

39 Historically, English became the *lingua franca* in the more industrialised areas, such as the South Wales Valleys, where there were large numbers of immigrant workers in the late 19th and early 20th centuries.

40 The areas with the lowest proportion are: East Ayrshire, Midlothian, Fife, Dumfries & Galloway, North Lanarkshire, South Lanarkshire, Falkirk, Scottish Borders, South Ayrshire, Aberdeenshire, East Lothian, North Ayrshire and West Lothian. Those with the highest proportion are: Westminster, Newham, Denbighshire, Brent, Conwy, Ceredigion, Carmarthenshire, Isle of Anglesey, Eilean Siar and Gwynedd.

41 The areas with the greatest increase are: Bridgend, Neath Port Talbot, Harrow, Caerphilly, Rhondda Cynon Taf, Pembrokeshire, Monmouthshire, Southwark, Blaenau Gwent, Newport, Torfaen and Newham. Those with decreases are: Dungannon, Derry, Cookstown, Down and Melton, while Easington, Staffordshire Moorlands, Cannock Chase, West Somerset and Richmondshire have seen no or only a very small increase in the proportion who may know another language.

42 Under 15% of the population of Monmouthshire, Blaenau Gwent, Newport and Torfaen know Welsh; these districts show the greatest increase of over 10%. Over 50 % of the population of Ceredigion, Carmarthenshire, Isle of Anglesey, and Gwynedd have some knowledge of Welsh; the smallest increases of under 7% are in Ceredigion, Gwynedd, Flintshire and Carmarthenshire.

43 The Scottish districts where fewer than 1% know Gaelic are: East Ayrshire, Midlothian, Dumfries & Galloway, Falkirk, Fife, North Lanarkshire, South Lanarkshire, Aberdeenshire, East Lothian, North Ayrshire, Scottish Borders, South Ayrshire, West Lothian, Angus, Dundee City, Orkney Islands and the Shetland Islands. The smallest increases of under 0.4% were in: Fife, East Ayrshire, Midlothian, Dumfries & Galloway, North Lanarkshire, South Lanarkshire, Scottish Borders, South Ayrshire and West Dunbartonshire.

44 In the districts of Omagh, Magherafelt, Dungannon and Newry & Mourne, over 15% of people know some Irish; the districts with the lowest proportion, under 4%, are: Carrickfergus, North Down and Ards. The greatest increases (over 2%) are in Coleraine, Moyle, Belfast and Limavady, while Dungannon, Derry, Cookstown and Down have seen decreases, Dungannon having the greatest decrease of −3.8%.

45 Ealing, Tower Hamlets, Kensington & Chelsea, Westminster, Newham and Brent have over 30% of people born in non-English speaking countries, while at the other end of the scale are Knowsley, Derwentside and Easington with 1%. The districts with the greatest increase are: Redbridge, Merton, Hounslow, Lewisham, Hackney, Ealing, Tower Hamlets, Brent, Harrow, Southwark and Newham, with rises of over 7%; those with no change are Easington, Staffordshire Moorlands, Cannock Chase, West Somerset and Richmondshire, while Melton had a decrease of −0.1% over the course of the decade.

Homes and cars

Maps in this section include:

No cars (p 157)	One car (p 158)	Two cars (p 159)	Three or more cars (p 160)	Commuting by car (p 161)	Commuting by foot (p 162)
Commuting by bus (p 163)	Commuting by train (p 164)	Commuting by underground (p 165)	Commuting by bicycle (p 166)	Owned outright (p 167)	Mortgaged (p 168)
Private renting (p 169)	Housing associations (p 170)	Local authority housing (p 171)	Communal establishments (p 172)	Temporary dwellings (p 173)	Shared dwellings (p 174)
Flats (p 175)	Houses (p 176)	Central heating (p 177)	Teachers and nurses (p 178)	Doctors and dentists (p 179)	Other services (p 180)

The material goods and services people have access to are vital in maintaining their standards of living. These services measured here include estimates of those provided in education and health. We also look at the local transport infrastructure available to different populations, and how this is used by people travelling to work; and at how the population is housed and some aspects of the quality of that housing.

We begin this chapter by looking at where people have access to cars. Cars have become an essential part of living in the UK for the majority of its population. They are more needed in some areas than in others, but even in the mostly densely built-up urban environment, taking your weekly shopping home without a car, especially when you have children, has become more and more difficult as local shops are converted into dwellings and supermarkets say they sell the cheapest. People's scope to find work in different areas, for leisure and recreation, and even to choose where their children may go to school, if they have a choice, can be curtailed if they do not have access to a car. Cars, which once were a luxury, are increasingly seen as a necessity.

It is still in the North of England, in Scotland and in Wales, that most households without access to a car or van can be found, although these areas have seen the greatest rises in car use over the course of the 1990s. The car is now dominant almost everywhere but in the core of Glasgow and the inner London boroughs. Its use is also restricted, even in affluent areas, where many of the population are elderly and living on their own. Single car ownership is now most common in the North, Scotland and Wales, and has become relatively rare in the Home Counties. It is in parts of the Home Counties that up to a third of people

now live in households with access to two cars, although again growth in this group has been highest further North and West. This group has also shrunk in size in the Centre of London where people are now less likely to have access to more than one car compared to those living there a decade ago. In London you are an increasingly unusual individual if you live in a household that has two or more vehicles parked outside your home.

Where car ownership has not become more evenly spread across the country is in the proportions of people living in households with access to three or more cars. These proportions have risen most where they were highest to begin with, in the Home Counties, where up to one person in six can now live in a household with three or more vehicles in the drive. It is also likely that the quality and value of cars is higher in the more affluent parts of the UK. Thus, the apparent evening out of cars in total may in fact be due to a northwards migration of second- and third-hand vehicles, rejected from the South.

More and more people are now travelling to work by car, the most popular form of such transport. Up from a quarter of the population a decade ago, approaching 30%, now commute by car daily. Such commuting is most common in the rings of districts surrounding London and Birmingham, but as car availability has spread North so too has car commuting, most obviously in Scotland and Northern Ireland. Only in London and a scattering of other places has congestion, lack of parking and other factors led some of the population to seek alternative means of getting to work. The most popular alternative to commuting by car has been to work at home or to walk to work. Traditionally a rural phenomenon, travel by foot is rising in the cities of the South but falling in areas where it was traditionally practised in the North and Wales, most obviously where there were large mines and factories close to people's homes. Commuting by bus has also become rarer outside of the South East other than in Scotland, which has experienced something of a revival in this form of often now privatised public transport.

In contrast, commuting by train remains a largely southern occupation and is vital for large parts of South East London. It has generally risen in popularity but is falling in areas most distant from the city centres. Perhaps in these areas people have taken to their cars in greater numbers, rather than endure long and unreliable journeys to work on a service now taking more customers from nearer afield? The London Underground has also seen a decline in its furthest out customers, but rises in those living closer to the centre. The changing experience of other forms of railed transport across the UK has been mixed, while commuting by bicycle is becoming less common despite the attempts to promote it. Practised most where the land is flatter and the weather better, cycling to work is generally only rising in popularity within the most congested larger cities. Where cars travel faster, and now in greater numbers, fewer bicycles are found than were a decade ago.

Where more people own more cars so too do they own more homes, and where there has been the largest rise in people with access to three or more cars, outright ownership of property has also increased the most.

However, ownership of property is closely linked to age, and so it is on the coast that more homes are owned than anywhere else in the UK. The numbers of people involved in buying their home with a mortgage have fallen in almost equal proportions to the rise in outright ownership, and most where property is most expensive to buy. An increase in private renting has taken up part of the shortfall in provision, as have rising numbers of people living in housing association property. The largest fall has been in the state-owned sector of housing, highest where right to buy became popular latest, in Scotland. There are also slightly more people living in communal establishments than before, with large rises seen in university cities and in some areas with growing numbers of elderly residents. Housing demands of a different kind mean that temporary dwellings, mostly caravans, are most common in the South of England, but are rising most in number, surprisingly, within London, where sharing a dwelling is becoming less common. Far more people are also living in flats in the South than before, and fewer in the North, especially in Scotland, where the quality of housing, measured by whether it has central heating, is increasing by most where it is most needed; although the census does not allow us to measure who may now have trouble affording to heat their home.

In measuring more tenuous amenities we found that the proportions of working teachers and nurses per person are quite even across England and Wales (the two countries to have asked the relevant question in 2001). Both groups are a little more likely to live where housing is cheaper and near to where there is more need for their skills, although the numbers of working qualified teachers and nurses living in some northern boroughs are low. In contrast, doctors and dentists are much more concentrated towards the South of these countries, and particularly around a few hospitals and other areas with high paying demand for their services. Where the population is most likely to be ill there are the fewest of these better paid health professionals living. This is most clearly the case for people working in other categories of health profession, many of which are supplied by the private market. These people are almost all found in their highest concentrations in the South. However, most concentrated in these areas are people who were trained in medicine or teaching but who no longer work in those professions and are working in other forms of employment. Given a choice, it is to the South that the more wealthy caring professions, as with almost all other affluent groups, tend to migrate.

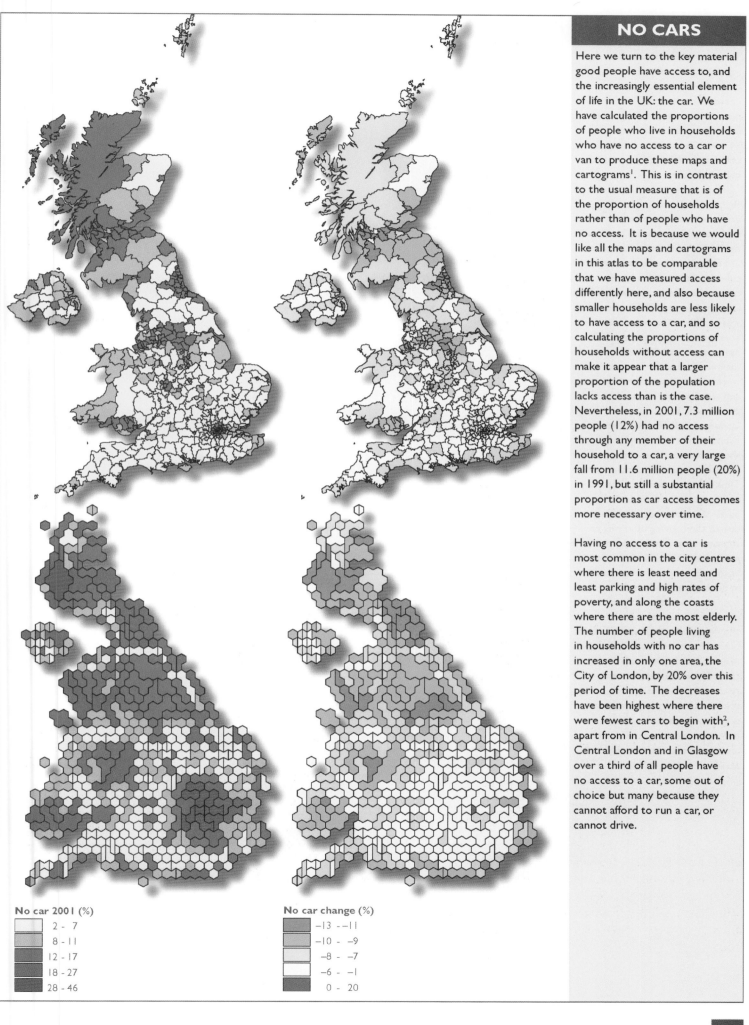

NO CARS

Here we turn to the key material good people have access to, and the increasingly essential element of life in the UK: the car. We have calculated the proportions of people who live in households who have no access to a car or van to produce these maps and cartograms[1]. This is in contrast to the usual measure that is of the proportion of households rather than of people who have no access. It is because we would like all the maps and cartograms in this atlas to be comparable that we have measured access differently here, and also because smaller households are less likely to have access to a car, and so calculating the proportions of households without access can make it appear that a larger proportion of the population lacks access than is the case. Nevertheless, in 2001, 7.3 million people (12%) had no access through any member of their household to a car, a very large fall from 11.6 million people (20%) in 1991, but still a substantial proportion as car access becomes more necessary over time.

Having no access to a car is most common in the city centres where there is least need and least parking and high rates of poverty, and along the coasts where there are the most elderly. The number of people living in households with no car has increased in only one area, the City of London, by 20% over this period of time. The decreases have been highest where there were fewest cars to begin with[2], apart from in Central London. In Central London and in Glasgow over a third of all people have no access to a car, some out of choice but many because they cannot afford to run a car, or cannot drive.

No car 2001 (%)

- 2 - 7
- 8 - 11
- 12 - 17
- 18 - 27
- 28 - 46

No car change (%)

- −13 - −11
- −10 - −9
- −8 - −7
- −6 - −1
- 0 - 20

ONE CAR

The proportion of people living in households with access to only one vehicle fell by 3% over the decade, not as quickly as the 8% fall in those without any access but substantial nevertheless, from 34% to 30% of the population of the UK, or from 19.5 to 17.8 million people.

People are most likely to live in households that have the traditional single car in Scotland, the Welsh Valleys, the North East of England and in some London suburbs. Such access is most common in places such as the London borough of Wandsworth, where 36% of the population have access to a single car (and 25% have no car). In Wandsworth they would have more cars, were parking not so problematic, and were people not so well served with buses, taxis and the Underground. The proportion in Wandsworth has risen by 1% as the proportion with two cars has fallen by a single percentage point. Thus the increases in people having access to a single car in parts of London such as here is due to them giving up trying to run two cars. The highest the rate reached is 37% of people, both in Barrow-in-Furness and in Berwick-upon-Tweed. In both these areas, and the other parts of the UK outside London showing increases, the rise is part of the general increase in car use in areas that traditionally had few cars. Given these contrasting reasons for the changes seen, the list of the small number of areas that have seen a rise in people with access to a single car contains many different types of area[3].

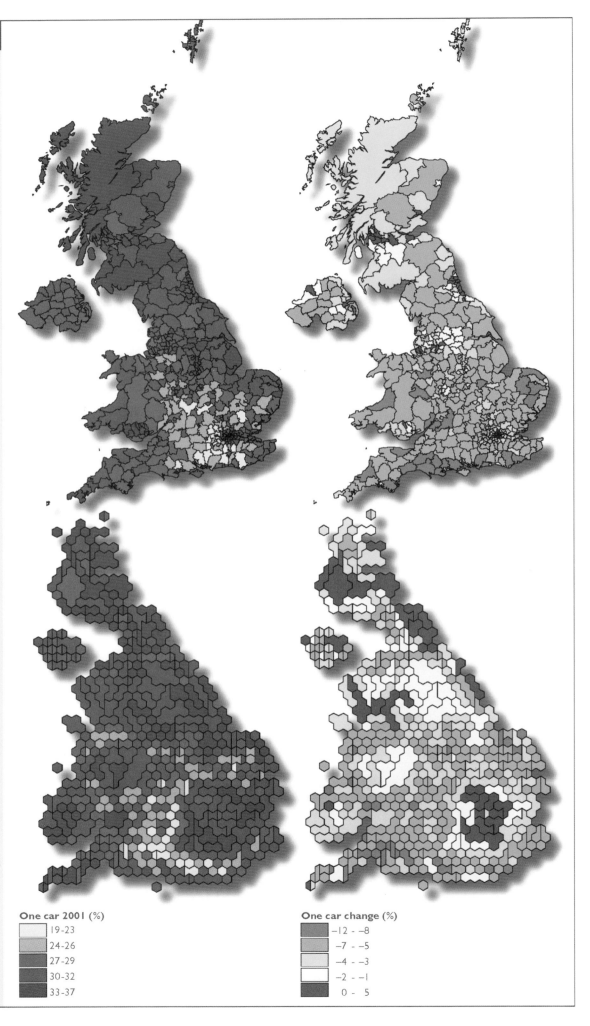

One car 2001 (%)

- 19-23
- 24-26
- 27-29
- 30-32
- 33-37

One car change (%)

- -12 - -8
- -7 - -5
- -4 - -3
- -2 - -1
- 0 - 5

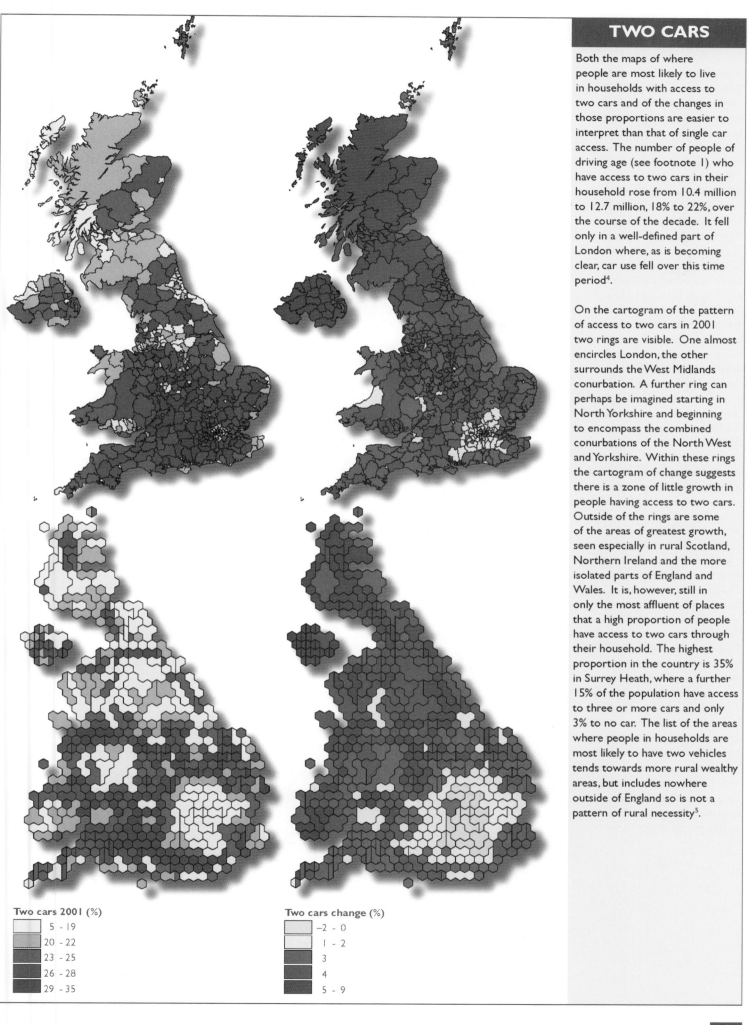

TWO CARS

Both the maps of where people are most likely to live in households with access to two cars and of the changes in those proportions are easier to interpret than that of single car access. The number of people of driving age (see footnote 1) who have access to two cars in their household rose from 10.4 million to 12.7 million, 18% to 22%, over the course of the decade. It fell only in a well-defined part of London where, as is becoming clear, car use fell over this time period[4].

On the cartogram of the pattern of access to two cars in 2001 two rings are visible. One almost encircles London, the other surrounds the West Midlands conurbation. A further ring can perhaps be imagined starting in North Yorkshire and beginning to encompass the combined conurbations of the North West and Yorkshire. Within these rings the cartogram of change suggests there is a zone of little growth in people having access to two cars. Outside of the rings are some of the areas of greatest growth, seen especially in rural Scotland, Northern Ireland and the more isolated parts of England and Wales. It is, however, still in only the most affluent of places that a high proportion of people have access to two cars through their household. The highest proportion in the country is 35% in Surrey Heath, where a further 15% of the population have access to three or more cars and only 3% to no car. The list of the areas where people in households are most likely to have two vehicles tends towards more rural wealthy areas, but includes nowhere outside of England so is not a pattern of rural necessity[5].

Two cars 2001 (%)
- 5 - 19
- 20 - 22
- 23 - 25
- 26 - 28
- 29 - 35

Two cars change (%)
- −2 - 0
- 1 - 2
- 3
- 4
- 5 - 9

THREE OR MORE CARS

The highest number of vehicles that both the 1991 and 2001 Censuses enumerated people as having access to through their households was three or more. These numbers have increased rapidly, from 2.9 million people in 1991 (5%) to 4.1 million by 2001 (7%). Here we begin to see the emergence of teenage children having cars along with both of their parents. The geography to the distribution of these vehicles would suggest that they are not, in the main, rusted old vehicles blocking up driveways, although numbers are high in a very few remote rural areas where vehicles are likely to be older and cheaper. South Buckinghamshire is the area where the most people live (16%) who have access to three or more vehicles in their household, and the other areas, which top the list, are similarly wealthy places[6].

Just as with people having access to two cars, the numbers having access to three or more have fallen in Central London and have hardly risen in the London suburbs nor in the other metropolitan areas of the country. Numbers have fallen too in Cambridge and the Isles of Scilly, so it is not just in London that a limit to car ownership appears, finally, to be being met. The rises have been greatest in Northern Ireland, where rates were low, mainly in areas that are rural and in economic times that have been relatively good. Outside of the Province rates are still rising most in the ring of places where they were highest in 1991. Only once every late teenage child, parent and grandparent here has their own vehicle can we expect to see a halt, or in cities which have simply run out of car parks[7].

Three+ cars 2001 (%)

	1 - 4
	5 - 6
	7 - 8
	9 - 11
	12 - 16

Three+ cars change (%)

	-1 - 0
	1
	2
	3
	4 - 6

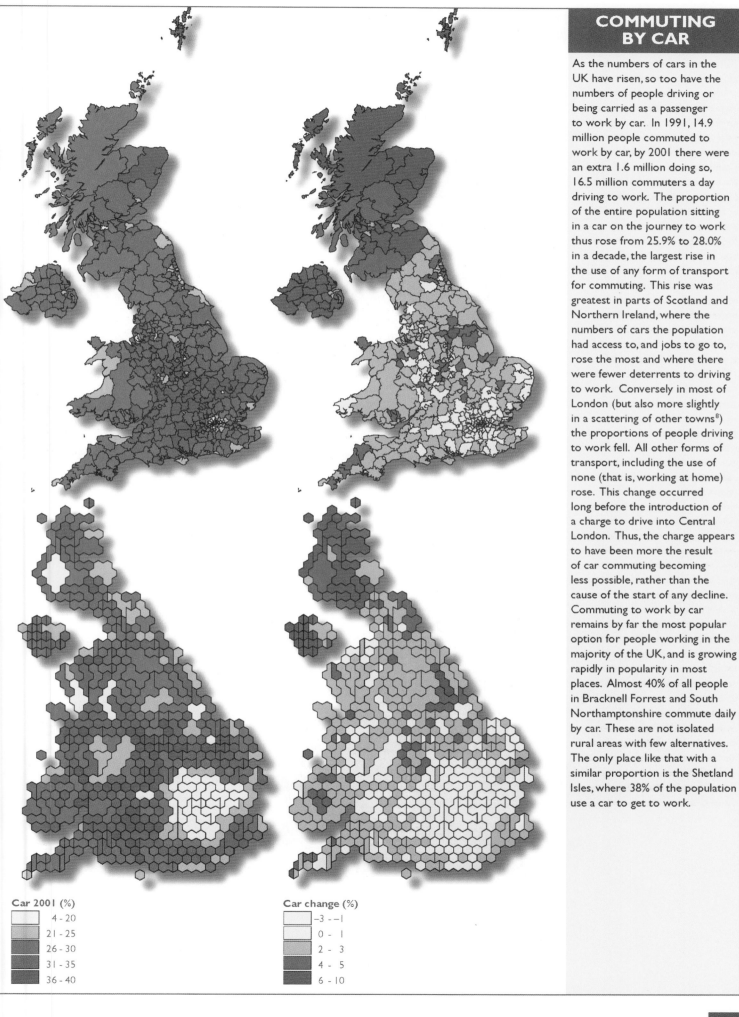

COMMUTING BY CAR

As the numbers of cars in the UK have risen, so too have the numbers of people driving or being carried as a passenger to work by car. In 1991, 14.9 million people commuted to work by car, by 2001 there were an extra 1.6 million doing so, 16.5 million commuters a day driving to work. The proportion of the entire population sitting in a car on the journey to work thus rose from 25.9% to 28.0% in a decade, the largest rise in the use of any form of transport for commuting. This rise was greatest in parts of Scotland and Northern Ireland, where the numbers of cars the population had access to, and jobs to go to, rose the most and where there were fewer deterrents to driving to work. Conversely in most of London (but also more slightly in a scattering of other towns[8]) the proportions of people driving to work fell. All other forms of transport, including the use of none (that is, working at home) rose. This change occurred long before the introduction of a charge to drive into Central London. Thus, the charge appears to have been more the result of car commuting becoming less possible, rather than the cause of the start of any decline. Commuting to work by car remains by far the most popular option for people working in the majority of the UK, and is growing rapidly in popularity in most places. Almost 40% of all people in Bracknell Forrest and South Northamptonshire commute daily by car. These are not isolated rural areas with few alternatives. The only place like that with a similar proportion is the Shetland Isles, where 38% of the population use a car to get to work.

Car 2001 (%)
- 4 - 20
- 21 - 25
- 26 - 30
- 31 - 35
- 36 - 40

Car change (%)
- -3 - -1
- 0 - 1
- 2 - 3
- 4 - 5
- 6 - 10

COMMUTING BY FOOT

The second most popular form of transport to work in the UK involves no vehicles. Here we have included people who work at home as they presumably have to walk from the bedroom! In rural areas, of course, many farmers live where they work and walk. Thus, the distinction between walking to work and working at home can be easily blurred. A total of 5.7 million people commute to work by foot each day, 0.6 million more than a decade ago. This form of transport is most popular outside of the major cities other than in Edinburgh. It does account, however, for a majority of trips in the City of London (36.7%), where there has also been the greatest rise in 10 years (of 10.9%). Almost all of the largest rises have been in towns and cities, especially in Scotland[9].

The proportion of the population walking to work has only fallen in a few rural areas. As the numbers of people working (some hours) in the UK rises, almost everywhere, more and more people are using different ways to get to work and more are working from home than before. This increase has been greatest in the South of England for a large part of the population, but fastest within the densely populated Scottish cities. In reality, many people walk as well as take the train, bus or another form of transport to commute. Here we are only including those whose main form of transport is walking and many who may not be walking very far if their office is in their home. Part of the reason for the rise is that more people in the South may now be working from home for three days a week, rather than, say, one or two.

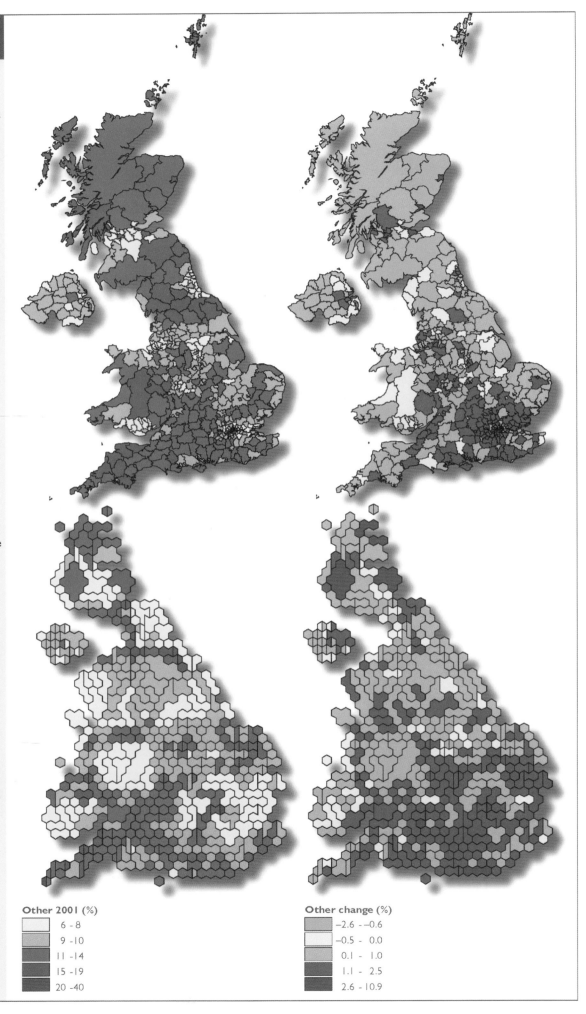

Other 2001 (%)

	6 - 8
	9 -10
	11 -14
	15 -19
	20 -40

Other change (%)

	−2.6 - −0.6
	−0.5 - 0.0
	0.1 - 1.0
	1.1 - 2.5
	2.6 - 10.9

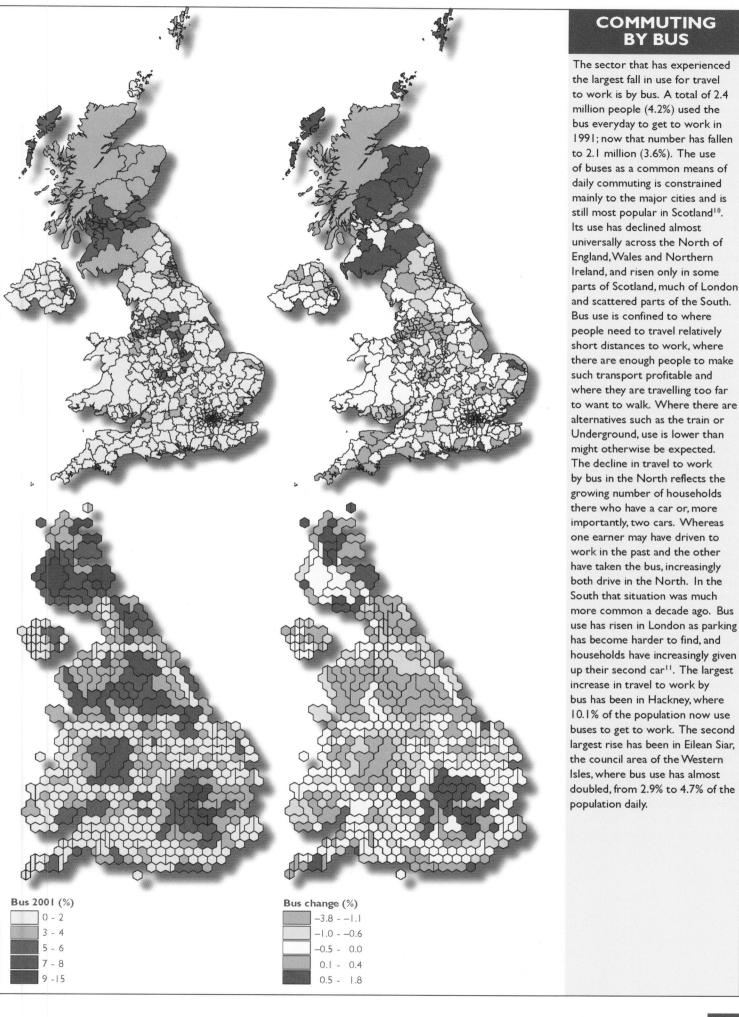

COMMUTING BY BUS

The sector that has experienced the largest fall in use for travel to work is by bus. A total of 2.4 million people (4.2%) used the bus everyday to get to work in 1991; now that number has fallen to 2.1 million (3.6%). The use of buses as a common means of daily commuting is constrained mainly to the major cities and is still most popular in Scotland[10]. Its use has declined almost universally across the North of England, Wales and Northern Ireland, and risen only in some parts of Scotland, much of London and scattered parts of the South. Bus use is confined to where people need to travel relatively short distances to work, where there are enough people to make such transport profitable and where they are travelling too far to want to walk. Where there are alternatives such as the train or Underground, use is lower than might otherwise be expected. The decline in travel to work by bus in the North reflects the growing number of households there who have a car or, more importantly, two cars. Whereas one earner may have driven to work in the past and the other have taken the bus, increasingly both drive in the North. In the South that situation was much more common a decade ago. Bus use has risen in London as parking has become harder to find, and households have increasingly given up their second car[11]. The largest increase in travel to work by bus has been in Hackney, where 10.1% of the population now use buses to get to work. The second largest rise has been in Eilean Siar, the council area of the Western Isles, where bus use has almost doubled, from 2.9% to 4.7% of the population daily.

Bus 2001 (%)

- 0 - 2
- 3 - 4
- 5 - 6
- 7 - 8
- 9 - 15

Bus change (%)

- −3.8 − −1.1
- −1.0 − −0.6
- −0.5 − 0.0
- 0.1 − 0.4
- 0.5 − 1.8

COMMUTING BY TRAIN

After the car, the biggest rise in any form of commuting was by train during the 1990s, but the absolute numbers of train travellers are still low. In 1991, 0.9 million people travelled to work by train every day (1.5% of all people). By 2001 that number had risen to 1.1 million (1.8% of the population). Although a small proportion of the population in most parts of the UK now use the train as their main means of getting to work, its main use is still concentrated to the South and East of London, to areas where the Underground does not extend[12].

Despite the overall rise in commuting by train, its use has actually declined to the far East of London, in parts of the North West of England, the West Midlands and a scattering of smaller towns where more people now prefer, or are able, to take the car. Travel by train has increased the most in London, and this is not of people whose main form of transport is the Underground. Increasing numbers of people live in London but work outside of the Capital. The largest increase has been in Wandsworth in London (of 3.1% more train commuters), outside of London in Reading (1.3% more), Epsom & Ewell (1.3% more) and St Albans (2.1% more), in Scotland in North Ayrshire (plus 1.6%) and West Dunbartonshire (2.0% more train commuters).

Where there are convenient stations, where traffic is bad, the route to work long, or parking difficult to find, then more people are taking the train, especially where there are couples who work in different congested towns and who can only live in one if they wish to live together.

Train 2001 (%)

- 0
- 1 - 3
- 4 - 6
- 7 - 9
- 10 - 13

Train change (%)

- −1.4 - −0.1
- 0.0
- 0.1 - 0.4
- 0.5 - 1.5
- 1.6 - 3.1

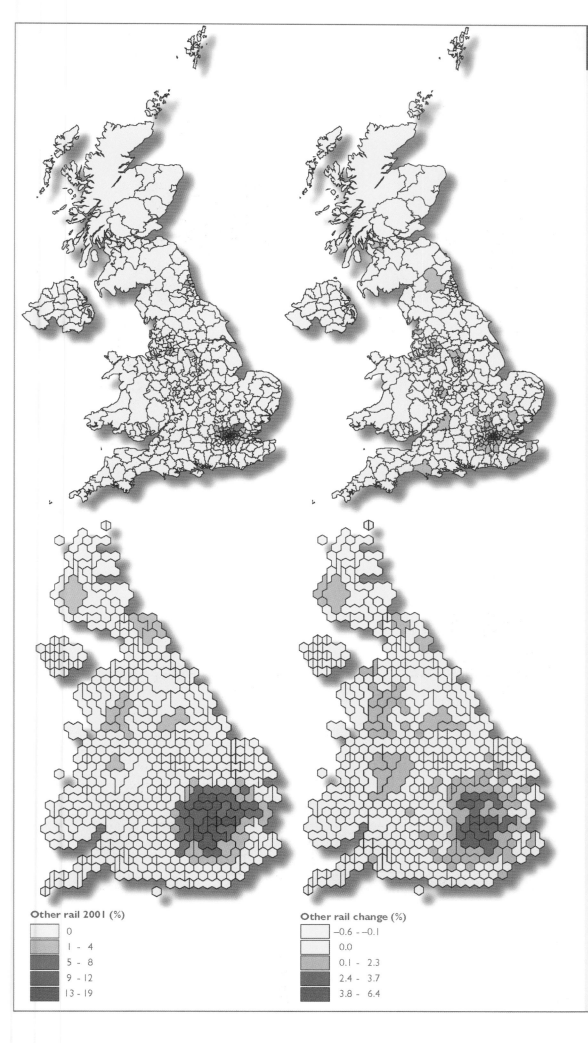

COMMUTING BY UNDERGROUND

This category of commuting includes other forms of light rail and trams that may travel also on roads. The large majority of people falling into this category of 'other rail' commuters do travel Underground, in London, but also in Glasgow and Newcastle. In total, 0.7 million people now use light rail as their main means of getting to work in the UK, 1.2% of the population. In 1991 that number was only 0.5 million, or 0.9%. Thus the rise in light rail use has been almost as great as that seen in train use more generally[13].

In Manchester the new trams travel partly on old tracks but also on roads, and increasing numbers of people use a variety of modes of transport to get to work, and so the rise there and any elsewhere in Britain where light rail has been introduced may appear a little diluted from the actual increase. We can only report what people say was their major means of travel at each point in time, given the options that they were presented with on the census forms. The largest increases over time were recorded in Tower Hamlets, where an extra 6.4% of the population use the Underground as compared to 1991. Outside of London the largest increases have been in Bury (2.0% more) and Trafford (2.3% more), following the introduction of light rail into those areas. The use of light rail has fallen most on the outskirts of London (fewer there use the Underground), in parts of Tyneside and Gateshead where fewer people now use the metro, and on the Wirral.

As more and more people are commuting in a wider variety of directions from each district it becomes harder to accommodate their needs by rail.

Other rail 2001 (%)

- 0
- 1 - 4
- 5 - 8
- 9 - 12
- 13 - 19

Other rail change (%)

- −0.6 - −0.1
- 0.0
- 0.1 - 2.3
- 2.4 - 3.7
- 3.8 - 6.4

COMMUTING BY BICYCLE

The only form of transport to work to have fallen in popularity along with the bus is the bicycle. In 1991 the bicycle carried 1.3% of all people to work, 0.72 million; it is now the least popular form of transport, in 2001 carrying 0.69 million cyclists to work in the UK, 1.2% of the population. The bicycle is traditionally most popular in the more rural areas of southern England, where the ground is flatter and where distances to travel are not too far away. At its peak it accounts for 11.7% of the population of Cambridge's daily commute to work (down from 12.5% in 1991), 7.1% of Scilly Isles commutes (down from 8.4%) and 6.6% of people travelling to work in Oxford (down from 7.4%). Elsewhere, only in Gosport (5.2%) and York (5.8%) do bicycles convey more than a twentieth of the population to work in the UK. The bicycle is falling in popularity where it was most popular to begin with, and it is rising in popularity in the cities of the North of England, in parts of Wales, Scotland, especially in Edinburgh, and in London (especially Central London), Bristol and Reading[14]. These increases in its popularity are too slight despite being spread over many areas to outweigh the overall declines in its popularity at the national level. On country and small town lanes fewer people are cycling to work as more and more drive past them in their cars. The list of areas where the bicycle is becoming more and more a vehicle of past commuting is growing[15]. Whether its rise in popularity in a few places that could be typified as young, trendy and urban leads to any greater revival has yet to be seen.

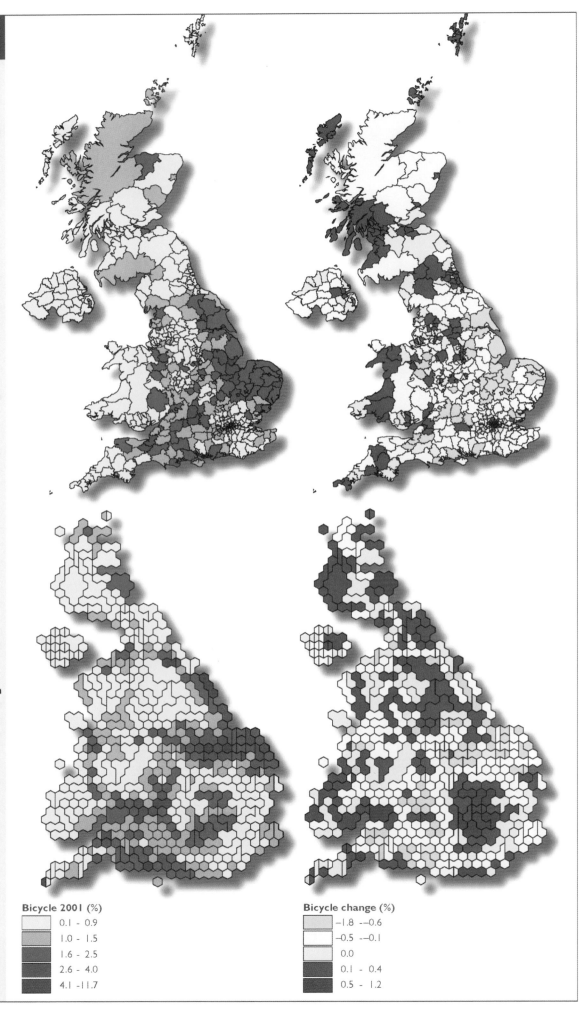

Bicycle 2001 (%)

	0.1 - 0.9
	1.0 - 1.5
	1.6 - 2.5
	2.6 - 4.0
	4.1 - 11.7

Bicycle change (%)

	-1.8 - -0.6
	-0.5 - -0.1
	0.0
	0.1 - 0.4
	0.5 - 1.2

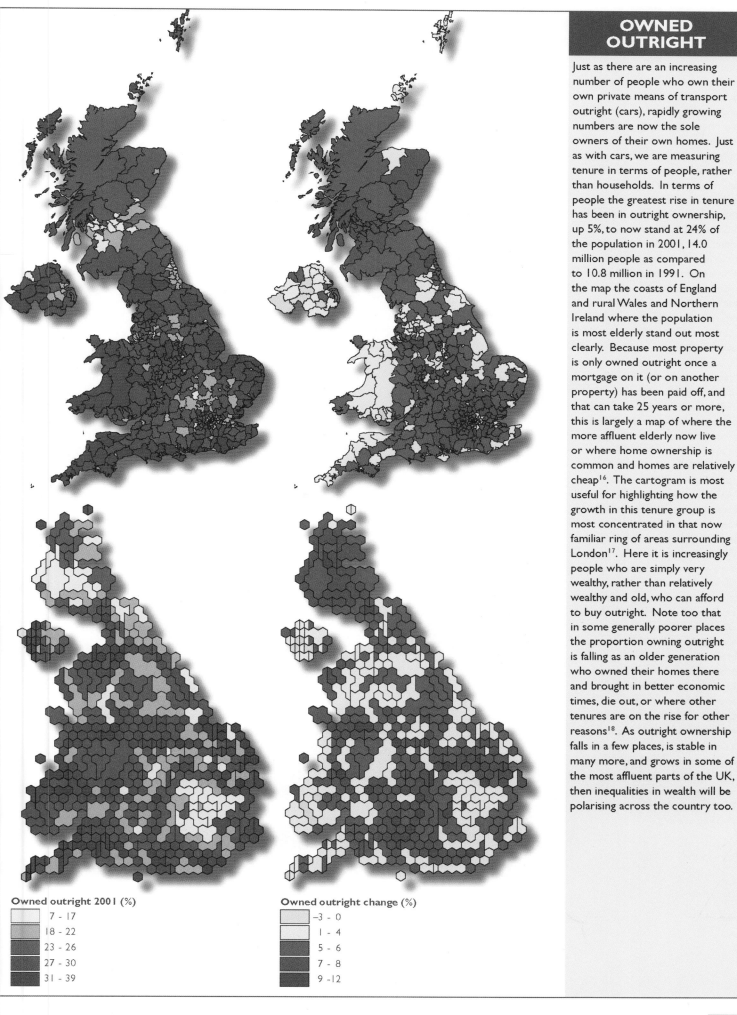

OWNED OUTRIGHT

Just as there are an increasing number of people who own their own private means of transport outright (cars), rapidly growing numbers are now the sole owners of their own homes. Just as with cars, we are measuring tenure in terms of people, rather than households. In terms of people the greatest rise in tenure has been in outright ownership, up 5%, to now stand at 24% of the population in 2001, 14.0 million people as compared to 10.8 million in 1991. On the map the coasts of England and rural Wales and Northern Ireland where the population is most elderly stand out most clearly. Because most property is only owned outright once a mortgage on it (or on another property) has been paid off, and that can take 25 years or more, this is largely a map of where the more affluent elderly now live or where home ownership is common and homes are relatively cheap[16]. The cartogram is most useful for highlighting how the growth in this tenure group is most concentrated in that now familiar ring of areas surrounding London[17]. Here it is increasingly people who are simply very wealthy, rather than relatively wealthy and old, who can afford to buy outright. Note too that in some generally poorer places the proportion owning outright is falling as an older generation who owned their homes there and brought in better economic times, die out, or where other tenures are on the rise for other reasons[18]. As outright ownership falls in a few places, is stable in many more, and grows in some of the most affluent parts of the UK, then inequalities in wealth will be polarising across the country too.

Owned outright 2001 (%)
- 7 - 17
- 18 - 22
- 23 - 26
- 27 - 30
- 31 - 39

Owned outright change (%)
- −3 - 0
- 1 - 4
- 5 - 6
- 7 - 8
- 9 -12

MORTGAGED

The increase in people owning their properties outright has largely arisen from increasing numbers of people coming to the end of their period of mortgage payments. These people have not been replaced by similar numbers starting new mortgages and people are starting families later in life. Thus the proportion of the UK population who live in property that they are buying has fallen by 3.6% over the period, from 28.6 million people (49%) to 27.0 million people (46%). Owner-occupation (buying and owned outright) as a whole has risen by only 1.6% over the course of the decade to now stand at 69.7% of the population of the UK.

Had it not been for the rises seen in Scotland, Northern Ireland and the North East of England in buying property in the 1990s, that overall rate of owner-occupation in the UK would have fallen[19]. These rises are mainly due to some Scottish Homes, Northern Ireland Housing Executive, and local authority tenants exercising their rights to buy later than in most of England and Wales. Where the proportions of people living in mortgaged property have fallen in England, this is mainly due to increases in private renting or outright ownership. In the UK as a whole people are least likely to be buying their home in inner London[20]. The highest proportions of home buyers are found in a ring of areas many people move to, from Inner London, once they do not wish to rent anymore, are willing to buy a car (or two or three) and/or begin to commute by train to the Capital. Note that we now include shared ownership in this category but the numbers involved are tiny.

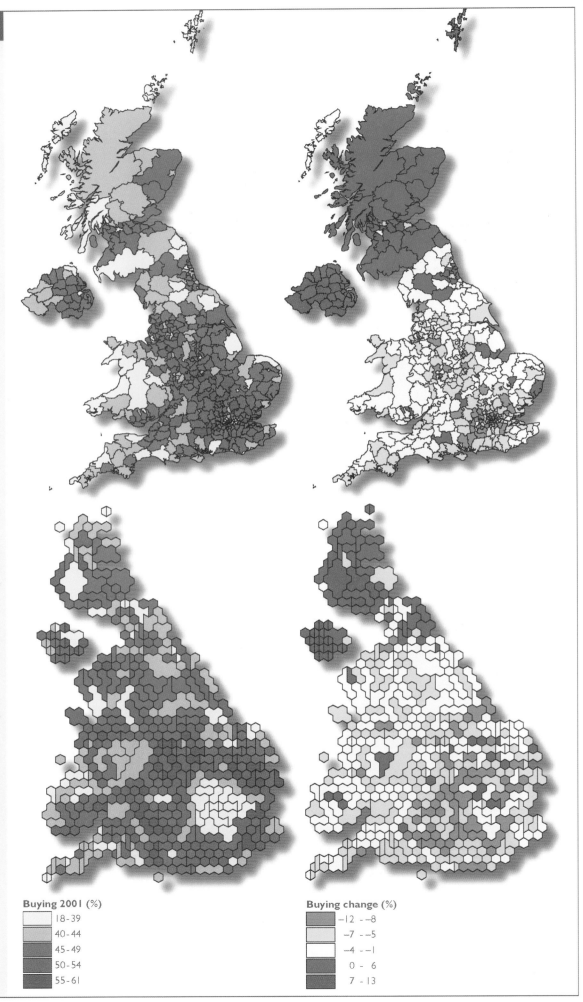

Buying 2001 (%)

	18-39
	40-44
	45-49
	50-54
	55-61

Buying change (%)

	−12 - −8
	−7 - −5
	−4 - −1
	0 - 6
	7 - 13

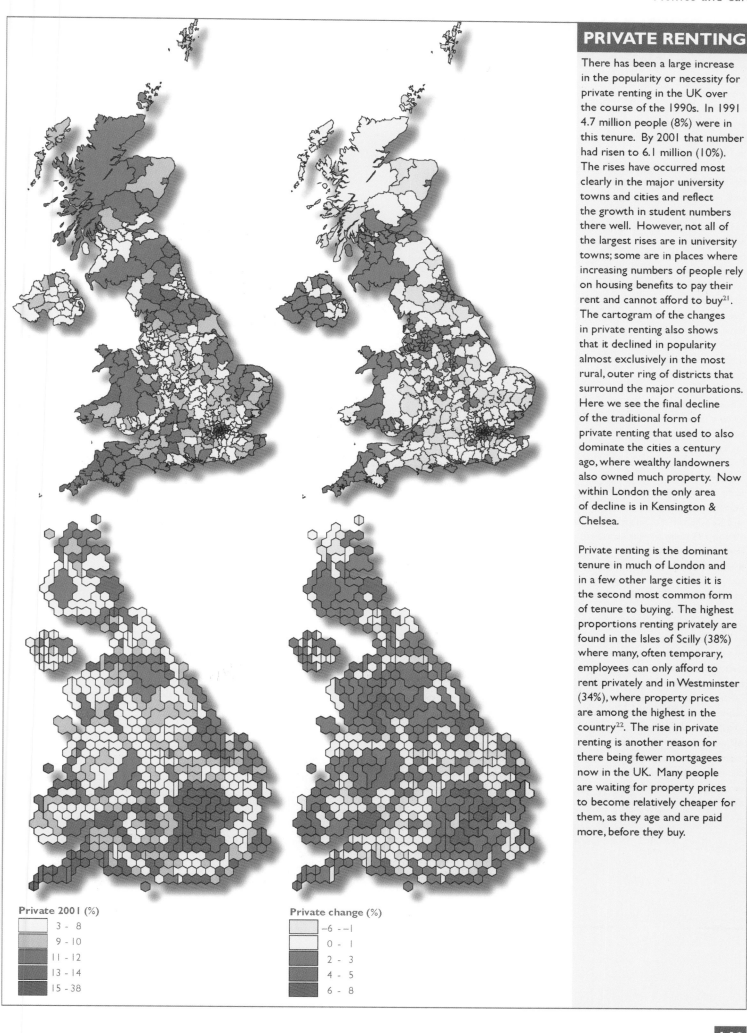

Private 2001 (%)
- 3 - 8
- 9 - 10
- 11 - 12
- 13 - 14
- 15 - 38

Private change (%)
- −6 - −1
- 0 - 1
- 2 - 3
- 4 - 5
- 6 - 8

PRIVATE RENTING

There has been a large increase in the popularity or necessity for private renting in the UK over the course of the 1990s. In 1991 4.7 million people (8%) were in this tenure. By 2001 that number had risen to 6.1 million (10%). The rises have occurred most clearly in the major university towns and cities and reflect the growth in student numbers there well. However, not all of the largest rises are in university towns; some are in places where increasing numbers of people rely on housing benefits to pay their rent and cannot afford to buy[21]. The cartogram of the changes in private renting also shows that it declined in popularity almost exclusively in the most rural, outer ring of districts that surround the major conurbations. Here we see the final decline of the traditional form of private renting that used to also dominate the cities a century ago, where wealthy landowners also owned much property. Now within London the only area of decline is in Kensington & Chelsea.

Private renting is the dominant tenure in much of London and in a few other large cities it is the second most common form of tenure to buying. The highest proportions renting privately are found in the Isles of Scilly (38%) where many, often temporary, employees can only afford to rent privately and in Westminster (34%), where property prices are among the highest in the country[22]. The rise in private renting is another reason for there being fewer mortgagees now in the UK. Many people are waiting for property prices to become relatively cheaper for them, as they age and are paid more, before they buy.

HOUSING ASSOCIATIONS

The largest rise in any tenure group other than outright owners is in people living in housing association or other registered social landlord owned property. In 1991 only 1.3 million people were in this tenure group (2%). By 2001 that number had grown to 3.1 million (5%). The growth has been largely at the expense of the local authority sector, as in many districts the entire sector has been transferred to housing association ownership (which accounts for most of the very large increases[23]), but it is also due to new home building by housing associations, especially in more rural areas. Nowhere has there been a decline in the size of this tenure group.

Housing associations continue to be a largely southern English based movement. With the inclusion of registered social landlords in this category, the highest proportions of people living in this tenure are now found in Hackney (21%, 10% in 1991) and Kensington & Chelsea (17%, 12% in 1991 and the highest then); both areas still have substantial proportions of residents living in local authority accommodation as well, but much less than they had in 1991. Successive British governments have encouraged the transfer of homes to this tenure, and have tried to ensure that the bulk of any new social housing is built in this tenure, an odd – neither state nor private – sector. The piecemeal way in which this massive state transfer of ownership, control and responsibility has played out is clear from the map and cartogram of change over the course of the decade.

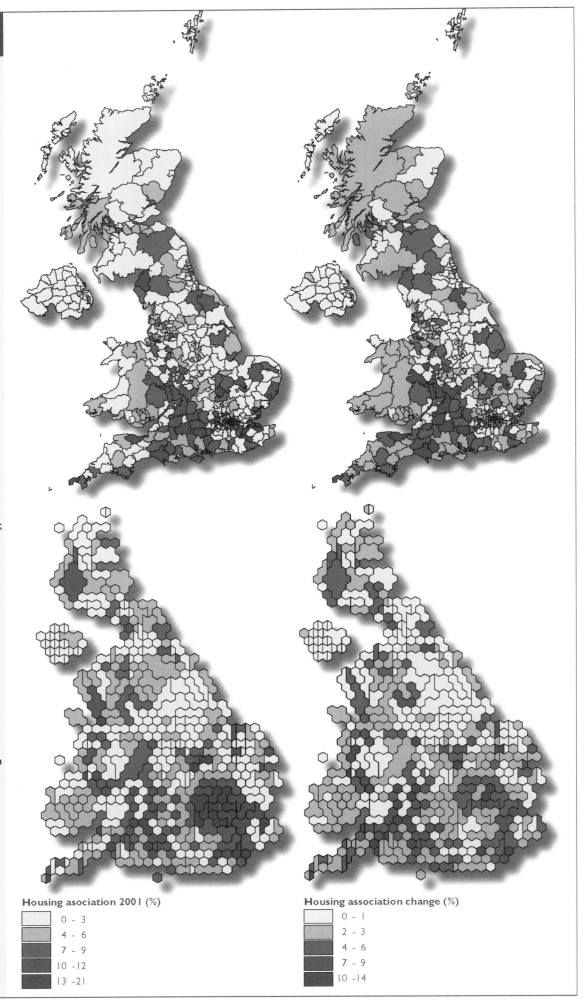

Housing asociation 2001 (%)

- 0 - 3
- 4 - 6
- 7 - 9
- 10 -12
- 13 -21

Housing association change (%)

- 0 - 1
- 2 - 3
- 4 - 6
- 7 - 9
- 10 -14

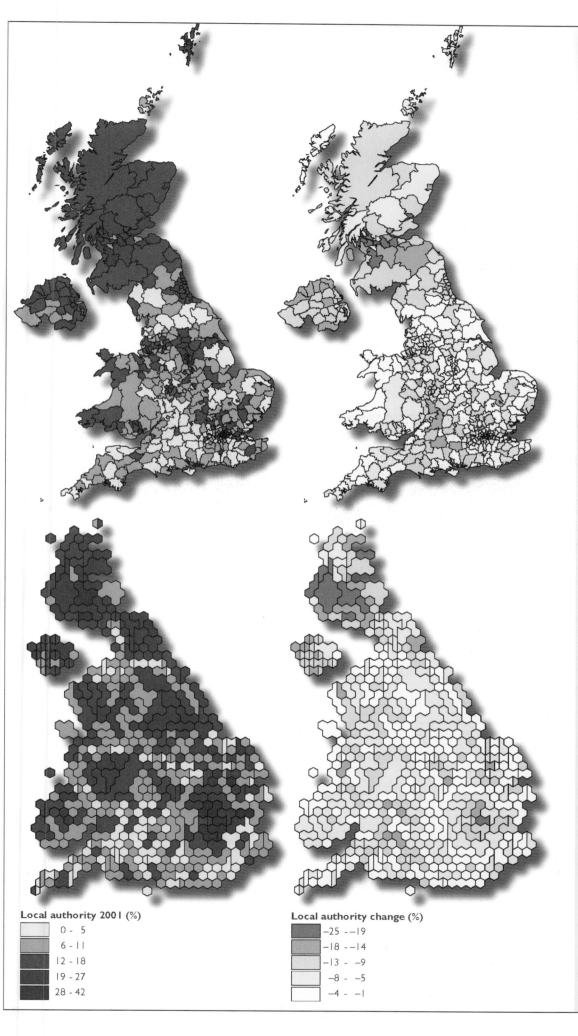

LOCAL AUTHORITY HOUSING

In England and Wales the state sector of social housing is termed 'local authority', in Scotland, Scottish Homes, and in the Province, Northern Ireland Housing Executive. In the UK as a whole by 2001 only 13% of the population lived in this tenure, 7.6 million people, down most rapidly from 20% in 1991, 11.5 million people. In 1991 a majority of the people of Southwark, Tower Hamlets and North Lanarkshire lived in this tenure. Now nowhere is the proportion more than 42% (in Southwark). Although the highest concentrations of local authority housing are still found in London, the list of areas where over a quarter of people are housed in this tenure is much more diverse than that[24].

Council housing, as it used to be collectively known, has declined fastest in Scotland, with right to buy rising across that country in the 1990s and the large-scale stock transfer of large parts of Glasgow's housing. No district in the UK has seen an increase. The smallest decreases have been in areas where there was very little council housing to begin with. If this volume of stock continues to be brought or transferred at 1990s rates then within 20 years there will be no strictly state-owned housing left in the UK. The areas which have been most affected by these changes have been those which often had the most council housing to begin with, where that housing is no longer the responsibility of their elected officials, and may now be their new home owner's responsibility, or the responsibility of some not-for-profit organisation[25].

Local authority 2001 (%)

- 0 - 5
- 6 - 11
- 12 - 18
- 19 - 27
- 28 - 42

Local authority change (%)

- −25 - −19
- −18 - −14
- −13 - −9
- −8 - −5
- −4 - −1

COMMUNAL ESTABLISHMENTS

A small but growing proportion of the population do not live in households and hence do not have a household tenure. These are people who live in communal establishments that range from student halls of residence, to prisons, to long-stay hospitals, to care and nursing homes. In total, 1.0 million people were housed in communal establishments in 2001 (1.8% of the UK population), as compared to 0.8 million in 1991 (1.4%). The populations of many communal establishments continue to fall due to factors such as closing psychiatric hospitals. Furthermore, the changing way in which people's address is recorded between censuses has also led to artefactual falls in some of the populations counted[26]. Despite this the sector has risen in size overall. As should be clear from the cartogram of change, a large part of that rise is due to the increased numbers of students living in places where new halls of residence were built over the course of the 1990s[27].

The falls in the population living in communal establishment shown on the map and cartogram opposite may not be as substantial as they appear. Many are in places that have a high number of hotels and boarding houses. People staying for long periods of time in these areas in 1991 may have been included in that census as being resident there, but not so in 2001 (see footnote 26). However, the general picture is largely correct. Communal living is now most common near large universities, but also along the south coast of England and north coast of Wales, where there is a preponderance of care and nursing homes for the elderly.

Communal 2001 (%)
- 0 - 1
- 2
- 3
- 4 - 8
- 9 - 13

Communal change (%)
- −8 - −1
- 0
- 1
- 2
- 3 - 10

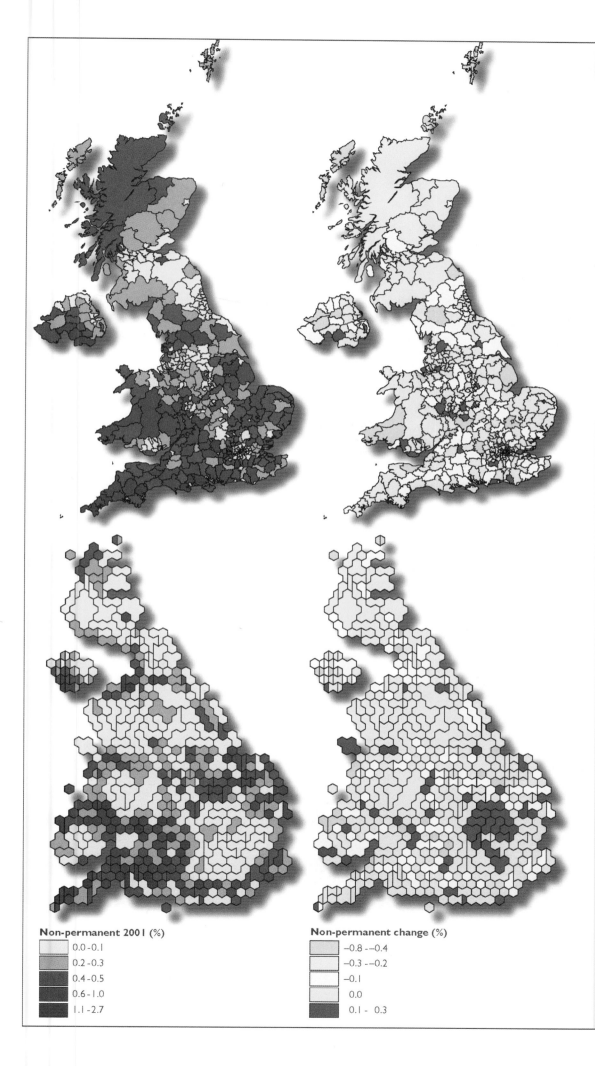

Non-permanent 2001 (%)

- 0.0 - 0.1
- 0.2 - 0.3
- 0.4 - 0.5
- 0.6 - 1.0
- 1.1 - 2.7

Non-permanent change (%)

- −0.8 - −0.4
- −0.3 - −0.2
- −0.1
- 0.0
- 0.1 - 0.3

TEMPORARY DWELLINGS

The censuses are used to count those people not living in communal establishments by the type of dwelling they occupy. Of the 98.2% of people living in households in 2001, 0.3% were living in temporary structures such as caravans, the same proportion as in 1991 and just under 0.2 million people at both points in time. Such temporary dwellings are most prevalent in the more rural areas of the South West of England, but large caravan sites and other areas where many people live in temporary structures can be found across the country[28].

In many of the places where temporary dwellings were most common in 1991, their numbers have declined. Less and less space in the countryside is being given up for those who wish to live there permanently in caravans. However, this decline has been countered by a rise in temporary dwellings being sited in other areas, most interestingly, in London. In Hackney 400 people were recorded to be living in temporary dwellings in 2001 as compared to just over 100 in 1991. It is possible that pressure for living space in the Capital has reached such proportions that in gardens and on other land not used for permanent housing more and more temporary structures are appearing. It is equally possible that these rises in the Capital are due to an increasing number of workers such as builders sleeping during the week in mobile homes on worksites. The census does not provide enough information to gauge the cause of this change. It can be used simply to point out that such a change appears to have occurred.

SHARED DWELLINGS

Across the UK as a whole, a slightly smaller number of people live in dwellings they share with another household or households than did a decade ago. These are mostly bed-sit flats that have a common front door behind which people rent individual rooms. In 1991, 0.5% of the population, 0.3 million people, lived in such accommodation. By 2001 the numbers had fallen greatly to 0.1 million or 0.2% of the population. Bed-sit accommodation is often viewed by landlords as being unprofitable, by local councils as being dangerous, and by many of its tenants as being a last resort. However, there is still a high demand for such accommodation, and thus it may not be surprising that where shared dwellings have declined the most in number, in London, temporary dwellings appear to have sprung up in their place the most. Shared dwellings remain most common in Central London boroughs, in a few other large cities such as Leeds, and in a string of towns dotted along the south coast of England[29]. Areas with high numbers of students are more likely to have more shared dwellings, but their numbers are highest of all in the royal borough of Kensington & Chelsea, where more than 3,000 people live in the centre of the densest part of the UK (see Chapter 1, footnote 8 and accompanying text). Decades ago shared dwellings were a temporary solution to a general lack of housing across the UK. Today they are common only where there is the most extreme pressure of space in areas, or where the generally younger and poorer members of the population cannot afford to rent their own home.

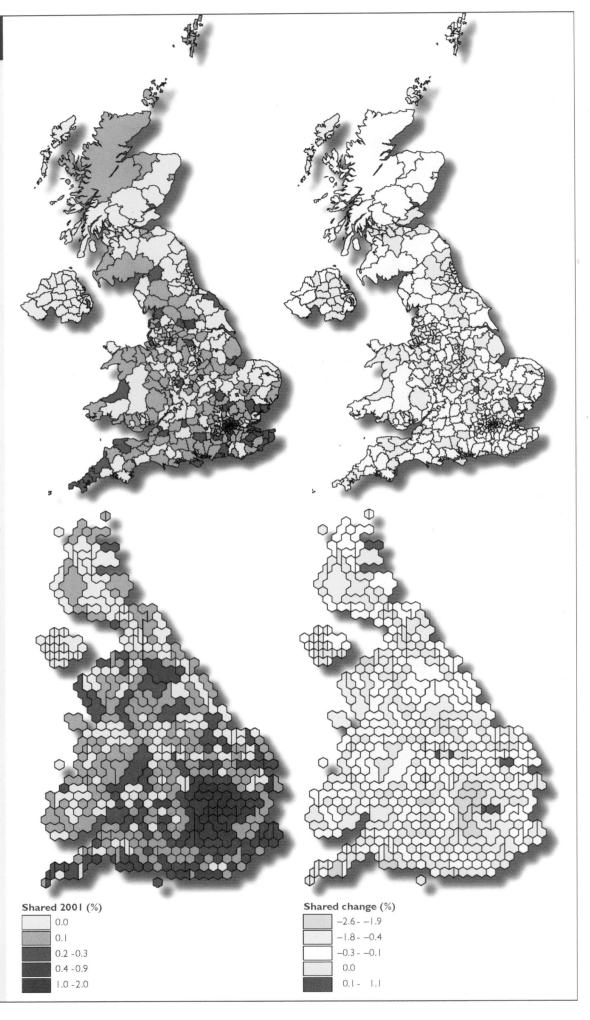

Shared 2001 (%)

- 0.0
- 0.1
- 0.2 - 0.3
- 0.4 - 0.9
- 1.0 - 2.0

Shared change (%)

- −2.6 − −1.9
- −1.8 − −0.4
- −0.3 − −0.1
- 0.0
- 0.1 − 1.1

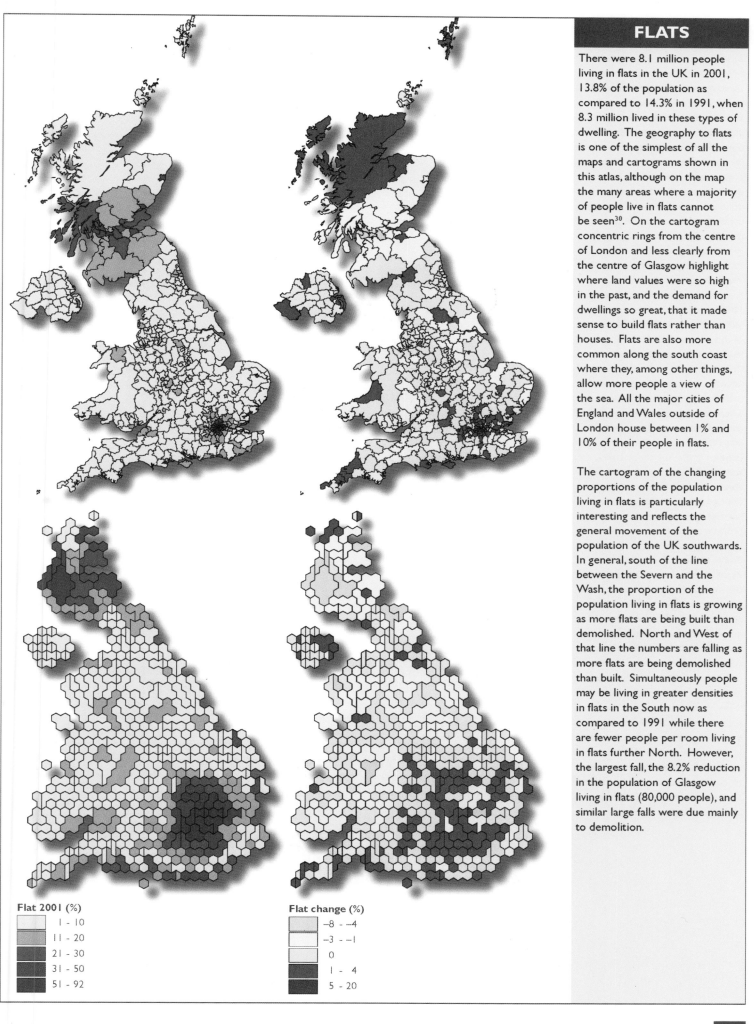

FLATS

There were 8.1 million people living in flats in the UK in 2001, 13.8% of the population as compared to 14.3% in 1991, when 8.3 million lived in these types of dwelling. The geography to flats is one of the simplest of all the maps and cartograms shown in this atlas, although on the map the many areas where a majority of people live in flats cannot be seen[30]. On the cartogram concentric rings from the centre of London and less clearly from the centre of Glasgow highlight where land values were so high in the past, and the demand for dwellings so great, that it made sense to build flats rather than houses. Flats are also more common along the south coast where they, among other things, allow more people a view of the sea. All the major cities of England and Wales outside of London house between 1% and 10% of their people in flats.

The cartogram of the changing proportions of the population living in flats is particularly interesting and reflects the general movement of the population of the UK southwards. In general, south of the line between the Severn and the Wash, the proportion of the population living in flats is growing as more flats are being built than demolished. North and West of that line the numbers are falling as more flats are being demolished than built. Simultaneously people may be living in greater densities in flats in the South now as compared to 1991 while there are fewer people per room living in flats further North. However, the largest fall, the 8.2% reduction in the population of Glasgow living in flats (80,000 people), and similar large falls were due mainly to demolition.

Flat 2001 (%)

- 1 – 10
- 11 – 20
- 21 – 30
- 31 – 50
- 51 – 92

Flat change (%)

- −8 – −4
- −3 – −1
- 0
- 1 – 4
- 5 – 20

HOUSES

The large majority of people in the UK live in houses. Successive censuses have classified these as being terraced, semi-detached and detached. However, the published tabulations from the 1991 Census omitted to record the numbers of people living in each of these types of dwellings, merely the numbers of households, and so we are unable to differentiate between them to show changes by type of dwelling. So we have chosen to show the category as a whole. The numbers of people living in houses rose from 48.2 million in 1991 to 49.4 million in 2001, an increase from 83.4% to 84.0% of the population of the UK. A few more houses were built than those that had to be pulled down due to age or condition. It is also likely that in many areas where housing demand was low, pairs of flats were converted into houses. Similarly in parts of London and a few other cities, some houses appear to have been converted into flats according to the cartogram of change. There has also been an increase in the proportion of the population of Central London living in houses that is most probably due to more people living in roughly the same numbers of houses. In Glasgow and much of the North of England and Scotland, the proportions have risen much faster than the numbers of people living in houses as there is overall population decline. Where the proportion of the population living in houses has fallen the most, part of that fall may be due to houses being occupied at lower densities than they were in 1991. But the falls tended to be clustered where there is most demand for homes, where more houses are becoming flats[31].

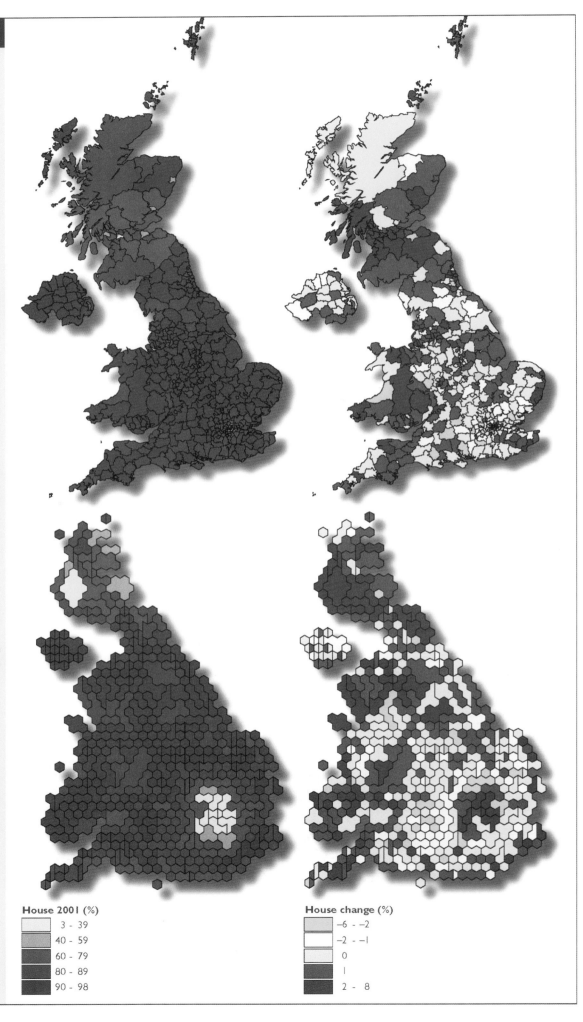

House 2001 (%)

	3 - 39
	40 - 59
	60 - 79
	80 - 89
	90 - 98

House change (%)

	−6 - −2
	−2 - −1
	0
	1
	2 - 8

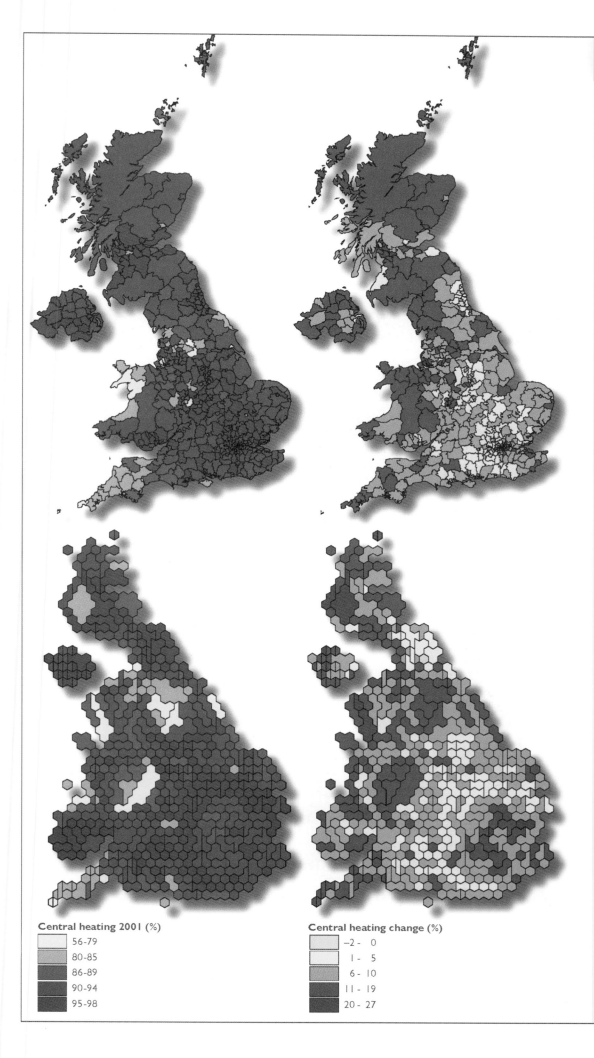

CENTRAL HEATING

The censuses have over time recorded the amenities that various households enjoy as well as their tenure and the types of dwelling they live in. In 1971 the census asked whether a household had access to hot running water. In 1981 there were still significant numbers of households using an outside toilet and more who did not have exclusive use of their own bath or shower. The latter group is now almost all confined to a small proportion of people living in bed-sits and we no longer ask about outside toilets, their numbers being so low. In 1991 a question was asked for the first time as to whether a household had central heating and this was repeated in 2001. The numbers of people living in such households rose quickly over the course of the decade, from 47.3 million (81.8%) to 57.8 million (91.3%). The people most likely to not be living in such households are now most concentrated in a few larger northern towns and cities[32] (although the lowest proportion of all is found on the Isles of Scilly).

The installation of central heating has been most evident in the northern cities where there was most need, particularly where large quantities of housing were owned by local councils and could be converted block by block. Within London too almost all homes have now been converted to this form of heating. The rises have been slowest where there were almost no homes left to convert, most obviously in the Home Counties. The proportions have fallen only in Cambridge (by 1.5%) and Durham (2.2%), where more students now live in property that has yet to be renovated.

Central heating 2001 (%)
- 56-79
- 80-85
- 86-89
- 90-94
- 95-98

Central heating change (%)
- −2 - 0
- 1 - 5
- 6 - 10
- 11 - 19
- 20 - 27

TEACHERS AND NURSES

The census now measures local amenities not directly related to those within each individual's household. In 2001 a question was asked for the first time as to whether a person was qualified to be a teacher, nurse, doctor, dentist or other health professional. Coupled with information as to whether these people were working in their chosen profession, it is now possible to map the provision of qualified education and health service personnel across the country. Unfortunately, in Scotland and Northern Ireland these qualifications were not distinguished and so the maps and cartograms we show here can only include England and Wales.

In 2001 there were 0.66 million qualified teachers teaching in England and Wales, 1.2% of the population of those countries. The map and cartogram show where they lived and hence where they most probably worked, although many live on the outskirts of large cities and commute in. They are fairly evenly spread across these countries. Similarly, the second map and cartogram show a generally even spread of the distribution of qualified nurses working in nursing, 0.40 million people, 0.8% of the population. Teachers live in their greatest concentrations in the Ribble Valley, 2.5% of people there are teachers. Nurses are slightly more numerous in the North and West where more people are ill. It is the areas in which there are fewest people qualified and working in these professions and their neighbouring districts where services may be poorest and authorities have least choice over who to employ[33].

Teachers 2001 (%)
- 0.5 - 0.9
- 1.0 - 1.2
- 1.3 - 1.4
- 1.5 - 1.9
- 2.0 - 2.5

Nurses 2001 (%)
- 0.4 - 0.6
- 0.7
- 0.8
- 0.9 - 1.0
- 1.1 - 1.3

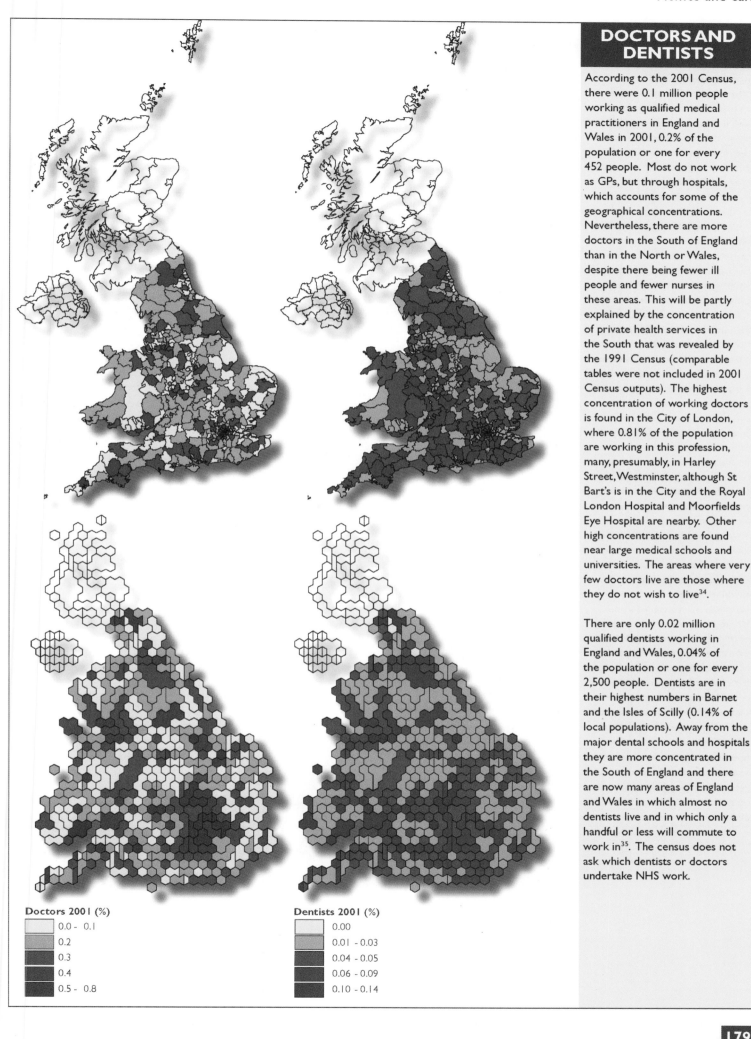

DOCTORS AND DENTISTS

According to the 2001 Census, there were 0.1 million people working as qualified medical practitioners in England and Wales in 2001, 0.2% of the population or one for every 452 people. Most do not work as GPs, but through hospitals, which accounts for some of the geographical concentrations. Nevertheless, there are more doctors in the South of England than in the North or Wales, despite there being fewer ill people and fewer nurses in these areas. This will be partly explained by the concentration of private health services in the South that was revealed by the 1991 Census (comparable tables were not included in 2001 Census outputs). The highest concentration of working doctors is found in the City of London, where 0.81% of the population are working in this profession, many, presumably, in Harley Street, Westminster, although St Bart's is in the City and the Royal London Hospital and Moorfields Eye Hospital are nearby. Other high concentrations are found near large medical schools and universities. The areas where very few doctors live are those where they do not wish to live[34].

There are only 0.02 million qualified dentists working in England and Wales, 0.04% of the population or one for every 2,500 people. Dentists are in their highest numbers in Barnet and the Isles of Scilly (0.14% of local populations). Away from the major dental schools and hospitals they are more concentrated in the South of England and there are now many areas of England and Wales in which almost no dentists live and in which only a handful or less will commute to work in[35]. The census does not ask which dentists or doctors undertake NHS work.

Doctors 2001 (%)
- 0.0 - 0.1
- 0.2
- 0.3
- 0.4
- 0.5 - 0.8

Dentists 2001 (%)
- 0.00
- 0.01 - 0.03
- 0.04 - 0.05
- 0.06 - 0.09
- 0.10 - 0.14

OTHER SERVICES

A further 0.16 million people are working and qualified to work in other health professions such as chiropodists, dispensing opticians, pharmaceutical dispensers, physiotherapists, occupational therapists and so on, 0.3% of the population. Many of the services they provide are delivered through the private sector, and so they tend to be located most where people have most money, not where people are more likely to be ill. The 10 areas containing the highest proportion of people working and qualified in these other health professions are: Camden, Wandsworth, Carrick, Exeter, South Hams, Tynedale, Rushcliffe, Oxford, Shrewsbury & Atcham and Waverley. The areas of the country they avoid living in are places with the fewest paying customers[36].

Finally, a very large number of people with professional qualifications in health or in teaching work in neither of these professions despite having been trained in them, and are working in other employment. The map and cartogram labelled 'other occupation' show where these people trained in teaching or medicine/health but not working in those jobs tend to live. They are clustered in the Home Counties and other rural enclaves of England and Wales. With the exception of nurses (who probably could not afford the choice), professionals trained in teaching or medicine tend to want to live in these areas even when they are working in their trained profession. When they cannot work there, many work in another job that allows them to live where their skills, if they were using them, would be in least demand[37].

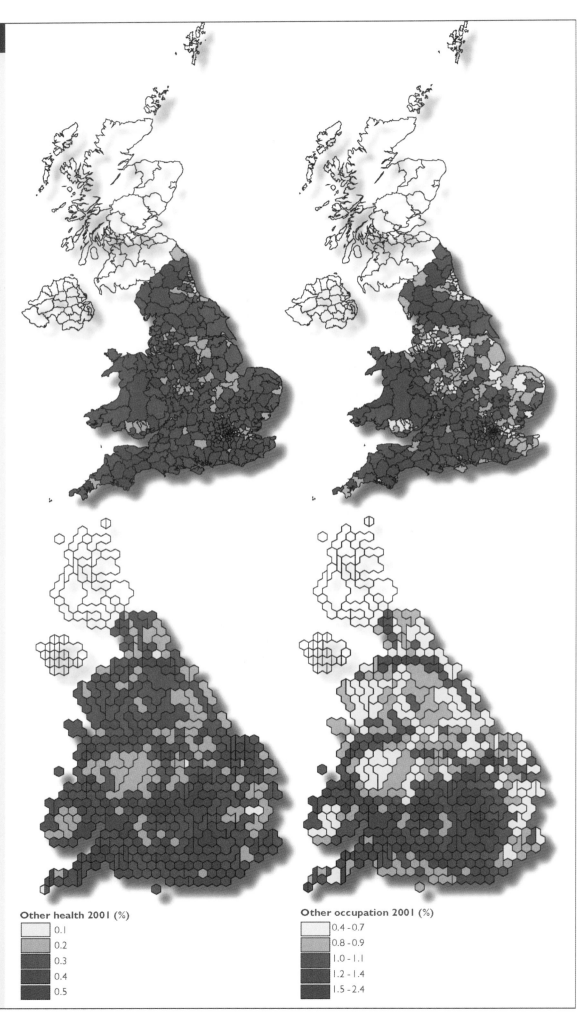

Other health 2001 (%)

- 0.1
- 0.2
- 0.3
- 0.4
- 0.5

Other occupation 2001 (%)

- 0.4 - 0.7
- 0.8 - 0.9
- 1.0 - 1.1
- 1.2 - 1.4
- 1.5 - 2.4

NOTES

[1] We only include people aged 17+ in 1991 and aged 16-74 in 2001, as this is how the data was tabulated. We do not believe the exclusion of people aged 75+ should have a great effect on these figures and is a little outweighed by the inclusion of 16-year-olds in 2001 (who are too young to be able to drive legally).

[2] An extra one person in 10 now has access to a car in the following areas: Manchester, Salford, Knowsley, Liverpool, Barnsley, Doncaster, Rotherham, Sheffield, Gateshead, Newcastle upon Tyne, North Tyneside, South Tyneside, Sunderland, Sandwell, Bolsover, Chesterfield, Derwentside, Easington, Hartlepool, Wear Valley, Eastbourne, Thanet, Wansbeck, Blaenau Gwent, Merthyr Tydfil, Rhondda Cynon Taf, Dundee City, East Ayrshire, East Lothian, Falkirk, Glasgow City, Inverclyde, North Lanarkshire, Renfrewshire, West Dunbartonshire and Belfast.

[3] The following places have seen an increase in the proportion of people living in households with access to a single car or van: Camden, Hackney, Hammersmith & Fulham, Haringey, Islington, Lambeth, Lewisham, Newham, Southwark, Tower Hamlets, Wandsworth, Westminster, Manchester, Knowsley, Liverpool, Gateshead, Newcastle upon Tyne, North Tyneside, South Tyneside, Sunderland, Isles of Scilly, Easington, Hartlepool, Kingston upon Hull, Dundee, Glasgow, Inverclyde, North Lanarkshire, West Dunbartonshire, Belfast and Derry.

[4] City of London, Camden, Croydon, Hammersmith & Fulham, Islington, Kensington & Chelsea, Richmond upon Thames, Tower Hamlets, Wandsworth and Westminster.

[5] More than 30% of people of driving age in the following areas have access to two cars through their household: Mid Bedfordshire, Bracknell Forest, West Berkshire, Windsor & Maidenhead, Wokingham, Aylesbury Vale, Chiltern, South Bucks, Wycombe, South Cambridgeshire, Congleton, Macclesfield, East Dorset, Maldon, Uttlesford, Basingstoke & Deane, East Hampshire, Eastleigh, Fareham, Hart, Test Valley, East Hertfordshire, St Albans, Three Rivers, Blaby, Harborough, Daventry, South Northamptonshire, South Oxfordshire, Lichfield, South Staffordshire, Mid Suffolk, Elmbridge, Mole Valley, Surrey Heath, Tandridge, Waverley, Stratford-upon-Avon, Horsham, Bromsgrove and Wychavon.

[6] More than 13% of the people of the following districts are of driving age and live in households with access to three or more vehicles: Wokingham, Chiltern, South Bucks, Wycombe, East Dorset, Maldon, Uttlesford, East Hampshire, Hart, Sevenoaks, South Northamptonshire, Mole Valley, Surrey Heath, Tandridge and Waverley.

[7] In Oxford 5% of people have access to three cars or more, a rise of only 1% on the proportion in 1991. With the falls seen in London and Cambridge we can perhaps see an affluent urban trend beginning partly where people may hire cars when they need them, rather than own them to have access at any time, but also requiring a permanent parking space for them.

[8] Wokingham, Chiltern, South Bucks, Wycombe, Cambridge, Macclesfield, Exeter, Lewes, Brentwood, Epping Forest, Broxbourne, St Albans, Welwyn Hatfield, Oadby & Wigston, Bridgnorth, Lichfield, South Staffordshire, Elmbridge, Guildford, Mole Valley, Runnymede, Spelthorne and Tandridge.

[9] The numbers of people working from home or walking to work have increased by 2% or more in: City of London, Hammersmith & Fulham, Islington, Kensington & Chelsea, Richmond upon Thames, Southwark, Bracknell Forest, Reading, West Berkshire, Wokingham, Milton Keynes, Wycombe, Brighton & Hove, Castle Point, Rochford, Uttlesford, Cheltenham, Fareham, Gosport, Dacorum, Watford, South Northamptonshire, Cherwell, Bridgnorth, Elmbridge, Guildford, Mole Valley, Reigate & Banstead, Surrey Heath, Waverley, Aberdeen City, Dundee City, Edinburgh, City of, Glasgow City, Stirling and North Down.

[10] More than 5% of people travel to work by bus in: Brent, Camden, Croydon, Ealing, Greenwich, Hackney, Hammersmith & Fulham, Haringey, Hounslow, Islington, Kensington & Chelsea, Lambeth, Lewisham, Southwark, Wandsworth, Westminster, Manchester, Tameside, Liverpool, Rotherham, Sheffield, Gateshead, Newcastle upon Tyne, Sunderland, Birmingham, Sandwell, Wolverhampton, Calderdale, Leeds, Reading, Bristol, Plymouth, Kingston upon Hull, Brighton & Hove, Southampton, Leicester, Broxtowe, Gedling, Nottingham, Oxford, Aberdeen City, Dundee City, East Ayrshire, East Dunbartonshire, East Lothian, East Renfrewshire, Edinburgh, Glasgow City, Inverclyde, Midlothian, North Ayrshire, North Lanarkshire, Renfrewshire, South Lanarkshire, Stirling, West Dunbartonshire, West Lothian and Belfast.

[11] And, perhaps, also partly as a result of pro-bus local government policies in London, resulting from the Underground being so overcrowded.

[12] Five percent or more of the population travel to work by train daily from: Bexley, Bromley, Croydon, Greenwich, Havering, Kingston upon Thames, Lambeth, Lewisham, Merton, Richmond upon Thames, Southwark, Sutton, Wandsworth, Basildon, Brentwood, Castle Point, Chelmsford, Rochford, Southend-on-Sea, Thurrock , Broxbourne, East Hertfordshire, Hertsmere, St Albans, Dartford, Sevenoaks, Tunbridge Wells, Elmbridge, Epsom & Ewell, Mole Valley, Reigate & Banstead, Tandridge, Woking, Mid Sussex and West Dunbartonshire.

[13] More than 5% of people travel to work by light rail in: City of London, Barking & Dagenham, Barnet, Brent, Camden, Ealing, Enfield, Hackney, Hammersmith & Fulham, Haringey, Harrow, Hounslow, Islington, Kensington & Chelsea, Lambeth, Merton, Newham, Redbridge, Southwark, Tower Hamlets, Waltham Forest, Wandsworth, Westminster, and only outside of London, in Epping Forest.

[14] An extra half a percent or more of the population now travel to work by bicycle in: Camden, Hackney, Hammersmith & Fulham, Islington, Lambeth, Southwark, Wandsworth, Reading, Bristol, Brighton & Hove and Edinburgh.

[15] Of the population as a whole, half a percent fewer people now cycle to work in: Bedford, Mid Bedfordshire, Cambridge, East Cambridgeshire, Fenland, Huntingdonshire, Peterborough, Crewe & Nantwich, Ellesmere Port & Neston, Isles of Scilly, Barrow-in-Furness, Erewash, Purbeck, East Riding of Yorkshire, Chelmsford, Maldon, Cheltenham, Cotswold, Gosport, New Forest, Portsmouth, Rushmoor, Wyre, Boston, East Lindsey, North Lincolnshire, South Holland, Broadland, King's Lynn & West Norfolk, North Norfolk, South Norfolk, East Northamptonshire, Selby, York, Bassetlaw, Newark & Sherwood, Oxford, South Oxfordshire, Vale of White Horse, West Oxfordshire, North Shropshire, Shrewsbury & Atcham, Mendip, Sedgemoor, Taunton Deane, Ipswich, Waveney, Runnymede, Spelthorne, Surrey Heath, Stratford-upon-Avon, Warwick, Chichester, North Wiltshire and West Wiltshire.

[16] Over 35% of people own their property outright in: East Devon, Christchurch, East Dorset, Rother, Tendring, South Shropshire, West Somerset, Ceredigion, Powys, Eilean Siar, Orkney Islands, Cookstown, Fermanagh, Magherafelt and Omagh.

[17] Not all of the 10 areas which have seen outright ownership grow the fastest are in this ring: City of London, Chiltern, South Bucks, Brentwood, Hart, Sevenoaks, Castle Morpeth, South Staffordshire, Surrey Heath and East Dunbartonshire.

[18] The 10 areas which have seen the smallest increases in this tenure group, or actual decreases are: Isles of Scilly, Blackpool, Hyndburn, Blaenau Gwent, Rhondda Cynon Taf, Banbridge, Cookstown, Dungannon, Fermanagh and Magherafelt.

[19] Rates of buying rose by between 8% and 13% in: East Ayrshire, Glasgow, Inverclyde, North Lanarkshire, West Lothian, Antrim, Armagh, Ballymoney, Banbridge, Cookstown, Dungannon, Fermanagh, Limavady, Magherafelt, Moyle, Newry & Mourne and Strabane.

[20] The 10 lowest proportions of buyers, all below 25% of the local population, are found in: the City of London, Camden, Hackney, Hammersmith & Fulham, Islington, Kensington & Chelsea, Southwark, Tower Hamlets, Westminster and the Isles of Scilly.

[21] An additional 5% or more of the population rent privately now in: Haringey, Islington, Lambeth, Newham, Redbridge, Tower Hamlets, Wandsworth, Manchester, Bristol, Kingston upon Hull, Brighton & Hove, Hastings, Southampton, Blackpool, Pendle, Lincoln, North East Lincolnshire, Nottingham, Rhondda Cynon Taf, Dundee, Edinburgh and Coleraine.

[22] More than 20% of people rent privately in: the City of London, Camden, Hammersmith & Fulham, Haringey, Kensington & Chelsea, Lambeth, Wandsworth, Westminster, Isles of Scilly, Brighton & Hove, Richmondshire (military), Oxford and Forest Heath (military). Note that the two military areas are included because we include home being provided by employer as private renting.

[23] More than a tenth of the populations of the following areas are now in this tenure who were not in 1991 (in 1991, 25,000 people living in areas where the stock had been transferred still thought they were in local authority tenure so not all of these areas might have seen stock transfer in the 1990s): Hackney, East Cambridgeshire, Penwith, North Dorset, West Dorset, Hastings, Cotswold, Basingstoke & Deane, Rushmoor, Hertsmere, Tunbridge Wells, Breckland, Hambleton, Telford & Wrekin, West Somerset, Lichfield, Stratford-upon-Avon, Kennet, Malvern Hills and Wychavon.

[24] Barking & Dagenham, Camden, Greenwich, Hackney, Islington, Lambeth, Lewisham, Southwark, Tower Hamlets, Manchester, Gateshead, Newcastle upon Tyne, South Tyneside, Kingston upon Hull, Harlow, Stevenage, Norwich, Corby, Nottingham, Clackmannanshire, East Ayrshire, Falkirk, North Lanarkshire and West Dunbartonshire.

[25] An additional 15% or more of the populations of the following areas no longer live in this tenure: Hackney, Tower Hamlets, Basingstoke & Deane, Hertsmere, Telford & Wrekin, Kennet, Aberdeen City, Clackmannanshire, Dundee, East Ayrshire, Falkirk, Glasgow, Inverclyde, North Ayrshire, North Lanarkshire, Renfrewshire, South Lanarkshire, West Dunbartonshire, West Lothian, Antrim, Ballymoney, Derry, Limavady, Moyle and Strabane.

[26] People only staying for a short time in a communal establishment, such as a homeless hostel, may not have been recorded as being resident there, or anywhere, in 2001. In 1991 they would have been recorded as resident in the hostel under the same circumstances.

[27] The proportion of the local population living in communal establishments has risen by 2% or more in: Manchester, Cambridge, Exeter, North Dorset, Durham, Teesdale, Winchester, Lancaster, Charnwood, Oadby & Wigston, Norwich, Richmondshire, Oxford, Rutland, Bridgnorth, Newcastle-under-Lyme, Runnymede, Kennet and Ceredigion.

[28] More than 1,000 people lived in temporary dwellings in the following areas in 2001: Doncaster, Bracknell Forest, West Berkshire, Windsor & Maidenhead, South Cambridgeshire, Vale Royal, Kerrier, Restormel, Teignbridge, East Dorset, Wealden, Epping Forest, South Gloucestershire, Tewkesbury, New Forest, Herefordshire, Medway, Wyre, East Lindsey, South Oxfordshire, Vale of White Horse, North Somerset, South Staffordshire, Mole Valley, Runnymede, Stratford-upon-Avon and Arun.

[29] More than half a percent of the population live in shared dwellings in: the City of London, Brent, Camden, Hackney, Hammersmith & Fulham, Haringey, Islington, Kensington & Chelsea, Kingston upon Thames, Lambeth, Lewisham, Newham, Southwark, Tower Hamlets, Wandsworth, Westminster, Cambridge, Bournemouth, Brighton & Hove, Eastbourne and Oxford.

[30] More than half the population of the following areas live in flats: the City of London, Camden, Hackney, Hammersmith & Fulham, Islington, Kensington & Chelsea, Lambeth, Southwark, Tower Hamlets, Wandsworth, Westminster, Edinburgh and Glasgow.

[31] The proportion of the population living in houses has fallen by 1% or more in: Enfield, Haringey, Kingston upon Thames, Newham, Manchester, Bracknell Forest, Reading, West Berkshire, Windsor & Maidenhead, Wokingham, Cambridge, Isles of Scilly, Exeter, North Dorset, Durham, Teesdale, Chelmsford, Winchester, Watford, Welwyn Hatfield, Canterbury, Chorley, Charnwood, Oadby & Wigston, Norwich, Richmondshire, York, Nottingham, Oxford, Vale of White Horse, Rutland, Bridgnorth, Oswestry, Mendip, Newcastle-under-Lyme, Guildford, Runnymede, Waverley, Adur, Kennet, Ceredigion, Midlothian, Belfast and North Down.

[32] More than 15% of the population do not live in homes with central heating in: Knowsley, Liverpool, Birmingham, Sandwell, Bradford, Calderdale, Kirklees, Leeds, Cambridge, Caradon, Carrick, Kerrier, North Cornwall, Penwith, Restormel, Isles of Scilly, Barrow-in-Furness, Exeter, Mid Devon, Plymouth, Teignbridge, Torbay, Torridge, West Devon, Kingston upon Hull, Portsmouth, Blackpool, Burnley, Hyndburn, Lancaster, Pendle, Preston, Scarborough, Oxford, Bridgnorth, East Staffordshire, Isle of Wight, Ceredigion, Conwy, Gwynedd, Isle of Anglesey, Dundee and Glasgow.

[33] Less than 0.7% of local populations are teachers in the following areas, which range from places too expensive for them to live in to areas which they appear not to wish to live in, as they could afford to live there and there are many children there to be taught: Barking & Dagenham, Kensington & Chelsea, Westminster, Knowsley, Sandwell, Slough, Easington, Kingston upon Hull, Blackpool, Corby, Ashfield, Stoke-on-Trent and Crawley. For similar reasons, less than 0.5% of the population are nurses in the following areas: Barking & Dagenham, Kensington & Chelsea, Tower Hamlets, Fenland, Castle Point, Epping Forest, Tendring, Thurrock, Broxbourne, Swale, Corby and Crawley.

[34] Less than a twentieth of a percent of the local population are working as qualified medical practioners living in: Barking & Dagenham, Hyndburn, Corby, Blyth Valley, Ashfield, Cannock Chase, Tamworth and Blaenau Gwent. In these districts only 290 doctors live and presumably work in areas where 728,000 people live. A few others will commute in but they are often the centres of larger areas that are under-served.

[35] Less than one hundredth of a percent of the local population are working as qualified dentists living in: Barking & Dagenham, Knowsley, Halton, Bolsover, Erewash, Easington, Kingston upon Hull, Thurrock, Blackpool, Blyth Valley, Wansbeck, Ashfield, Tamworth, Blaenau Gwent and Merthyr Tydfil. In these districts only 126 working dentists live among a population of 1.69 million people, one dentist for every 13,400 people. It is unlikely that dental services here are adequate.

[36] The 10 districts in England and Wales in which the fewest people live who are qualified and work in these professions are: Barking & Dagenham, Newham, South Tyneside, Sandwell, Walsall, Isles of Scilly, Easington, Broxbourne, South Holland and Corby.

[37] Over 1.5% of the local populations of the following areas are trained in teaching or health/medical professions, are in work, but not in a directly related job, although many may be working in universities: the City of London, Camden, Haringey, Richmond upon Thames, Southwark, Westminster, Cambridge, South Cambridgeshire, Isles of Scilly, South Lakeland, Derbyshire Dales, High Peak, South Hams, Winchester, Tynedale, Craven, Oxford and Ceredigion.

Conclusion

9

Map in this section

London and the Archipelago (p 187)

The patterns to people's lives in the UK, when mapped, can appear as layer after layer of a complex changing mosaic. Each place is unique in many ways; each map of these places is a collective snapshot of life histories that suggests particular places tend towards one group of collective trajectories rather than another. A census atlas is at best the crudest of summaries of a tiny number of facets of millions upon millions of photo albums, shared memories and collective experiences. Within each place, each tile of the mosaic, another mosaic may be drawn of the difference that a few streets' separation makes, of parts of town on the rise, of villages that are changing slowly, of the edges of cities beginning to decay, of homes being repopulated by new kinds of people. Moreover, each of those specks on the map appears woven from dozens of unique events in the passage of the hundreds or thousands of the lives that have passed through there.

The business of stereotyping such detail, of summarising what is common from what is peculiar, is speculative, and the result is often unique to those who try to interpret the changing picture. However, through drawing map after map, common patterns begin to form in the mind. After a time, when plotting something new, you are unsurprised to see the colours turning out as they are. The same things are happening in the same places enough, and often similarly enough, to the previous decade you drew these maps, such that you begin to imagine that something quite simple is at work beneath all the subtle differences you see between people and places. We bring the atlas to an end by giving one take on what this pattern to the processes might be: what it is that we are looking at.

At the start of the 21st century, the human geography of the UK can be most simply summarised as a tale of one metropolis and its provincial hinterland. These two areas cover the whole of the nation and divide it along an ancient boundary. In the past this boundary was thought of as the North–South divide, separating one group of cities, towns and villages from another. The last 10 years of changes to the human geography of the UK has cumulated a longer running process whereby this divide is no longer a regional division; it now marks the boundaries

of two places which are ever more dissimilar to each other across that divide, but much more homogenous within themselves. On each side of the divide there is a great city structure with a central dense urban core, suburbs, parks and a rural fringe. However, to the south these areas are converging as a single great metropolis, while to the north is a provincial archipelago of city islands.

These two areas are each made up of many cities and towns but function as two separate entities and in two different ways. On the southern side of the line is the great *world metropolis of London*, while on the northern side lies its antithesis, the *provincial archipelago*. The archipelago lies west and north of the old counties of Gloucestershire, Warwickshire, Leicestershire and Lincolnshire. These are no longer counties: they are the city limits of London. You could quibble as to the exact route London's city limits run, but they follow a line that corresponds closely to those county boundaries, from the estuary of the Severn to a few miles south of the Humber, running along the foothills of what used to be called upland Britain. This is no longer the North–South divide. It is the dividing line between a new Greater London, and the rest. In everyday speech we no longer talk of Greater London. That area, demarcated in 1965, is now simply referenced to as London. Greater London should now be seen as the metropolis that extends from Gainsborough in the North to Penzance in the West. Like any great city, its outer fringes are less populated but are the weekend retreats of its more affluent inhabitants. It is only when they cross the new city limits that Londoners really leave London.

The archipelago of the provinces is perhaps harder to envisage. It extends west throughout Wales, the West Midlands, up all of northern England and throughout Scotland and Northern Ireland. Grimsby and Scunthorpe, Nottingham and Derby, Coventry and Cardiff all lie just inside its border; they are its southern limits. The archipelago of the provinces has no common name as it is defined through its exclusion from the capital, but the building of more bridges over the Severn and the Humber, and of new road links through the Midlands, have only heightened its degree of separation. It is not separate because travel is difficult from London. It is separate because it is *different* from London. To define the archipelago of the provinces we must first redefine Greater London.

Built-up Greater London now extends as far north as its suburbs of Leicester and Northampton, as far west as its edge suburbs of Bristol and Plymouth. Between these places are green fields, but they are now the parkland of this city. Hardly anyone living near those fields works on the land. Greater London is defined here by where it appears to have an immediate and connected geographical effect. It ends where, when you look at the maps in these pages, its immediate impact appears to peter out. Such immediate impacts of Greater London encompass Cambridge, Norwich and Ipswich, Oxford, Swindon, Reading and Southampton. When the patterns to the changing human geography of the UK are considered in total, these places are all swallowed up by the trends emanating from the capital. Half the population of the UK now live within its immediate influence, within that metropolis. In London's suburbs are the universities of Oxford and Cambridge, its educational enclaves; at its extremities are the beaches of Devon and Cornwall, where many Londoners spend their summer weekends. London's edge suburb is not Croydon, but Bristol. Its parks are not in Hampstead but in Hampshire. Its commuter belt extends up to the ends of the M3 and M11, up to Leamington Spa on the M40, to Chepstow on the M4. The M25 is now its inner ring road. You drive to the M25 down one motorway, around it and out again to where you are going within the metropolis; it does not relieve traffic from within old London, it helps move it around the new. The South is London and London is the South; and regional divisions within are meaningless. This is a single functioning place: the London metropolis.

The archipelago of the provinces is made up of a series of city cluster islands and their immediate hinterlands. It is a human geography archipelago because these city clusters are functionally separate. It is an archipelago because each cluster of towns and cities looks to London rather than to its neighbouring islands for its greatest, but now distant, influence. These are separate islands which together have had a common transformation of increased subservience to the metropolis. At the centre of the archipelago is a huge cities island, a conurbation as great as the old London in population, but a conurbation which does not even have a name; a collection of towns and cities which are increasingly living in the shadow of that distant capital which has engulfed the South. This island is shaped like a ring, broken only to the South. The great northern conurbation's borders stretch from Liverpool in the West, through Knowsley, St Helens, Wigan, Bolton, Blackburn with Darwen, Hynburn and Burley, to Calderdale, Bradford and Leeds in the East, then down through Wakefield, Doncaster, Rotherham, Sheffield

and southwards to North East Derbyshire and Chesterfield, then back across through the High Peak to Stockport, Manchester, Trafford, Warrington and Halton, encircling Pennine towns and boroughs within those borders. This centre lies directly in the rain-shadow created by the London metropolis separating the north from Europe. It lies too far North to benefit from any spill-over effect at the borders. Within its core is a park, a national park, the Peak District, and the largely uninhabited southern Pennines Hills. In those hills, and at the centre of this great metropolis is Stott Hall Farm, which stands between two lanes of the M62 motorway. In antithesis to London, the centre of the archipelago of the provinces is not the Greenwich Meridian, Big Ben or Buckingham Palace. It is a farm high up on a bleak moor crossed by the UK's highest motorway.

Between the metropolis of London, with its great old port to the East, and this central conurbation with its old port to the West, are the southern suburbs and outer estates of the archipelago of the provinces. A string of islands run like border forts on the southern limits of this northern sea: Nottingham, Derby, Coventry, Birmingham, Hereford and Cardiff. All benefit from being near the border with London, all achieving little from their allocation to the other pole. The western edges of the archipelago of the provinces extend into North Wales and Snowdonia. North are more people but before them lie the parks of the Lake District, the Yorkshire Dales and Moors. The main island's eastern boundary is the sea and river Trent, south is the Peak District and the Cheshire plain and nestled among all this scenery are enclaves, small islands, towns and villages as affluent as many London suburbs, yet still different. Many of the people who run the archipelago of the provinces originally came from the metropolis, and commute in from these countryside islands to govern the uplands. It is because the archipelago is so diffuse and even its largest island has no obvious single core, that it is not one giant metropolis. Its provincial nature includes the encapsulation of another three countries, the larger formed of two medium-sized islands amid a scattering of atolls, the next of just one medium-size island and a few smaller parts, and the smallest a single city state island.

Scotland's two medium-sized islands are Edinburgh and Glasgow. Above there are the atolls of Dundee and Aberdeen at the northern extreme of the archipelago. South of Edinburgh and Glasgow is an island chain which has little connection to its northern neighbours. The main islands of that chain are the clusters of people living near the mouths of the rivers Tyne, Wear and Tees. To the West, the only medium-sized island in Wales is Cardiff. South Wales is the border country of the archipelago. The boundaries of the new Greater London are just over either of two Severn bridges and a short trip on the M4. The North of Wales consists of a cluster of tiny atolls which lie too far away to benefit. Between here and London is the island of the Black Country dominated by Birmingham, benefiting a little from being the largest island near to the shores of the metropolis, but still a member of the archipelago. Most remote of all is the island of Belfast, more closely connected to London than anywhere else, like all the other islands of the archipelago. Other minor outlining islands include Hull, Swansea and the Wirral. The archipelago is typified by places that appear more separated from their neighbours than distances alone could explain. The explanation is that they all live in the shadow of the metropolis.

Flicking through the pages of this atlas it is clear that the population of the metropolis has grown. Almost all of the islands of the archipelago are slowly sinking as they become less densely occupied and drift further from where the core of people in the UK live. Although there is great poverty in the centre of the metropolis, poverty is scattered throughout the islands and very few of the rich or wealthy live outside the metropolis. When they do they recreate its image in tiny pockets of places that will never really be anything like Islington, Westminster or Oxford. Even the official classification of areas in the UK has six types of place (out of 13) which are almost exclusively only found outside of the archipelago. There are slightly more men in the metropolis than in the archipelago, and more children are being born there. Although many more venture into the archipelago to attend university than before, more than ever move back (or travel South for the first time) to the metropolis in their twenties and thirties. A few return to govern the archipelago from within, more when services are supposed to be provided universally such as in health (but less than there ought to be). The elderly are being pushed out of the core of the metropolis, to live on its outskirts, return to or leave for the archipelago in their retirement. However, it is only in the metropolis that significant numbers reach a very old age.

In the archipelago quaint customs are still followed. On a few islands a majority of the population are married and almost everywhere on the islands a majority of the population are Christian. It is in the metropolis that the most people believing in other religions live. The metropolis is more cosmopolitan, trendy and liberal despite as a whole tending to vote Conservative. Nowhere else contains such clusters of the UK's smallest religions. In the provinces areas are still divided along Christian lines. Outside of the main and Black Country islands, the population is almost exclusively White; and, as with religion, people from the UK's smallest ethnic groups live almost exclusively outside of the archipelago islands. Most people in the archipelago were born in the countries they live in. People from the smallest birthplace groups, those collectively born 'elsewhere' in the world, are least likely to choose to live on these islands. The metropolis is the home of the vast majority of people born overseas in Europe, the Caribbean, North America, Africa, Asia and

Australasia. It is to the metropolis that most people come when travelling to the UK from abroad to live. The islands hold little attraction to people considering moving to the UK.

In the metropolis are found the most qualified people and the fewest with no qualifications. That centre of the metropolis swarms with university graduates, those swarms becoming denser year by year. Only in the very core of the metropolis are significant numbers of people still out of work. Youth unemployment is lowest just outside that core; here people are in greatest demand when they are young and fit to work. Almost no one in the metropolis is sick or disabled in comparison with the archipelago. People retire young only to the edges of the metropolis, its core is largely reserved for those in full-time work or for a few looking for such work. There is greater poverty in the very heart of the metropolis, but these people are not living in unconnected areas. Most are employed on low wages to keep the infrastructure of the core of the Capital running. People are more willing to live there in those circumstances than venture North. The majority of self-employed people live in the metropolis where a higher proportion of people work in total, even if it is just for a few hours a week. Moreover, the metropolis is the centre of the long hours culture in the UK. Around its core people claim to work the longest and within its core working hours are rising most quickly.

The metropolis employs the bulk of managers, with numbers rising most in its centre. It is the workplace of preference for professionals and they too are increasing in numbers fastest in the UK in the core of the metropolis, so, too, with those working in associate professional jobs, and in administration and secretarial work, although that sector as a whole is declining. The metropolis is running out of space for those employed in the less lucrative fields of sales, customer services, and personal services, and has lacked space for people employed in skilled trades for some time. However, it is in the islands of the archipelago that skilled trades are declining most. Similarly, there, where machine operatives were most common, they are also falling most in number. Only people working in the most elementary of occupations are increasing in number more in these archipelago islands. The islands have lost almost all of the mining work they once monopolised. Employment in energy, water, agriculture, forestry and fishing has fallen most on the islands too during the 1990s. There is less room in the metropolis for people to live now who work in construction, distribution and catering, the state sector and transport. Near London transport is only increasing significantly around the major airports. These airports surround the old Greater London area, and are booming with trade. What most typifies industrial changes in these two places is the continued loss of manufacturing jobs in the archipelago, and the continued massive growth of finance in the metropolis. Beneath all these changes it is banking and money which has caused the metropolis to rise, and the continuous decline of manufacturing industry, without significant replacement, which causes the archipelago to sink. The UK no longer manufactures for the rest of the world, but it is one of the world's key bankers, and that sector is growing rapidly. However, the archipelago islands are of little use for this growth sector.

It is in the archipelago islands that people are mostly likely to need to care for family or friends who are ill, and to spend many hours a week providing such care, where most lone parents without work are found, and where the fewest households have two earners. It is only in the centre of the metropolis that almost no one provides unpaid care for 50 hours or more a week. People need to work to afford to live in all but the poorest parts of the metropolis, and because of this there are very few people living there in poor health. There is thus least need for such care away from the islands. It is on the islands that children and adults are most likely to be seriously ill. It is away from the islands that young people move most, particularly following graduation, to share homes with others in the metropolis.

Young people are also most likely to be living alone in the metropolis, to cohabit here, but not to have children until they are a little older. The core of the metropolis is ringed by outer suburbs typified by married couples living with their children. In the archipelago there are relatively more married couples whose children have now left home, more of them are pensioners, other than on the metropolis limits. Single pensioners in the metropolis are squeezed out to those limits. They are more often the inhabitants of the ageing archipelago. The metropolis, especially its centre, is becoming yet more crowded in relation to the norm. A growing plethora of languages from around the world are understood and spoken in the metropolis. At the outer reaches of the archipelago three ancient Celtic languages survive, but more through the classroom than the home.

Apart from in its very core, where they are least needed, households in the metropolis almost all own cars, and the more cars a household owns the more likely it is to live in the metropolis. It is thus in the metropolis that people drive to work the most, but here also they are most likely to commute on foot, bicycle, by train, other rail or work at home. Commuting by bus is most common on the islands. Just as more households own cars in the metropolis, so slightly more own their property outright, and those numbers are growing as have the values of those homes. More people here have a mortgage, more are renting privately but there are also more people living in housing association property. In contrast, more of the islands' population live in council tenure, but more people in the metropolis live in communal housing, particularly where the old (who live for longer in the metropolis) can afford

to retire to, and there are far more temporary dwellings, in the metropolis and more shared dwellings, all reflecting the higher demand for land there. It is only in the metropolis, to any significant degree, that more people are now living in flats. Most of the islands are predominantly built up with houses. There is more space there and many flats are being turned back into houses on the islands where the state of housing in terms of its heating has improved over the course of the last decade. Just as basic housing amenities are improved and that gap between places appears to diminish, other inequalities appear. Despite the greater need on the islands, there are more doctors and dentists per head in the metropolis, many more people working in other health professions and large numbers of people trained in medicine or teaching working in other occupations in the metropolis in favour of their vocation, and in favour of living where there is most demand for their work, on the islands. Increasingly those who can, move South. The world city is strong; its hinterland, made up of an archipelago of city clusters, prospers only where it does in London's wake.

Every decade a census is taken and its results drawn in new, fuller and brighter detail to reveal the complexity of the human geography of the UK. In each decade a clearer and clearer picture is revealed despite the improved technology increasing the possibilities for confusion. The picture is a snapshot of the tale of the metropolis and the archipelago of the provinces, a tale of two places intertwined and ever more separate.

We end this story with a picture of what it is we imagine we can see between the lines of numbers in the data and the pages of this atlas that were drawn from them: an image of London and the archipelago. If the UK continues to change in the ways of recent decades then this is where we are heading.

LONDON AND THE ARCHIPELAGO

Our last image in this atlas is a fictitious map and cartogram of the country based on the trends we have just tried to summarise. These pictures are not derived from data directly. They are instead our impression of how the country is becoming more and more divided.

We draw a line separating the new London metropolis from the rest of the UK. Beneath that line lies the metropolis.

Its core is in the centre of the Capital, where the population is most densely concentrated, increasing, becoming younger and where finance is centred. That core is surrounded by the new inner London, an extension of what was outer London and which functionally includes cities as far away as Bristol and Norwich. London's suburbs now extend to North Somerset. Outer London reaches as far as Exeter and Dover.

The edge of London is along the coasts of Cornwall and Suffolk.

To the north of the line is the archipelago that has numerous centres surrounded by core areas, inner areas, the new suburbs of these northern and Welsh islands, their outer areas and remoter edges. The archipelago is an amalgam of places, which have most in common in not being in the

London metropolis. They are the places in this atlas where in general the population is less concentrated, is often reducing in numbers, becoming older away from its centres where southern youth venture North to university before returning South. They are the centres of industries that have died or are dying. They are places that now still exist because there remains a population there to be served.

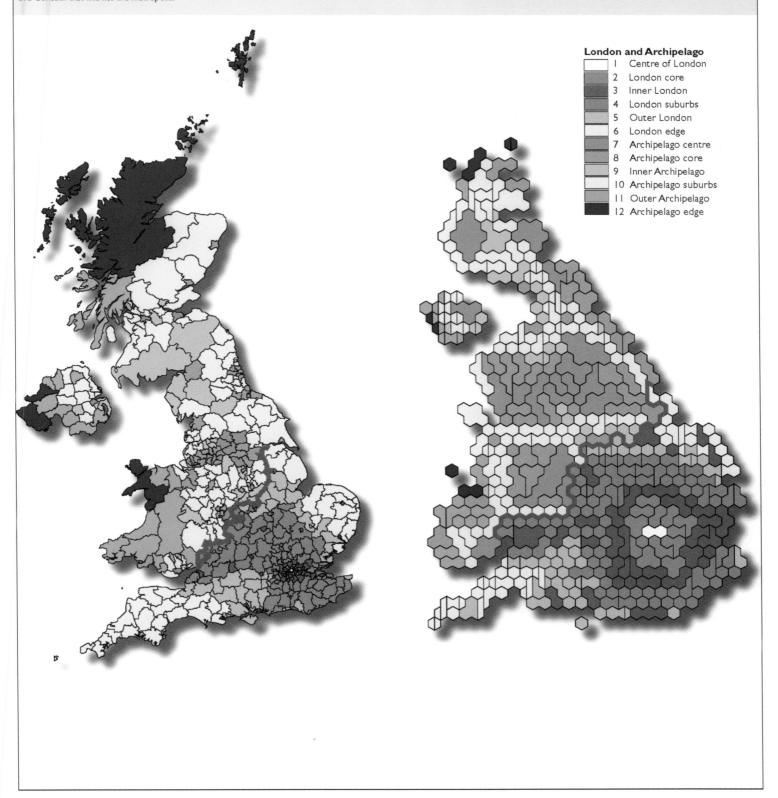

London and Archipelago
1. Centre of London
2. London core
3. Inner London
4. London suburbs
5. Outer London
6. London edge
7. Archipelago centre
8. Archipelago core
9. Inner Archipelago
10. Archipelago suburbs
11. Outer Archipelago
12. Archipelago edge

Appendix

This Appendix contains the data mapped in the Poor, Rich and Wealthy maps and cartograms on pages 14–16 of the Introduction and Overview. Additionally, it include the ranking of each Local Authority in Great Britain. The City of London and the Isles of Scilly have not been included due to their extremely low populations. Northern Ireland is also excluded from this Appendix.

Top and bottom 20 change in high income households					Top and bottom 20 high income households				
Local Authority	% 2001	Rank 2001	Rank 1991	% change	Local Authority	% 2001	Rank 2001	Rank 1991	% change
Top 20					**Top 20**				
Wandsworth	7.48	6	54	3.07	Wokingham	8.54	1	2	0.50
Tower Hamlets	4.01	128	359	2.98	Hart	8.10	2	1	−0.27
Westminster	6.11	25	130	2.96	Richmond upon Thames	7.88	3	8	1.76
Hammersmith & Fulham	6.40	18	91	2.72	St Albans	7.77	4	5	1.25
Kensington & Chelsea	6.50	15	73	2.47	Surrey Heath	7.68	5	3	0.43
Lambeth	4.90	72	187	2.31	Wandsworth	7.48	6	54	3.07
Islington	4.54	88	208	2.24	Chiltern	7.31	7	6	1.06
Camden	5.43	52	116	2.15	Windsor & Maidenhead	7.23	8	4	0.71
Southwark	3.78	146	284	2.11	Elmbridge	7.13	9	7	0.99
Merton	5.99	27	66	1.87	South Bucks	7.12	10	12	1.27
Richmond upon Thames	7.88	3	8	1.76	Bracknell Forest	6.98	11	11	1.12
Cherwell	4.82	77	135	1.75	Woking	6.71	12	10	0.83
Oswestry	2.72	241	361	1.71	Wycombe	6.56	13	14	0.95
South Northamptonshire	6.22	21	49	1.66	Guildford	6.51	14	18	1.02
Ealing	5.49	47	81	1.61	Kensington & Chelsea	6.50	15	73	2.47
North Shropshire	3.64	153	229	1.56	Kingston upon Thames	6.48	16	17	0.99
Brent	4.18	112	174	1.53	West Berkshire	6.43	17	13	0.68
Hounslow	4.97	68	101	1.46	Hammersmith & Fulham	6.40	18	91	2.72
Richmondshire	3.22	189	278	1.46	East Hertfordshire	6.40	19	26	1.11
Milton Keynes	5.18	62	89	1.46	South Oxfordshire	6.27	20	21	0.86
Bottom 20					**Bottom 20**				
Blyth Valley	2.11	303	249	0.11	Liverpool	1.36	387	397	0.72
Lewes	2.98	217	150	0.09	Great Yarmouth	1.36	388	350	0.26
Bexley	3.29	179	122	0.09	Hartlepool	1.36	389	376	0.44
Weymouth & Portland	1.95	321	263	0.08	West Somerset	1.35	390	399	0.79
East Renfrewshire	4.84	75	41	0.05	Gwynedd	1.33	391	391	0.56
Hertsmere	5.44	50	23	0.05	Pembrokeshire	1.33	392	377	0.42
Havant	3.15	197	133	0.04	Orkney Islands	1.32	393	381	0.46
North Ayrshire	1.54	368	302	0.03	Berwick-upon-Tweed	1.31	394	393	0.56
Tewkesbury	4.15	114	65	0.02	South Tyneside	1.31	395	387	0.50
Shetland Islands	1.81	339	269	−0.01	Blackpool	1.27	396	369	0.31
Welwyn Hatfield	4.76	80	39	−0.04	Neath Port Talbot	1.24	397	388	0.44
Mid Sussex	5.49	48	15	−0.06	Stoke-on-Trent	1.24	398	394	0.49
Oadby & Wigston	3.41	167	105	−0.07	Eilean Siar	1.19	399	390	0.41
Purbeck	2.59	254	172	−0.08	Dundee City	1.17	400	403	0.69
Stevenage	3.93	135	72	−0.11	Merthyr Tydfil	1.10	401	396	0.43
Durham	2.39	274	190	−0.15	Dumfries & Galloway	1.09	402	383	0.25
Mole Valley	5.85	32	9	−0.15	Kingston upon Hull	0.99	403	402	0.48
East Dunbartonshire	4.09	119	61	−0.17	Penwith	0.97	404	398	0.39
Hart	8.10	2	1	−0.27	Easington	0.86	405	405	0.57
Angus	1.95	319	199	−0.45	Blaenau Gwent	0.83	406	406	0.61

Top and bottom 20 change in poor households					Top and bottom 20 poor households				
Local Authority	**% 2001**	**Rank 2001**	**Rank 1991**	**% change**	**Local Authority**	**% 2001**	**Rank 2001**	**Rank 1991**	**% change**
Top 20					**Top 20**				
Newham	42.93	3	16	12.55	Tower Hamlets	46.46	1	1	8.93
Brent	34.75	15	53	10.18	Hackney	44.36	2	2	7.44
Tower Hamlets	46.46	1	1	8.93	Newham	42.93	3	16	12.55
Camden	40.31	7	8	8.90	Islington	41.66	4	4	6.08
Haringey	36.68	10	22	8.34	Southwark	41.41	5	5	6.25
Westminster	38.93	8	12	7.96	Glasgow City	40.93	6	3	5.05
Kensington & Chelsea	35.65	13	29	7.91	Camden	40.31	7	8	8.90
Enfield	25.98	83	184	7.88	Westminster	38.93	8	12	7.96
Waltham Forest	31.49	27	62	7.83	Lambeth	37.85	9	7	5.53
Ealing	29.04	44	110	7.67	Haringey	36.68	10	22	8.34
Hounslow	28.16	51	124	7.46	Manchester	36.26	11	6	3.04
Hackney	44.36	2	2	7.44	Hammersmith & Fulham	35.79	12	20	6.63
Slough	26.89	66	143	7.28	Kensington & Chelsea	35.65	13	29	7.91
Luton	25.90	86	162	7.27	West Dunbartonshire	34.86	14	13	4.21
Croydon	24.44	121	213	7.15	Brent	34.75	15	53	10.18
Redbridge	23.42	142	251	7.10	Liverpool	34.21	16	9	2.90
Harrow	21.83	188	308	6.74	Dundee City	34.08	17	10	2.88
Hillingdon	22.63	168	269	6.73	North Lanarkshire	33.54	18	15	2.92
Hammersmith & Fulham	35.79	12	20	6.63	Inverclyde	33.38	19	11	2.38
Barnet	23.98	130	205	6.41	Lewisham	33.37	20	28	5.56
Bottom 20					**Bottom 20**				
West Lothian	27.14	62	45	1.75	Mole Valley	15.47	387	381	2.54
Wansbeck	27.31	59	43	1.68	Waverley	15.44	388	365	2.02
Shetland Islands	23.35	144	104	1.67	Blaby	15.39	389	401	4.16
Berwick-upon-Tweed	25.12	102	65	1.64	South Cambridgeshire	15.39	390	368	2.04
Newcastle upon Tyne	31.02	32	17	1.64	Broadland	15.29	391	398	3.44
Chester	19.33	258	200	1.63	South Northamptonshire	15.14	392	371	1.87
Sheffield	27.25	60	42	1.59	Epsom & Ewell	15.12	393	399	3.74
Salisbury	19.15	271	204	1.56	Tandridge	15.09	394	392	2.88
Rutland	17.07	349	286	1.56	Wealden	14.98	395	390	2.66
North Wiltshire	16.49	367	311	1.52	Horsham	14.79	396	383	2.04
Bromsgrove	15.67	384	345	1.47	Elmbridge	14.78	397	394	2.61
Derwentside	25.72	91	55	1.42	South Bucks	14.69	398	397	2.63
Chester-le-Street	22.20	179	123	1.42	Mid Sussex	14.59	399	386	2.17
Falkirk	27.86	53	35	1.39	East Dorset	14.48	400	402	3.34
Salford	29.34	43	27	1.36	Fareham	14.29	401	403	3.24
Kennet	18.99	277	195	1.21	Harborough	14.22	402	391	1.96
Alnwick	22.19	181	119	1.20	Chiltern	14.09	403	400	2.76
Durham	23.33	145	86	1.12	Surrey Heath	13.82	404	404	3.17
Cotswold	17.35	337	245	0.86	Hart	13.07	405	405	2.69
North Tyneside	25.32	99	48	0.28	Wokingham	12.54	406	406	3.41

Top and bottom 20 change in wealthy households					Top and bottom 20 wealthy households				
Local Authority	% 2001	Rank 2001	Rank 1991	% change	Local Authority	% 2001	Rank 2001	Rank 1991	% change
Top 20					**Top 20**				
Maldon	10.73	10	25	2.75	Hart	12.67	1	1	1.56
Castle Morpeth	8.73	68	114	2.68	South Bucks	12.52	2	2	1.78
South Northamptonshire	10.97	7	13	2.60	Surrey Heath	12.38	3	3	1.70
Forest of Dean	9.03	57	86	2.52	Chiltern	12.26	4	4	1.69
East Cambridgeshire	9.14	51	80	2.47	Uttlesford	12.05	5	6	2.17
Horsham	9.96	24	38	2.44	Wokingham	11.84	6	5	1.95
Congleton	9.17	49	73	2.39	South Northamptonshire	10.97	7	13	2.60
East Hampshire	10.74	9	12	2.36	Tandridge	10.78	8	7	1.37
East Dorset	9.69	31	48	2.34	East Hampshire	10.74	9	12	2.36
Aberdeenshire	7.46	138	184	2.33	Maldon	10.73	10	25	2.75
Mid Suffolk	9.84	29	39	2.33	Waverley	10.71	11	9	1.63
Bromsgrove	9.98	23	33	2.32	Mole Valley	10.70	12	8	1.33
North West Leicestershire	7.87	110	149	2.29	South Cambridgeshire	10.46	13	16	2.25
Hinckley & Bosworth	7.65	125	168	2.26	Daventry	10.32	14	15	2.09
South Cambridgeshire	10.46	13	16	2.25	Harborough	10.24	15	23	2.24
North Shropshire	9.34	41	61	2.25	Malvern Hills	10.20	16	22	2.19
Harborough	10.24	15	23	2.24	Elmbridge	10.18	17	10	1.24
Rutland	9.99	22	29	2.24	Winchester	10.12	18	11	1.57
South Derbyshire	7.81	113	151	2.24	Sevenoaks	10.11	19	14	1.79
Selby	7.78	115	154	2.24	Wychavon	10.08	20	20	2.05
Bottom 20					**Bottom 20**				
Norwich	3.17	377	355	0.53	Haringey	2.92	387	344	0.15
Manchester	2.73	390	382	0.52	North Lanarkshire	2.87	388	403	1.28
Crawley	5.90	221	167	0.48	Nottingham	2.83	389	378	0.57
Glasgow City	1.30	405	406	0.43	Manchester	2.73	390	382	0.52
Croydon	5.08	273	210	0.41	Kensington & Chelsea	2.63	391	354	−0.02
Greenwich	2.97	384	360	0.40	Lewisham	2.62	392	372	0.23
Barking & Dagenham	2.06	398	399	0.36	Lambeth	2.45	393	381	0.22
Hammersmith & Fulham	2.36	394	388	0.25	Hammersmith & Fulham	2.36	394	388	0.25
Lewisham	2.62	392	372	0.23	Kingston upon Hull	2.34	395	397	0.60
Lambeth	2.45	393	381	0.22	Dundee City	2.31	396	402	0.69
Newham	1.87	400	401	0.22	West Dunbartonshire	2.16	397	404	0.61
Wandsworth	3.10	379	332	0.21	Barking & Dagenham	2.06	398	399	0.36
Tower Hamlets	1.02	406	405	0.15	Camden	1.99	399	389	0.03
Haringey	2.92	387	344	0.15	Newham	1.87	400	401	0.22
Hackney	1.83	402	400	0.14	Southwark	1.85	401	396	0.08
Southwark	1.85	401	396	0.08	Hackney	1.83	402	400	0.14
Camden	1.99	399	389	0.03	Islington	1.72	403	398	0.00
Islington	1.72	403	398	0.00	Westminster	1.72	404	391	−0.17
Kensington & Chelsea	2.63	391	354	−0.02	Glasgow City	1.30	405	406	0.43
Westminster	1.72	404	391	−0.17	Tower Hamlets	1.02	406	405	0.15

Local Authority	Households receiving very high income				Poor households				Wealthy households			
	% 2001	Rank 2001	Rank 1991	% change	% 2001	Rank 2001	Rank 1991	% change	% 2001	Rank 2001	Rank 1991	% change
Aberdeen City	3.10	203	164	0.37	26.76	68	56	2.52	3.46	368	348	0.72
Aberdeenshire	3.08	207	191	0.55	20.71	216	192	2.82	7.46	138	184	2.33
Adur	2.74	238	200	0.37	19.56	251	272	3.68	4.69	299	295	1.19
Allerdale	1.85	334	341	0.65	22.78	164	135	2.66	6.25	207	213	1.60
Alnwick	2.28	287	285	0.62	22.19	181	119	1.20	6.30	199	250	2.16
Amber Valley	3.19	193	186	0.60	20.41	226	238	3.75	6.02	218	215	1.39
Angus	1.95	319	199	−0.45	24.74	113	78	2.16	4.97	283	320	1.78
Argyll & Bute	2.15	300	265	0.32	25.35	98	91	3.45	4.80	295	287	1.16
Arun	2.54	258	262	0.66	18.64	290	317	3.73	5.69	234	226	1.20
Ashfield	1.94	323	339	0.73	24.90	110	133	4.71	4.14	333	327	1.07
Ashford	3.67	150	143	0.71	19.19	269	232	2.42	8.09	99	111	2.01
Aylesbury Vale	5.99	28	35	1.05	17.26	339	342	2.92	9.36	40	47	1.99
Babergh	3.89	137	98	0.35	17.55	330	329	2.93	9.12	53	56	1.94
Barking & Dagenham	1.57	364	392	0.81	32.80	24	36	6.41	2.06	398	399	0.36
Barnet	5.71	40	60	1.43	23.98	130	205	6.41	6.13	211	146	0.54
Barnsley	1.59	362	349	0.48	27.72	54	54	3.34	3.70	357	374	1.35
Barrow-in-Furness	1.71	351	379	0.83	23.92	131	145	4.38	3.53	363	358	0.92
Basildon	3.52	162	147	0.63	22.54	171	173	4.13	6.10	214	188	1.11
Basingstoke & Deane	6.14	22	16	0.60	17.60	327	314	2.64	8.92	62	65	1.88
Bassetlaw	2.42	271	279	0.67	23.28	147	141	3.57	6.26	205	233	1.84
Bath & North East Somerset	3.90	136	127	0.73	19.31	262	229	2.49	7.31	146	133	1.47
Bedford	4.20	110	78	0.22	21.30	200	230	4.50	7.54	134	128	1.64
Berwick-upon-Tweed	1.31	394	393	0.56	25.12	102	65	1.64	4.95	285	292	1.40
Bexley	3.29	179	122	0.09	20.00	239	303	4.76	5.29	262	241	1.00
Birmingham	2.15	301	293	0.54	31.18	29	46	5.79	4.06	340	323	0.92
Blaby	4.49	91	79	0.52	15.39	389	401	4.16	7.51	135	110	1.42
Blackburn with Darwen	2.08	306	315	0.66	27.37	57	77	4.74	4.25	325	335	1.39
Blackpool	1.27	396	369	0.31	26.92	65	113	5.76	3.63	360	334	0.76
Blaenau Gwent	0.83	406	406	0.61	30.31	35	40	4.48	3.41	370	370	0.97
Blyth Valley	2.11	303	249	0.11	25.06	103	83	2.80	3.99	345	368	1.50
Bolsover	1.95	320	362	0.94	25.57	95	108	4.17	4.36	317	329	1.41
Bolton	2.74	239	226	0.63	25.00	106	112	3.70	4.53	310	307	1.22
Boston	1.44	379	357	0.39	23.05	155	157	4.20	5.82	225	254	1.72
Bournemouth	2.57	257	281	0.87	22.93	159	170	4.44	5.57	244	229	1.10
Bracknell Forest	6.98	11	11	1.12	17.56	329	279	1.87	8.83	64	69	1.93
Bradford	2.48	263	257	0.56	26.74	69	105	5.09	4.86	291	302	1.47
Braintree	4.22	109	119	0.99	19.19	268	235	2.45	8.26	92	103	2.06
Breckland	2.51	261	287	0.87	20.08	236	256	3.90	7.41	142	158	1.89
Brent	4.18	112	174	1.53	34.75	15	53	10.18	4.13	334	325	1.04
Brentwood	5.17	63	46	0.49	16.22	372	384	3.60	8.65	71	31	0.93
Bridgend	2.06	310	325	0.70	23.09	153	148	3.84	5.67	236	227	1.18
Bridgnorth	4.38	96	103	0.88	18.87	280	266	2.90	9.54	35	46	2.16
Brighton & Hove	3.25	184	224	1.12	26.26	74	102	4.56	3.51	365	341	0.71
Bristol	3.23	186	218	1.05	24.69	117	115	3.58	4.88	289	267	0.95
Broadland	3.22	188	159	0.45	15.29	391	398	3.44	7.58	132	109	1.49
Bromley	4.92	70	53	0.50	18.78	284	336	4.26	6.65	178	138	0.89
Bromsgrove	5.34	55	80	1.38	15.67	384	345	1.47	9.98	23	33	2.32
Broxbourne	4.16	113	104	0.67	19.30	263	346	5.19	7.72	119	107	1.63
Broxtowe	3.57	160	106	0.11	19.82	244	271	3.93	5.27	265	260	1.20
Burnley	2.07	309	334	0.82	25.77	90	101	4.02	3.82	353	352	1.16
Bury	3.37	172	155	0.53	21.59	193	203	3.97	5.31	260	262	1.26
Caerphilly	1.80	340	351	0.70	25.95	85	84	3.70	4.56	307	303	1.18
Calderdale	3.07	209	221	0.91	24.15	128	130	3.92	4.72	298	300	1.30
Cambridge	4.49	92	90	0.77	25.97	84	79	3.50	4.75	297	253	0.65
Camden	5.43	52	116	2.15	40.31	7	8	8.90	1.99	399	389	0.03
Cannock Chase	2.84	229	238	0.80	22.67	165	181	4.53	6.04	217	239	1.71
Canterbury	2.51	260	244	0.50	21.28	202	216	4.14	6.39	192	189	1.40

Local Authority	Households receiving very high income				Poor households				Wealthy households			
	% 2001	Rank 2001	Rank 1991	% change	% 2001	Rank 2001	Rank 1991	% change	% 2001	Rank 2001	Rank 1991	% change
Caradon	2.17	296	276	0.40	19.21	267	285	3.69	7.08	159	171	1.73
Cardiff	3.11	202	204	0.77	23.80	133	127	3.11	6.14	210	208	1.44
Carlisle	1.99	317	303	0.49	22.51	173	138	2.52	5.29	263	273	1.43
Carmarthenshire	1.53	369	386	0.71	22.84	161	163	4.22	7.23	149	141	1.55
Carrick	1.87	331	320	0.49	20.41	227	239	3.76	6.72	174	186	1.60
Castle Morpeth	3.65	151	107	0.21	18.58	293	236	1.84	8.73	68	114	2.68
Castle Point	3.39	170	136	0.32	17.15	345	393	4.96	7.99	106	97	1.60
Ceredigion	1.43	380	389	0.64	21.26	203	246	4.78	8.62	72	68	1.72
Charnwood	3.61	157	131	0.47	19.04	276	326	4.37	6.83	170	150	1.25
Chelmsford	5.25	58	38	0.42	16.50	366	370	3.19	8.56	75	67	1.60
Cheltenham	3.70	149	145	0.77	19.63	248	220	2.56	5.89	222	228	1.41
Cherwell	4.82	77	135	1.75	18.12	308	260	2.02	7.68	123	142	2.03
Chester	4.32	100	100	0.79	19.33	258	200	1.63	7.33	145	134	1.51
Chesterfield	2.31	282	280	0.59	24.94	108	76	2.20	4.12	335	345	1.34
Chester-le-Street	2.87	225	237	0.84	22.20	179	123	1.42	4.86	290	326	1.78
Chichester	3.47	164	175	0.82	18.13	306	277	2.41	8.56	74	76	1.82
Chiltern	7.31	7	6	1.06	14.09	403	400	2.76	12.26	4	4	1.69
Chorley	4.02	127	86	0.28	19.06	275	320	4.24	7.17	155	148	1.59
Christchurch	2.44	270	216	0.23	17.92	317	356	3.95	5.37	256	265	1.37
Clackmannanshire	1.87	332	304	0.37	29.37	42	41	3.60	3.83	352	363	1.28
Colchester	3.79	145	167	1.09	20.01	238	259	3.92	7.04	162	161	1.54
Congleton	5.20	59	55	0.80	15.69	383	380	2.74	9.17	49	73	2.39
Conwy	1.72	348	372	0.78	21.70	191	194	3.88	6.30	198	183	1.17
Copeland	1.78	341	300	0.26	24.72	115	103	3.03	5.30	261	271	1.39
Corby	1.95	322	344	0.80	28.53	48	49	3.50	4.02	343	337	1.20
Cotswold	4.12	116	112	0.77	17.35	337	245	0.86	9.54	34	44	2.10
Coventry	2.45	265	255	0.51	26.10	78	109	4.70	3.69	358	350	0.96
Craven	3.18	195	234	1.13	17.64	326	289	2.24	7.02	166	162	1.52
Crawley	3.88	138	160	1.12	21.68	192	169	3.16	5.90	221	167	0.48
Crewe & Nantwich	3.30	178	228	1.20	20.00	240	198	2.25	6.87	169	191	1.89
Croydon	4.23	108	68	0.13	24.44	121	213	7.15	5.08	273	210	0.41
Dacorum	5.73	38	34	0.79	18.86	281	247	2.39	8.38	87	85	1.86
Darlington	2.62	249	254	0.65	23.46	141	122	2.61	4.52	312	308	1.20
Dartford	3.34	174	153	0.48	20.26	232	267	4.30	5.57	245	218	0.95
Daventry	5.61	44	62	1.39	17.11	346	347	3.01	10.32	14	15	2.09
Denbighshire	1.91	327	352	0.81	22.12	183	190	4.17	6.53	187	182	1.40
Derby	2.76	235	201	0.39	24.26	124	116	3.25	4.44	316	316	1.21
Derbyshire Dales	3.97	132	151	1.09	18.11	309	294	2.75	8.72	69	88	2.22
Derwentside	1.89	328	368	0.92	25.72	91	55	1.42	4.10	336	373	1.73
Doncaster	1.83	337	338	0.61	25.68	93	75	2.92	4.28	322	339	1.47
Dover	1.86	333	290	0.25	22.47	175	152	3.36	5.53	249	255	1.44
Dudley	2.91	223	180	0.28	23.75	134	151	4.59	5.46	252	243	1.24
Dumfries & Galloway	1.09	402	383	0.25	26.07	81	98	4.24	5.03	278	277	1.25
Dundee City	1.17	400	403	0.69	34.08	17	10	2.88	2.31	396	402	0.69
Durham	2.39	274	190	−0.15	23.33	145	86	1.12	5.32	259	274	1.50
Ealing	5.49	47	81	1.61	29.04	44	110	7.67	4.05	341	315	0.80
Easington	0.86	405	405	0.57	30.91	33	25	2.88	3.03	382	394	1.22
East Ayrshire	1.60	358	343	0.45	31.17	30	24	2.88	3.46	367	384	1.27
East Cambridgeshire	4.53	89	120	1.31	18.26	304	270	2.36	9.14	51	80	2.47
East Devon	2.05	311	327	0.72	17.22	341	331	2.64	7.23	150	172	1.88
East Dorset	3.87	141	115	0.59	14.48	400	402	3.34	9.69	31	48	2.34
East Dunbartonshire	4.09	119	61	−0.17	19.31	261	321	4.52	6.27	204	193	1.30
East Hampshire	5.67	42	44	0.93	15.71	381	387	3.30	10.74	9	12	2.36
East Hertfordshire	6.40	19	26	1.11	15.93	376	372	2.66	9.51	37	27	1.63
East Lindsey	1.55	366	354	0.47	21.89	187	228	5.05	6.75	173	185	1.63
East Lothian	2.64	248	268	0.82	25.53	96	71	2.55	4.26	323	340	1.46
East Northamptonshire	4.42	95	129	1.27	18.15	305	298	2.85	8.22	94	104	2.03

Local Authority	Households receiving very high income				Poor households				Wealthy households			
	% 2001	Rank 2001	Rank 1991	% change	% 2001	Rank 2001	Rank 1991	% change	% 2001	Rank 2001	Rank 1991	% change
East Renfrewshire	4.84	75	41	0.05	18.08	310	355	4.09	6.33	196	177	1.14
East Riding of Yorkshire	2.99	215	202	0.62	18.62	292	281	2.99	7.13	156	173	1.79
East Staffordshire	3.26	183	225	1.15	20.78	215	202	3.15	6.58	183	179	1.41
Eastbourne	1.77	344	336	0.54	23.67	137	142	4.01	4.17	332	321	1.00
Eastleigh	4.63	84	71	0.59	15.88	377	385	3.39	8.15	96	120	2.13
Eden	2.16	298	296	0.62	18.56	294	287	3.06	8.85	63	63	1.77
Edinburgh	4.02	126	132	0.89	25.82	89	82	3.47	3.06	381	377	0.75
Eilean Siar	1.19	399	390	0.41	24.62	118	114	3.47	5.46	253	288	1.84
Ellesmere Port & Neston	2.88	224	213	0.66	21.16	209	156	2.31	6.43	190	217	1.81
Elmbridge	7.13	9	7	0.99	14.78	397	394	2.61	10.18	17	10	1.24
Enfield	3.75	148	139	0.73	25.98	83	184	7.88	4.82	294	252	0.70
Epping Forest	4.49	90	94	0.89	19.12	273	334	4.59	8.55	76	43	1.09
Epsom & Ewell	5.67	43	30	0.57	15.12	393	399	3.74	8.50	82	64	1.44
Erewash	3.07	208	194	0.60	20.68	217	207	3.21	5.03	280	284	1.30
Exeter	2.34	278	283	0.66	23.13	152	144	3.55	4.79	296	289	1.18
Falkirk	2.22	292	307	0.75	27.86	53	35	1.39	3.81	354	383	1.62
Fareham	5.00	66	43	0.23	14.29	401	403	3.24	8.42	85	91	1.93
Fenland	2.31	281	326	0.98	21.45	196	233	4.68	6.60	182	202	1.83
Fife	2.10	304	295	0.52	26.39	73	59	2.61	4.05	342	351	1.32
Flintshire	2.85	227	245	0.85	20.26	231	243	3.71	7.31	147	155	1.77
Forest Heath	3.13	200	241	1.12	22.10	184	153	3.03	5.93	220	232	1.48
Forest of Dean	3.06	210	165	0.35	19.17	270	291	3.78	9.03	57	86	2.52
Fylde	3.81	143	108	0.37	17.54	331	325	2.87	6.70	175	160	1.20
Gateshead	1.60	359	360	0.58	30.18	36	23	1.89	2.95	386	392	1.06
Gedling	3.31	176	140	0.32	18.94	278	306	3.82	5.62	241	225	1.12
Glasgow City	1.46	375	385	0.64	40.93	6	3	5.05	1.30	405	406	0.43
Gloucester	2.85	226	196	0.41	21.26	204	201	3.59	5.54	248	248	1.38
Gosport	2.39	273	259	0.48	21.19	206	180	3.04	4.55	308	304	1.19
Gravesham	2.99	216	203	0.63	22.49	174	189	4.54	6.28	200	178	1.10
Great Yarmouth	1.36	388	350	0.26	24.83	112	128	4.37	5.03	279	281	1.29
Greenwich	2.95	220	230	0.88	33.01	21	30	5.64	2.97	384	360	0.40
Guildford	6.51	14	18	1.02	16.77	357	351	2.75	9.58	33	30	1.83
Gwynedd	1.33	391	391	0.56	23.18	150	149	3.96	7.08	161	125	1.17
Hackney	2.71	243	323	1.34	44.36	2	2	7.44	1.83	402	400	0.14
Halton	2.26	289	312	0.82	26.96	64	64	3.42	4.82	293	330	1.89
Hambleton	4.04	124	125	0.87	17.27	338	319	2.46	9.53	36	35	1.95
Hammersmith & Fulham	6.40	18	91	2.72	35.79	12	20	6.63	2.36	394	388	0.25
Harborough	5.71	39	36	0.85	14.22	402	391	1.96	10.24	15	23	2.24
Haringey	4.06	121	168	1.36	36.68	10	22	8.34	2.92	387	344	0.15
Harlow	3.08	206	171	0.41	26.06	82	63	2.43	4.46	314	293	0.94
Harrogate	4.63	85	113	1.30	16.81	355	316	1.87	8.11	97	98	1.77
Harrow	5.77	36	48	1.18	21.83	188	308	6.74	6.57	184	156	1.05
Hart	8.10	2	1	−0.27	13.07	405	405	2.69	12.67	1	1	1.56
Hartlepool	1.36	389	376	0.44	29.54	41	39	3.51	3.97	346	338	1.16
Hastings	1.83	338	306	0.36	26.24	75	117	5.23	4.30	321	312	1.00
Havant	3.15	197	133	0.04	21.45	197	217	4.36	6.36	195	180	1.19
Havering	3.18	194	183	0.57	20.28	230	300	5.00	5.75	229	219	1.14
Herefordshire	2.85	228	272	1.06	19.86	243	244	3.32	8.52	79	87	2.02
Hertsmere	5.44	50	23	0.05	18.49	298	318	3.61	7.83	112	90	1.33
High Peak	3.61	156	134	0.51	19.51	254	221	2.47	6.64	179	192	1.67
Highland	1.78	342	319	0.39	24.42	122	96	2.58	5.11	270	286	1.42
Hillingdon	4.36	99	82	0.49	22.63	168	269	6.73	5.70	233	203	0.95
Hinckley & Bosworth	4.09	118	109	0.66	17.79	321	362	4.22	7.65	125	168	2.26
Horsham	5.59	45	37	0.73	14.79	396	383	2.04	9.96	24	38	2.44
Hounslow	4.97	68	101	1.46	28.16	51	124	7.46	4.35	318	294	0.85
Huntingdonshire	5.18	61	47	0.52	16.89	354	337	2.39	9.02	58	71	2.17
Hyndburn	2.08	305	271	0.28	24.34	123	150	5.17	3.86	350	356	1.22

Local Authority	Households receiving very high income				Poor households				Wealthy households			
	% 2001	Rank 2001	Rank 1991	% change	% 2001	Rank 2001	Rank 1991	% change	% 2001	Rank 2001	Rank 1991	% change
Inverclyde	1.62	357	356	0.55	33.38	19	11	2.38	2.98	383	393	1.10
Ipswich	2.61	251	252	0.62	24.88	111	125	4.18	4.23	327	317	1.02
Isle of Anglesey	1.48	373	365	0.48	22.99	156	166	4.45	7.68	124	116	1.63
Isle of Wight	1.71	350	335	0.48	20.95	212	223	3.99	5.75	230	236	1.39
Islington	4.54	88	208	2.24	41.66	4	4	6.08	1.72	403	398	0.00
Kennet	4.36	98	110	0.96	18.99	277	195	1.21	9.31	43	58	2.17
Kensington & Chelsea	6.50	15	73	2.47	35.65	13	29	7.91	2.63	391	354	−0.02
Kerrier	1.43	381	332	0.15	21.16	210	240	4.52	6.25	206	190	1.26
Kettering	3.58	159	197	1.14	19.23	265	241	2.64	6.67	177	201	1.87
King's Lynn & West Norfolk	2.00	315	322	0.63	21.18	208	211	3.81	7.03	165	165	1.54
Kingston upon Hull	0.99	403	402	0.48	32.74	25	18	3.38	2.34	395	397	0.60
Kingston upon Thames	6.48	16	17	0.99	20.26	233	302	4.98	5.56	246	195	0.61
Kirklees	3.02	213	205	0.69	24.92	109	129	4.52	4.95	284	291	1.37
Knowsley	1.36	386	404	0.96	32.95	22	14	2.32	3.41	369	371	0.97
Lambeth	4.90	72	187	2.31	37.85	9	7	5.53	2.45	393	381	0.22
Lancaster	1.88	329	331	0.60	22.13	182	167	3.59	5.36	257	246	1.17
Leeds	2.98	218	219	0.80	26.50	72	68	3.29	4.53	311	309	1.22
Leicester	1.60	361	353	0.52	32.22	26	37	5.95	3.22	376	364	0.67
Lewes	2.98	217	150	0.09	18.44	300	324	3.74	6.45	189	196	1.50
Lewisham	3.44	165	188	0.86	33.37	20	28	5.56	2.62	392	372	0.23
Lichfield	4.90	71	56	0.51	17.71	325	357	3.83	9.38	39	37	1.82
Lincoln	1.73	347	314	0.31	25.87	88	69	2.87	3.94	347	347	1.18
Liverpool	1.36	387	397	0.72	34.21	16	9	2.90	3.35	371	361	0.78
Luton	2.98	219	185	0.38	25.90	86	162	7.27	4.46	313	314	1.17
Macclesfield	5.75	37	31	0.69	16.03	374	350	2.00	9.13	52	45	1.71
Maidstone	4.64	83	75	0.63	18.01	312	312	3.03	8.60	73	84	2.06
Maldon	4.60	87	77	0.62	16.80	356	379	3.79	10.73	10	25	2.75
Malvern Hills	4.31	101	85	0.52	17.19	344	343	2.89	10.20	16	22	2.19
Manchester	1.78	343	374	0.86	36.26	11	6	3.04	2.73	390	382	0.52
Mansfield	1.70	352	348	0.59	25.65	94	118	4.66	4.09	337	331	1.17
Medway	3.15	198	170	0.47	21.56	194	250	5.24	5.81	226	237	1.46
Melton	3.98	131	154	1.13	17.79	322	295	2.42	8.52	80	92	2.05
Mendip	3.20	191	198	0.77	18.77	285	296	3.41	8.36	89	77	1.62
Merthyr Tydfil	1.10	401	396	0.43	29.95	39	44	4.36	4.07	339	328	1.06
Merton	5.99	27	66	1.87	23.46	140	164	4.88	4.25	326	298	0.80
Mid Bedfordshire	5.88	31	24	0.52	16.22	371	352	2.21	9.30	44	52	2.07
Mid Devon	2.53	259	246	0.53	19.61	249	273	3.74	8.45	84	72	1.63
Mid Suffolk	4.04	125	146	1.12	16.92	353	341	2.55	9.84	29	39	2.33
Mid Sussex	5.49	48	15	−0.06	14.59	399	386	2.17	9.16	50	49	1.82
Middlesbrough	1.42	383	345	0.29	30.57	34	32	3.74	3.85	351	333	0.97
Midlothian	2.44	268	274	0.65	27.33	58	60	3.62	3.80	355	367	1.29
Milton Keynes	5.18	62	89	1.46	21.37	198	208	3.90	6.76	172	216	2.14
Mole Valley	5.85	32	9	−0.15	15.47	387	381	2.54	10.70	12	8	1.33
Monmouthshire	4.01	129	111	0.64	18.55	296	307	3.43	9.18	48	41	1.71
Moray	1.74	345	384	0.91	23.83	132	97	2.00	5.21	267	283	1.48
Neath Port Talbot	1.24	397	388	0.44	25.90	87	99	4.07	4.84	292	279	1.07
New Forest	3.27	181	158	0.48	16.23	370	378	3.20	8.35	90	99	2.06
Newark & Sherwood	2.95	221	220	0.79	20.95	211	206	3.39	6.70	176	187	1.68
Newcastle-under-Lyme	2.65	247	247	0.65	22.61	169	161	3.90	5.58	242	247	1.40
Newcastle upon Tyne	2.03	314	321	0.64	31.02	32	17	1.64	3.60	361	386	1.41
Newham	1.88	330	373	0.95	42.93	3	16	12.55	1.87	400	401	0.22
Newport	2.57	256	250	0.58	24.99	107	95	3.14	5.41	254	256	1.32
North Ayrshire	1.54	368	302	0.03	30.18	37	31	3.30	3.30	374	380	1.07
North Cornwall	1.44	377	370	0.50	20.85	213	263	4.81	7.72	120	124	1.79
North Devon	1.72	349	366	0.72	20.41	225	234	3.66	7.09	158	152	1.53
North Dorset	2.76	234	233	0.71	17.90	318	301	2.63	8.53	78	79	1.84
North East Derbyshire	3.06	211	195	0.60	21.75	189	185	3.66	6.28	203	222	1.71

Local Authority	Households receiving very high income				Poor households				Wealthy households			
	% 2001	Rank 2001	Rank 1991	% change	% 2001	Rank 2001	Rank 1991	% change	% 2001	Rank 2001	Rank 1991	% change
North East Lincolnshire	1.48	374	347	0.37	25.03	105	126	4.34	4.32	320	310	1.01
North Hertfordshire	5.51	46	45	0.80	19.32	260	215	2.05	7.46	140	117	1.41
North Kesteven	3.12	201	179	0.49	17.51	332	293	2.13	7.22	152	170	1.86
North Lanarkshire	1.84	335	340	0.63	33.54	18	15	2.92	2.87	388	403	1.28
North Lincolnshire	2.12	302	309	0.68	21.91	186	159	3.16	5.89	223	240	1.58
North Norfolk	1.69	354	367	0.71	20.06	237	226	3.17	6.88	168	169	1.51
North Shropshire	3.64	153	229	1.56	19.68	246	252	3.39	9.34	41	61	2.25
North Somerset	3.94	134	114	0.61	17.20	342	348	3.15	8.10	98	94	1.66
North Tyneside	2.20	295	297	0.66	25.32	99	48	0.28	3.79	356	366	1.26
North Warwickshire	3.64	152	169	0.96	20.45	222	248	4.04	7.65	126	115	1.60
North West Leicestershire	3.88	139	166	1.18	19.53	252	249	3.14	7.87	110	149	2.29
North Wiltshire	5.26	57	84	1.45	16.49	367	311	1.52	9.19	47	66	2.15
Northampton	3.79	144	178	1.16	22.26	178	158	3.50	5.80	228	245	1.60
Norwich	1.99	318	316	0.57	28.69	47	38	2.54	3.17	377	355	0.53
Nottingham	1.73	346	358	0.69	32.85	23	21	4.37	2.83	389	378	0.57
Nuneaton & Bedworth	2.79	231	256	0.86	22.20	180	183	4.10	5.28	264	275	1.48
Oadby & Wigston	3.41	167	105	−0.07	17.39	336	388	5.00	6.38	193	163	0.88
Oldham	2.30	284	288	0.68	27.53	56	70	4.53	3.56	362	359	0.96
Orkney Islands	1.32	393	381	0.46	22.91	160	168	4.37	6.54	186	209	1.85
Oswestry	2.72	241	361	1.71	20.51	221	182	2.40	7.64	127	144	2.02
Oxford	3.63	155	177	0.99	26.72	70	61	3.03	4.95	286	242	0.73
Pembrokeshire	1.33	392	377	0.42	22.80	163	176	4.50	7.12	157	139	1.39
Pendle	2.34	280	299	0.82	24.57	119	155	5.68	4.60	303	322	1.45
Penwith	0.97	404	398	0.39	23.73	136	146	4.24	5.39	255	230	0.93
Perth & Kinross	2.70	244	294	1.10	22.98	157	136	2.92	5.64	240	259	1.57
Peterborough	3.21	190	206	0.88	23.74	135	131	3.51	5.24	266	268	1.32
Plymouth	1.70	353	333	0.43	25.22	101	106	3.64	4.32	319	296	0.84
Poole	3.27	182	182	0.65	17.85	320	333	3.32	6.46	188	174	1.12
Portsmouth	2.71	242	253	0.74	25.25	100	89	3.25	4.17	331	324	1.07
Powys	2.04	313	328	0.71	20.64	218	219	3.57	8.36	88	82	1.78
Preston	2.79	232	235	0.74	25.06	104	87	2.87	5.07	274	276	1.28
Purbeck	2.59	254	172	−0.08	18.52	297	290	3.12	7.69	122	132	1.84
Reading	5.42	53	67	1.31	23.51	139	147	4.10	5.49	251	251	1.36
Redbridge	4.28	103	124	1.09	23.42	142	251	7.10	5.58	243	223	1.05
Redcar & Cleveland	1.64	356	337	0.41	26.20	77	85	3.98	4.54	309	313	1.25
Redditch	4.11	117	83	0.29	22.58	170	154	3.65	6.99	167	198	2.14
Reigate & Banstead	5.82	35	29	0.65	15.77	380	377	2.71	9.05	56	28	1.25
Renfrewshire	2.60	252	239	0.57	29.02	45	33	2.23	3.29	375	387	1.18
Restormel	1.42	382	378	0.53	21.52	195	218	4.43	6.62	180	181	1.47
Rhondda Cynon Taff	1.60	360	371	0.66	26.21	76	94	4.35	4.62	302	301	1.23
Ribble Valley	4.24	106	121	1.03	15.82	379	382	3.05	8.81	66	55	1.62
Richmond upon Thames	7.88	3	8	1.76	18.65	288	254	2.40	5.53	250	199	0.72
Richmondshire	3.22	189	278	1.46	19.89	242	196	2.12	7.77	117	122	1.82
Rochdale	2.38	275	275	0.61	27.56	55	58	3.76	4.21	329	346	1.44
Rochford	4.28	104	96	0.70	16.00	375	396	3.87	8.40	86	70	1.53
Rossendale	3.13	199	181	0.51	23.06	154	174	4.66	5.68	235	257	1.59
Rother	2.28	286	266	0.46	18.31	303	328	3.65	7.29	148	159	1.79
Rotherham	2.05	312	301	0.54	26.08	80	66	2.66	4.26	324	349	1.53
Rugby	4.23	107	137	1.20	18.45	299	261	2.36	7.04	163	153	1.49
Runnymede	5.48	49	33	0.54	17.09	347	354	3.09	8.93	60	40	1.43
Rushcliffe	5.71	41	42	0.94	15.84	378	369	2.51	8.52	81	74	1.74
Rushmoor	5.09	65	64	0.88	19.25	264	258	3.13	7.19	153	147	1.61
Rutland	4.73	82	87	1.00	17.07	349	286	1.56	9.99	22	29	2.24
Ryedale	2.50	262	291	0.90	19.46	257	227	2.59	7.94	107	83	1.37
Salford	2.07	308	330	0.78	29.34	43	27	1.36	3.49	366	357	0.87
Salisbury	3.81	142	152	0.94	19.15	271	204	1.56	8.05	102	119	2.03
Sandwell	1.54	367	364	0.53	31.17	31	34	4.54	3.13	378	379	0.88

Local Authority	Households receiving very high income				Poor households				Wealthy households			
	% 2001	Rank 2001	Rank 1991	% change	% 2001	Rank 2001	Rank 1991	% change	% 2001	Rank 2001	Rank 1991	% change
Scarborough	1.44	378	355	0.37	23.23	149	140	3.36	5.07	275	272	1.19
Scottish Borders	1.92	325	324	0.56	24.47	120	88	2.42	5.03	276	280	1.28
Sedgefield	1.67	355	346	0.55	26.99	63	52	2.19	4.02	344	353	1.37
Sedgemoor	2.75	237	242	0.73	19.47	256	276	3.66	8.06	101	93	1.61
Sefton	2.48	264	258	0.56	23.39	143	137	3.37	5.94	219	211	1.28
Selby	3.94	133	144	1.01	18.13	307	288	2.68	7.78	115	154	2.24
Sevenoaks	5.09	64	40	0.30	16.55	364	363	3.00	10.11	19	14	1.79
Sheffield	2.31	283	267	0.48	27.25	60	42	1.59	3.93	348	342	1.14
Shepway	2.23	291	261	0.34	22.09	185	188	4.12	6.28	201	224	1.76
Shetland Islands	1.81	339	269	−0.01	23.35	144	104	1.67	6.62	181	214	1.98
Shrewsbury & Atcham	3.24	185	214	1.02	19.13	272	237	2.46	7.47	137	140	1.75
Slough	4.24	105	128	1.09	26.89	66	143	7.28	5.09	272	306	1.76
Solihull	4.80	79	51	0.29	18.91	279	304	3.70	8.18	95	78	1.46
South Ayrshire	2.16	297	240	0.14	24.74	114	90	2.77	4.44	315	311	1.14
South Bedfordshire	4.99	67	57	0.64	17.94	316	338	3.49	7.46	139	121	1.48
South Bucks	7.12	10	12	1.27	14.69	398	397	2.63	12.52	2	2	1.78
South Cambridgeshire	5.97	29	27	0.71	15.39	390	368	2.04	10.46	13	16	2.25
South Derbyshire	4.04	123	142	1.06	17.99	313	322	3.26	7.81	113	151	2.24
South Gloucestershire	4.75	81	93	1.09	15.63	386	395	3.47	8.00	105	96	1.58
South Hams	2.68	246	223	0.53	17.07	348	353	3.06	8.00	104	100	1.74
South Holland	2.40	272	313	0.96	19.67	247	275	3.84	7.77	116	143	2.14
South Kesteven	3.76	147	156	0.95	18.64	289	231	1.85	7.87	109	136	2.06
South Lakeland	2.77	233	251	0.78	17.44	334	305	2.25	7.08	160	145	1.47
South Lanarkshire	2.59	253	210	0.31	28.33	50	50	3.32	3.87	349	369	1.39
South Norfolk	3.37	173	184	0.76	16.59	363	374	3.38	8.71	70	75	1.93
South Northamptonshire	6.22	21	49	1.66	15.14	392	371	1.87	10.97	7	13	2.60
South Oxfordshire	6.27	20	21	0.86	15.64	385	358	1.85	9.83	30	18	1.68
South Ribble	3.60	158	148	0.71	17.01	352	340	2.64	6.81	171	204	2.08
South Shropshire	2.38	277	311	0.94	18.83	283	284	3.24	9.32	42	54	2.13
South Somerset	3.01	214	193	0.53	18.08	311	283	2.48	7.78	114	123	1.85
South Staffordshire	4.63	86	58	0.29	17.87	319	373	4.64	9.25	45	50	1.93
South Tyneside	1.31	395	387	0.50	31.27	28	19	1.96	2.96	385	390	1.05
Southampton	2.44	269	270	0.64	27.17	61	81	4.80	4.67	300	299	1.22
Southend-on-Sea	2.92	222	209	0.62	22.67	166	199	4.95	5.19	268	235	0.82
Southwark	3.78	146	284	2.11	41.41	5	5	6.25	1.85	401	396	0.08
Spelthorne	4.96	69	52	0.49	17.20	343	389	4.84	7.23	151	108	1.13
St Albans	7.77	4	5	1.25	15.70	382	375	2.51	8.76	67	57	1.58
St Edmundsbury	3.64	154	141	0.64	19.32	259	209	1.87	7.83	111	129	1.93
St Helens	2.08	307	308	0.61	26.08	79	92	4.21	4.57	306	305	1.22
Stafford	4.00	130	117	0.75	18.43	301	282	2.82	8.08	100	89	1.58
Staffordshire Moorlands	3.05	212	215	0.83	18.37	302	360	4.65	7.89	108	126	1.98
Stevenage	3.93	135	72	−0.11	23.27	148	111	1.93	5.64	238	244	1.45
Stirling	3.38	171	163	0.63	23.67	138	100	1.92	6.13	212	207	1.42
Stockport	4.04	122	99	0.51	19.22	266	264	3.21	6.14	209	175	0.91
Stockton-on-Tees	2.61	250	260	0.72	24.17	127	107	2.64	5.33	258	297	1.85
Stoke-on-Trent	1.24	398	394	0.49	28.52	49	72	5.58	3.08	380	376	0.74
Stratford-upon-Avon	5.38	54	59	1.04	16.37	369	332	1.81	10.05	21	21	2.04
Stroud	4.06	120	97	0.51	17.22	340	327	2.56	9.21	46	59	2.08
Suffolk Coastal	3.49	163	149	0.60	17.57	328	297	2.26	8.47	83	101	2.21
Sunderland	1.51	371	380	0.63	30.01	38	26	2.01	3.52	364	385	1.33
Surrey Heath	7.68	5	3	0.43	13.82	404	404	3.17	12.38	3	3	1.70
Sutton	4.47	93	74	0.46	20.20	235	292	4.82	5.75	231	194	0.79
Swale	2.76	236	189	0.20	22.52	172	214	5.24	6.23	208	206	1.51
Swansea	1.92	326	305	0.43	24.21	126	120	3.22	5.66	237	234	1.27
Swindon	4.13	115	126	0.96	20.43	224	210	2.99	5.86	224	249	1.71
Tameside	2.20	293	292	0.60	25.71	92	80	3.27	3.65	359	365	1.12
Tamworth	3.42	166	222	1.27	22.65	167	160	3.94	6.28	202	258	2.19

Local Authority	Households receiving very high income				Poor households				Wealthy households			
	% 2001	Rank 2001	Rank 1991	% change	% 2001	Rank 2001	Rank 1991	% change	% 2001	Rank 2001	Rank 1991	% change
Tandridge	5.83	34	19	0.36	15.09	394	392	2.88	10.78	8	7	1.37
Taunton Deane	2.68	245	232	0.62	19.52	253	224	2.60	7.03	164	176	1.83
Teesdale	2.58	255	264	0.72	21.36	199	177	3.11	7.63	129	102	1.41
Teignbridge	2.44	266	286	0.79	18.63	291	313	3.66	7.17	154	157	1.65
Telford & Wrekin	3.33	175	227	1.22	23.31	146	139	3.33	6.57	185	212	1.91
Tendring	1.84	336	342	0.66	21.21	205	255	5.01	5.64	239	238	1.30
Test Valley	5.33	56	63	1.11	16.75	360	315	1.80	9.44	38	34	1.84
Tewkesbury	4.15	114	65	0.02	16.38	368	344	2.16	8.25	93	81	1.66
Thanet	1.57	363	375	0.66	24.71	116	132	4.51	5.00	281	278	1.23
Three Rivers	6.02	26	25	0.66	17.03	351	330	2.42	9.06	55	36	1.49
Thurrock	2.82	230	289	1.20	22.83	162	172	4.39	5.09	271	266	1.10
Tonbridge & Malling	4.83	76	50	0.32	17.43	335	339	3.05	8.93	61	62	1.84
Torbay	1.56	365	363	0.56	22.94	158	191	5.05	5.03	277	264	1.01
Torfaen	1.99	316	298	0.47	25.36	97	74	2.59	4.98	282	290	1.37
Torridge	1.52	370	395	0.81	20.44	223	278	4.73	7.61	131	112	1.54
Tower Hamlets	4.01	128	359	2.98	46.46	1	1	8.93	1.02	406	405	0.15
Trafford	4.37	97	123	1.18	20.35	228	193	2.48	6.40	191	166	0.98
Tunbridge Wells	4.88	73	76	0.89	18.71	287	280	3.07	8.53	77	51	1.26
Tynedale	3.31	177	161	0.55	19.76	245	197	2.00	7.64	128	164	2.14
Uttlesford	6.13	23	32	1.14	16.05	373	367	2.67	12.05	5	6	2.17
Vale of Glamorgan	3.28	180	162	0.53	19.60	250	242	3.03	7.49	136	106	1.33
Vale of White Horse	5.92	30	22	0.51	16.55	365	359	2.81	9.66	32	32	2.00
Vale Royal	4.43	94	95	0.85	18.71	286	257	2.57	8.32	91	95	1.88
Wakefield	2.20	294	310	0.76	26.52	71	67	3.30	4.07	338	343	1.29
Walsall	2.24	290	277	0.47	28.09	52	73	5.26	4.65	301	282	0.92
Waltham Forest	3.20	192	211	0.93	31.49	27	62	7.83	3.33	373	362	0.76
Wandsworth	7.48	6	54	3.07	28.98	46	51	4.13	3.10	379	332	0.21
Wansbeck	1.36	385	401	0.84	27.31	59	43	1.68	3.33	372	395	1.52
Warrington	4.30	102	118	1.06	19.93	241	212	2.60	6.38	194	221	1.78
Warwick	5.43	51	69	1.33	18.55	295	265	2.56	7.43	141	130	1.53
Watford	5.19	60	70	1.11	20.82	214	222	3.85	5.81	227	205	1.09
Waveney	1.50	372	318	0.11	22.37	177	186	4.33	5.55	247	261	1.49
Waverley	6.12	24	20	0.67	15.44	388	365	2.02	10.71	11	9	1.63
Wealden	4.19	111	102	0.69	14.98	395	390	2.66	9.92	26	24	1.93
Wear Valley	1.45	376	382	0.60	26.85	67	57	2.75	4.58	305	336	1.74
Wellingborough	3.40	169	192	0.90	22.44	176	178	4.20	6.31	197	200	1.49
Welwyn Hatfield	4.76	80	39	-0.04	21.18	207	171	2.71	7.63	130	118	1.59
West Berkshire	6.43	17	13	0.68	16.75	359	361	3.17	9.89	27	26	1.98
West Devon	2.44	267	212	0.18	17.71	324	349	3.66	9.02	59	53	1.80
West Dorset	2.30	285	243	0.29	17.95	314	274	2.11	7.39	143	137	1.60
West Dunbartonshire	1.39	384	400	0.83	34.86	14	13	4.21	2.16	397	404	0.61
West Lancashire	3.23	187	157	0.43	21.28	201	179	3.05	7.70	121	127	1.80
West Lindsey	2.73	240	236	0.69	19.12	274	253	2.83	8.04	103	131	2.15
West Lothian	3.10	204	217	0.91	27.14	62	45	1.75	4.20	330	375	1.85
West Oxfordshire	4.82	78	92	1.14	16.72	361	335	2.19	9.09	54	60	1.96
West Somerset	1.35	390	399	0.79	20.23	234	225	3.32	7.36	144	135	1.54
West Wiltshire	3.41	168	176	0.76	17.95	315	310	2.95	7.73	118	105	1.54
Westminster	6.11	25	130	2.96	38.93	8	12	7.96	1.72	404	391	-0.17
Weymouth & Portland	1.95	321	263	0.08	21.70	190	175	3.34	5.16	269	270	1.26
Wigan	2.34	279	282	0.65	24.03	129	121	3.07	4.59	304	318	1.39
Winchester	5.85	33	28	0.68	17.03	350	309	2.02	10.12	18	11	1.57
Windsor & Maidenhead	7.23	8	4	0.71	16.68	362	364	3.13	9.88	28	17	1.71
Wirral	2.38	276	248	0.38	23.14	151	134	2.95	6.04	216	197	1.10
Woking	6.71	12	10	0.83	16.76	358	376	3.69	8.82	65	42	1.35
Wokingham	8.54	1	2	0.50	12.54	406	406	3.41	11.84	6	5	1.95
Wolverhampton	1.92	324	317	0.51	29.78	40	47	4.72	4.21	328	319	1.02
Worcester	3.88	140	173	1.22	20.58	220	187	2.56	5.75	232	263	1.71

Local Authority	Households receiving very high income				Poor households				Wealthy households			
	% 2001	Rank 2001	Rank 1991	% change	% 2001	Rank 2001	Rank 1991	% change	% 2001	Rank 2001	Rank 1991	% change
Worthing	3.08	205	207	0.77	19.50	255	268	3.56	4.89	288	269	0.98
Wrexham	2.15	299	329	0.84	24.24	125	93	2.38	6.12	213	231	1.66
Wychavon	4.84	74	88	1.11	17.49	333	323	2.78	10.08	20	20	2.05
Wycombe	6.56	13	14	0.95	17.76	323	366	4.37	9.94	25	19	1.84
Wyre	2.28	288	273	0.49	18.86	282	299	3.58	6.10	215	220	1.50
Wyre Forest	3.54	161	138	0.51	20.63	219	262	4.59	7.54	133	113	1.49
York	3.17	196	231	1.09	20.34	229	165	1.79	4.90	287	285	1.21

Patterns of poverty across Europe
Richard Berthoud

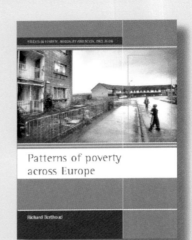

Using new EU-wide data, this report shows very different patterns of poverty across Europe, depending on the benchmark used. From a European perspective, the poor are heavily concentrated in Portugal, south-western Spain, southern Italy and Greece. The research also tests two methods of calibrating poverty lines to show which level of area offers the most sensitive indicator of social exclusion. The results fail to corroborate the conventional view that nationally based poverty lines are the most appropriate basis for international comparisons.

The findings have important implications for the spatial distribution of poverty within and between countries (including the UK) and for the development of anti-poverty policy across the EU.

Paperback • £12.99 (US$20.95) • ISBN 1 86134 574 7
297 x 210mm • 60 pages • March 2004

Child poverty in the developing world
David Gordon, Shailen Nandy, Christina Pantazis, Simon Pemberton and Peter Townsend

This report provides a summary of the results from a major international research project, funded by UNICEF, on child rights and child poverty in the developing world.

The report presents the first ever scientific measurement of the extent and depth of child poverty in developing regions. This measurement is based upon internationally agreed definitions arising from the international framework of child rights.

The study findings indicate that considerably more emphasis needs to be placed on improving basic infrastructure and social services for families with children, particularly with regards to shelter, sanitation and safe drinking water in rural areas. Anti-poverty strategies need to respond to local conditions; blanket solutions to eradicating child poverty will be unsuccessful.

Paperback • £9.99 (US$15.00) • ISBN 1 86134 559 3
297 x 210mm • 44 pages • October 2003

World poverty
New policies to defeat an old enemy
Edited by Peter Townsend and David Gordon

World poverty is an authoritative analysis of how to tackle poverty worldwide. With contributions from leading scholars in the field both internationally and in the UK, the book asks whether existing international and national policies are likely to succeed in reducing poverty across the world. It concludes that they are not and that a radically different international strategy is needed.

The interests of the industrialised and developing world are given equal attention and are analysed together. Policies intended to operate at different levels – international, regional, national and sub-national - ranging from the policies of international agencies like the UN and the World Bank through to national governments, groups of governments and local and city authorities – are examined. Key aspects of social policy, like 'targeting' and means-testing, de-regulation and privatisation, are considered in detail.

Paperback • £25.00 (US$35.00) • ISBN 1 86134 395 7
Hardback • £55.00 (US$69.95) • ISBN 1 86134 396 5
234 x 156mm • 480 pages • September 2002